can crocodiles cry?

Daily Mail

can crocodiles cry?

500 answers to correspondents

andy simpson

hamlyn

An Hachette Livre UK Company

First published in Great Britain in 2007 by
Hamlyn, a division of Octopus Publishing Group Ltd
2–4 Heron Quays, London E14 4JP
www.octopusbooks.co.uk

ISBN: 978-0-600-61745-7

A CIP catalogue record for this book is available from the
British Library

Printed and bound in Great Britain by Mackays of Chatham

10 9 8 7 6 5 4 3 2 1

Every effort has been made to contact individuals whose letters
are contained within this volume; if anyone has been overlooked,
we would be grateful if he or she would contact Octopus Publishing
Group Ltd.

General Editor: Andy Simpson
Editorial Assistance: Margaret Jonas

Contents

Introduction

The Victorian era, well known as an age of confidence and certainty, when the 'progress' of history was likened to the progressive development of the steam engine, was also an age of investigation and exploration, when the boundaries of social enquiry were being expanded as fast as the boundaries of Empire.

As the 1890s dawned, Alfred Harmsworth was developing the interest in journalism he had begun at school where he had edited the school magazine. The great publishing success at the time was *Tit-Bits* magazine, selling 900,000 copies a month. In 1888 Alfred and his brother Harold set up their rival: the weekly *Answers to Correspondents*, promising their readers that every question sent in would be answered.

To answer them, they relied on the vast body of knowledge and experience provided by their ever-growing readership among the great British public. No sooner were the questions asked than the answers rolled in. *Answers to Correspondents* miscellaneous collection of information, jokes, anecdotes and serial stories by popular authors was a great success, selling more than a million copies a week within four years.

Looking back, the preoccupations of that time were curiously similar to our own: Should there be more Bank Holidays? Are taller people more likely to be successful? Should you consult your parents before marrying? Is criminality hereditary? All these issues, answered more than 100 years ago in a friendly and informative fashion, which doesn't look out of place today, have strong echoes in discussions currently taking place in our newspapers and magazines.

Dotted around this book in tinted boxes you'll find several examples of Harmsworth's questions and answers from 1892. Down all these years the concerns – and attitudes – of readers are still surprisingly relevant.

Along with them you'll find here the best of the recent enquiries from *The Daily Mail*'s ever-popular column – in some cases remastered for clarity, brevity and contemporaneity. Intriguing questions eliciting erudite, informative and always entertaining responses from the great pool of knowledge which is the paper's readership.

So, is such a book really needed in the Internet age, when all the information you could want – and more – is just three clicks away? The answer is that *Answers* is as popular as ever, not just because of the individual experiences it brings to the knowledge that it shares, but also because, in many cases, until you saw it queried here you just didn't think to ask ...

Andy Simpson

CAN crocodiles cry?

WHEN a crocodile is basking out of the water, for respiratory reasons it leaves its jaw gaping wide open, opening its tear ducts.

This leads to a flow of tears which, accompanied by the animal's apparent broad grin, encourages people to use the expression 'crocodile tears' to refer to someone who is feigning sadness when in fact they're happy.
Alan Marston, Wellingborough, Northants.

THE crocodile is said to fool its prey into presenting itself as the animal's next meal by emitting a piercing cry, easily mistaken for a human being crying out in great pain or shock.

Crocodiles may have learned this trick from observations made when they took a human victim: the snack shrieked and – as if by magic – another one came running to the scene.
Les Roberts, Swindon, Wilts.

TO get an accurate reading, what's the best time of day to weigh yourself?

TO obtain comparable readings of weight gain or loss, it's best to weigh oneself first thing in the morning after going to the toilet and before any food or drink is consumed. No clothes or jewellery should be worn – and it's important to make sure that the dial on the scales is set to zero.

Normal fluctuations in weight due to food and waste in the intestine and variations in body fluids and tissues, including fat stores, are likely to be minimal early in the morning.

Where people are trying to lose weight, dieticians recommend weighing only once a week to avoid individuals becoming disheartened when short-term increases occur due to these normal fluctuations.
Jane Earland, Centre for Human Nutrition, Sheffield University.

WHERE is the narrowest thoroughfare in Britain?

TEMPLE Bar in the fishing village of Port Isaac on the north Cornish coast is generally held to be the narrowest thoroughfare in England: it's just 18in wide in places. It features in the *Guinness Book Of Records* as the narrowest thoroughfare in Britain but the world record is held by Vicolo della Virilita, in the Italian village of Ripatransone. It is less than 17in wide.

Temple Bar is named after a Mr Temple who, it's said, constructed a bar across the thoroughfare to stop people from using it. He failed. The more common name for this thoroughfare today is 'Squeeze-ee-Belly Alley' and, although very narrow, it's wider now than it was in the 1950s when it was widened marginally when one of the side walls was replaced.

P. Kelly, Port Isaac, Cornwall.

❓ WAS there ever a racehorse called Christmas Day which fell on a Good Friday?

I CAN find no record of a horse called Christmas Day falling at any race on a Good Friday and this is highly unlikely as, traditionally, horse races aren't held on Good Friday or Christmas Day.

This story is probably a distortion of the famous incident during the Thorneycroft Chase at Wolverhampton on Boxing Day, 1899, when a horse called Good Friday fell, thus Good Friday fell on the day after Christmas Day, the source of many a wager between friends.

Simon Clare, Ladbrokes, London.

WHEN I was agent for The Memory Man, Leslie Welch, who played the principal variety theatres in the Fifties, he used to begin his act with a stooge in the audience asking whether Good Friday ever fell on Boxing Day. Leslie would reply that a horse named Good Friday fell at Wolverhampton in a race on Boxing Day.

George Knapman, Twickenham, Middx.

❓ CAN the Northern Lights be seen from Bournemouth?

THE Northern Lights (aurora borealis), caused by a cascade of magnetic particles from a solar flare hitting the earth's atmosphere, are generally attracted by magnetism to the North Pole and are rarely seen in latitudes such as the south of England.

When they hit the atmosphere, the particles give off brilliant colours, arcs, flashes and curtains of light. They have a strange effect on electrical and communications equipment, jamming radio and satellite systems.

Several displays of the Northern Lights have occurred in the south of the country, for instance on January 25, 1938, February 11, 1958, March 25, 1958, March 14, 1989, and June 14, 1991, any of which could have been seen from

Bournemouth and other south-coast areas.

The chances of seeing the Northern Lights from Bournemouth or any other built-up area are decreasing as street lights obscure our view of the night sky.
Thomas Davenport, Lincoln.

I'LL never forget seeing the Northern Lights from Bear Wood, just outside Bournemouth, in about 1958 or 1959. We had no street lights then and they showed up better than in the town. Bournemouth airport and Purbeck coast-guards confirmed the sightings that night and they were seen even in northern France.
Norman Foot, Lilliput, Dorset.

Ⓠ WHY doesn't England have a national costume?
OUR national costume is the smock, worn for many centuries, plain for work and embroidered for best, with needlework and colour indicating regional variations and strapwork – side panels – indicating the trade of the wearer.

In countries whose nationality is most threatened, people cling most strongly to their national dress. Perhaps now we are feeling a little uneasy at our apparent merging with Europe, it's time to bring out our smocks. I wore mine on St George's Day.
Elizabeth Horton, King's Heath, Birmingham.

ENGLISH national dress can be seen in our towns and villages around May Day. Men wear sleeveless coats, full shirts, hose, knee breeches, buckled shoes and cloth cap. For the ladies, it's the peasant-girl look with a blouse, lace waistcoat, three-quarter length panniered skirt, petticoat, buckled shoes and a bonnet.
Catherine Stock, Bristol.

OUR national dress has always been regarded by foreigners as pin-striped suit, bowler hat, brogues and umbrella for men and the Mary Poppins look for women. This is now being replaced by the reality these same foreigners see when we visit their countries. The Brit-on-Tour look consists of Union Jack shorts, 'I'm with this idiot' T-shirt, scruffy trainers and knotted hankie for men; sandals, Lycra shorts and football top for women.
Tony Youlton, Hove, Sussex.

ENGLAND'S lack of 'traditional' national dress used to be most evident during Miss World contests. The sight of our nation's hopeful having to wear a mock Beefeater costume always left me in fits of laughter.

The plus side is that our constantly evolving approach to clothes shows what an independent lot we really are.

Thomas Gresham, Lincoln.

THIS is something of which we should be proud. Today's national costumes are merely elaborate and fanciful forms of a peasant's dress, mostly created for 19th-century tourists. In Scotland, tartans, with four or five exceptions, were the work of designers and entrepreneurs cashing in on the popularity of Sir Walter Scott's novels. England, alone in Europe at that time, had seen her peasants become free, landowning yeomen. No peasantry, no peasant costumes, and no national costume.

J. Brian Blacklock, Stradbroke, Suffolk.

AS most national dress is based on a country's climate, may I suggest hooded anorak, waterproof bottoms and green wellies.

Julie Tucker, Gillingham, Kent.

？ WHERE did the swastika originate? Why did the Nazis adopt it as their symbol?

THE swastika has been associated with the Nazis for much of the past century but has been around in various forms for at least 3,000 years. The Indian name swastika comes from the Sanskrit *svastika*, comprising *su* (good) and *asti* (to be), referring to any lucky or auspicious object. The addition of *ka* makes it a diminutive, as we might say, a lucky charm.

The swastika shape has been found all over the world including Japan, Ireland and among several American Indian tribes. The name for the shape depended on the country in which it was found.

In Indian it's a swastika but in Chinese it's *wan*, in Old English *fylfot* and in Ireland it's known as Brigit's Cross. The German is *hakenkreuz* or 'hooked cross'. The pre-Christian Anglo-Saxon ship burial at Sutton Hoo, Suffolk, contains gold cups and shields bearing swastikas.

Before unification in 1871, Germany consisted of many separate states. Even before the turn of the 19th/20th centuries, German nationalists had adopted the swastika to try to establish a Germanic/Aryan history.

In August 1920, the swastika was emblazoned on the flag of the National-sozialistische Deutsche Arbeiterpartei (Nazi Party). Its black and red colours were said to represent Blut und Boden (Blood and Soil), taken from the black, red and white colours of the North German Confederation flag produced by Otto von Bismarck.

Michael J. W. Cassidy, Kenley, Surrey.

ADOLF Hitler decided on the swastika as the Nazi Party emblem. In his book *Mein Kampf* he explains how he came to choose red, black and white for the colours of his national flag: 'I myself always came out for the retention of the old colours, because in their aesthetic effect they are by far the most compatible with my feeling.

'After innumerable attempts, I laid down the final form; a flag with a red background, a white disk and a black swastika in the middle.

'After long trials, I found a definite proportion between the size of the flag and the size of the white disk, as well as the shape and thickness of the swastika.'

Russ Jones, Rugby.

THEORIES abound as to why the Nazis adopted the swastika as their symbol. In *Mein Kampf*, Hitler claimed the form in which the Nazi Party used the symbol was based on a design submitted to him by Friedrich Krohn, a dentist from Starnberg.

Some historians claim Hitler first saw the swastika when he was a young pupil at the Abbey of Lambackam-Traum in upper Austria where it was carved in the four corners of the monastery and above the chapel organ on the order of abbot Theodorich Hagen. Hagen had come across the symbol in 1856 on a tour of the Middle East.

There is photographic evidence of various designs of the symbol in the early days of the Nazi Party. At the first Nazi rally in Munich in January 1923, there were different flags on display. The next year, the official programme of the first meeting of the National Socialist Freedom Movement of Greater Germany, held in Weimar, depicted an anti-clockwise swastika lying flat on its side.

As late as October 2, 1932, Hitler was photographed in Potsdam standing in front of a large flag depicting the swastika in a square, not a circle.

Ian R. Lowry, London SW3.

CONTRARY to popular belief, the direction in which the arms of the sign point holds no significance for black magic. The symbol used by the Nazis was the same as that used by Hindus or Buddhists.

The Nazis adopted the swastika as their symbol through the mistaken belief that it represented an ideal of Aryanism, a link with earlier Scandinavian and Germanic peoples and the idea of racial superiority.

Joseph D. Jean, Hale Barns, Cheshire.

IT has been suggested that Winston Churchill deployed his famous V gesture as a cabalistic sign, intended to dilute the lethal potency of the ancient swastika used by the Nazis.

Churchill is said to have decided on this particular retaliation after secret consultations with the necromancer Aleister Crowley, the 'most evil man in Britain' – and we still won the war.

John Madracki, Bolton, Lancs.

———

? WHAT'S the different between a 'public' school and an 'independent' school?

ALL schools have to be registered with the Department of Education. 'Independent' schools are those which are funded by fees from parents whose children attend them, plus whatever endowments or other private resources a school may have.

'Public school' was a term used to describe those independent schools for senior pupils whose heads were members of the Headmasters' Conference, a body that dates from 1869. This archaic term has been largely replaced by 'senior independent school'.

Ian Ross, Independent Schools Information Service, London.

———

? WHAT'S the origin of the recently popularised greeting 'Yo!'?

'YO' has been around since the time of ancient Rome, as any good Latin dictionary will show. It originally had the form 'Io' and was a friendly salutation.

J. McDonald, Whiston, Merseyside.

? WHAT'S the significance of the tears which clowns paint under their eyes?

CLOWNS and clowning can be traced to earliest history but the appearance of modern clowns owes much to the *commedia dell'arte* of late medieval Italy, which developed the characters of Harlequin, Pulcinella, Pantalone, etc.

The clown with a tear on his face is Pierrot who first appeared among troupes touring France in the early 18th century. With his wan complexion and long white peasant smock, his roots lie among the apprentice bakers who made merry once a year, fooling around with flour.

As his character developed, the naive and vulnerable Pierrot became a symbol of unrequited love; always too shy to win his sweetheart, who invariably went off with Harlequin. His humour lay in his being thwarted and depressed.

The stylised tear represents the converse side of happiness, the point where sadness becomes ludicrous.

Elizabeth Morgan (Fizzie Lizzie the clown), Clowns International Gallery and Archive Co-ordinator, London.

THE legend in France is that St Peter found a waif outside the gates of Heaven and took him in, calling him Pierrot, Little Peter. He gave him a white suit and allowed him to play outside the Pearly Gates but forbade him to play with mortal children.

Of course, he disobeyed and St Peter knew he had done so because where the children touched Pierrot's white suit, black marks appeared (his black pom-poms and skull cap).

With tears in his eyes, Little Peter was banished from Paradise for ever.

Monty Wells (Bonzo the Clown), London.

? WHO was Trelawney, about whom Cornish rugby supporters sing?

THIS is 'The Song Of The Western Men', sung to the French tune 'Petit Tambour' as an anthem at assemblies of native Cornish people. It was written by Rev Robert Stephen Hawker, the eccentric vicar of Morwenstow who died in 1875.

The song challenges the monarchy and confirms Cornish national identity. It's generally believed that the Trelawney referred to was Sir Jonathan Trelawney, 1650–1721, of Pelynt in East Cornwall, Bishop of Bristol, Exeter and Winchester.

He was sent to the Tower for refusing to promulgate James II's declaration allowing toleration of Roman Catholics but was subsequently acquitted.

Bishop Trelawney is buried in the family vault at Pelynt Church.

Graham Long, Liskeard, Cornwall.

BISHOP Jonathan Trelawney was a member of a staunchly royalist Cornish family who were a thorn in the flesh of Cromwell's Commonwealth government.

After the Stuart restoration, Sir Jonathan supported Charles II and James II and, with his younger brother, Major General Charles Trelawney, helped put down Monmouth's Rebellion in 1685. He was rewarded with the Bishopric of Bristol but didn't approve of James's move to accommodate Roman Catholicism and was imprisoned in the Tower. When he was acquitted he was greeted in Cornwall with an old refrain, adapted to:

And shall Trelawney die?
And shall Trelawney die?
Here's 20,000 Cornishmen
Will know the reason why.

Robert Hawker, vicar of Morwenstow from 1834, elaborated on this in his 'Song Of The Western Men':

A good sword and a trusty hand,
A merry heart and true,
King James's men shall understand,
What Cornish lads can do.
And have they fixed the where and when?
And shall Trelawney die?
Here's 20,000 Cornishmen
Will know the reason why.

J. C. Cornish, Head of politics, Truro School.

? WHO invented the parachute? Who was brave enough to try it out?

LEGEND has it the first parachutist was Chinese Emperor Shun (*c*.2200 BC) who, as a youth, escaped an arsonist's attempt on his life by leaping from a tower under two traditional reed hats.

Or perhaps it was the Siamese acrobat who was reported in 1688 to have entertained his king by leaping from the roof under two umbrellas fixed to his girdle.

Leonardo da Vinci and other 15th-century visionaries designed fall-breakers, though there's no evidence they were put to the test.

It wasn't until the late 18th century that Frenchman Louis Sebastian Lenormand tested the first practicable fall-breaker and gave us the word 'parachute' (from the Latin *parare* – prepare – and Old French *chute* – fall). He dropped domestic animals in a wicker basket suspended by cords from a domed canopy of linen from the tower of Montpelier Observatory.

Other French aeronauts (the balloon first took to the air in 1773) such as Montgolfier and Blanchard also introduced livestock to the pleasures of parachuting.

But the first human to cast himself off was André Garnerin. In Paris on October 22, 1779, this very brave aeronaut ascended in a small basket suspended beneath a semi-rigid parachute, dangling from an unmanned balloon, and cut himself loose at a height of about 2,000ft.

He oscillated wildly back to earth, to rapturous applause and lasting fame. His wife, Jeanne Labrosse, is said to have been the first woman balloonist and parachutist.

In 1802, Garnerin made the first parachute descent in England, ascending beneath his balloon from Grosvenor Square and landing near the present-day site of Marylebone station.

Thirty-five years later, Robert Cocking, the first Briton to make a parachute descent, died in the attempt when his inverted cone chute collapsed and he fell to his death in a Kentish field. The first successful British parachutist was John Hampton, who jumped a year after Cocking's death.

Peter Hearn, parachutist and author: The Sky People, The History Of Parachuting, Abingdon, Oxon.

THE first person to have their life saved by a parachute was Jodaki Kuparento, a Pole, whose balloon caught fire in 1808.

Albert Berry, an American, was the first person to descend from an aircraft in flight – on March 1, 1912, over St Louis.

On April 19, 1919, Leslie Leroy Irvin, also an American, was the first person to use a ripcord – over McCook Field, Dayton, Ohio.

Sally Cheshire, Cambridge.

HOW did our recognised use of various symbols, such as commas, semi-colons, question and exclamation marks, come about?

CLASSICS scholar Aldus Manutius (1450–1515) is credited with the introduction of all punctuation, with the exception of the full stop and the question mark.

Funded by his pupil Albertus Pico, he founded the Aldine Press in Venice in 1494, the first person to print and bind his own work, first to use italic type and first to produce pocket editions of the classics.

Eric Green, Isleworth, Middx.

WHO wrote the first 'Dear John' letter? Which John was the victim?

A 'DEAR John' letter is a missive telling somebody their relationship with a wife or girlfriend is over. The expression entered our language during World War II when, for military personnel on all sides, it was the type of letter they most dreaded. During that war, and in all others before or since, many women couldn't cope with the prolonged separation and uncertainty, and took solace with other men.

The term is thought to be of British origin, but spread widely through U.S. forces when they entered the war. The first recipient of a Dear John will, however, never be known.

K. P. Barnes, Aldershot, Hants.

MY mother may have played a part in the origin of Dear John letters early in World War II, when we lived in Wimbledon. I returned there after being evacuated to the West Country where I had been in the Duke of Cornwall Light Infantry Army Cadets.

Once back home, I joined the local East Surrey Cadets and was promoted to Sergeant, details of which appeared in the press, along with a photo.

Within days I was receiving affectionate letters from young ladies, some of which included locks of hair. Our postman started an avalanche of letters, though, when he answered a news reporter's query about how the bombing was affecting deliveries by saying that no matter what, all the young ladies' letters to Dear John would get through.

After my mother placed an ad in the Press saying: 'No more Dear John letters please; his love is for another' the letters still poured in but instead of 'Dear John, yours forever, etc' the new intake said, 'Dear John, get lost', or

'Dear John, drop dead'. My demise was duly reported in the Press.
John Cuffley, Wimbledon, London.

IN the RAF before the war, we knew Dear John letters as 'Mespots', an abbreviation of Mesopotamia, now called Iraq, where RAF aerodromes were way out in the desert.

Service overseas then was five years and wives weren't permitted. Iraq was an unpopular posting and to receive a 'Mespot' letter was most dispiriting.

It was, nevertheless, the practice to pin the Mespot letter on the canteen or mess dartboard to allows one's colleagues to throw darts at it while jugging up to help drown the sorrows of their heartbroken oppo.
Jock Prior, Bangor, Co. Down.

? WHAT'S the origin of the expression 'beyond the pale'?

THE word 'pale' in this context comes from the Latin *palus* – a fence stake used to define a border, from the same route which gives us a paling fence today.

In the 14th century, there were two areas known as the 'English Pale', around Calais in France and a large part of Ireland.

Within these areas, English rule was effective, allowing, for example, the settlement of Ireland during Henry II's reign. To go 'beyond the pale' was to leave an area of civilised jurisdiction, just as today it means to go into unacceptable or intolerable areas in conversation, action or deed.
Nigel Wilcockson, editor, Brewers Phrase And Fable, *Cassell Publishers, London.*

? WHY do some old documents have an 'f' where you would expect an 's'? When did this die out?

THIS alphabet character, distinguished from the 'f' by its horizontal bar protruding only on the left, is the 'long s', indicating a longer, stronger 's' sound. It was found in early books produced by scribes and religious orders.

Movable type printing was modelled on the written word, including the 'long s'. The first book to discard the 'long s' was *Ames Typographical Antiquities* in 1794, but John Bell (1745–1831) first removed it from his newspaper the *English Chronicle* in 1786, followed by *The World* in 1787, in the 'interest of readability'.
Eric Green, Isleworth, Middx.

I THOUGHT use of the 'long s' had died out in the early 1800s until I found a dictionary in which my great-aunt had pencilled her name as 'Mifs Mary Burgefs' when she was a teenager in about 1875.

John Willis, Rugby.

❓ WHAT'S the origin of the pub name The Crooked Billet?

NO definitive origin has been discovered for this sign, though much has been written about it and the history of each pub bearing the name seems to be different.

One theory is that in medieval times, when armed retainers accompanied a local baron on his journeys and had to seek lodgings overnight while their master was offered more fitting accommodation, they looked for a simple sign offering them a 'billet'. This was often an untrimmed stick suspended over the door as could once be seen at Wold Newton, now in Humberside, with this verse on one side:

When this comical stick grew in the wood;
Our ale was fresh and very good.
Step in and taste, O do make haste,
For if you don't 'twill surely waste.

Gordon Wright, co-author: Pub Names Of Britain, Wollaton, Notts.

THIS pub sign may have originated after the Battle of Towton, the bloodiest battle on English soil, when 30,000 were killed in one day. It occurred on March 29, 1461, during the Wars of the Roses between Yorkists and Lancastrians.

The Yorkists, under the Earl of Warwick and Lord Fauconberg, were centred on Pontefract and set up their HQ at an inn about two miles from Towton village.

This inn subsequently became known in the local dialect as the *kreukt billet* – the crossed sticks – which may derive from the silver saltire of the Neville family arms which Warwick would have set up above the entrance.

The present inn is called The Crooked Billet and has a sign with the full Warwick heraldic arms, with the Neville saltire at lower left.

S. Smith, Pontefract, Yorks.

IS IT ABSOLUTELY NECESSARY TO CONSULT PAPA WHEN THINKING OF MATRIMONY?

DEAR *Answers*,—I don't see why we should consider our parents at all in this matter. Just think of it! Two young people, both having reached years of discretion, being obliged to obtain their parents' consent before entering the matrimonial state.

If two young people love each other and feel they are in every way suited to each other, let them take the law into their own hands.

Matrimony, Exeter.

Certainly papa should be consulted and, for that matter, mamma. I suppose it is one of the abominable so-called up-to-date ideas that young people nowadays should be so entirely self-reticent in matters matrimonial.

In my young days, age and experience were revered and no young man or woman would dream of taking any important step – not to mention the matrimonial one – without first consulting their elders.

Surely the young people's parents are in a better position to judge whether they are suited to each other than they are themselves, if only from the fact that the 'outsider sees most of the game.'

At the risk of seeming very conservative I would certainly say let children consult their parents in everything and, what is more, adopt their advice in preference to their own inclinations.

T. H., Truro.

Some deference is due to parents. They should be consulted and, if possible, their consent gained before marriage takes place. They have (in most cases) through the whole of our lives done their best for us and proved themselves willing to sacrifice many things on our account to further our interest and happiness.

They have presided over our education and we have trusted entirely to their guidance, at least during the earlier years of our lives.

What reason have we to suppose that their wisdom has failed just at this particular point and that it is their mistake if they do not view the proposed union of their child with favourable eyes?

I think if consent to a union be asked and refused, a wise parent will be sure to give good reasons for the refusal, and these should be considered carefully, and if the objections are such as can be removed by waiting a little time or by some small sacrifice of the will, I maintain that it is not too much for the parent to expect.

I am speaking chiefly of young people just out of parental control. Such would very likely be all the better for waiting to obtain the desired consent.

In every case, I believe the parties wishing to marry should seriously view each side of the question and, if possible at all, do everything they can to win the old folks' blessing. But after waiting a reasonable time and still seeing no reason to change their minds one toward another, I think they might marry even if consent were not given.

In any case, young people about to marry against their parents' wishes ought to be very careful before they do so, as marriage is an irrevocable step and once the knot is tied no power on earth can break it. It is well to realise this before tying it.

Common-Sense, Manchester.

I do not think it necessary to ask parents consent to a marriage provided the young people have both reached an age of discretion but to all under age it is very essential.

Hundreds of unhappy marriages are undoubtedly caused by young people marrying in opposition to their parents' wishes and while they are yet inexperienced in the ways of the world.

Whether married or single, parents are our best friends. I myself am not 19 yet but would marry immediately if my parents would consent; but rather than incur (as I feel sure I should do) their lasting displeasure, I am waiting two long years.

Myra, Brixton.

? WHO invented the wood screw?

GREEK mathematician, physicist and engineer Archimedes of Syracuse (*c.*287–212 BC) is the first person recorded to have used a screw structure. Its earliest uses were for moving loads or pressing olives for oil and grapes for wine.

In modern times, patent number 4117, taken out in 1817 by James Colbert of the John Sutton Nettlefold Company, was for the production of screws in various metals.

Peter Milne, B & Q, Chandlers Ford, Hants.

? I'VE heard that the youngest British military casualty in World War II was a 14-year-old Merchant Navy cadet and that the oldest taken prisoner of war was a 74-year-old on a commando raid. Are these details correct?

THE oldest British prisoner of the 1939–45 war was Admiral Sir Walter Henry Cowan, captured by the Italians during a commando raid, trying single-handedly to subdue a tank while armed only with a revolver, at Bir Hacheim in North Africa on May 27, 1942 – 15 days short of his 71st birthday.

Cowan, though highly fit, shouldn't have been in the war at all. He had retired from the Navy in 1931 after an amazing career but the lure of another 'good fight' was too much for him and he pulled some strings to serve as a commander in the Royal Marine Commandos.

He was held by the Italians for a year but repatriated in a mass exchange for Italian soldiers. He rejoined the Commandos and took part in several operations throughout the Italian Campaign.

In 1945, at 73, he decided he was too old for active service and reverted to the retired list. He had been in the Navy since the age of 13 and had become one of the most highly decorated and respected Naval men this country had ever seen. On November 22, 1946, he was appointed honorary colonel of the 18th King Edward VII's Own Cavalry and stayed with them in India in 1947 before finally retiring, this time to Kineton, having never been injured in any of his battles. He died in 1956.

John Costello, Harrogate, North Yorks.

THE youngest service casualty of World War II was our Royal Marine bugler on HMS *Fiji*, sunk in the Battle of Crete in May 1941. He was Peter Avant, aged 15, and he went down with the ship. His name is on the Naval War Memorial on Southsea Common.

Albert Howden, Horncastle, Lincs.

HOLIDAYING in the Outer Hebrides, we came across a group of Merchant Navy graves, among which was one of Able Seaman W. Daley, of the SS *Oak Crest*, who died on December 7, 1940, aged ten.

J. R. Gordon, Bexhill, Sussex.

WHY are American lawyers and police shown on TV always so concerned about something called Miranda?

THIS refers to Ernesto Miranda, arrested in Arizona in 1963 and charged with rape. He made a written confession but during his trial defending lawyers argued he hadn't been made aware of his right to have a legal representative present during questioning.

He was found guilty and sent to jail but the American Civil Liberties Union took his case all the way to the U.S. Supreme Court which ruled 5-to-4 in his favour in 1966.

This established the ruling that an arrested person must be informed of their rights under the Fifth Amendment of the Constitution: the right to silence, the fact that what they may say may be used against them and their right to legal representation. Since 1966 U.S. police officers have referred to reading an arrested person their rights as 'giving them the Miranda'.

Ernesto Miranda was retried on new evidence, reimprisoned and paroled after ten years. He later died of knife wounds sustained in a bar fight.

Ian Preece, Poole, Dorset.

WHO first put tea in teabags? Is there any difference between teabag tea and that which is sold loose?

TETLEY'S first put tea in teabags in Britain, launching it in 1953. Today, teabags account for about 86 per cent of tea brewed in the UK. The difference between teabag tea and loose-leaf tea is only in the appearance of the leaf, not in the quality. The teabag version is in smaller particles to assist quicker brewing in the bag.

Illtyd L. Lewis, The Tea Council.

ON a tea plantation in Kenya, I was told teabags enabled them to use the fine dust from the tea-making process which still makes excellent tea.

Pamela Sippitt, Portsmouth, Hants.

❓ MANY older people suggest it would be a good idea to 'bring back the birch' – but was birching ever used in Britain?

JUDICIAL corporal punishment was regularly administered in England from medieval times. Referred to as 'whipping' in earlier times, around the middle of the 19th century the whip gave way to the birch as the instrument used.

From around that time, the sentence was applied mainly to youths and young boys. Birching was officially abolished in England in 1967.

Peter Fellows, Birmingham.

ABOUT 70 years ago, when I was 12, a poor man and his wife displayed outside West Cornwall Hospital, Penzance, a photograph of their small son, aged seven or eight, who had been birched for stealing coal from a horse-drawn truck.

It showed the effect of the birching on his back and legs – a mass of raised weals and sores. It was a shocking display of medieval torture.

K. A. Kew, Southbourne, Dorset.

WHEN I was at school in the mid-1930s, three boys in my class were birched for stealing from the offertory box in a church and breaking into a café on the beach. After their punishment they all decided 'no more, thank you'. All three served in World War II and were good citizens.

C. B. Dodd, Cheltenham, Gloucs.

IN 1934, as a young constable in a county force in the South of England, I was present when a youth was given six strokes by court order. The inspector applied the birch to the offender's bare buttocks but it had little effect on the boy apart from enhancing his status with his circle of ne'er-do-wells.

J. Bond, Dunsford, Devon.

HERE in Jersey, until recent years, the birch was administered for vandalism. There's no doubt that it deterred would-be wrong-doers. Details of the punishments were displayed on buses and in cinemas and phone boxes, with names of offenders for all to see.

Various people I've spoken to who had the task of carrying out the sentence all agreed that not one offender they punished came back for more and many went on to become decent law-abiding citizens.

John Lloyd, Grouville, Jersey.

MY father was birched in 1902 at the age of ten. His crime was playing on the railway line and the magistrate sentenced him to three strokes. During his punishment, however, a police sergeant came in and said: 'I know this boy, he's always being a nuisance to his mother, let me have a go' and he was given three extra strokes.

The birch was kept at the police station, pickled in brine. After his punishment my father had to do his lessons standing up because it was too painful to sit down.

He didn't grow up to be resentful of authority but was a good citizen, a patriotic soldier and loving father – and jolly good fun.

Miss J. Upson, Bracknell, Berks.

? ARE judges in court still given a pair of white gloves if there are no cases to deal with on a particular day?

HISTORICALLY, gloves were regarded as tokens of faith and purity and there have been times in history when only clergymen and emperors were allowed to wear them.

Wearing white gloves used to signify innocence and the idea was adapted by the legal profession when judges at assize courts were presented with a pair of white gloves if there were no cases for trial at a particular session.

The tradition almost died out when the assize court system was replaced with crown and county courts in 1971. With all courts used to their full potential today, the likelihood of there being no cases to try on any particular day is very low, but a pair of white gloves is still handed to judges at Oxford Crown Court at the opening of each legal year (normally October 1) in ceremonial form by both city and university.

Dominique Baldy, Lord Chancellor's Department, London.

? WHAT is the latest date at which snow has fallen in our English summer?

I HAVE a picture of snow on August 6, 1956, at Tunbridge Wells, Kent. But should this be regarded as late summer snow or early winter, bearing in mind Lord Byron's view that the English winter starts in August and ends in July?

Dennis Parker, Woking, Surrey.

I HAVE a photo and cutting from the *London Evening News*, dated June 26, 1980, showing Sevenoaks High Street, Kent, under snow. The heading is: Snow in Flaming June.
Jane Salt, Christchurch, Dorset.

I WAS studying in Muswell Hill, London, on June 2, 1975 when it snowed. I ran outside to verify this but, afterwards, the only people who would believe it were those who heard John Arlott mention it while commentating on a cricket match at Lord's.
Len Eavby, Alton, Hants.

? MY reference dictionary defines a billion as a million million but points out that in France and America it's a thousand million. Which of these definitions is currently being used when describing Britain's National Debt or international trade balance?
THE word 'billion' originated in 16th-century French meaning a million million. It was adopted in English in the late 17th century at around the time that its meaning was changing in France to refer to a thousand million.

This use of the word had established itself in American English by the 19th century, causing predictable confusion between the U.S. and Britain.

From about 1951, most writers, newspapers and magazines in Britain have adopted the American use, to avoid confusion. The Treasury uses the financial world's accepted meaning of a billion as a thousand million.
Birte Twisselmann, Collins English Dictionary, London.

? WHY are things described as 'piping' hot?
PEOPLE use the term 'piping hot' as an allusion to the heat of boiling water escaping from a tap or pipe. 'Piping' is used in the sense of a shrill voice or noise. This can be experienced with food that is so hot it actually makes a noise.
David Teacher, Canterbury, Kent.

'PIPING hot' comes from the Royal Navy method of piping orders with a bosun's pipe. If your mess was near the galley, when Hands to Dinner was piped, food was soon on the mess table, delivered 'piping hot'.
E. W. Whitley, RN (retd), Southport.

WHERE is the hill up which the Grand Old Duke of York is supposed to have marched 10,000 men?

THIS nursery rhyme is usually said to be based on the events of the brief invasion of Flanders by Prince Frederick, Duke of York and Albany (1763–1827), second son of King George III and Commander-in-Chief of the British Army in the Napoleonic Wars.

In 1793, a painstakingly prepared attack on the northern conquests of the French Republic was led by the Duke himself. In April 1794, he won a small cavalry victory at Beaumont but was heavily defeated at Tourcoing in May and recalled to England.

The hill in the rhyme has long been presumed to be where the small town of Cassel rises 176m (570ft) above the otherwise flat lands of Flanders, close to the current France/Belgium border.

Simon Andrews, London NW5.

AN alternative location, often alluded to in Yorkshire, claims the rhyme originated with people watching the activity of a vast army of workers ascending and descending the hill at Allerton Castle, ten miles east of Harrogate, where the Duke – having acquired the estate in 1786 – was busy reconstructing a house and building a prominent Temple of Victory monument.

Or the hill could be in the Suffolk town of Ipswich, a former shipbuilding town, where Woodbridge Road has a pub named after the Duke.

Robin Simmonds, Sheffield.

ACCORDING to research by Geoffrey Hudson MC, the hill in the rhyme is Bincombe Hill, Dorset, part of an area used for military manoeuvres. The rhyme relates to 1804–05, during the Napoleonic Wars, when Britain was preparing for possible invasion and the whole of the South Coast was on alert.

The Duke was stationed in Dorset and made ready for any possible invasion. Frequent visits were made by King George and the men were often deployed on training exercises.

A force of about 10,000 men was assembled in the Bincombe Down area and, according to novelist Thomas Hardy, they were to be seen 'busily engaged in making continuous and easy track from the crest of the down to the bottom of the steep'.

Maureen Attwool, local historian, Weymouth, Dorset.

? **WHO was Woodbine Willie?**

WOODBINE Willie was Rev Geoffrey Anketell Studdert-Kennedy, legendary padre-poet of the World War I trenches. He was born in June 1883, the son of a Leeds vicar, ordained in 1909 and appointed vicar of St Paul's, Worcester, in 1914. A kindly man, he was well known for his generosity to the poor and gave away his coat and bed at times when others needed them.

In December 1915, he was appointed Chaplain to the Forces in France and established a reputation as a gifted orator. Many soldiers went to the trenches strengthened by his words of comfort. When troop trains left for the front, he moved through the carriages, shaking the hand of every man, offering copies of the New Testament and the Woodbine cigarettes which earned him his nickname.

At Messines Ridge, he was awarded the Military Cross for gallantry and devotion to duty, tending wounded soldiers under heavy fire.

After the war, thousands flocked to hear him preach. In 1922 he was appointed to St Edmunds, Lombard Street, and became Chief Missioner to the Industrial Christian Fellowship.

His relentless hard work took its toll and he died on March 8, 1929, aged 45, while on a visit to Liverpool. Thousands thronged the streets to pay their respects to him and as his coffin was about to be put on the ferry, en route for its final resting place at St Paul's, Worcester, an old man pushed through the crowd and placed a packet of Woodbine cigarettes on the casket before disappearing back into the crowd: a touching tribute to Woodbine Willie whose generosity touched the heart of the nation.

John W. Brown, Streatham, London.

REV Geoffrey Studdert-Kennedy wrote many moving poems about the life of the troops in the trenches, some in common dialect, which he entitled *Rough Rhymes*. In one he explains his own nickname thus:

Woodbine Willie.
They gave me this name like their nature,
Compacted of laughter and tears,
A sweet that was born of the bitter,
A joke that was torn from the years,
Of their travail and torture, Christ's fools,
Atoning my sins with their blood,
Who grinned in their agony sharing,
The glorious madness of God.

Their name! Let me hear it – the symbol
Of unpaid – unpayable debt,
For the men to whom I owed God's Peace,
I put off with a cigarette.
G. P. Ellis, Bexley, Kent.

❓ DOES Mrs Victor Bruce's 2,164-mile solo drive in 24 hours in a borrowed three-litre Le Mans Bentley in the 1930s still stand as a record?

THE Hon Mrs Victor Bruce, born Mildred Mary Petre on November 10, 1895, was one of this country's most amazing automobile and aviation adventurers, breaking many speed records, in the air, on land and at sea.

She's perhaps best noted for her record solo flight (after only 40 hours flying experience) to Tokyo in 1930. But her famous automobile record, at the Montlhery track, when she covered 2,164 miles in 24 hours, is no longer a record.

The Le Mans Grand Prix d'Endurance is presently championed by Dr Helmut Marko of Austria and Gils van Lennep of the Netherlands. Together, in a 24-hour period ending on June 13, 1971, the two men covered 3,315.2 miles in a 4,907cc flat-12 Porsche 917K Group 5 sports car.

Mrs Bruce died in May 1990 aged 94, not before she had looped the loop in a Chipmunk after being away from flying for 37 years.
Simon Courtney, Andover, Hants.

❓ WHY is the Groundnut Scheme referred to whenever there's talk of grandiose government projects which come to nothing? Whose idea was it and what happened?

IN 1946/7, when Britain was critically short of cooking oils, the Labour government hatched a scheme to grow groundnuts in Africa. It asked Unilever, which was growing them with good results in West Africa, to start a scheme in Tanganyika, East Africa, to run it for three years and hand it over to the Government as a going concern.

My late husband and his brother got jobs setting up the first workshop, at Kongwa, in May 1947. Former World War II tractors, jeeps and farming equipment from various parts of the world arrived at Dar es Salaam and were driven in convoy 250 miles to Kongwa. The journey, by indifferent roads, took weeks – it took three days even by train.

At first everything went well. Planting started in small *shambas* – fields surrounded by hedges to keep the winds from blowing away the topsoil. Kongwa expanded, experimental units were established and after about a year, wives and families of Unilever staff were allowed to join their husbands. We lived in tents with concrete floors, mats on the floor, nice furniture, china, etc, and a houseboy. We all ate in a communal mess and it was great fun.

Soon my husband, baby daughter and I moved to Unit 2 at Urambo, where he started another workshop and at last we had a bungalow, which was built in a couple of days. Planting and harvesting of groundnuts went according to plan and we grew sunflowers and corn-on-the-cob as well.

When the time came for Unilever to hand over the project to HM Government, lots of VIPs came for the first time to see what was happening. They stayed only a couple of days but the visiting experts decided the shambas were too small. The hedges were taken out and for weeks there was a lot of bush-bashing to open it up for easier planting and ploughing.

Unilever and local Africans warned against this but the Government and officials in Britain thought they knew better. We had to watch the disintegration as three years of hard work turned into a red dust bowl – and so ended the Groundnut Scheme in 1951–52.

I wonder what happened to all those cases of Angostura Bitters?
Esme Horton, Hayling Island, Hants.

? ENGLISH is written from left to right, Hebrew from right to left and Chinese downwards. Is any language written upwards?

ALTHOUGH no major language is nowadays written upwards, examples are found in ancient inscriptions of languages written in all possible combinations of horizontal lines or vertical columns.

Some texts are written in circles and spirals, and some 'boustrophe don' fashion ('as the ox ploughs' – left to right then right to left in the way computers print out).

Sometimes the up–down or right–left orientation of individual letters is reversed between lines.

Modern Chinese, Japanese and Korean can be written equally well in horizontal lines, right–left or left–right, or in vertical columns top to bottom.
Michael Healey, Sheffield.

I'VE long maintained that we address our envelopes wrongly in that they read from the bottom up. The first thing a Royal Mail sorter looks at is the country, the bottom line, then the county or town, then the street and lastly the number and name.

It would make more sense if we addressed envelopes the other way up.

F. C. Luff, Bognor Regis, Sussex.

GULLIVER observed of the inhabitants of Lilliput that 'their manner of writing is very peculiar, being neither from the left to the right, like the Europeans, nor from the right to the left, like the Arabians, nor from up to down, like the Chinese, nor from down to up like the Cascagians, but aslant from one corner of the paper to the other, like ladies in England'.

T. Cross, Dereham, Norfolk.

⟨?⟩ IF you pull a grey hair out by the root, will another grey one grow in the same place?

GREY hair is like any other hair, but lacks pigment cells to give it colour. The common myths that if you pull out a grey hair, two will grow in its place, and that grey hair is coarser, are untrue.

Philip Kingsley, Philip Kingsley Trichological Clinic, London.

⟨?⟩ WHERE and when was the first public telephone box installed?

THE first was installed by Connecticut Telephone Company in its office at New Haven, Connecticut on June 1, 1880.

'Call office suites' were installed in Britain at the Stock Exchange and Baltic Exchange, London and the Wool Exchange in Bradford by the National Telephone Company in 1882.

Callers had to pay an attendant, who locked up the booth when he went off duty. Regular callers were supplied with a 'subscriber's trunk pass' key to give them access to the phone at any time. The first Post Office call boxes, described as 'silence cabinets', were authorised in August 1884.

Patrick Robertson, New Shell Book Of Firsts, London.

OUTDOOR phone boxes didn't arrive until a fair while after the first version. The first one was erected outside Staples Inn, High Holborn, in 1903.

Tim Mickleburgh, Grimsby, Lincs.

? WHY do fingers go wrinkly in the bath?

IT has been suggested this is God's way of allowing us to get a better grip on the soap. In fact, the outer layer of the skin, the epidermis, is composed of layers of cells which are themselves mainly formed from a fibrous protein called keratin.

One of the physical properties of keratin is to swell and expand in water. When we wash our hands, especially in hot water, the keratin in our skin absorbs a little of the water and expands, throwing the surface of the skin up into the characteristic folds and wrinkles.

The wrinkling tends to be confined to the fingers, the palms, and soles of the feet, as the skin in these areas has the thickest superficial layer of keratin in order to protect our hands and feet from damage from friction.

Tony Dawlish, Plymouth.

? IS there any connection between Northumbria and North Umbria in Italy?

THERE is no known connection. Northumbria was an Anglo-Saxon kingdom, extending at one time from the Humber to the Forth, formed in the seventh century by the union of the kingdoms of Deira and Bernicia.

With its capital at Bamburgh, it became one of the cradles of Northern European Christian civilisation, one of its famous sons being the historian The Venerable Bede.

By 829, Northumbria had recognised the overlordship of Wessex and its unity was destroyed by the Danes in the late ninth century. The name now applies only to the police force which covers Northumberland, Durham and Tyne and Wear.

Umbria is a region of central Italy, comprising the provinces of Perugia and Terni. It was part of the papal states during the Middle Ages.

Richard Luty, Bolton, Greater Manchester.

? WHAT World War II tales of seamen taking on impossible odds do the Germans like to celebrate?

GERMAN seamen still remark on the daring raid by Lieutenant-Commander Gunther Prien's submarine U-47 which entered the British home fleet HQ at Scapa Flow on October 14, 1939, less than six weeks into the war, and sank the 29,000-ton battleship *Royal Oak*.

German aerial reconnaissance spotted that Scapa's defences in the Orkney Isles were incomplete. U-47 spent a whole day on the seabed before surfacing late in the evening and sailing into the harbour through the 50ft gap at the entrance to Kirk Sound. The current was so strong that the sub had to stay on the surface. The aurora borealis lit the sky brightly on a moonless night.

The sub fired seven torpedoes, three of which hit the *Royal Oak*, sinking it in minutes with the loss of 810 lives. Fortunately for the Royal Navy, most of the fleet was at sea, or the attack might have had even worse consequences.
John Salmon, Southampton, Hants.

? ASSUMING rain falling vertically and evenly between points A and B, 50 yards apart, would I get wetter if I walked from A to B at Xmph rather than running the same distance at 2Xmph?

AS a maths teacher I have done the algebra involved. There are two areas to think about: the horizontal (top of your head) and the vertical (your front).

Your speed doesn't affect how wet your front becomes. If you run more quickly your front gets wetter faster but as A to B is a fixed distance, it is exposed to the rain for less time and the result is the same, however fast you go.

Your head, however, just gets wetter the longer it is in the rain, so you should run faster to keep this time as short as possible. So the short answer is run fast – or buy a hat.
John Smith, Bracknell, Berks.

WE can determine the logic of this by speeding up the runner so he goes as fast as an Olympic sprinter and slowing down the walker to the pace of a man on crutches.

The walker will arrive at point B wetter, having been in the rain longer. As the difference in speed between runner and walker increases, the difference in time spent in the rain increases and the walker ends up the wetter. In light or moderate rain the difference would be marginal but in a torrential downpour I would choose to run.
Andrew Kernick, St Helens, Lancs.

❓ DOES the U.S. Constitution really give all Americans the right to bear arms?

THE second amendment to the U.S. Constitution (the first being the right to free speech) reads: 'A well-regulated militia being necessary for the defence of a free state, the right of the people to keep and bear arms shall not be infringed.'

There has been considerable debate recently as to whether 'well-regulated militia' means the police, national guard and Armed Forces or the people as a whole. The history behind the drafting of this amendment seems to indicate the latter.

Despite this, there are more than 20,000 widely varying gun laws in the U.S. at federal, state and municipal levels. In New York State, where gun crime is soaring, handgun ownership has been licensed and guns registered since 1911 while the small town of Kennesaw, Georgia, where crime is negligible, has a 1982 law making it mandatory for all households to have a gun.

More than 40 states issue permits allowing private citizens to carry handguns for self-defence.

Alexander Hughes, London SW19.

❓ HOW much money might a writer expect from their first novel? Has any novelist become a millionaire from their first book?

CERTAINLY not a fortune. A first novel might render the author a royalty of up to ten per cent of the price of each hardback copy sold. Writers usually receive an advance which the publisher recoups from the royalties. The final income depends on the number of copies sold and whether the book is published later in paperback. First prints of novels are often as few as 750 copies though they may be several thousand.

Charlotte Burrows, Writers' And Artists' Yearbook, London.

GONE With The Wind was Margaret Mitchell's first and only work.

Published in June 1936, it sold a million copies in six months, including 50,000 on a single day. By the end of 1939 sales had reached two million in the U.S. alone. Before she died in 1949, eight million copies of the book had been sold in 40 countries. Not a bad first effort and obviously very lucrative.

D. B. Madden, Faversham, Kent.

HAS ANYONE ACTUALLY SEEN A SEA SERPENT?

DEAR *Answers*,—In the year 1849, I was serving on board HMS *Cleopatra* in the Indian Ocean, on our way to China.

One evening, when in the forecastle netting on the look-out, I saw, about three points to the lee bow, at a distance of two miles from the ship, an object projecting out from the water, I should judge, about 50 feet.

The head of the monster was much like a dog's, the body being about eight feet in circumference, as far as we could judge. Its colour was of a greenish brown and, as it passed astern it left such a wake as would be caused by a large steamer, and in a few minutes was out of sight.

The serpent was seen not only by myself but by several of the ship's company who were on deck at the time.

George Lucas, Cannahall Road, Wanstead.

Having had over 35 years at sea, visiting all parts of the world, one sees many curious and interesting things in one's travels but I never saw the tall sea-serpents that some profess to have seen and which, I believe, exist mostly in their own imagination. What I have seen, however, in the way of sea-serpents I will tell without exaggeration.

About three years ago, when going up the Mediterranean and when half-way between Gibraltar and Algiers, and 20 miles from the land, I saw, as I thought at first, two masts or wreckage of some ship standing out of the water, but presently seeing that they were moving, and evidently something alive, I naturally was very intent in watching them. They gradually drew nearer, until they got within half a mile or so of us.

I saw then that they were large snakes or sea-serpents. They kept up on a parallel line with us for fully half an hour (ship going 8½ knots). They then struck off in another direction.

I had a good view of them with the naked eye but with the telescope I could see them as distinctly as if they had been on the ship's deck. One was a little longer than the other. I judged the longer to be not less than 30 feet, the other four or five feet shorter. The longer carried its head

? HAD the RAF been equipped with just one squadron of modern fighters such as F-15s or Tornados during the Battle of Britain, what difference would it have made?

THE major physical difference posed by this highly hypothetical question would lie in the ability of today's jets to shoot down enemy aircraft without actually seeing them. The psychological effect on the enemy would also have been a major factor.

Wing Co. Pat Hancock OBE, DFC, Battle Of Britain Fighter Association, Portsmouth.

? CAN jet airliners glide?

AN aircraft's ability to glide and the angle at which it can do so is represented by its lift/drag ratio. A jet airliner has to fly very fast to support its weight so, in the absence of engine thrust, it has to go into steep descent.

J. Andrews, Roker, Sunderland.

IN about 1983, an Air Canada Boeing 787 wide-bodied twin-engined airliner on an internal flight ran out of fuel at 29,000ft. It had been refuelled before take-off but the plane's instruments were calibrated in U.S. gallons and the crew was working in Imperial gallons, so the tanks contained less than they thought.

By chance one of the pilots was an experienced glider pilot and the other knew the terrain they were flying over. Between them they controlled the plane in a glide for 30 miles and set it down on a disused airfield near the small town of Gimli, 40 miles north of Winnipeg.

R. D. Thomson, Kirkcudbright, Dumfries and Galloway.

? WHAT happens to torpedoes which miss their targets?

● THE first torpedo launched was by the Confederate submarine the *Hunley*, the first submarine to sink a warship.

The *Hunley*, constructed from a 25ft x 4ft boiler and powered by hand cranks, attacked the USS *Housatonic*, one of several Union warships guarding the harbour of Charleston, South Carolina, on February 17, 1864.

After sinking the *Housatonic*, the *Hunley* disappeared without trace until recently when divers exploring the coast of South Carolina found the long-lost submarine.

Jeffrey Blyth, Madison Avenue, New York.

BACK in 1940, members of our unit, 3 GHQ Coy RASC were waiting among the sand dunes at Malo les Bains, Dunkirk. Amid all the activity of men getting into boats and the din of Stukas dive-bombing the beach, two torpedoes suddenly came out of the sea with a tremendous whoosh and ploughed straight up the beach.

We flattened ourselves, expecting them to explode but, thankfully, they didn't, though there were flames coming from one of them.

Kenneth Mill, Mapperley Park, Notts.

I SPENT three days with the Royal Corps of Signals on the Dunkirk beaches for the evacuation and saw the two torpedoes arrive. I was quite close to them and thought they must have been jettisoned by a vessel in trouble. I was worried that they might explode but have since learned that in those days torpedoes exploded on impact rather than by timed fuses.

D. C. Chandler, Diss, Norfolk.

FURTHER to the two torpedoes which came up the beach at Dunkirk, I was serving on the destroyer HMS *Jaguar* and we had just loaded almost 1,000 soldiers and had cleared the harbour when we were dive-bombed and developed a considerable list.

We had to get rid of as much top weight as possible so set all our torpedoes to safe and fired them off. Several headed for the beach and I've always hoped none of them hurt anybody.

A. D. Saunders, Southend-on-Sea, Essex.

WHERE did the phrase 'being sacked' originate when referring to losing one's job?

THE phrase 'to get the sack' has been around since at least the mid-17th century and stems from the days when most workers used their own tools.

An employer wanting to get rid of someone would collect his employee's tools and hand them back inside the bag they were normally carried in: hence 'getting the sack'.

B. W. Jennings, Leeds.

WHAT causes white specks in fingernails?

CONTRARY to popular belief, these aren't caused by a lack of calcium but by damage to the area just below the nail. The white specks are simply the evidence of the damage as the nail grows out.

The time taken by a nail to grow and its visibility makes the nails one of the best areas of the body in which to examine a person's general health. Lung disease, heart disorders, cirrhosis of the liver, circulation problems, nutritional deficiency, stress, skin disorders etc, can all be seen in a change of shape, thickness or colour of nails.

George Tyson, London W1.

I KNOW of only one other occurrence of my Christian name, in the Bible, in Romans 16:12. 'Salute Tryphena and Tryphosa, who labour in the Lord' and I've never met anyone else with this name. Are there any other Tryphenas about? Tryphena M. Perry, Swansea, West Glamorgan.

I'M Tryphena Jenkins (née House), one of seven children born in the village of Nettleton, Wilts. My mother chose my name from a dictionary of names.

Years ago, I met a Tryphena who lived in a village a few miles from mine and there's a lady called Tryphena buried in Little Badminton churchyard. I also spotted it as the name of the personnel manager of a company in Bristol.

The *Bristol Evening Post* ran an article on a lady called Tryphosa who had celebrated her 100th birthday. I wrote to her and received a nice reply from her son on her behalf. He said that one of her elder sisters was Tryphena and that two of her mother's sisters had been Tryphena and Tryphosa. Perhaps we're not such a rare breed after all.

Tryphena Jenkins, Bristol.

I'M the Tryphena who Tryphena Jenkins met in 1977. Mine is a family name on my father's side from Dorset, where the name is not uncommon – it means tasty or delicious.

My maternal grandmother had two cats called Tryphena and Tryphosa.
Tryphena Jordan, Badminton.

TRYPHENA Sparks was a cousin of Thomas Hardy with whom he is said to have been in love. He gave her a ring but it was returned when she married hotelier Charles Gale. She died young, in 1890, after bearing him three sons.

She was a handsome girl and a bright one. She trained at Stockwell College, Clapham, passing out with a first-class certificate, and became headteacher of the girls' department of Plymouth Public Free School. She is the subject of Thomas Hardy's moving poem 'Thoughts Of Phena' which begins: 'Not a line of her writing have I, not a thread of her hair.'
C. H. Watson, Petts Wood, Kent.

? ALMOST every page of The Times from December 18, 1914, mentions a 'Yellow Book'. What was this book about?

ALL mentions of the *Yellow Book* in the *The Times* for that date are advertising a special 32-page supplement called the *Yellow Book*, to be published the following day.

This was a translation of the full text of the diplomatic documents relating to the French Government's reasons for being at war with Germany. French Government documents (equivalents of our Blue Books) were known as Yellow Books.
Lewis J. Black, Kilwinning, Ayrshire.

? HOW did veterans of the Battle of Waterloo celebrate its 50th anniversary in 1865?

THE Duke of Wellington held an annual banquet at his London home, Apsley House, on the anniversary of the Battle of Waterloo, June 18, 1815, with guests including surviving high-ranking officers and other dignitaries. In 1836, the banquet was recorded in a 6ft x 11ft painting by William Salter, now on show at Apsley House. The annual tradition continued until the Iron Duke's death in 1852.
Fleur Mainwaring, National Army Museum, Chelsea, London.

THE average life expectancy of a man in the early 19th century was a mere 55 years so very few of the 24,000 British soldiers who returned from Waterloo were still alive on the 50th anniversary, June 18, 1865.

Newspapers of the time have no mention of the half-century anniversary. Celebrations were confined to individual regiments which had taken part.
David Junker, London SW1.

THE last survivor of the Battle of Waterloo, Bombardier John Riley, lived in Speedwell Terrace, Staveley, Derbys, until he was 95.

He was born on April 26, 1793, took his place at Waterloo at the age of 22 and worked until he was 90, dying on July 28, 1888. His gravestone in Staveley cemetery records his Army service.
Fred Wood, Chesterfield, Derbys.

ON June 18, 1965, 150 years after the battle, a Grand Ball was held in the Great Hall of the Law Courts.

The 1,500 guests wore outfits of the period which made wonderful pageantry as everyone danced to the music of Joe Loss and dined on curried melon, Scotch salmon, coq au vin and strawberry meringue. My daughter and five nieces cooked the banquet.
Evelyn Payne, Highcliffe, Dorset.

A SET of 500 cigarette cards, now very rare, depicting the uniforms of Napoleonic war armies, was made for the 100th anniversary. They were due for release in 1915 but as Britain and France were then allies fighting together in World War I, this was considered insensitive and the cards were withheld.

A set came up for auction a few years back at Winterton's Fine Arts, Lichfield. They are among a unique collection of cigarette cards, the life's work of the late Joseph Henry Stafford, a leading authority, particularly on Wills and Players issues.
David Smith, Stratford Marketing Ltd, Lichfield, Staffs.

❓ WHY do we boo to express disapproval?

THE simple answer is because other people do. People who are alone, watching things on TV, rarely boo or make any other sound. We tend to boo when a performance is live and we are in company. So booing isn't instinctive but a learned act of communication, used most often when there are competing groups watching the same event. As one side cheers to support a speaker's point while others boo loudly to show it's unpopular.

Booing crowds at football matches normally face opposing supporters rather than the players. First recorded use of the word 'boo', said by some to derive from the lowing of a cow, to express disapproval, comes from 1801. Forms of disapproval vary widely across situations: some contexts would prohibit a 'boo' but allow a polite 'tut-tut' which could be every bit as devastating. In another context, 'tut-tut' would sound ludicrous.

Dr Stephen Reicher, social psychologist, Exeter Unversity.

⊙ HAS anyone in real life ever slipped on a banana skin, or does this happen only in comedy films?

STUDYING for my Extra Master Mariner's Certificate in 1957 under the tutelage of eminent consultant naval architect John Cook (the man who cured the Royal Yacht's 'swinging propeller') he told us that in India during the 1940s and 1950s it was quite common to launch new ships from ramps lined with thousands of banana skins.

It was cheaper than using mineral grease and very effective – and it was not April 1 when he told us.

Graham Danton, author: Theory And Practice Of Seamanship, *Plymouth.*

⊙ WAS printing with movable metal type in use in Korea before Gutenberg was credited with its invention in 1448?

THE printing of books with carved wooden blocks, one block per page, dates back to eighth-century China or Korea. Movable clay type was first produced in China in 1041, and movable wooden type was also known. But clay is fragile and wears down quickly, while the uneven grain of wood absorbs too much ink and can give illegible results.

The technical breakthrough of movable metal type came in Korea, where the world's oldest surviving example of bronze type is in the National Museum, dating from between 1102 and 1234. Many examples survive of Korean books printed with movable type long before the German Johannes Gutenberg produced his printed Bible in 1448.

Graham Healey, School of East Asian Studies, University of Sheffield.

THE introduction of a phonetic alphabet, making characters easier to manipulate, allowed the Koreans to improve printing techniques used for centuries in China. Gutenberg's contribution was the invention of a mould for casting metal letters.

Tony Martin, Nunhead, London SE15.

❓HOW many changes of costume did Vivien Leigh have as Scarlett O'Hara in *Gone With The Wind*?

A TOTAL of 4,118 costumes were produced for *Gone With The Wind*, of which 44 were Scarlett's, 36 Rhett's, 21 Melanie's and 11 for Ashley.

The costumes cost $153,818 and the women's outfits accounted for 35,000 yards of material. The movie also used 700 false moustaches, 500 pairs of false sideburns and 700 two-and-a-half ounce bottles of greasepaint.

Vivien Leigh was one of 1,400 initial candidates for Scarlett but Clark Gable was the only choice for Rhett.

Katherine Day, Billericay, Essex.

OF Vivien Leigh's 40-odd costume changes in the film, she had four scenes in her underwear, five in different nightdresses, three in dressing gowns and three in mourning dress.

Paul Dew, Hillingdon, Middx.

❓IN my schooldays, atlases showed the world's second highest mountain as Mount Godwin-Austen. Now it's K2. Who was Godwin-Austen and why was he dropped in favour of K2? Is Everest K1?

LIEUTENANT-COLONEL Henry Haversham Godwin-Austen (1834–1923) was appointed surveyor to the Kashmir section of the Indian Survey Department in 1857.

In 1861, he plotted the position of a range of high mountains in the remote Karakoram area and, unable to discover any local names, listed them from left to right as he looked at them, as K (for Karakoram) 1, K2, K3, etc.

He calculated the height of K2 as the second highest mountain so far recorded, Mount Everest having been measured a few years earlier.

In 1888, a former Surveyor-General of India proposed that the mountain be officially named Mount Godwin-Austen but the colonel modestly declined such recognition. It was used unofficially for a time but has now been over-taken by K2.

Mount Everest, 700 miles away at the other end of the Himalayas, was originally designated Peak 15 in a different sequence by Surveyor-General Colonel A. S. Waugh during preliminary surveys in the 1850s.

David McNeill, Royal Geographical Society.

❓ WHAT is the toxic substance in many varieties of bean. How is it removed or neutralised by cooking?

RAW kidney, haricot, butter and runner beans contain natural toxins called lectins which, if eaten, cause nausea, vomiting and diarrhoea within two hours. About ten years ago there were many reports of poisoning when there was a trend for eating raw kidney beans, and doctors reported 25 outbreaks affecting about 100 people.

There were some reports of red beans still being toxic after slow cooking. Since then, all packets of dried beans include a health warning on the label with advice to soak them overnight, throw the water away and boil the beans vigorously in fresh water for ten minutes. This process destroys the lectins and the beans can then be enjoyed.

Heinz Baked Beans, now celebrating 100 years, are made with a type of haricot bean called a navy bean. They are soaked in hot water during preparation then sealed in cans with special tomato sauce and cooked in steam at a very high temperature to finish the cooking process.

Dr Nigel Dickie, nutrition consultant, H. J. Heinz Co Ltd, Hayes, Middx.

❓ DID the Germans recruit an army of Indian nationals to fight against British Allied Forces in World War II?

IN 1941, Indian nationalist leader Subbas Chandra Bose arrived in Berlin, intent on obtaining German help to free his country. He persuaded the Germans to recruit a volunteer group from among the many Indian troops of British forces captured in North Africa.

By the end of 1942, the force had a strength of 2,000 men, had become known as Legion Freies Indian, and was officially formed into Indisches Inf. Regt. 950 of the German Army. This comprised three four-company battalion companies of infantry, anti-tank guns, engineers and also a depot battalion of honour guard. The Legion was led by German officers and the volunteers wore the standard German Army uniform. In 1943, Chandra Bose travelled to Japan to organise the Indian National Army while the Free Indian Legion remained in Europe where they were stationed south of Bordeaux as part of the Atlantic wall garrison.

After D-Day, the legion was withdrawn to Germany and on August 8, 1944, came under the control of the Waffen-SS. They never saw combat and were disbanded on Hitler's orders

C. W. Daniels, Alderley Edge, Cheshire.

❓ HOW does someone like Rod Stewart arrive on the central stage at Wembley in the middle of his 22-piece band without walking through the audience?

MY sister-in-law and I were in the front row at a Rod concert, directly in front of the understage entrance. The stage was built with a room underneath. The band walked through the audience and arrived on stage through the understage entrance, but without Rod Stewart. We then noticed a large tour crate, with 'Rod Stewart' written on the side, being carefully wheeled through the audience and up the ramp leading to the understage entrance. We asked one of the security guards if Rod was in it and he simply winked at us and nodded.

Lesley Alabaster, Bow, London.

❓ HAS any batsman scored a century against all the opposition counties, including the county side for which he originally played?

THE inclusion of Durham in the County Championships brought the number of first class counties to 18.

Graham Gooch, of Essex, and Tim Curtis, of Worcestershire, have made centuries against all the counties except their own. West Indian batsman Viv Richards, who played county cricket with Somerset and Glamorgan, scored hundreds against all 17 counties competing for the championship. He played against Durham twice and in his last innings against them made 62 not out, so he came as close as anyone to scoring a century against all 18.

Philip Crofton, East Peckham, Kent.

IS AERIAL NAVIGATION DESIRABLE?

DEAR *Answers*,—In a few years, the first flying-machine will appear – not the huge cigar-shaped balloons such as the French Government has been recently experimenting with but compact, heavier than air vessels, that will rise from Mother Earth and glide through the vast ocean of air with a velocity never yet attained by any man.

As Mr Maxim says: 'It would appear that we are within measurable distance of a successful machine for navigating the air, and I believe it is certain to come within the next ten years, whether I succeed or not.'

When they do appear the first use they will be put to will be a military one. It will at once become an engine of war, not only to reconnoitre the enemy's position, as has been attempted by the so-called dirigible balloons, but also for carrying and dropping into the enemy's line and country large bombs charged with high explosives. If I can rise from the coast of France, sail through the air across the Channel, and drop half a ton of nitro-glycerine upon an English city, I can revolutionise the world.

It does not require a prophet to foresee that successful machines of this character would at once make it possible for a nation possessing them to paralyse completely an enemy by destroying in a few hours the important bridges, armouries, arsenals, gas and water works, railway-stations, public buildings, etc, and that all the modern means of defence, both by land and sea, which have cost untold millions, would at once be rendered worthless.

Of what use then will be the enormous armies of today if one of these flying-machines, gliding calmly along beyond the range of the rifles, could send thousands of brave men to 'kingdom come' simply by dropping a few dynamite bombs? Of what use our armour-clad forts, when they could in the same way be blown to atoms? Of what use our huge navy, with its costly ironclads, which could be shivered to splinters? Of what use our murderous artillery if, for want of elevation, it could not respond to the attacks of its aerial foes?

Interested, of Stockwell.

Mr Maxim is a clever inventor and able mechanical engineer but his theory of revolutionising the world by means of a flying-machine is somewhat visionary.

The flying-machine must be brought to practical perfection and the half-ton of nitro-glycerine dropped on the exact spot selected – which would not be easy. When this is done, the only effect would probably be to destroy the lives of a certain number of non-combatants, and to raise in their fellow-countrymen a determined spirit of resistance.

As soon as a war flying-machine is a practical success, means will be found to make matters very unpleasant for the aeronauts. Remember that the machine gun, submarine, nitro-glycerine shell, etc, have not fulfilled the expectations placed in them.

And an aeronaut would have a very bad time in anything like rough weather – no rare thing over our shores.

W. H., Bideford.

If we do not succeed in inventing a flying-machine, someone else will but I cannot coincide with the opinion that the successful aerial machine will be a means of wholesale destruction.

Civilised war-making nations have agreed among themselves that methods of destruction shall be confined within certain limits. An explorer may use explosive bullets against African savages but it was decided long ago at Geneva that such fiendish methods should have no place in civilised warfare.

If dynamite is to be dropped like rain from heaven upon the just and the unjust, upon fighting men and peaceful townsfolk, why not poison the enemy's water supply, or smuggle cholera-infected rags across his frontier? Such a thing has only to be regarded for a moment in its practical aspect to be seen to be utterly out of the range of possibility.

I should like to see a safe and easily manageable machine invented and I believe it will be done very shortly. When we once get it, the human race will soon find out to what use it can be put. Let us hope it will be of a more peaceful nature than some seem to think. Perhaps in the near future we will be gliding over the tops of those hills which we formerly had to grind up on a bicycle, looking down on the dear old earth below and seeing that the flying-machine has altered its face very little.

Leo, Cambridge.

In consequence of the phenomenal amount of interest shown in this discussion, Answers went to interview American-born Briton Sir Hiram Maxim, inventor in 1884 of the Maxim machine gun and asked him: 'Don't you think the possession by a nation of such a fearful machine would result in the total annihilation of their adversaries?'

DEAR *Answers*,—'No. Something would be done to combat it. I don't think any invention that would put additional power into the hands of man is to be deprecated. I think it good that rich, cultured countries like England and France should possess such weapons, although it is undoubtedly a fact that the possession of such a weapon by a great power would perhaps result in a decided alteration in the map of Europe.

'No man in the world would be more pleased than me to see the problem of aerial navigation successfully solved. I am experimenting every day, with a staff of assistants; the result is purely a question of time.

'I have succeeded in making an engine in which one horse power is compressed into a body the size of a chicken. My aerial machine at present is run along on a railway, tied down in such a way that if it did lift it could not get away and thus I am able to make the necessary calculations, etc.

'If I fail, I shall have the satisfaction of knowing that I have moved a step in the right direction. Others who follow will take my drawings and go on with the work.

'As for successful aerial navigation as a medium of passenger traffic, I don't think that is likely to come about; at least, not yet. It will be done some day but when, I am unable to say.'

Hiram T. Maxim.

WHAT are the duties and responsibilities, if any, of a non-executive director?

NON-EXECUTIVE directors are required to act in the interest of the company with the same legal duties as executive directors.

Their other important contributions are to bring experience, skill and knowledge to the board, to monitor management performance, and to ensure that company interests are safeguarded where they conflict with the personal interests of individual directors.

Nicola Rampling, Institute of Directors, London.

❓ WHAT are the longest one-word palindromes in the English language?

THE longest palindromes I can think of are of nine letters: rotavator and Malayalam, the language of the peoples of the Malabar coast of India.

Other than these, I can come up with only six-letter ones such as denned and redder or the five-letter ones, civic, kayak and level.

Doug Douglas, Southport, Lancs.

THE longest palindrome listed in the second edition of the *Oxford English Dictionary* is 'tattarrattat', employed by James Joyce in his *Ulysses*, written in 1922 ('I knew his tattarrattat at the door'), but if we are to include the offerings of writers who, like Joyce, set out deliberately to invent words, then the hunt for the longest one will be endless.

If I get the word 'whooombmooohw' – the sound an exhaling water buffalo makes under water – included in my next book, will its 13 letters beat Joyce's 12?

I suggest a word isn't worth considering if it doesn't appear in two separate publications.

A. Simmons, London N5.

❓ HAS Britain been known to use chemical weapons?

ROBERT Harris and Jeremy Paxman's book *A Higher Form Of Killing* says Britain used arsenic smoke during the Russian Civil War in 1919 and is also thought to have used gas against Afghan tribesmen on the North-West Frontier, also in 1919.

During the Malayan Emergency of the Forties and Fifties, a herbicide called 245T was used against guerrilla food plantations and to remove jungle cover.

M. G. Thornton, Sheffield.

❓ HOW was it possible for Crystal Palace in London to burn down with such ferocity when it was made of glass and steel?

ALTHOUGH the main structure of the Crystal Palace was of glass and wrought iron (large-scale steel manufacture for construction use was not yet available when it was built), the internal galleries, auditorium in the main transept where the great organ was situated, and other features were largely of timber.

It was also very dry and dusty, having been under glass since 1854 when it was re-erected after being moved to Sydenham from the 1851 Great Exhibition site in Hyde Park.

When the fire broke out on the night of November 30, 1936, the wind was blowing along its length and there were no fire-breaks. Consequently, the building acted as a large horizontal flue, spreading flames rapidly from end to end.

It was situated on a hill and water pressure was low so, despite the best efforts of the fire brigade, the blaze got completely out of hand.

It wasn't the first fire at the palace. In 1866, the north end of the building, including the north transept, was destroyed by fire and never rebuilt. Intriguingly, part of the north aisle was the last part left standing for a few days after the main fire until it finally succumbed.

In any case, the Crystal Palace would not have survived World War II. There were no less than three direct hits by V1 flying bombs on the site of the main structure.

R. H. Tunstall, Farnham, Surrey.

❓ DO the colours of the uniforms in *Star Trek* have any significance?

IN the original series, blue shirts – as worn by Dr McCoy and Mr Spock – denoted Science Division, red shirts – worn by Mr Scott, Lt Uhura and various security officers (whom you knew were shortly to get killed) – denoted Engineering, Security and Technical Services, while gold – worn by Chekhov, Sulu and Captain Kirk – meant command.

Just to confuse matters, from time to time Kirk wore a green top of a different design for no apparent reason.

By the time the first cinema film appeared, characters were wearing what appeared to be jump suits in pastel shades with a waist frill – grey standing for science and fawn for everything else.

These were soon ditched and for the remaining films red tunics were adopted, with the different divisions denoted by polo neck jumpers worn underneath: white (for command), sky blue (sciences), gold (services, including engineering and security), olive (medical), grey (operations) and red (cadet).

When *Star Trek: The Next Generation* appeared, styles and colours had changed again. Jump suits were back, but of a different design, with blue tops meaning science (Dr Crusher), gold for security/engineering/technical services (Data, Worf and La Forge) and red for command (Picard and Riker).

This style changed a little for *Deep Space Nine* and *Voyager* but the colours kept their meanings.

Chris Gornall, Penwortham, Lancs.

? WHEN were Royal Navy seamen issued with cutlery instead of having to eat with their hands?

ALL naval seamen brought their own cutlery aboard ship until the middle of the 19th century.

In 1842, officers were issued with solid silver Admiralty cutlery. Lower ranked seamen weren't given cutlery until at least the 1890s.

Michael Barrett, National Maritime Museum, Greenwich, London.

? WHEN footballing greats Tommy Lawton and Dixie Dean met, Dean said: 'Call me Billy; that's OK. Call me Dixie and I'll thump thee.' So why Dixie?

ONE of soccer's finest centre forwards, William Ralph Dean (1907–80) was nicknamed Dixie because of his dark complexion. It was used as an allusion to Dixieland and he didn't like it.

He played for Everton, scoring 379 goals in 437 games, including an all-time record of 60 in one season (1927–28).

Steve Cottley, Liverpool.

? IS there really a breed of sheep-killing parrot in New Zealand?

THE Kea parrot (*Nestor notabilis*) is a remarkably intelligent bird, about 19in long, that lives in the South Island of New Zealand. It is a dull, brownish green with patches of red and yellow. Its beak is long, slender and hooked, with a brush-like tongue.

In summer, the birds live above the tree line, nesting in rocky fissures and feeding on fruit, nectar, seeds and insects.

In winter, they descend from the snow-capped mountains and adopt a more cosmopolitan diet, including fat bitten from around the kidneys on the backs of sheep.

Elizabeth Wright, pet manager, Eastbourne, Sussex.

? WHAT is the significance of the black metal horses along the railway lines between Birmingham and Wolverhampton?

THERE are 12 of these horses, six running in the direction of Birmingham, six in the direction of Wolverhampton. They were commissioned in 1985 as part of Operation Greenline, an environmental awareness campaign that aimed to improve areas left desolate with the loss of heavy industry.

The sponsors were British Rail, West Midland County Council, West Midlands Arts and the local authorities of Birmingham, Sandwell, Dudley and Wolverhampton. The sculptor was Isle of Man-born Kevin Atherton, who was visiting lecturer at the University of Central England in Birmingham.

The iron horses were finished at Corley Welding and installed in March 1987.

The sculpted horses are supposed to represent the speed of the railway and the history of the area as a cradle of the industrial revolution whose 'iron horses' powered the first industries.

Richard Brooks, Regional Railways Central, Birmingham.

? IS it true that the concrete used to make the 1936 Hoover Dam has still not set properly?

THE 726.4ft high Hoover Dam spans the Colorado River at a point called Black Canyon, on the boundary between Nevada and Arizona, 30 miles southeast of Las Vegas.

The dam holds back about 247 square miles of reservoir, known as Lake Mead. This extends about 110 miles upstream with a width between a few hundred feet to eight miles.

Work began on the dam on April 20, 1931, and was completed by March 1, 1936. During this time, 5,218 workers used 3,250,000 cubic yards of concrete in the dam and a further million cubic yards in the power plant – enough to build a monument 100ft square rising to a height of 2.5 miles. More than five million barrels of cement were required.

To counter the problem of chemical heat caused by the setting cement, a series of one-inch-thick pipes was embedded in the concrete through which water was circulated via a refrigeration plant capable of producing 1,000 tons of ice in 24 hours.

It was estimated that the cooling of the concrete was complete in March 1935. Today, the concrete, although solid, still hasn't fully set and the best estimates suggest this will happen around 2030.

Colleen Dwyer, Hoover Dam, Nevada.

WHERE is the cholesterol in an egg, in the yolk or in the white?

THE fat-soluble compound cholesterol is found only in the yolk of an egg.

In the past, it was thought that people should limit the number of eggs they ate because of their cholesterol content. But it is now known that saturated fat, of which eggs have little, is more influential in raising blood cholesterol than dietary cholesterol itself.

Research at the Radcliffe Infirmary, Oxford, concluded that people following a high-fibre, low-fat diet could eat up to seven eggs a week without increasing their blood cholesterol levels.

Anna Jones-Perrott, British Egg Information Service, London.

WE'VE all sung 'Sire, he lives a good league hence . . .' from the carol 'Good King Wenceslas' and read Jules Verne's *20,000 Leagues Under The Sea*, but how far was a league?

A LEAGUE is an obsolete measurement which varied in distance, but is commonly equal to three miles.

It would not be possible to travel to a depth of 20,000 leagues under the sea as this would measure 60,000 miles and the diameter of the Earth is only 7,926 miles so the title of the book clearly refers to the distance travelled underwater and not to the depth attained.

Neil Blake, Flitwick, Beds.

Q HAVE there been any feature films with an all-female or all-male cast?

FAR and away the most outstanding example of this must be David Lean's 1962 epic *Lawrence of Arabia* in which Peter O'Toole and Omar Sherif appeared to such good effect.

Albert Simmons, Oxford.

WALT Disney's 1954 film of Jules Verne's *20,000 Leagues Under The Sea* had an all-male cast, led by James Mason as Captain Nemo, with Kirk Douglas, Peter Lorre and Paul Lukas. It was Disney's first live-action cinemascope production and cost $5 million. The mechanical giant squid that attacked the *Nautilus* submarine cost $200,000, weighed 20 tons and required 28 men to operate it.

Karen McCreedy, James Mason Appreciation Society, London.

THE Lives Of A Bengal Lancer, often quoted in this instance, is not an all-male film.

Mrs Kathleen Burke had a small but important role as a romantic interest leading to the kidnapping of the colonel's son.

J. H. Ashley, Staxton, Scarborough.

Q NEW York is called the Big Apple: what are other major cities in America nicknamed?

MANY U.S. cities have several nicknames, created by incident, person, comment, etc plus their 'official' nicknames dreamed up as slogans by public relations staff.

Among the genuine names are: Dogwood City (Atlanta); Beantown (Boston); Earthquake City (Charleston); Windy City (Chicago); Porkopolis (Cincinnati); Armpit of America (Cleveland); Big D (Dallas); Mile High City (Denver); Motor City (Detroit); Oil Centre (Houston); Mushroomopolis (Kansas City); Glitter Gulch (Las Vegas); Derby Town (Louisville); Bluff City (Memphis); Little Cuba (Miami); Beer City (Milwaukee); The Big Easy (New Orleans); Rock City (Nashville); City of Brotherly Love (Philadelphia); Valley of the Sun (Phoenix); Forest City (Portland); The Big No (Reno); The Gateway (St Louis); Mormon City (Salt Lake City); Bag Town (San Diego); Skid Row (Seattle) and Foggy Bottom (Washington DC).

Rachel Gordon, Harold Washington Library, Chicago, Illinois.

WHY 'nick' in nickname?

'NICKNAME' comes from the 15th century, when 'nekename' was mistakenly derived from the earlier 'an ekename' (an additional name), made up from *eke*, an addition, and *name*.

A similar mistake turned 'an ewt', through mispronunciation, into 'a newt'.
Lorna Gilmour, Collins Dictionaries, Glasgow.

THE process by which the 'n' slid off 'an' and attached itself to 'eke' making 'a nekename' occured in reverse with the words 'adder' and 'orange', originally 'naddre' and 'norange' as the Spanish *naranja* demonstrates.

This proves the French must have derived *l'orange* from us rather than from their continental neighbours.
Louise Jones, Witney, Oxon.

AS a child, my father comforted me during storms by saying: 'It's just God moving his furniture.' Has anyone a better explanation?

WHEN I was in junior school, our teacher used to assure us that the sound of thunder was God playing bowls in the sky.

This caused me to spend many an hour imagining what was going on up there rather than concentrating on my schoolwork.
Julia Guerard, Reigate, Surrey.

WHAT is the origin of the aiguillette decoration that hangs from the shoulder of some military uniforms?

IT is suggested that aiguillettes are the descendants of horse picketing pegs, kept by senior officers and worn over the shoulder so they could be easily distinguished from ordinary soldiers. They were worn in the Army long before they were introduced into the Navy in 1879.

Royal aiguillettes are plain gold, Naval aiguillettes are gold and blue and other military aiguillettes are red and gold.

Flag lieutenants and admirals' secretaries wear aiguillettes on the left shoulder while other wearers of Naval aiguillettes, such as ADCs to royalty, viceroys and governors general, wear them on the right shoulder.
Jerry Apted, Bridport, Dorset.

I WAS told that aiguillettes were there to help the parrot get a better grip.
Mary C. Travers, East Didsbury, Manchester.

WHAT percentage of the world's population can speak English? At what speed is the figure progressing towards 100 per cent?

ABOUT 330 million people speak English as their mother tongue or first language and the number is increasing.

Another 300 million use it as a second language, while up to 300 million use it as a foreign language. That means up to 1,000 million people, roughly a fifth of the world's population, speak English.

English is proving very popular in Eastern Europe, where Russian was traditionally taught in schools. It's difficult to see when the rapid expansion of English might level off.
Simon Freeman, The English-Speaking Union, London.

WHY do cricket commentators refer to a score of 111 as 'a Nelson'?

MICHAEL Rundell's *Dictionary of Cricket* says 'a Nelson', supposedly unlucky, is a total of 111 runs, made by a team or an individual player.

It's named after the great British admiral who was said to have had one arm, one eye and one leg. The ill effects of this score can be countered by the umpire standing on one leg while the figure remains on the scoreboard.

In fact, although Nelson lost an arm and the sight in one eye, he retained both his legs.
Claire Fathers, Test and County Cricket Board, Lord's, London.

TEST Umpire David Shepherd used to lift one foot off the turf whenever he spotted a Nelson on the scoreboard but no one seems to know when this superstition began.

Our research in the early Nineties established that only 33 scores of 111 had been made in the 1,200-odd Test Matches played until then. More batsmen had seen their innings end on other scores in that area – 105 (39), 109 (46), 112 (44), 114 (34) and 117 (36) so any apprehension at that point is illogical.

Australians, however, may be reluctant to agree. When Frank Tyson's express bowling brought England victories in Melbourne and Adelaide in

1955, Australia were shot out for 111 on both occasions. And the same total returned to haunt them at Headingley in 1981, when Bob Willis (8 for 43) snatched a famous 18-run victory for England.

David Frith, editor, Wisden Cricket Monthly, Guildford, Surrey.

BATSMEN think there's a jinx on the score 111 because the figures resemble the three stumps of the wicket with no bails.

E. A. Stebbing, Potters Bar, Herts.

IN 1994, I saw a match at Hove which would have had umpire David Shepherd standing on his head, let alone lifting a foot off the turf.

Sussex Second XI played Middlesex Seconds in a 55-over match. Middlesex scored 221, so Sussex needed 222 to win. Sussex reached 111 for one, at which point the scoreboard showed that score and 111 on the 'runs to win' section.

Then the curse struck: Sussex lost a wicket and subsequently, the match.

John Devonshire, Burgess Hill, Sussex.

? WHAT is the origin of places known as 'hundreds' in the British countryside?

THE term 'hundreds' originates from English medieval feudal settlements where land was leased to tenants for cultivation.

The standard length of a furrow was a furlong (from the Old English *furlang*) equal to 220 yards. Cultivated land was farmed out in strips one furlong by 22 yards: hence one acre (from the Old English *aecer*, a field) equals 4,840 square yards, or one-tenth of a square furlong.

Settlements were, in principle if not in practice, built up: one homestead equalled four acres (four strips of land held by one farmer): one shareland equalled four homesteads (16 acres): one holding equalled four sharelands (64 acres): one vill (township) equalled four holdings (256 acres): one maenor (as in 'lord of the') equalled four vills (1,024 acres): one commote equalled 12 maenors and two vills or 50 vills (12,800 acres) and one hundred equalled 100 vills or two commotes (25,600 acres).

The best-known hundreds are the Chiltern Hundreds, the stewardship of which is a nominal office for which an MP applies in order to resign his seat. A successful applicant receives the appropriate sum of £100. A similar office exists for the Manor of Northstead at Scarborough.

Dr Anthony R. Allen, Harrogate, North Yorks.

A 'HUNDRED' is a unit of land going back to Anglo-Saxon times, dating from a time when a 'hide' was an area of land large enough for one family to live off.

The size of the hide was not constant; it depended on the quality of land and the size of the family. A 'hundred hide', later called a 'hundred', was, in essence, an administrative area which could hold 100 families comfortably.

There is a place near Bere Regis in Dorset called Barrow Hundred, so called after a 'barrow', a Bronze Age burial mound, and because it was used as a meeting place for the people of the area or 'hundred'.

Adrian Room, author: Dictionary Of Place Names In The British Isles, *Bloomsbury Publishing, London.*

? DID Jonathan Swift write about two small satellites of the planet Mars which are invisible to the naked eye, long before they were discovered by telescope?

JONATHAN Swift wrote about these planets in *Gulliver's Travels* in 1726, including fairly accurate descriptions of their distances from Mars and times of rotation. They weren't actually discovered until 1877, when Asaph Hall, at the U.S. Naval Observatory in Washington DC, tired of reading in textbooks that Mars had no moons, spent many nights looking for one with the observatory's new 26in refractor.

He was on the point of giving up when his wife persuaded him to try once more. Delayed for several nights by fog, he eventually saw Phobos and Deimos, which Swift had mentioned 150 years earlier.

But rumours that Swift was a Martian are untrue. He was looking for a feasible bit of science fiction and seized upon Johannes Kepler's third law of planetary motion. Kepler (1571–1630) succeeded, after several futile attempts, in borrowing Galileo's telescope and with it confirmed the existence of the four largest moons of Jupiter. Knowing that Venus had no moon, Earth one and Jupiter four, he formulated a mistaken geometrical progression, predicting two moons for Mars.

John Ridge, Carmarthen.

? WHO is the greatest outsider ever to win a major sporting contest?

IT must be Boris Becker, the 1985 Wimbledon tennis champion. I saw him play a tournament on television in 1984 and thought then that he could win Wim-

bledon the next year. I was even going to put a £100 bet on him at 1,000–1. Unfortunately, I was in France on holiday and overlooked my little wager.
Alan White, Purbrook, Hants.

AT the beginning of the televised stages of the Embassy World Snooker Championships of 1986, Joe Johnson was the biggest outsider at odds of 5,000–1. I remember thinking he was worth risking £1 but I was only 16 and unable to place a bet. Johnson went on to win the championship, leaving me a potential £5,000 down.
J. Laker, Tonbridge, Kent.

❓ HOW many miles of coastline does Great Britain have?

TAKING purely the island of Britain, the total using our 1:625 000 scale OS Travel Map is 9,551.30 miles of continuous coastline. This can be broken down into 3,164.24 miles in England, 830.82 miles in Wales, and the majority of coastline, 5,556.24 miles, in Scotland.
Paula Curtis, Ordnance Survey, Southampton.

THIS question has no finite answer because the coastline isn't one dimensional but a fractal. A fractal has a non-whole-number dimension, in this case 1.26 or more precisely log4 divided by log3.

This arises because the coastline is jagged on all measurement, whatever the scale.

The apparent length varies according to the length of a pacing stick or smallest division on a ruler used to measure it.

A long pacing stick would measure from major headland to major headland, missing out minor promontories. Using a smaller and smaller pacing stick, on a circle, the apparent length steadily approaches pi times the diameter. But in the case of the coastline the apparent length gets longer and longer.

This problem was first considered by Lewis F. Richardson early this century and more recently by Benoit Mandelbrot.
Frederick A. Fryer, American University, London N19.

❓ I'VE never seen frogs strong-arming other frogs, so why 'frog-marched'?

FROG-MARCHING originally meant four people carrying a resisting person along, face down, by holding a limb each, in an outstretched manner resembling a frog. Later, the word was used for any means of forcibly moving a person against their will.

Ian Timpson, Harrogate.

IN the years before the end of World War II, inhabitants of military towns will have witnessed the true frog-march as carried out on errant members of the Armed Forces during their nights 'on the town'.

The offenders, thus treated, were usually intoxicated to the extent that their behaviour had exceeded the limit beyond which the Shore Patrols and/or Military Police were prepared to countenance.

Should an offender decide to resist the patrol's efforts to persuade him to come quietly, he would be pushed to the ground, turned face down, and four patrolmen would each take hold of an arm or a leg, lift the captive and march him to the patrol wagon.

In transit, he would look like a frog leaping. Struggles were sometimes rewarded by the struggler being dropped to the ground.

Today's description of 'frog-marching' refers to an offender being impelled in a required direction by two peace offenders, each taking the offender by an arm. Mild stuff that!

G. H. Reed, Newton Stewart, Wigtownshire.

? DESPITE reassurances, I'm terrified of being trapped in one of those modern, self-cleaning toilet cubicles. Has this ever happened to anyone?

THERE has so far never been any substantiated cases of a person being trapped in any of these toilets. However, several people using an automatic superloo in Alnwick, Northumberland, were blasted with dye and soaked with high-pressure jets of water after the 'anti-vandal' system was accidentally triggered. Two pensioners were knocked off their seats, with one having her skin dyed orange for several days.

This is nothing, though, compared with the many amazing things that can happen to unsuspecting 'penny-users' in many other kinds of toilet.

A frightening example of the dangers of vacuum toilets, as used on aircraft and boats, came in 1987 when a 70-year-old woman aboard a cruise ship off the coast of Vancouver flushed the toilet while still sitting down. The pressure was so great she had to have immediate major surgery.

New Scientist reported a male airline passenger who was stuck to his seat after flushing and was only able to free himself after the plane lost altitude.

And the worst case must be the death of a man electrocuted while using a temporary public toilet in Ryde, Isle of Wight, after a broken light fitting made the all-metal cubicle 'live'.

Craig Ross, Aberdeen.

❓ DOES Bolsover MP Dennis Skinner possess more than one jacket and tie?

WORKING in a picture library, I pulled out the file we have on the Labour MP to confirm this. Of 30 or so shots going back over five years, I could see at least two jackets, both a very similar grey colour, which he mostly wears with black or grey trousers and white, single-stripe shirt.

I also counted three different though very similar ties, all red with diagonal black stripes.

My own theory for his clothing constancy is that as he is known as the hardest-working parliamentarian in the country, with an unbeaten record of taking part in 98.8 per cent of votes in the Commons. He has hardly any time for shopping and just buys the clothes he likes.

He's not always a fuddy dresser. I found a picture of him wearing a baseball cap and trendy winter jacket, with a scarf over his face and fashionable back-pack.

Lisa Mellor, Streatham, South London.

❓ WHEN and by whom was the term 'special relationship' first used to describe Anglo-American relations?

THE idea of a 'special relationship' between Britain and the U.S. was pushed heavily by Winston Churchill during the early days of World War II.

He emphasised our two nations' great similarities of language, history and culture as part of his attempt to persuade the U.S. that it should join in against a common enemy.

The actual words 'special relationship' are thought not to have been coined by Churchill until after the war in a speech in the Commons in late 1945.

Hugh Jones, Wrexham, Clwyd.

? OUR European neighbours are rudely referred to as krauts, wops, dagos and frogs. By what name do inhabitants of other European countries refer to us British?

MOST European countries, including Norway, Spain, Italy and The Netherlands, use the words 'Brits', 'British' or more often 'English' which, if you come from Wales or Scotland, is probably as offensive as you're likely to hear.

Exceptions include the Germans who call us *Inselaffen*, translatable as 'island monkeys' and the French, who use *rosbifs*, meaning 'roast beefs'.
Katey Chivell, Ilford, Essex.

I'M told by Breton friends that the French call us *rosbifs* not because we eat beef but because of our tendency to turn red-faced when we don't get our way.
Steve Cowling, Nesscliff, Shropshire.

SO the Germans call us *Inselaffen*, or Island Monkeys. A monkey wrench is known in Germany as *Ein Englander*. Perhaps they're trying to tell us something.
M. J. W. Cassidy, Kenley, Surrey.

———

? WHICH building in Britain has the most number of storeys underground?

A DEVELOPMENT in Aldersgate, East London, in which my company was involved as main contractor, needed a deep excavation to accommodate 14 levels of underground car parking.

I am not aware of any other Central London building which has this number of floors below ground.
M. P. Peskin, Costain Construction Limited, London SE1.

———

? WHO was the Rorke who gave his name to Rorke's Drift?

JAMES Rorke was born in the Cape Colony in 1827, the son of a soldier in an Irish regiment. After serving in the Frontier War of 1846, he arrived in Durban, married, and in 1849 acquired a 3,000-acre farm on the west bank of the Buffalo River, the boundary between Natal and the Zulu kingdom.

He built a homestead – which subsequently became an army hospital – farmed and knocked down the banks on both sides of the river to ease the passage of traders to and from Zululand, creating the 'drift'.

Rorke was popular with the Zulus living nearby, who called him Jimu, and the trading post he set up became known as 'TkwaJimu' or 'Jim's Place'.

Rorke became a Field-Cornet, a lieutenant of irregular cavalry with local administrative and sometimes magisterial duties, in the Buffalo Border Guard, and died about 1875.

His property was subsequently acquired by the Swedish missionary, Otto Witt, who opted to join his wife and children at Helpmakaar, 12 miles away, rather than stay for the battle there in 1879.

The film *Zulu*, although shot many miles away in the Royal Natal National Park, was very accurate about the Battle of Rorke's Drift and the Zulu's victory except for its depiction of Witt.

Robin Elliott, Hampstead, London.

AT school I was taught an alphabetical poem which began: 'An Austrian army, awfully arrayed/Boldly, by battery, besieged Belgrade....' Can anyone remember the rest?

THERE are several versions of this poem under such titles as 'An Austrian Army', 'Alliterations Artful Aid' and – probably the best known – 'The Siege Of Belgrade'.

Authorship of the work is also in doubt, many giving credit to poet Alaric A. Watts (1797–1864) who first published it in the *Literary Gazette* in 1820, while others feel it is a few years older.

An Austrian army awfully arrayed / Boldly by battery besieged Belgrade.
Cossack commanders cannonading come / Dealing destruction's devastating doom;
Every endeavour engineers essay / For fame, for fortune fighting-furious fray.
Generals 'gainst generals grapple, gracious God! / How honours heaven heroic hardihood!
Infuriate-indiscriminate in ill / Kinsmen kill kindred – kindred kinsmen kill;
Labour low levels loftiest longest lines / Men march 'mid mounds, 'mid moles, 'mid murderous mines:
Now noisy noxious numbers notice nought / Of outward obstacles opposing ought;
Poor patriots! Partly purchased – partly press'd / Quite quaking, quickly, Quarter! Quarter! quest.
Reason returns, religious right redounds / Suwarrow stops such sanguinary sounds.

*Truce to thee, Turkey, triumph to thy train / Unwise, unjust, unmerciful
Ukraine!*

*Vanish, vain victory! vanish, victory vain! / Why wish we warfare? Wherefore
welcome were*

*Xerxes, Ximenes, Xanthus, Xavier / Yield, yield, ye youths, ye yeomen, yield
your yell:*

Zeno's Zampatee's, Zoroaster's zeal / Attracting all, arms against acts appeal!
Patricia Lenny, Markethill, Co Armagh.

THIS poem first appeared in the Westminster School magazine, *The Trifler*, in
1817, dedicated to lovers of alliteration and 'presented to us by a friend'.

It was almost the same version though with Zorpator instead of Zampetee.
The lack of a J line reflects the fact that even in the early 19th century, dictionaries intermingled I and J words in a single series.

'Suwarrow', who 'stops such sanguinary sounds', is an Anglicised name of
Count Suvorov, one of Russia's great military commanders. He distinguished
himself in the Russo-Turkish War of 1787–91 during which Belgrade was
occupied for a while by Russia's ally, Austria.
Ernest Brook, Weston-super-Mare, Avon.

ℚ WHY is the zip area of a man's trousers known as his 'flies'?

THE idea of the zip fastener is generally credited to Whitcomb Johnson of
Chicago who patented a 'slide fastener' on August 29, 1893. This was originally meant for use on shoes and boots.

The first zip to look anything like the ones we know today was patented by
Swedish-American engineer Gideon Sundback in 1913.

The name 'flies', however, comes from the arrangement in the flies area
before zips came along. The use of buttons was the norm and, although generally protective, they did have a habit of occasionally popping open or leaving
tell-tale gaps. This meant that the use of loose flaps of material was used, two
to ensure closure and a third to overlap and cover the join.

The term 'flies', stemming from the word meaning 'to move through the air',
was already applied to other things such as loose ends of ropes, flags, sails,
even tent flaps, and was therefore quite a natural term to use for the clothing
layout at the zip area.
Val Savage, fashion stylist, London.

? IF the Hubble telescope were pointing towards Earth, how much detail would we expect to see?

TECHNICAL jargon about the Hubble camera's resolution being 0.043 arc seconds per pixel doesn't mean much to most people but it can be translated into being able to distinguish something the size of a football from the telescope's orbital altitude of around 380 miles – assuming that weather and atmospheric conditions generally co-operate (which is a big 'if'). But that's nothing exceptional.

While they are still kept very much under wraps, U.S. Air Force reconnaissance satellites can do at least as well as that, and civilian earth resources satellites are close to a time when they'll be able to distinguish objects a few feet across on the surface.

The Hubble space telescope's great capabilities would be wasted on looking at the Earth. High above the obscuring layers of the Earth's atmosphere, its various instruments are devoted to looking deeper into the universe than has been possible hitherto.

Orbiting at many thousands of miles per hour, nothing is more dramatic than its ability to lock onto a distant, dim object and hold steady for hours while its cameras and other sensors study it. It can keep pointing to within 0.007 of an arc second – roughly the equivalent of locking onto a penny on the Scottish borders from the South Coast of England.

H. J. P. Arnold, Space Frontiers, Havant, Hants.

? WHY do we 'turn the tables' on someone?

THIS expression to describe a reversal of fortune or circumstance, dates from around the 15th century and refers simply to altering the course of a game of chess, draughts, cards etc from close to defeat to certain victory, making it seem is if the board (table as it was commonly known) had been physically turned.

Heather Wallace, Aberdeen.

IS ANOTHER BANK HOLIDAY NECESSARY?

DEAR *Answers*,—I thoroughly enjoyed the August Bank Holiday but now it is a thing of the past, what is there to look forward to in the way of another? One is coming certainly – so is Christmas! In fact, they both come together. Nearly five months' interval? Is not this far too long?

There are a vast number of people to whom Bank Holidays are their only ones. A Bank Holiday is urgently required in the autumn, say the middle of October, when the leaves are falling though the bleakness of winter is not yet upon us.

Think what a boon it would be to millions of us who have nothing but hard work to look forward to till Yule-tide. Surely one more day could be spared; it is not so very much to ask.

B. A. N. Klarke, The City.

Undoubtedly, another Bank Holiday is necessary at the period stated. The difficulty is in obtaining it.

I beg to throw out the suggestion that some member of parliament should pilot a new Bank Holiday Bill into the House. He would gain, I feel sure, both the thanks of the working classes and the support of his fellow-members.

May this discussion be the means of procuring for the great masses, whose time of pleasure is so limited, another day's liberty.

The national holiday frequently falls on a day when the weather is exceedingly unpropitious; another day in the autumn will in some measure atone for this, it being more likely to be fine.

Interested, London E.C.

I am not quite sure that another Bank Holiday is necessary. No doubt it would be a desideratum to bank clerks and others whose salaries thereby would not suffer. But what about those tradesmen and artisans who are paid by the hour or day, and who would thus lose a day's pay? Would they appreciate a holiday which means a reduced exchequer with an increased expenditure?

Would another day in the autumn atone for an earlier holiday when the weather has been unpropitious? I hardly think so, for the weather in England at the time suggested for the extra Bank Holiday is, to use a slang expression, no great 'catch,' it usually being very murky about the beginning or middle of October; and if we do happen to get a pleasant day we regard it more as a rara avis than anything else.

Dubious, Liverpool.

Living, as I do, in the heart of the coal district, I see the establishment of a set of holidays which are at once a necessity and a blessing to many. I refer to that known as 'Mabon's Day,' by which the colliers obtain as a free day the first Monday in each month. They thus have 12 working days in the year accorded to them, which is no more than they deserve, considering the nature of their occupation and the terrible risks they run daily.

To one class of the community a fair quantum of holidays has been, therefore, conceded and, such being the case, may we not extend the field of operations by obtaining at any rate one extra day for the general public, especially for that portion of it to whom the word holiday is an 'unknown number.'

Each succeeding summer sees the well-to-do portion of the community disporting themselves 'by mount and stream and sea,' wooing thereby health and strength for the ensuing winter. To many of these the thought of anything so commonplace, not to say plebeian, as a 'bank holiday' never occurs and yet, if they knew what a world of pleasure and expectation is bound up in those two words to very many of their poorer brethren, would they not at once give their vote and influence towards the obtaining of another holiday before the golden skies of summer have been changed for the leaden ones of winter?

Pro Bono Publico, Cardiff.

WORD endings, particularly '-ence' and '-ance' always make me think twice. Is there any rule as to which is correct in a particular circumstance?

THERE'S no particular rule to follow when using words ending 'ence' or 'ance', suffixes originating from the Latin *'entia'*, which was superseded by *'antia'*.

This suffix evolved from Latin, through Old French, into modern English. *The Oxford Companion to the English Language* explains: 'Its uses are for forming states, conditions, situations and instances.'

So 'ence' and 'ance' have the same meaning, the different spellings having evolved with the individual word through the creation of the modern language.

Suzanne Blumson, Writers' Monthly, Turnpike Lane, London.

? WHAT is the oldest magazine in publication in the world, or in Britain?

THE oldest continuing periodical in the world is the *Philosophical Transactions of the Royal Society*, published in London, which first appeared on March 6, 1665. Britain's oldest weekly periodical is *The Lancet*, first published in 1823.

The most durable annual is *Old Moore's Almanack*, published since 1679, when it appeared as a broadsheet produced by Dr Francis Moore (1657–1715) of Southwark, London, to advertise his 'physiks'. Published by W. Foulsham & Co Ltd of Slough, Berks, its aggregate sale to date is more than 113 million.

Carole Jones, Guinness Book of Records, Enfield, Middx.

? WHY do older people talk about their 'salad days'?

IT has been suggested they're referring to the days when they could eat celery without their teeth falling out. In fact, they're quoting words Shakespeare gave to Cleopatra in his *Antony and Cleopatra* (Act I, scene v).

The full line is 'My salad days, when I was green in judgment', a metaphor for the time of inexperienced youth, before cynicism and knowledge of one's limitations set in.

Elizabeth Ward, Dundee.

? WAS London's Seven Sisters Road named after seven sisters? If so, who were they?

WHEN Seven Sisters Road, connecting Holloway and Tottenham, was built in 1831–33, it was named after the circle of seven elm trees on Page Green at its Tottenham end, said to have been planted by seven sisters who were about to separate.

These trees were first recorded in 1631 but by 1840 they were dying and seven new trees were planted in 1852 by seven sisters called McRae.

Thirty-four years later, 2,000 people attended the ceremony when four local people arranged for more new elms, the planting being carried out by seven sisters of the Hibberd family.

The spade used in both the 1852 and 1886 ceremonies is in Bruce Castle Museum in the house where the historic meeting took place of Henry VIII and his sister Margaret, Queen of Scotland, in 1516.

Another ceremony in 1953 involved seven local sisters replacing the dying elms with Lombardy Poplars. These are still going strong in Seven Sisters Gardens, near the junction of Seven Sisters Road and Broad Lane.

Tim Pyall, arboricultural officer, Haringey Council.

THE seven elm trees on Page Green are marked as the '7 Sesters' on a map of 1754 and 'Seven Systers' on one from 1805.

J. J. Tuthill, London SW9.

THE Seven Sisters was the sign of an old pub at Page Green, Tottenham, opposite the circle of seven elms, with a walnut tree in the middle, where local tradition said a martyr was burnt to death.

J. C. Meekins, Hassocks, Sussex.

THE tale I heard is that a wealthy merchant planted seven trees for his seven daughters. Six grew tall and straight but one withered, like one of his daughters, who had a withered arm.

Seven roads in the Seven Sisters area had the names Ida, Roslyn, Elizabeth and so on, which I like to think were the names of the seven sisters, though some of these roads have now disappeared.

Ms. S. B. Elis, Hertford, Herts.

? EVERY episode of ITV's *The Bill* ended with credits and a WPC and PC's legs walking down a cobbled street. Who do they belong to?

IN the long history of *The Bill*, there were three versions of the closing shot. The most recent was produced to speed up the closing sequence and save a few more seconds for the action.

Actress Karen England has put her best foot forward as the female officer in all three versions. She had walk-on parts in the series between 1984–92 and appeared in four different speaking parts in 1988–91.

The size nines of the latest male officer belong to Paul Page-Hanson, who had walk-on parts from 1984–90 and a speaking part in June 1990.

Mariette Overeynder, The Bill press office, London.

? HAS anyone really been swallowed by a whale and survived?
APART from the Biblical story of Jonah, French scientist M. de Parville, in his *Journal des Debats* of 1914, claimed that on February 7, 1891, two crew members of the American whaler *Star of the East* were lost overboard from a small boat while trying to harpoon a sperm whale off the Falklands.

He says the whale was eventually harpooned, killed and winched on deck to face the flensing knives.

The next morning its stomach was split open to reveal the unconscious but miraculously alive seaman James Bartley. His hair and parts of his face, limbs and body were bleached snowy white by his 16-hour ordeal in the whale's digestive fluids, and when he came round he was raving mad.

However, he recovered his senses within three weeks although his skin retained its 'ghastly pallor'.

Mike Barwell, editor, Alternative Book of Records, Hedon, Hull.

THE old chestnut about James Bartley being swallowed by a whale was investigated by Sydney G. Brown and Ray Gambell and shown to be an old sea dog's tale.

In *Mariners' Mirror* Volume 79 (1993), they say whalers of that period never brought whales' stomachs aboard ship, there was no whaling ship of that name and there's no record of a sailor of that era called James Bartley.

The idea of a whale swallowing a human seems less likely than of a human swallowing the tale.

Bruce Laing, Aberdeen.

? WHAT is the history of the ruined house which can be seen close to the M25/M11 junction?
THIS is Hill Hall, originally built before the Norman Conquest when it was owned by a Saxon called Godric. The house was rebuilt in the Tudor period by Cambridge classical scholar Sir Thomas Smith, Regius Professor of Civil Law

from 1542 and later Secretary of State in Somerset's government.

He was Chancellor of the Order of the Garter and, on the accession of Elizabeth I, became ambassador to France. He was much travelled and influenced by architecture he had seen and endeavoured to introduce many such features in the construction of Hill Hall.

The building remained in the Smith family until the 20th century but was sold in 1923 and passed through various owners and uses – maternity home, RAF officers' billet, accommodation for soldiers and prisoners of war – before becoming a women's open prison in 1952. Its most famous inmate was Christine Keeler.

Hill Hall was gutted by fire in 1969 and is now administered by English Heritage. There are plans for its restoration.

Vernon W. Jackson (descendant of the Smith family), Wellingborough, Northants.

THERE are in fact two ruined mansions near this motorway junction. Hill Hall, in Theydon Mount, east of the Bell Common tunnel over the M25, and Copped (or Copt) Hall, west of the tunnel, in Epping.

Copped Hall was built in 1753–58 for John Conyers MP. After his death in 1775, James Wyatt remodelled some of the rooms but the whole building was destroyed by fire in May 1917.

After the opening of the M25, the building became the subject of many speculative development proposals but none came to fruition and in 1993 Copped Hall Trust was formed to secure preservation of the mansion and its outbuildings.

Hill Hall is currently owned by English Heritage, which allows limited tours of its internal period wall paintings. There are also a number of private apartments within it.

Paul Sutton, Epping Forest District Council.

THE early history of Copped Hall estate dates from about 1150 and the name Coppedehalle was used as early as 1258.

The Hall and estate have had a chequered history. In the 12th and 13th centuries, it was held by families who served the kings as huntsmen in the Royal Forest of Essex, one of whose remnants is Epping Forest.

Henry VIII visited Copped Hall and Mary Tudor became almost a state prisoner there during Edward VI's reign.

When the building was demolished in the 1750s so a new Hall could be built, a stained glass window from it was sold for £400 to St Margaret's

Church, Westminster, where it still stands.

K. H. Gray, Clacton, Essex.

AFTER the 1917 fire, Copped Hall wasn't occupied except by ghosts of victims of the fire and, if you read James Herbert's book *Lair*, by a plague of mutant rats.

P. A. Buxton, Luton, Beds.

MANY years ago, I spent many nights inside ruined Copped Hall, looking for the various ghosts supposed to haunt the building. The only thing of note that happened was one night at about 2am when several armed men jumped in through the windows and demanded to know why I was there.

They laughed at my ghost-hunting venture and told me they were after Martians they claimed used Copped Hall as a regular landing site. As we swopped ghost and Martian tales, I was never sure who was the most ridiculous.

R. C. Woodhouse, Hunstanton, Norfolk.

MY grandfather drove a horse-drawn fire engine, one of several local appliances called to the fire at Copped Hall on Sunday, May 5, 1917. He travelled ten miles there, only to find no adequate water supply and almost all the Hall destroyed.

George Butcher, Broxbourne, Herts.

ACCORDING to Lady Lucinda Lambton's TV programme about historical architecture, this house was built on the site of a much older house which is reputed to be where William Shakespeare was staying when he wrote *A Midsummer Night's Dream*.

S. Mabey, Cardiff.

HOW does the puzzling points system in county championship cricket operate?

THE points system is designed to give a fair balance between bat and ball, with 16 points given for a win, none for a draw or loss. In addition, batting and bowling points can be gained during the first 120 overs of each first innings as follows: one point for 200–249 scored, two for 250–299, three for 300–349 and the maximum four for 350–plus; one point for 3–4 wickets taken, two for 5–6 wickets, three for 7–8 wickets and the maximum four points for 9–10 wickets.

In a tied match (very rare), each side scores eight points plus any batting or bowling points. In a drawn match with the scores level (also rare), the side batting in the fourth innings scores eight points plus any batting or bowling points.

If bad weather or any other reason reduces play to less than eight hours from the start of play, a one-innings-a-side match is played, with 12 points going to the winners, six points each if it is tied, and a drawn match with the scores level earns the side batting second six points. There are no batting or bowling points in a single-innings match.

Points can be deducted for providing a pitch deemed unsuitable for First Class cricket.

Ian Elsdon, Buscot Park Cricket Club, Oxon.

WHEN Pope John Paul visited Brazil in 1980, he was so moved by the poor residents of Favela do Vidigal that he gave his ring to be used to help them. What happened to the ring and did the villagers benefit from it?

POPE John Paul was obviously moved by conditions in the slum. 'A society that is not socially just and does not intend to be puts its own future in danger,' he said. To the amazement of the crowd and Vatican officials, he took off his gold ring and said to parish priest Father Italo Coelho: 'I want to give this ring to your parish.'

The Pope had worn the ring since 1967. It was given to him by Pope Paul VI when he was made a cardinal.

The slum's residents were so overcome by the Pope's generosity that they decided not to sell the ring but to keep it as a symbol of the Pope's stand against poverty and an inspiration to themselves.

Kieran Conry, Catholic Media Office, London.

MY radio station says Clumber Street, Nottingham, is the busiest street in the world. Is this true?

CLUMBER Street, Nottingham's main commercial road, may seem pretty busy but the most likely contender for the busiest street in the world is Nathan Road, Kowloon, Hongkong, named after a former governor of the territory.

The road is in the Tsim Sha Tsui shopping and entertainment district, also known as the Golden Mile, and is busy 24 hours a day.

Marie Prince, Hongkong Tourist Association.

? IN the 1930s, I took excursion trains from Romford, Essex, across London to Aldershot, Hampshire, without changing trains. Would this still be possible?

VIRTUALLY all the lines used by such a train in the Thirties are still in use and it would be possible to run trains from Romford to Aldershot. The most likely route would be via Stratford, Dalston, Willesden, Kew, Staines and Woking to Aldershot.

However, such a route would be unlikely to attract sufficient interest nowadays to be commercially viable.

Graham J. Coombs, London.

THESE excursions were run for the annual Aldershot Tattoo which used to last for about seven days in the 1930s. The Tattoo in June 1935 attracted 483,000 spectators.

The last one was held in 1939, not long before the outbreak of World War II, since when only a much-reduced Army Show has been performed.

An excursion train from Romford to Aldershot today would be most unlikely unless Romford were playing Aldershot Town Football Club in an important cup match.

Paul Henham, Aldershot, Hants.

ALTHOUGH no passenger or freight train makes this direct journey, it's still perfectly possible. Thanks to the extensive rail network built up since the 19th century, travel between most stations in Britain is possible without changing trains.

Stephen Milton, Railtrack, London.

? IS there a historical origin to the 'Sing A Song Of Sixpence' nursery rhyme?

LEONARD B. Lubin says the rhyme is based on Henry VIII's seizure of church lands, his divorce from Catherine of Aragon and later disposal of Anne Boleyn.

The 'sixpence' and 'rye' are the money and grainfields confiscated by Henry from the Church. The 'pie' was presented to the King by the Abbot of Newstead, containing the title deeds of 24 church properties. The 'blackbirds' are black-robed monks. The King added this gift to his other wealth in the counting house.

Meanwhile Queen Catherine, sure she wouldn't be divorced, sat in her parlour eating 'bread' (Henry's slights) and 'honey' (the belief that Spain and the Church would preserve her marriage).

The 'maid' (Anne Boleyn, once a maid-in-waiting to the Queen) was first noticed by the King in the gardens of Whitehall Palace. Later, when she upset Henry by producing a girl instead of a boy, another 'blackbird' in the form of a royal headsman, relieved Anne of not just her nose, but her entire head.
Linda Luff, Tonbridge, Kent.

THE version of the song I know concludes: 'It caused so much commotion/ That little Jenny Wren/Flew down into the garden/And put it back again,' which doesn't exactly square with the Anne Boleyn theory.
Mrs F. Marshall, Halifax.

WHEN I was in charge of the Patent Office Library, one of its treasures was a 15th-century recipe book which gave advice on how to serve a pie full of live birds. One had to line a pie dish with thick paste and pack it with rye to keep its shape. The rye is removed after baking and replaced with the birds.

I've always been intrigued at the thought that the original rhyme was: 'Sing a song of thick paste, Pack it full of rye...'

This pie used to be prepared for visiting notables, including kings, when much mirth was promised.
Miss M. F. Webb, Sutton, Surrey.

WHO was Beatrice Blore Browne (1887–1921) who 'feared naught but God', according to her headstone, which incorporates a marble motor vehicle roadwheel, in the cemetery on Great Ormes Head in Llandudno?

ONE of the most beautiful and original gravestones in the country, the grave of Beatrice Blore Browne at St Tudno's churchyard is one of Llandudno's more peculiar tourist attractions.

It's just yards from the tomb of Alfred Tennyson Smith, the man responsible for American Prohibition, and the graves of Jess Yates, father of Paula and one-time host of TV's *Stars On Sunday*, as well as a man who deserves a mention for having such a good name, Frank Plank.

Little is known about the woman and the circumstances of her death other than local rumours about her being a committed suffragette with family connections to a local coach company, the first people to drive a motorised vehicle along the Great Orme – hence the winged wheel gravestone.

The double burial plot was purchased by her husband, George Wilkins Browne, of Delamere, in the village of Penmaen Mawr, although the second part wasn't used.

This old quarrying village is about ten miles from the cemetery and it was quite exceptional in those days to be buried in a different parish. The quality of the headstone suggests some wealth.

Local newspapers of the time have no mention of her death in 1921 at the age of only 34.

John Sumbland, former sexton, Aberconwy Borough Council, Penrhynside, Gwynedd.

A SIMILAR gravestone in St Peter's churchyard, Harborne, Birmingham, commemorates the death of a local schoolgirl, killed in a road accident in the 1920s.

Mrs B. L. Carter, Plympton, Devon.

? WHERE in the world does the highest rise and fall of the sea tide occur?

THE greatest tides on Earth occur in the Bay of Fundy, between Nova Scotia, Canada, to the east and New Brunswick, Canada, and Maine, U.S., to the west.

In this area, Burncoat Head in the Minas Basin, Nova Scotia, has the greatest mean spring range, with 14.5m (47ft 6in). A range of 16.6m (54ft 6in) was recorded in Leaf Basin in Ungava Bay, Quebec, Canada, in 1953.

By contrast, Tahiti, in the Pacific Ocean, experiences virtually no tide.

The greatest mean spring range in Great Britain is at Beachley, on the River Severn, with a range of 12.4m (40ft 8.5in). The average for the British Isles is 4.6m (15ft).

Carole Jones, Guinness Book Of Records.

IN pre-war Sunderland the Sundays in Lent were known as Tid, Mid, Miseray, Carling, Palm and Paste-egg days. We still have Palm Sunday and Easter eggs on Easter Sunday. What were the other four?

THERE are variations of this in different parts of the North of England. When I was a boy living in Newcastle upon Tyne in the Twenties, I knew Tid, Mid, Miseray, Carling, Palm and Paste-egg Day.

Tid was a contraction of Te Deum, sung on the second Sunday in Lent. Mid came from Mi Deus and Miseray was Miserere, the beginning of the penitential Psalm 51.

Carling, Carline, Carlin, Carle or Care Sunday was the fifth Sunday in Lent, Passion Sunday. The old meaning of the word 'Care', until about 1600, was mourning and sorrow. Carlings, named from this Sunday, were peas steeped overnight to soften them, then parched, fried in butter and eaten with salt and pepper.

In some areas of the North, there were customs associated with eating carlings, such as the person who ate the last one from the dish would be the first to be married.

Palm Sunday needs no explanation. Paste-eggs or pace-eggs were associated with Easter Sunday or Monday. The name is derived from Paschal, used for the Jewish Passover and by Christians for Easter. They were hard-boiled eggs coloured by boiling in water containing a dye, or painted afterwards.

Trevor Hopkinson, Harrogate, North Yorks.

HAS anyone ever seen a car door being locked in a film?

ROGER Moore locked the door of his white Lotus Esprit while spying on the hideout of a Cuban hitman in Madrid in the 1981 James Bond film *For Your Eyes Only*.

The Lotus self-destructs when a thug ignores the 'Burglar Protected' label and tries to break one of its windows.

Roger, car keys in one hand and Carole Bouquet in the other, arrives seconds too late and says to the girl: 'I hope you have a car.' They escape in her battered Citreon 2CV.

The doors of the same Lotus were also locked by Roger Moore in his 1977 third Bond outing, *The Spy Who Loved Me*.

Ian Guard, Kidderminster, Worcs.

NOT only is it rare to see a car door being locked during a film, it's also unusual to see an everyday parking manoeuvre being performed instead of just driving up and leaping out.

Both of these can be seen in the 1968 film *Bullitt* when Steve McQueen reverses his 1968 Ford Mustang Fastback into a space and then purposefully locks the door before entering a corner shop to buy a handful of TV dinners.

Not so much care was exercised later in the film when, during the car chase that ranks as one of the best filmed, McQueen uses his Mustang to ram the villains in their black Dodge Charger off the road and into a petrol station, causing a huge explosion.

Alan Davies, Stroud, Gloucs.

WERE there many successful escapes by Allied PoWs from Japanese prison camps during World War II?

ALTHOUGH some escapes were successful within a few days of capture, few succeeded from permanent PoW camps because it is easy to identify Westerners roaming the oriental world.

One that is recalled involved three officers who, aided by Hong Kong Chinese, escaped from Sham Shui Po Camp, Kowloon. One was a New Zealander, another a medical officer.

While passing through Japanese-occupied Kwangtung Province, they were hidden and passed between many communist military and guerrilla groups, before reaching safety in Nationalist territory. They eventually reached Ceylon. After recovering, at least one returned to active duty.

Jim Jacobs, Fareham, Hants.

AFTER the fall of Hong Kong, my father, Bombadier B. H. Parrott RA, escaped with three colleagues from the camp at Sham Shui Po. He travelled across China to rejoin British forces and was awarded the Military Medal for this achievement.

After his escape, he went on to serve with Brigadier Orde Wingate on the Chindits expeditions.

Pamela Skinner, Leighton Buzzard, Beds.

WHAT'S the difference between a trout, a salmon and a salmon trout?

ALL these fish are members of the Salmonidae family. Trout (brown trout) live in rivers and lakes and, though their colour varies from area to area, are normally golden brown and heavily spotted.

Salmon are born in rivers and the juvenile fish look much like small brown trout. After three or four years, they turn silvery and migrate to sea, where they may stay for up to four years before returning to the river of their birth.

When they return to freshwater they are still silvery but the longer they're in the river, the more mottled and dark they become.

'Salmon trout' is the fishmongers' name for sea trout. These are nothing more than brown trout which migrate to sea and, like the salmon, return to the river of their birth. Like the salmon they're silvery when they enter the river, but when they have been in freshwater for some time, revert to the appearance of the brown trout.

Sandy Leventon, Trout and Salmon Magazine, Peterborough.

IF an Olympic sprinter and a top sprint cyclist started from stationary, how much ground could the runner make before the cyclist caught him?

EVERY race is different but the consensus among experts at the British Cycling Federation's sports science support programme at Chichester Institute is that a pursuit cyclist, starting acceleration for a 4,000m race, would cover the first 125m in about 11 to 12 seconds.

A sprint athlete covers 100m in about ten seconds. On this basis, the pursuit cyclist would probably overtake the runner at about the 100m mark.

For a sprint cyclist taking on a sprint athlete, it's estimated that the change of leader would be somewhere between the 80m and 90m points.

Kelly Simpson, National Coaching Foundation, Leeds, West Yorks.

WHAT was so Black about the Black Prince?

THE name 'Black Prince' wasn't used during the lifetime of Edward, Prince of Wales (1330–76), eldest son of Edward III and Philippa of Hainault. It wasn't until two centuries after his death that he was given this nickname.

Edward was a legend in his lifetime as he fought, jousted and lived a soldier's lifestyle. He was knighted at 16 and became a great military leader as a teenager.

This hero of Crécy, Poitiers and Nagere revolted against the extravagance of others by always wearing black armour at the head of his army. He stipulated in his will that all his followers should wear sombre black or grey at his funeral and didn't wish to have monuments erected to his memory.

He left a fine set of black hangings for the Church.

He died of dysentery in 1372, a year before his father. His son became Richard II. Oddly, his effigy in Canterbury Cathedral is in gold.

Audrey Openshaw, Weybridge, Surrey.

❓ HAS there ever been a half-crown note?

NEVER in Britain though on three occasions, all in wartime, low-denomination notes, including the half-crown, were considered.

In 1917, proofs were prepared for 5 shilling (25p) currency notes, and the following year for 1 shilling (5p) notes to help the Royal Mint cope with the increased demand for coins in World War I. The 5-shilling notes were printed but never distributed and were destroyed soon after the war.

In 1941, the Bank of England prepared eight million 5-shilling and the same number of half-crown notes as a contingency measure against a possible shortage of coin and to conserve silver which was imported mainly from the U.S. and had to be repaid after the war.

Both denominations were distributed to banks but remained unissued and were destroyed after the war.

Also in 1941, the Bank of England printed 259,660,000 notes for use by our armed forces in the Western Desert and other territories such as Libya, Italy and Greece. Known as British Military Authority notes, they came in £1, 10 shilling (50p), 5 shilling, 2/6 and 1 shilling denominations to a conventional design with the lion and crown of the General Staff and a metallic thread incorporated within the paper – an innovatory feature at the time.

Most of these notes were pulped in 1948/9.

John Keyworth, curator, Bank of England Museum, Threadneedle St, London.

SHORTLY after the outbreak of World War II, there was a shortage of coins and, as an emergency measure, postal orders, including half crown ones, were used as well as coins.

My father considered that a few postal orders in his wallet were more convenient than a pocketful of coins.

G. W. F. Archer, Oxford.

WHAT is the origin of the word 'twerp'?

'TWERP' and 'dwarf' may be different forms of the same word. There are several cases of such pairs of words in English (though sometimes with slightly differing meanings) as a result of the coming together of the Saxon and Norse peoples. Good examples are ship and skiff, yard and garth.

There may even be a third form of the word – 'twilp' or 'twillup', which I have used since childhood, meaning much the same, though less condemnatory.

It should come as no surprise that 'twerp' should not be found written before 1874 and only then in Australia. Many words in common local or national conversational use never achieve literary status.

Edwin Spring, Street, Somerset.

STATIONED at Bulford Camp early in 1940, I recall going on duty at Boscombe Down airstrip and hearing a sound like an express train in the air before seeing an aircraft with no propeller fly over. Was this the first flight of Frank Whittle's jet aircraft?

THE Frank Whittle W1 jet-engined Gloster E28/39 made its first short hops on April 17, 1941, and a flight of 17 minutes, piloted by Flight Lieut Jerry Sayer, on May 15, 1941 at Cranwell, Lincolnshire.

The aircraft was one of two built purely for test-flying, under serial number W4041/G, the G indicating it was secret and always under armed guard.

The second aircraft, W4046/G, didn't fly until March 1, 1943, and crashed on July 30 the same year. W4041 was presented to the Science Museum in April 1946 and is still a popular exhibit.

Peter Fitzgerald, Science Museum, South Kensington, London.

WAS there ever a case of survivors from a sunken ship refusing to be picked up by their rescuers?

ON May 17, 1941, the Blue Funnel Cargo ship *Peisander* was 350 miles southeast of Nantucket Island when it was torpedoed and began to sink. No one was hurt and the crew abandoned ship in three lifeboats.

They decided to steer a westerly course to bring them to land between Block Island and Cape Cod. During the night, the captain's boat became separated from the other two, commanded by the mate and second mate. After three days, these two were sighted by the steamer, *Baron Semple*, which stopped to pick them up.

The lifeboat crews held a conference and decided not to accept rescue. The *Baron Semple* was bound for Cape Town. She was quite a small ship and if they had allowed themselves to be picked up they would have had a very long voyage ahead, in cramped and uncomfortable accommodation. Food would be in short supply with another 43 mouths to feed and fresh water rationed.

Cape Town was not a port on their regular route and it might be difficult to find a ship to take them back to Liverpool. The *Baron Semple* had to traverse the whole Atlantic and there was every likelihood that she, too, would be torpedoed.

They were fit and well, the weather looked fine, they had two strong, well-provisioned lifeboats and were within a few days sail of the American coast, where undoubtedly a heroes' welcome awaited them.

They told the *Baron Semple*: 'We'll stay where we are.'

The two boats made land on Nantucket Island on May 24 and the captain's boat was picked up the next day by an American Coast Guard cutter. The *Baron Semple* made Cape Town safely but on November 2, 1943, was torpedoed by U-848 and sank in seconds with the loss of all on board.

C. H. Milsom, editor, Sea Breezes Magazine, Liverpool.

AS a crew member of the *Baron Semple* in 1941 to 1942, I could suggest an additional reason why people drifting in lifeboats might have elected to row on to America rather than take passage with us.

Baron Line ships were christened 'Hungry Hogarth ships' by the Merchant Navy due to a reputation won during the cut-throat pre-war tramp ship days.

K. Hardie, Woking, Surrey.

WHERE is the 'rhubarb triangle'?

THE area bounded by Wakefield, Leeds and Morley, in the middle of the Yorkshire coalfield, is famed for its forced rhubarb, grown in warm, dark sheds and picked by candlelight.

The climate in the area is just right for this kind of cultivation, with a short growing season, from Christmas to Easter. The plants are started outside, where the cold makes the roots dormant, before being transplanted into coal-fire warmed sheds and force grown.

At the turn of the century, a daily 'rhubarb express' left Wakefield for the London markets. The World Rhubarb Championships are held annually in February at a venue within the triangle.

Harlow Carr Gardens, outside the triangle at Harrogate, houses the National Rheum (Latin for rhubarb) Collection with 150 varieties out of a known 170, some of which are purely ornamental.

Tracey Highton, Wakefield Metropolitan Council.

? WHILE on a trip to Liverpool, I wondered: where is John Lennon buried?

SHORTLY after John Lennon's murder by deranged fan Mark Chapman outside Lennon's New York apartment on December 8, 1980, his widow Yoko Ono (who was by his side when he was shot) arranged for a private cremation in New York.

Rumours that his ashes were scattered across the River Mersey are untrue. Yoko still has his remains in her apartment in New York and Lennon has no gravestone as such.

Fans pay their respects in New York by visiting a garden of remembrance known as Strawberry Fields, in Central Park.

Here in Britain, the White Room, a section of The Beatles' Story exhibition, is dedicated to John's memory.

Shelagh Johnston, Beatles Story Exhibition, Albert Dock, Liverpool.

? WHICH was the last Lancashire theatre to have duckboards on the stairs to the galleries for people wearing clogs?

DUCKBOARDS in areas leading to the gallery, the cheapest seats, were installed to muffle the noise of the clogs on the concrete flooring. The last of the Lancashire theatres to use boards for this purpose was probably the Blackburn Palace which opened on September 10, 1900, with a promise of 'new low prices' ranging from 2d to 2 shillings (10p) for an evening's entertainment.

The gallery at the Palace, the largest of any theatre in Lancashire, bore the impressive sign '1,000 seats at 2d'. Sadly, just 30 years after opening, the Palace suffered a dip in its fortunes and competition from 'talkie' cinemas.

With dwindling audiences, the theatre became uneconomic to run, closed in 1932, and was demolished shortly afterwards.

Max Tyler, British Music Hall Society, Chichester, West Sussex.

SHOULD THE ARMY GIVE UP ITS RED COATS FOR KHAKI?

DEAR *Answers,*—To many people, bearing in mind the grand traditions of the 'thin red line,' such a proposal would, at first, seem almost treason; but a little thought will convince them that it is only reason.

The red coat has long since been abolished for active service by our army in India. Khaki, a dust or mud-coloured drill is there worn, and it has many advantages which are obvious.

It is hardly distinguishable at a few hundred yards' distance and is invisible when scarlet would be plainly seen. The advantage of this cannot be over-rated.

The red coat looks most slovenly when stained and every little stain shows on it. What then must its appearance be after even a few months' campaigning?

Khaki-coloured serge, thick and warm, is manufactured, so the plea of unsuitability to a cold climate cannot be urged. Why then retain the red coat at all?

A Marksman, Aldershot.

My only wonder is that the red coat was not abolished years ago. The advantages of a dust-coloured material over a scarlet one cannot, in times of war, be over-estimated, and I hope the earnest attention of the War Office authorities will be given to this very important subject.

I speak from experience, having served through the Crimean War in a red coat and through the late Burmah campaign wearing khaki, so my words should carry weight. It is an undoubted fact that whereas one man in scarlet can be seen at a distance of at least a mile and a half, it is possible to be within a few hundred yards of a whole company wearing khaki and not know it. Of course it is understood that the men are lying down, and in extended order.

It having been shown that the red coat is un-serviceable, why retain it? No good reason can be adduced. 'It is not so attractive, and would, therefore, lessen the number of recruits,' says someone. Not a bit of it! Let the uniform be well-fitting and of a stylish cut (which is more than can be said for the present infantry dress) and I will go so far as to say that the number of recruits would be increased.

Many of the native regiments of India have only khaki-coloured uniform and right soldierlike and smart they look in it.

Sentimentalists may say what a pity it is to do away with the 'thin red line.' It is a glorious tradition, of course, but a red line, however thin, taking the field in these days of perfected rifles would be very speedily erased.

A Colonel (rtd), Naval and Military Club, Piccadilly.

The adoption of khaki would mean an immediate and serious falling off of recruits. Hundreds of young men enlist solely on account of the uniform and if it were changed for clothing of a quieter hue the army would suffer accordingly in numbers.

It would not only appear like treason to abolish the scarlet coat, it would be such were our men to have taken away those clothes in which they have so often gone to victory.

Red is a grand colour, a noble colour and as it has so far served us so well, I say let it do so again. The British soldier is genuinely proud of his red coat. Let him keep it.

Conservative, Woolwich.

I was all for retaining the red coat but now the great advantages of an earth-coloured uniform in time of war have been brought home to me. I have no technical knowledge of soldiering but the proposed reform seems to be a matter of common-sense and humanity.

I trust that the War Office authorities will give this matter their attention and that the result will be the abolition of the red coat.

A Soldier's Mother, Edinburgh.

It has been assumed that the site of a battle must be parched, open ground. Were this so, there would be no doubt whatever as to the suitability of material that would harmonise with it – but this is not always the case.

What becomes of the argument if a fight takes place in a wood? And military history shows us that this is by no means rare. A green uniform would be requisite then, khaki would be as plainly discernible as red.

Seeing that it is impossible for our soldiers to have uniforms to suit every variety of ground, it is absurd to propose changing the present soldiers' dress.

Interested Civilian, Clapham.

Not only is the red coat dangerous to the men when in action but it is also an extremely unserviceable garment for general every-day wear.

Here at Aldershot we have blacksmiths, bricklayers, plumbers and men of all trades going about their work clothed in a gaudy red uniform, which is soiled by the slightest touch.

The Royal Engineers are only too anxious to experience a change of uniform.

A Sapper, Aldershot.

I am directed by Lord Wolseley to inform you that he considers there can be no doubt that khaki is the colour best suited for active service before an enemy.

Major J. S. S. Barker, The Royal Hospital, Dublin. July 15, 1892.

Our soldiers are very fond of their red coats, and the glorious traditions connected with them. Why not use the khaki for drill purposes and still retain the red coat for best wear?

In active service, the khaki is undoubtedly preferable but at other times I should feel less of a soldier if my coat was not red.

I think most private soldiers, whilst allowing that many improvements in pattern are required, will endorse my opinion as to retaining the honoured colour.

It is absolutely necessary that our soldiers should have a different uniform while on active service; but there is, as far as I am aware, nothing to prevent them from wearing a red coat of improved pattern while on home service.

In The Ranks, Aldershot

I know that on active service the red coat offers a splendid target for the enemy's marksmen, yet I think it would be very unwise in the interests of recruiting if the War Office authorities adopted the khaki uniform for home service.

Imagine our splendid regiments of Guards marching through London clad in the hideous, though serviceable, khaki-coloured uniform and, above all, the traditional bearskins being laid aside in favour of helmets! It will never do.

Enough was done to discourage recruiting when the territorial system came into force. Our gallant redcoats then were deprived of their glorious old titles, neat facings, badges, etc. They must be spared this last indignity.

To obtain good recruits for our infantry battalions, the authorities must make the home uniform more attractive than it is at present. For service in the field, khaki or gray is a most excellent colour but for home service let the soldier wear a uniform in which he will take a pride.

I was present, during the Boer War battles of Laing's Nek and Majuba where I saw at what a terrible disadvantage our brave redcoats were placed, their uniforms standing out in bold relief against a background of gray rocks or sun-dried grass. The Boers, being clad mostly in gray or a lightish brown corduroy, offered no mark at all for our men's rifles.

That magnificent body of men, the Natal Mounted Police, whose duties were the most arduous of any corps, were provided with a neat dark gray uniform, which proved very serviceable, their headgear being a soft gray felt hat, a la Buffalo Bill.

I met this corps many times during the campaign and, no matter what duty they were upon, they always presented a smart and comfortable appearance. I think the commanders of many of our Colonial regiments could give the War Office authorities a wrinkle or two in the matter of clothing our troops for service in the field.

An Old Sergeant-Major, West Hampstead.

WHO is the 'ghost boy' who appears briefly in the film *Three Men And A Baby*?

IN its day, the 1987 film *Three Men And A Baby*, starring Ted Danson, Tom Selleck and Steve Guttenberg, was one of the top ten all-time comedy films and Walt Disney's most successful film ever.

Three years after its release, a Los Angeles TV news channel showed a clip with what appeared to be a boy in the background of one of the scenes for just two seconds. Speculation at the time suggested he was a ghost, captured on film. Video sales soared as people tried to see for themselves what was hiding behind the curtain in the scene where Danson, with the baby (four-month-old Michelle Blair), confronts Celeste Holm.

Claims were made that the 'ghost' was that of a child who had died in the flat where the scene was shot, or that of a suicide victim who had become the ghostly protector of the baby. It was also suggested that the child was possibly put there as a prank by one of the film technicians.

In fact, the 'ghost' was a cardboard cut-out of Danson, awaiting use in another scene.

Bernie Clerkin, editor, TV And Satellite Week, London SE1.

I WONDER if there are two versions of this film. Residents of the apartment block where the movie was filmed say the rogue image is the spirit of a young boy who plunged to his death from the window in the scene some years earlier. But the production company, Disney-owned Touchstone Pictures, says it's a cardboard cut-out of Ted Danson.

When the film is viewed at a cinema, the figure can be seen clearly as a legless boy but when viewed on TV, it appears as the Danson cut-out. Some video copies of the film show the legless boy while others show the cut-out.

Alan Jarvie, East Kilbridge, Strathclyde.

? WHY are wind farm turbines designed with the blades revolving in a vertical plane?

WIND turbines are usually referred to as either horizontal axis wind turbines (HAWT), with the blades revolving on a vertical plane, or vertical axis (VAWT), with the blades revolving horizontally.

Theoretically, vertical axis models have potential and some machines have been designed and manufactured but they haven't caught on. Designers have stayed with the proven and technically easier HAWTs which are generally more efficient, have fewer technical problems and are more cost effective.

The cost of VAWTs per kilowatt-hour is higher because of engineering difficulties to do with power transmission and fatigue.

Power quality is poorer (less constant) because torque changes with position, they are not self-starting, the blades have been prone to buckling and noise has been very high on some models. But research continues.

Hugh Piggott's book *Windpower Workshop* explains how you can build your own wind turbine.

Julie Bromilow, Centre for Alternative Technology, Machynlleth, Powys.

❓ THE ancient Romans were magnificent engineers and administrators but how did they do their sums using Roman numerals?
THEY didn't. Roman numerals weren't used to perform calculations but to record the results of calculations performed on an abacus or counting board.

Our word 'calculation' comes from the Latin *calculus*, a pebble. The algebra of real numbers, using numerals as a direct means of calculation, is possible only with a symbol for zero, which the Romans lacked. This was a Hindu invention which came to us by way of the Arabs.

Michael Mullins, Glasgow.

❓ IS it true that the deaths of elm trees in Britain were due to a quantity of untreated timber being allowed into a Welsh port?
DUTCH elm disease was present in Britain in a non-aggressive, rarely fatal form from the late 1920s. The epidemic of the late 1960s and early 1970s, which wiped out an estimated 23 million elms, was caused by an aggressive form of the fungus which arrived from North America.

The elm bark beetles which transmitted the aggressive form of the disease arrived in Britain in untreated elm logs imported with intact bark.

Initially, Gloucestershire, Herefordshire, Worcestershire and the Thames Estuary, in Essex and Kent, were the worst-affected regions, suggesting entry to Britain via southern ports.

David Rose, Forestry Commission, Farnham, Surrey.

❓ WERE there ever joint No 1s in the *Top Of The Pops* chart?
BEFORE 1969, the BBC compiled its own chart from a weighted average of lists in the major music papers and there were several occasions when this resulted in joint No 1s. In April 1967, for instance, Nancy and Frank Sinatra's 'Somethin' Stupid' shared top spot with Sandie Shaw's 'Puppet On A String'.

On August 29, 1968, each of the three main music papers listed a different record at No 1. *Record Mirror* had the Beach Boys' 'Do It Again', *New Musical Express* listed Tom Jones's 'Help Yourself' and *Melody Maker* gave it to Herb Alpert with 'This Guy's In Love With You'.

That was the only time in its history when *Top Of The Pops* announced three No 1s.

After 1969, compilation of the BBC chart was taken over by an independent body and there has never been a joint No 1 since, though matters came close in August 1990 when the Steve Miller Band's 'The Joker' and Dee-Lite's 'Groove Is In The Heart' couldn't be separated on sales figures. 'The Joker' was listed at No 1 for having made the biggest sales gain over the previous week.

This caused such an uproar that the chart rules were changed to allow joint positions again.

Howard Pizzey, Staplehurst, Kent.

IN December 1953, David Whitfield and Frankie Laine shared the top spot for a week with their versions of 'Answer Me'.

'Singing The Blues' by Guy Mitchell and 'Garden Of Eden' by Frankie Vaughan were side by side at No 1 on February 1, 1957 and on July 4, 1958, Vic Damone's 'On The Street Where You Live' and The Everly Brothers' double-sider, 'All I Have To Do Is Dream/Claudette' jointly held the top position.

David Hutt, Stourbridge, West Midlands.

❓ WHO names hurricanes and how? Is there likely to be a hurricane Stephanie?

HURRICANES have been given personal names, issued every six years by the World Meteorological Organisation, since 1953. Originally named after girls, since 1979 they have alternated between male and female names. So far, none has been called Stephanie.

The names are international because hurricanes are tracked by many countries.

Since 2000, tropical cyclones in the North West Pacific have been given Asian names, most of which aren't personal names but birds, animals, trees and even foods.

When a disturbance intensifies into a tropical storm, the various authorities give it a name from the current list, allotted in alphabetical order (excluding Q, U, X, Y and Z). After a particularly damaging hurricane, its name is permanently retired and not used again.

If more storms arrive in a given year than there are names on the list, the Greek alphabet (Alpha, Beta, etc) is brought into play. This happened for the first time in the record-breaking 2005 season when there were 27 named tropical storms.

The scheduled names for northern hemisphere tropical cyclones in 2008 are: Arthur, Bertha, Cristobal, Dolly, Edouard, Fay, Gustav, Hanna, Ike, Josephine, Kyle, Laura, Marco, Nana, Omar, Paloma, Rene, Sally, Teddy, Vicky and Wilfred.

For 2009 they are: Ana, Bill, Claudette, Danny, Erika, Fred, Grace, Henri, Ida, Joaquin, Kate, Larry, Mindy, Nicholas, Odette, Peter, Rose, Sam, Teresa, Victor and Wanda.

The Meteorological Office, Bracknell.

? HAS anyone ever recognised themselves in one of those 'timeless' views on seaside postcards?

MY children, Robert and Louise, are on a postcard of Reculver Towers, near Herne Bay, Kent. On the day it was taken, there was a very high tide, it was very windy and they were told not to go near the sea.

They went anyway – but were found out when the postcard was published.

Mrs L. Simpson, Highgate N6.

A CARD on sale in the Weymouth/Portland area shows a view of Pulpit Rock and Portland Bill. The young man proudly standing on top of the rock is me, aged 20. I'm now considerably older.

Brandon Long, Lutterworth, Leics.

MY parents were surprised to see themselves on a historic postcard showing Pakefield in the 1930s. The houses and cliffs in the picture are now about 50 yards out into the North Sea.

V. Campbell, Hertford.

YEARS ago, my husband and I were on holiday with two friends in Cliftonville, Kent. The following year we were sent a postcard from friends on holiday there and it showed four people looking over the cliffs.

It was a photograph of the four of us.

Mrs S. M. Drinkwater, Caerphilly, Mid Glamorgan.

? WHAT conclusions were reached by the Institute for Consumer Ergonomics research project, funded by the Department of the Environment from 1972 to 1974, into the suitability of the British lavatory seat?

THIS early Seventies study, using 200 subjects, concerned the anthropometrics (body dimensions) for safe and effective use of toilet seats and pedestals.

It was part of a larger piece of research commissioned by the Building Research Establishment investigating whether the standard British WC needed redesigning to minimise the amount of water used with each flush.

The study concluded that the existing British Standard offered the minimum acceptable front-to-back aperture for UK adults, although the standard seat should be narrower, to help support the buttocks.

The report recognised that any change in seat aperture would mean a major redesign of the bowl and fail to make the intended water saving.

Matthew Trigg, ICE/Ergonomics, Loughborough, Leics.

? WAS the film *The Dirty Dozen* based on a real-life incident?

ROBERT Aldrich directed Lee Marvin, Ernest Borgnine, Telly Savalas, Charles Bronson, Jim Brown, John Cassavetes, Richard Jaeckel, George Kennedy, Trini Lopez, Ralph Meeker, Robert Ryan, Donald Sutherland, Clint Walker and Robert Webber in the 1967 film *The Dirty Dozen*, based on a novel by E. M. Nathanson.

It tells of a band of army prisoners recruited for a suicide mission to destroy a chateau housing Nazi top-brass in return for pardons in the unlikely event of them managing to get back.

The Pentagon says none of the 2,000 convicts who went into the military during World War II was recruited specifically for a mission like the Operation Amnesty depicted in the film, though many performed outstanding feats of heroism. Missions of that type were normally carried out by professional specialist units.

Today's U.S. Army is barred from drafting felons.

John Walker, Halliwell's Film Guide, London.

? WHICH bird is acknowledged as the world's finest songster?

THE Nightingale is the true master of song. From its arrival in this country in late April until the end of May, the male sings day and night to keep its territory and attract a mate. For such a small, drab brown bird, its song is remarkably loud, melodious and inventive.

It's not surprising that the great opera singer Jenny Lind was known as The Swedish Nightingale.

Derek Niemann, RSPB, Sandy, Beds.

? WHERE are all the wasps before late August?

THE life-cycle of the wasp begins when a fertilised queen overwinters in a place such as a garden shed or loft. In spring, she searches for a suitable nest site, below ground, in a tree, bush or the eaves of a roof.

She scrapes wood, chewing it into paper to create the first cells of the nest where she lays six or so eggs. These hatch into larvae and are fed by the queen until they turn into worker wasps, leaving the queen to produce more off-spring, which are cared for by the nursery workers and fed by the foragers.

The nest reaches peak population (15,000 to 30,000 wasps) by late August or early September, which is when we see most wasps. As winter approaches the queen begins to produce fertile males. These mate with fertile female workers which leave to become future queens. The old queen dies and the nest is never used again.

Harsh winters mean fewer queens survive to build nests.

Tony Stephens, Rentokil, East Grinstead, West Sussex.

? WHICH is the more efficient – to pull or to push?

AS a young practical engineer, it was impressed on me that pulling is a practical impossibility; the action is actually a mechanical form of pushing.

When a woman pushes a pram, she pushes with the palms of her hand, but when she pulls it, she is actually pushing it with her fingers. When a vehicle tows a trailer, the rope is inserted forward of the tow pin and pushed by the tow pin.

So my answer is pushing, because any attempt to pull is, if my mentors are to be believed, related to pushing anyway.

Brian Turner, Brandon, Suffolk.

? WHAT happened to Hitler's private yacht *Grille*?

HITLER suffered badly from seasickness and went on board the *Grille* only three times before it was given to Admiral Dönitz to use as a U-boat flagship.

My father George Arida, honorary British consul in Tripoli, Lebanon, bought the *Grille* from the British Admiralty in an auction. Its high-pressure boilers had been sabotaged before it was surrendered.

My brother George Jnr took the yacht to Genoa to be refitted as a Mediterranean cruise ship but King Farouk said he wanted to buy it, so it was refitted to the original plans.

On arrival in Egypt, Farouk received us on the pier in Alexandria and said he would promote my father to Pasha if he offered him the ship as a gift – a ruse to avoid being seen to buy it.

The yacht's home port was to be Beirut but while it was there the Israeli secret service, seeking revenge on the Führer, blew a gaping hole in its hull. The damage was repaired and the *Grille* went to U.S. to be put on show with the proceeds going to various charities.

However, with the Korean War in full swing and fears of a third world war, the U.S. Navy mobilised all its shipyards and the yacht had to leave in mid-refit. At this point my father decided to cut his losses and scrap it.

The family still has the ship's log, ship's bell and other mementoes.
Edward G. Arida, London.

I JOINED the crew in 1947 while the *Grille* was owned by Lebanese textile manufacturer George Arida and under repair in West Hartlepool. We sailed for Genoa but one of the high-pressure boilers burst and we had to be towed into Hull for repair. Further boiler failures left us drifting for a week in a stormy Bay of Biscay before an ocean-going tug finally towed us to Genoa.

In Italy, several prospective buyers, including representatives of Egypt's King Farouk, inspected the *Grille* but I decided yachting was too dangerous and returned to the UK.
Denis Barker, Dursley, Gloucs.

❓ DID St Patrick really banish all the snakes from Ireland?

MANY of the world's islands have no snakes at all but Britain, itself an island, has three species, the grass snake, adder and rare smooth snake.

At the end of the last Ice Age, what is now England was connected to the Continent by land, while Ireland was linked to Scotland.

As the glaciers retreated, various species of snakes and other reptiles moved northwards and colonised England. A few, such as the adder, made it as far north as Scotland but the low temperatures there didn't suit most reptiles.

By this time, the connecting strip of land between Scotland and Ireland had disappeared so no snakes could progress there.

Russell Tofts, Whittlesford, Cambs.

? DO ostriches really bury their heads in the sand and imagine their enemies cannot see them?

THE ostrich (*Struthio camelus*), the largest bird on the planet standing 3m (10ft) high and weighing 150kg (330lb), can run at more than 40mph and has a kick powerful enough to kill a predator. It can defend itself admirably and has little need to stick its head in the ground.

This common misconception has arisen because the ostrich, which lives up to 30 years in arid, open country, makes a nest by scraping a hollow in the ground. The nest holds between 10 and 30 eggs on which the male sits at night, giving way to the female by day.

The ostrich's keen eyesight can spot potential dangers and its grey/brown plumage is good camouflage. When threatened, ostriches sometimes lie down with their necks along the ground, attempting to look like stumps of grass.

Kirsty MacFarlane, London Zoo.

? COULD Dick Turpin have ridden from London to York in one day?

HE could, but it's doubtful that he did. 'Swift' John Nevison robbed a sailor at Gad's Hill, three miles north-west of Rochester, at 4am one day in 1676 and is said to have established an alibi by arriving in York (and playing bowls with the Mayor!) at 7.45pm that day.

For the 235-mile trip he would have needed to average about 15mph, and have hired a relay of horses.

Bold tales of Turpin's famous ride on Black Bess seem to have no basis in fact. Turpin (1705–39) was no hero, but a sadistic brute who went to York after killing an Epping Forest keeper, for which he was later hanged.

Kevin Heneghan, St Helens, Merseyside.

THE distance is about 190 miles which, at a moderate 20mph canter, would take nine-and-a-half hours. Baden Powell, founder of the Scouts, was an experienced long distance rider who considered that a fit horse could go on almost indefinitely if allowed to walk a mile and canter a mile alternately, with additional stops for food and water.

On a test ride in South Africa, he rode 112 miles in eight-and-a-half hours. At this pace, a really fit horse could probably reach York from London in less than 24 hours – but the RSPCA might have something to say about it.

In 1603, Sir Robert Carey rode from Windsor to Edinburgh in 66 hours to tell James VI of Scotland he had become King of England – but he had a succession of horses ready for him on the way.

In *Rookwood*, Victorian novelist Harrison Ainsworth's fictional account of Turpin's feat, Turpin's success is accounted for by stratagems including a secret drug – brandy poured down the horse's throat – and a refreshing swim in the river Ouse. And, of course, brave Black Bess drops dead at the end of it.

Ainsworth's account put Dick Turpin on the map – but it's only fiction.

Margot Lawrence, Edgware, Middx.

? WHAT is the significance of the name 'Brunswick' on many 19th-century Methodist chapels?

METHODIST chapels began to be called 'Brunswick' as a gesture of loyalty to the Crown during the Revolutionary and Napoleonic wars against France, culminating in the Battle of Waterloo in 1815.

John Wesley, the founder of Methodism, died in 1791, less than 60 years after the turmoil caused by Bonnie Prince Charlie's rebellion. Anyone taking secret oaths or forming societies was treated harshly, and Methodists, who had broken away from the Established Church, were often accused of being Jacobites. After 1789, the Government feared an uprising similar to the French Revolution and any 'outsiders' were regarded with suspicion.

Brunswick, in Germany, was the seat of the House of Hanover and putting this name on Methodist chapels, as in Newcastle and Birkenhead, demonstrated Wesleyans' support for George III.

Today, with hindsight, it can be seen that Methodists in the late 18th and early 19th centuries offered upward mobility to the working classes and acted as a form of social safety valve against the potential for revolution, stabilising society rather than fomenting revolution, as they were accused.

Geraldine Ranson, Methodist Church, London.

? AS barbers, we're often asked what we do with the hair we cut off. What can be done with surplus hair?

IN his Berlin diary, American correspondent William L. Shirer records for May 6, 1940, (four days before Hitler invaded France and the Low Countries): 'German schoolgirls were today asked to bring the combings from their hair to school. The combings will be collected to make felt.'

M. Foley, Aylesbury, Bucks.

? WHAT'S the most trivial or curious mobile phone conversation overheard?

ON a visit to Alton Towers, while waiting for our final ride of the day, a man in front of us was conducting a lengthy business conversation on his mobile phone.

The conversation continued while climbing up the stairs inside a huge plastic tree: then followed the bizarre sight of a grown man chatting away while sitting on a large, moving, brown plastic squirrel, suspended several feet in the air.

I wonder how seriously the other party would have taken the conversation had they been able to see the scene we did.

Mrs A. Higgins, Chester.

I WAS in a fast-food restaurant when another customer's mobile phone rang. He had no sooner answered it than his other mobile also rang. He answered that, too, at which point he had a mobile to each ear and was carrying on two conversations at the same time.

Trivial? Don't jump to conclusions.

He could have been advising President Bush on one line while helping to eradicate world famine on the other.

Martin Taylor, London E17.

? ARE there any examples of the 1957 Edsel Ford still on the road?

I'VE been an Edsel enthusiast since, as a boy, seeing the new model at the 1957 London Motor Show at Earl's Court. The Duke of Bedford was at the show and he bought the yellow and black Citation four-door hardtop on display, becoming the first person in Britain to own an Edsel.

I wrote to the Duke, who now lives in New Mexico, and he said he had fond memories of driving the car to Spain in 1958. It drew crowds wherever it went.

There's an Edsel Owners' Club in the U.S., which has a UK chapter.

There's a 1958 Edsel Corsair four-door hardtop in London's Science Museum and a 1959 Edsel Villager station wagon in the Haynes Motor Museum at Sparkford, Somerset.

Major A. A. Thompson, Wimborne, Dorset.

I OWNED that Edsel Citation directly after the Duke of Bedford. It had only 8,000 miles on the clock and was registered as MCC1. I was told the Duke acquired it as part of a sales promotion deal. I was a car dealer at the time and ran it for about 10,000 miles on trade plates.

Although the Edsel wasn't generally rated in the trade, I found it absolutely wonderful, with its two-tone black top and primrose bottom, its beautifully woven gold upholstery and pushbutton gear change, with a whole lot of refinements not found on British cars.

I bought the car in 1959, selling it after a year. Later, I learned that it had come off the newly built M1, ending up in a field on its side.

T. Compton, Rickmansworth, Herts.

MY husband spotted an Edsel Ford in a Havana sidestreet during our holiday in Cuba. Despite language difficulties, he managed to convey his admiration and enthusiasm for the vehicle to its proud owner and persuaded him to let us take a ride in it.

The drive was slow and far from smooth (the car would never have passed a British MoT test) and we got hopelessly lost. But viewing the sights of Havana through the cracked windscreen was an unforgettable experience.

The car has been in daily use, as have hundreds of other Fifties American classics, since the Cuban revolution cut off trade with the U.S.

Selena Quirke, Kingston Hill, Surrey.

? WHY did Flt Lt Gatward 'buzz' the Arc de Triomphe in occupied Paris in a Bristol Beaufighter in 1942?

ON June 12, 1942, Flt Lt Ken Gatward DFC and navigator Flt Lt George Fern DFM, in Beaufighter ND-C of 236 Squadron of RAF Coastal Command, took off from RAF Thorney Island, flew to Paris at heights rarely above 100ft and unloaded two French Tricolour flags, attached to metal bars.

The mission was the idea of Major Ben Cowburn who was working undercover in Paris for Special Operations Executive and wanted to stage a morale-boosting event for the French during the daily parade of German troops down the Champs Elysees.

The Air Ministry asked Fighter Command to send three Spitfires trailing red, white and blue smoke but they would have been at the limit of their range so Coastal Command asked for a volunteer Beaufighter crew.

They arrived in Paris at the correct time for the parade but the Germans didn't show up and very few people saw them drop the French flag over the Arc de Triomphe and fly on to the Place de la Concorde where Fern threw the second Tricolour out of the flare tube over the Gestapo headquarters and Gatward gave the building a burst of cannon fire.

They returned to RAF Northolt with not a sight of an enemy fighter or any anti-aircraft fire. No one knows why the regular parade was cancelled but the Germans may have had reports of a flight heading for Paris.

Mike Lunn, Whittlesey, Cambs.

⟨? ⟩ WHAT is the origin of calling someone 'a brick'?

● ACCORDING to Eric Partridge, the late great expert in this field, the origins of calling someone a 'brick' to describe them as a good fellow go back at least to the early 19th century.

It was first used in print in George C. Bell's *Rough Notes By An Old Soldier* published in 1867. The reference to a 'brick' is an allusion to solidity and reliability, someone who won't let the rest down.

Julian Knightley, International Phrase and Fable Society, London.

⟨? ⟩ DID Bill Bailey exist? Did he ever come home?

● THE song 'Bill Bailey, Won't You Please Come Home' was written in 1902 by Hughie Cannon. It was first recorded by Arthur Collins, but was popularised by Louis Armstrong. It had a revival in the Fifties when it was recorded by Pearl Bailey.

It is thought to have been written in honour of Willard Godfrey Bailey, known as Bill, a popular trombonist and music teacher in Jackson, Michigan – where the song was written – between 1894–1907.

Old Bill must have managed to get home OK as he continued teaching at the local school for five years after the song was composed.

Betty Baron, Sutton Coldfield Music Library, Birmingham.

IS EARLY RISING BENEFICIAL TO HEALTH?

DEAR *Answers.*—It may not be known to many that a German doctor has for some time past been collecting information about the habits of long-lived persons.

As a result of his researches he finds that the majority of long livers indulged in late hours and at least eight out of ten persons over 80 never went to bed till well into the small hours and did not get up again until late in the day.

He considers that getting up early tends to exhaust the physical power and to shorten life while the so-called invigorating early hours are, he thinks, apt to produce lassitude and are positively dangerous to some constitutions.

Rather hard on the 'Early to bed, early to rise' people, eh?

Late Up, Belfast.

It is with pleasure that I notice the decay of the old early-rising doctrine. To most young men, nine hours' sleep is absolutely necessary – say, from 11pm till 8am.

It is unnecessary to retire before 11 and surely 8 o'clock is early enough to rise in the morning, at least I always find it so.

Personal experience teaches me that very early rising makes its effects felt later in the day; therefore people who rise early should take a short nap in the afternoon.

Experience, Swindon.

I think one must be particularly lazy one to recommend the hour of 8am as the time for rising. I have tried both sides of the question – going to bed at 12 midnight and rising at 8am and retiring to rest at 10.30pm and rising at 6am and must certainly say that the latter is more beneficial to health.

What is better than to have an hour in the garden or to take a walk in the country before breakfast? Do not doctors advise two hours in bed before midnight as being far more conducive to a hardy constitution than two hours after?

I have heard Americans remark when in London that by the time we commenced business, their countrymen have done three or four hours' work. Is not this the secret of their success? I would recommend any late riser to try rising at 6am, not once, or for a week, but for three months and I feel sure they would not return to their old time of 8 o'clock.

J. O., Thornton Heath.

I maintain that early rising is beneficial to health and people will only give it a fair trial.

Did Nature ever intend that we should spend in bed the four brightest hours of the day and work a corresponding time by lamplight?

Any person who has studied in the morning will tell you how much fresher they are and how much clearer a grasp they have of a subject than when they numbered themselves amongst those benighted individuals who burned the midnight oil.

Common-Sense, Dublin.

WHAT were the Camptown Races referred to in the famous old song? Are they still held?

THERE never was a racetrack called Camptown but it's generally accepted that the song refers to an annual horse race, open to all-comers, which took place on a flat section of dirt road between the small town of Camptown and nearby Wyalusing, in Bradford County, Northern Pennsylvania. This, as the song says, is roughly five miles long.

The song was written in 1850 by Pittsburgh-born Stephen Collins Foster (1826–1864), whose primary education was at an academy in the area. It was one of 14 songs he wrote in 1850, six of them in Minstrel style. The song was originally called 'Gwine To Run All Night' but was changed later to 'Camptown Races'.

Dennis Irvine, editor of the local newspaper *The Daily Review*, says the Camptown Races still take place in spring each year but are today held on foot.
Simon Clare, British Horseracing Board, Portman Square, London.

WHY 'Wendy' house?

THIS stems from Peter Pan who brought Wendy to Never Never Land to be a mother to the Lost Boys. As she approached the island, a jealous Tinkerbell kept pinching her so she would cry out.

When the Lost Boys heard her crying, Tinkerbell called out that Peter wanted them to shoot the Wendy bird.

Tootles, the only one of the Lost Boys who had his bow and arrow, shot her. Wendy was saved by the button Peter had given her and which she wore round her neck on a chain.

No one wanted to move Wendy because it would not have been respectful to her so Peter decided to build a house around her. While they collected building materials, Wendy sang: 'I wish I had a pretty house, The littlest ever seen, With funny little red walls, And a roof of mossy green.'

To be a true Wendy House, there should be the sole of a shoe for a knocker and a top hat for a chimney.

W. R. Inglis, Kirkcaldy, Fife.

ON *Songs Of Praise*, it was said that Queen Victoria chose 'The Day Thou Gavest Lord Is Ended' for the service marking her Diamond Jubilee. Which hymns did she choose for her wedding?

ACCORDING to reports in newspapers of the time, the marriage of Queen Victoria at the age of 20 to the 'Pauper Prince', Albert of Saxe-Coburg and Gotha, at noon on Monday, February 10, 1840, at the Chapel Royal, St James's Palace, London, began with the national anthem.

The ceremony included 'Deus Miseratur' (Kings in B flat) under the direction of a Mr Hawes, with Sir George Smart at the organ.

Celia Harbridge-West, Bournemouth, Dorset.

QUEEN Victoria's choice of 'Deus Miseratur' for her wedding refers to an anthem rather than a hymn. Hymn singing, as we know it, was comparatively rare. In 1840, the year of her wedding, hymns were used mainly by the Methodists.

The habit of singing hymns in Anglican churches arrived during the 1850s and 1860s, a great boost being the publication of *Hymns Ancient And Modern*.

The custom had become very well established by the time of Queen Victoria's Diamond Jubilee in 1897.

Michael Farrer, London NW5.

? WAS there a naval engagement off Bridlington during the American War of Independence?

A MONUMENT erected on behalf of the Borough of Bridlington near the lighthouse on Flamborough Head, Humberside, commemorates a sea battle that took place off the headland on September 23, 1779, between Captain Richard Pearson RN of the frigate HMS *Serapis* and Captain John Paul Jones of the *Bonhomme Richard* sailing under the flag of the American Continental Congress.

In the ensuing close encounter, the *Bonhomme Richard* foundered. Although the Americans lost 150 of their 300 men, they still managed to capture HMS *Serapis* and sail her to France. Captain Pearson, with 49 of his crew dead, surrendered his sword but was secure in the knowledge that he had saved a convoy of 40 ships sailing along the Yorkshire coast.

John Paul Jones, who was born in Kirkbean, Dumfries and Galloway, is regarded by the Americans as the father of the U.S. Navy, though he was employed after the war as Rear Admiral of the Russian Black Sea Fleet, fighting in the Russo-Turkish War of 1788–89.

He died in Paris in 1792, aged 45, and his remains were moved in 1905 to a shrine at the U.S. Naval Academy in Annapolis, Maryland.

Vernon Moore, Penrhyn Bay, Gwynedd.

? IS it true that Welbeck Abbey in Nottinghamshire has an underground ballroom and riding school? Who built it?

ECCENTRIC Lord William John Cavendish-Scott-Bentinck (1800–75), 5th Duke of Portland, had an underground ballroom as well as other subterranean structures built at Welbeck Abbey.

He showed no early unusual signs and was MP for King's Lynn for a time but he is supposed to have gone off at a tangent after being thwarted in love.

He didn't marry but became a recluse, spending millions of pounds building miles of underground passages and rooms at Welbeck, all of which were gas-lit.

His underground ballroom is the largest in Europe without supporting pillars. He loved horses and built a riding school second only in size to the Spanish riding school in Vienna.

H. G. Denman, Manchester.

THE underground ballroom, now part of Welbeck College, a Ministry of Defence training establishment, still exists. The riding school, which was

above ground, has now gone, though the shell of the building is still in place.
Stan Lawrence, Brighton, Sussex.

THE Duke created a 236ft-long library, a ballroom which could accommodate 2,000 people (though he never gave so much as an intimate dinner party) and the second largest riding school in the world.

Most of the rooms aren't deep underground but have skylights and are light enough during the day.

One reason for all his building was perhaps a desire to relieve local unemployment. The Duke was a generous contributor to charities and a much respected landlord.
Leslie Grout, Windsor, Berks.

NONE of the tunnels connecting different parts of the Welbeck estate went as far as Worksop Station, as some people believe.

A 1.5-mile tunnel went from the Abbey to the outskirts of the estate. Called the Skylight Tunnel, it has an exit at the northern boundary of the estate, referred to locally as The Tunnel End. From there, the Duke travelled a further three miles overland by closed coach, through the Duke of Newcastle's Worksop Manor Estate, to reach Worksop Station without being seen.
Jack Edson, Worksop, Notts.

? WHAT'S the difference between a vaccination and an inoculation?

THE word 'vaccinate' was first used by British physician and vaccine pioneer Edward Jenner at the beginning of the 18th century.

The word derived from the Latin *vacca*, meaning 'cow', as he developed a technique of injecting people with the cowpox virus to prevent smallpox.

Though the verb 'to vaccinate' was coined in the 1700s, 'vaccine' was not used as a noun, meaning inoculated material, until the 1840s.

The word 'inoculate' derives from the Latin *oculus*, meaning 'eye'. By a metaphorical extension, *oculus* was applied to the 'bud' of a plant, and the verb 'inoculare' was coined to denote the grafting on of a bud or other plant part.

It was not modified until the early 18th century to the modern meaning of introducing antigens into the body, which was based on the notion of engrafting or implanting an immunising virus into a person. Similar to vaccination, its original use related to immunisation against smallpox, by placing the pocks on small incisions on the patient's body.

In the strictest sense, therefore, a vaccination refers specifically to the cow-pox inoculation. However, over time, the process of administering a vaccine has become both a vaccination and an inoculation.

Dr G. S. Murray, Wolverhampton.

WHY is Peterborough United FC known as 'The Posh'?

THE local football paper *The Pink 'Un* first used the nickname. The paper gave each club in its area a nickname and caricature. Fletton United were known as The Brickies, caricatured by a cartoon working-class clodhopper. On April 27, 1921, the club held a meeting to consider better-class football for Peterborough. *The Pink 'Un* picked up on this and the following season called them 'the posh boys in a posh team from a posh town'.

The clodhopper cartoon was changed to a posh man with trilby and cigar, later changed to top hat and monocle.

After a run of poor results *The Pink 'Un* reverted to its original Brickies nickname, with 'ex Posh' in brackets until they defeated Kettering Town 5–1 in the FA Cup on October 7, 1922.

'The Posh' reference then returned and continued after the merger of Peterborough and Fletton United in 1923 and has been used for the present Peterborough United FC since 1932.

Mel Hopkins, Kettering, Northants.

THE title track of the Roger Waters album *Amused To Death* mentions 'the Children of Melrose strutting their stuff' and *Melrose* is the title of a Tangerine Dream album. What is/are Melrose?

THE title track of Waters's album was taken from my book *Cheerful Sacrifice, The Battle Of Arras 1917*, published by Leo Cooper in 1990. 'The Ballad Of Bill Hubbard' tells the story of the savage World War I infantry battle fought near Arras from April 9 to May 3, 1917.

The book features the 8th (Service) Battalion The Royal Fusiliers and the story of two young soldiers Alf Razzell and Bill Hubbard.

The Germans forced Alf to leave his gravely wounded friend, Bill, alone in a shell hole in no man's land. Bill's body was never found and he is commemorated on the Arras memorial.

Roger Waters read my book and converted it into a bestselling album.
Jonathan Nicholls, Hemel Hempstead, Herts.

? WAS Fritz Haber, known as the godfather of fertiliser, more interested in chemical weapons?

THE name Fritz Haber has long been associated with the process of synthesising ammonia from its elements, the essential precursor for many important substances, particularly fertilisers and explosives used in mining and warfare.

Born on December 9, 1868, in Breslau, Fritz was the son of a prosperous German chemical merchant and threw himself into physical chemistry research. In 1911, he was appointed director of the Kaiser Wilhelm Institute For Physical Chemistry in Berlin. With the outbreak of World War I in 1914, he was put in charge of cross-disciplinary research in chemistry and physics.

His team of scientists developed a range of processes which significantly helped the German war effort. His process of ammonia synthesis allowed the large-scale production of nitric acid – an important ingredient in high explosives.

With the development of chemical warfare, he helped produce protective chemical devices for troops but, more infamously, directed the first gas attacks.

At Ypres on April 22, 1915, Haber directed the first large-scale release of chlorine gas. Figures vary, but it is thought that between 5,000 and 15,000 Allied troops were wounded or killed that day, with further losses among German troops due to the gas being blown back onto them.

Haber was controversially awarded the Nobel Prize in 1918 but his role in chemical warfare left him isolated from the scientific community.

He felt strongly some responsibility for the enormous war debt of the German state and tried to make a contribution to reduce it by formulating a process to extract gold from sea water.

When Hitler became Chancellor and Jewish academics were purged, Haber emigrated and was given a post at Cambridge in 1933 but he didn't stay long in Britain, as ill health and the climate depressed him. On route to visit Switzerland, he died suddenly at Basle on January 30, 1935, at the age of 65.
Barbara Gaver, London.

THE Haber process made Germany independent of imported nitrates and so able to wage a large-scale war without being bothered by the Royal Navy blockade.

Haber's involvement with chemical warfare upset his wife so much that she committed suicide.

Fred Jones, Great Sankey, Warrington.

❓ DOES any barber in Britain still use a cut-throat razor?

SEVERAL barbers still offer a traditional shave with a cut-throat razor, though the service almost died out in the late Eighties because of the public fear of contamination from such diseases as HIV.

As the only 'cut-throat' barber in Manchester, I'm doing my best at Smooth, my salon, to re-educate the male population and revive this noble art.

Cross-contamination is very rare and could occur only if a barber had an open wound on his hand and then cut a client.

Today, cut-throat razors have a traditional handle incorporating a cartridge system. This means that a new blade is used on each client – preventing cross-contamination between them. All of the equipment is sterilised using either an autoclave or disinfectant.

Allan Bulwich, Manchester.

I'VE been a barber for ten years at Salon 2 and regularly use a cut-throat razor with disposable blades. After use, the blade is disposed of and never used again.

I also use the more traditional hollow ground cut-throat razor, which looks very good, but isn't as hygienic.

Few barbers have the time to do face shaves nowadays, which is a shame. Like many barbers' traditions, it is at risk of becoming a thing of the past, but I won't stop as long as the customers keep turning up.

Stuart Clark, Lincoln.

IS THERE ALWAYS A 'MR RIGHT'?

DEAR *Answers,*—We are told there are four women to each man, therefore all women cannot expect to get married. Yet, to the contrary, we hear 'There is a Jack for every Jill.' If this is so, why are there so many Jills left without Jacks?

Personally, for instance, I am not engaged not through lack of suitors but because Mr Right has not yet appeared. Unfortunately, those who like me I do not care for and vice-versa.

We are informed by some people that if a young lady is not engaged before 20 or 21, she will have little chance after. Others say: 'Oh, there is plenty of time. Mr Right will surely come along some day' but time goes on, and still he doesn't appear.

I am aware that it is difficult to please yet I fully believe it is in my power to truly love. I have frequently tried to force myself to love those who have professed affection for me but each time without success.

I am now waiting, as advised, for Mr Right.

Twenty-one, London S.E.

With four women to every man, it may be taken for granted that many women never have a chance of meeting with a suitor at all, much less Mr Right. Few women who know and are continually meeting many men ever meet him.

My own case is a very good illustration. Here am I at 22, good-looking, well-educated, domesticated and possessing those faculties which make a good wife, isolated in a country village where I never even have the chance of seeing a suitable partner, not to speak of meeting one.

It seems too, judging by the number of incongruous couples about, that very few people find Mr Right. That a Jack exists for many Jills, I would not for one moment dispute but the difficulty lies in finding him.

There are in our small towns and villages hundreds of girls who never meet congenial men and, unless they marry for a home, are doomed to spend their life in single blessedness.

M. C., near York.

Is there always a Miss Right? I am a bachelor, 29 years of age, living in Liverpool (the second city in the United Kingdom), in business for myself and making a fair livelihood. I am of quiet and steady habits, a non-smoker, total abstainer, very fond of home life, of a very affectionate nature and would make any girl very happy who married me. And yet, with all these qualifications, I have not been able to find Miss Right, though I have been looking for her for the last half a dozen years.

Backed by such experience, I am beginning seriously to think she does not exist. I sympathise very much with M.C., so much so that if I could persuade our worthy Editor to give me the young lady's name and address, I would try and persuade her to change her nom de plume to 'Happy Wife,' which I feel sure would suit her to perfection.

I have often thought of advertising for a wife in the Liverpool papers but am doubtful of the result. At present, I am bent on deciding whether it is better to wait until Miss Right turns up or if I am to go and try and find her among the numerous young ladies I know.

Batchelor, Liverpool.

Of course there is a Mr Right. So many girls, however, in their impatience to possess a lover of their very own do not wait long enough for him to turn up.

Frequently I have heard girls who have tied themselves to men for whom they only entertain a slight affection remark: 'Ah, how Mr So-and-So's thoughts and ideas harmonise with my own. If only I had known him before.'

I sincerely believe that every girl will meet a Mr Right if she will only wait long enough and allow herself time and discretion in looking out for him.

In my own case, I have met Mr Right. Previous to meeting him, I had many offers of marriage but refused them all, feeling that not one of the parties was fitted to be Jack to my Jill.

I strongly advise girls to wait and exercise patience and thought before deciding on the great question of matrimony with a man who does not appear to them as being Mr Right.

Margery, Berwick.

In my young days, girls never asked if there was a Mr Right; they were only too pleased to accept any decent man who proposed to them. If there was less talk about an imaginary Mr Right who probably does not exist and more advantage taken of the proposals that are made by sensible, suitable men, matrimony would be less of a lottery.

In my young days, girls married for a comfortable home and then took a pride in it, and also in the comfort of their lord and master.

The *fin de siècle* young lady affects romance. Her lover must go on his knees, sigh, press his hands to his heart and look ridiculous. He must serenade the fair one in his best style and spend his cash on French almond rock and chocolate creams. In return, he gets worked slippers and pincushions. He hangs the former up and brags about them and uses the latter as a top-hat smoother. In fact, he wears leather slippers and sticks his pins in his waistcoat.

The gentleman who is usually thought to be Mr Right is usually the last man a girl should marry. He is foppish, fatuous and fashionable. He spends his income on collars, cuffs and ties, puts on 'side' or draws out a weary 'Indeed' and then, so far as his conversation is concerned, evaporates.

He keeps his tailor in horses, has a three-fold looking-glass to keep his profile in order, a suit, collar, tie and pair of boots for every day in the week and wears a single eyeglass. This is 'Mr Right', while the steady, plodding, truthful, modest young fellow, whose bump of domesticity is abnormally developed, takes a back seat. Such is love.

An Old Stager, London W.

? **GIVEN equal rider/driver expertise and staying power, what would be the likely outcome of a race between a superbike and a Formula 1 car?**

A SUPERBIKE, though light and manoeuvrable, operates on two wheels, which means it can accelerate and brake only within the adhesion limits of two relatively skinny tyres.

A Grand Prix car not only benefits from four (much wider) tyres in contact with the ground but also from the tremendous downforce created by its wings.

At 180mph, a Grand Prix car will have so much downforce that you could effectively drive it on the ceiling, which means cornering speeds are far higher in a grand prix car.

In terms of power-to-weight ratio, a typical saloon car would have around 80 horsepower per tonne. A superbike would produce around 700 and a Grand Prix car more than 1,300 horsepower per tonne.

In racing terms, the Grand Prix car would win 'by a country mile'. At the Catalunya circuit in 2000, Mika Hakkinen lapped the circuit in 1min 24secs. A superbike would take more than 20 seconds longer.

Over a Formula 1 race of 65 laps, the superbike would be 21 laps behind.
Steve Andrews, Bar Hill, Cambs.

WE'RE told that Tony Blair's nickname as a pupil at Fettes College and as a barrister at the Inns of Court was Miranda. Why?
THE reference to the nickname Miranda comes from one-time lawyer and one half of TV's *Two Fat Ladies*, Clarissa Dickson Wright, who said she knew Blair when he was a barrister, claiming 'we had a nickname for him then – Miranda – but I mustn't tell you why'.
Claire Taylor, Birmingham.

WHILE at the Inns of Court, Blair was known as a bit of a dandy, who was always well dressed and wore pungent aftershave. This, coupled with his somewhat effete mannerisms, led to the nickname Miranda.
Dominic Cooper, Stonehaven, Aberdeenshire.

THE Fettes nickname was not Miranda but Matilda, from Hilaire Belloc's poem which begins: 'Matilda told such dreadful lies, It made one gasp and stretch one's eyes ...'
P. Anderson, Edinburgh.

WAS there any practical use for the metal half-moons German military police wore in World War II?
THE metal half-moon, known in English as a gorget (*ringkragen*) is the last symbolic vestige of medieval armour worn by modern soldiers.

Its original purpose was to protect the throat, and it was normally the last piece of armour donned by a knight going into battle or tournament.

World War II German military police (*Feldgendarmerie*) wore a light alloy gorget on a chain at breast height to indicate their authority. Their role was to follow the fighting troops, round up stragglers and guard PoWs and booty.

They were disliked by rank and file troops and referred to as *Kettenhunden* (chained dogs).

The bosses, eagle, swastika and lettering on the *Feldgendarmerie* gorget were treated with luminous paint to retain the authority of its wearer in the dark.

Barry Jenkins, Ferring, West Sussex.

THE gorget was used as a badge of rank by commissioned officers in the British Army until the early 19th century.

Andy Gibbs, North Drayton, Middx.

'GORGET' was also the name given to the wimple which covered the throat and chest on women's clothing in the 14th century. It's used for a distinctive band of colour on the throat of animals and birds.

Bernard Hope, Roker, Sunderland.

? ARE bats' sonic steering devices audible to the human ear?

BATS aren't blind but do emit high frequency sounds to build up a 'sound picture' of their surroundings and catch their insect food in the dark.

Different bat species have different systems of echo-location, some emitting sounds through the nose and some through the mouth. Higher frequency sounds give more information but work over shorter distances.

The human ear can hear frequencies from about 20 Hz to about 20 KHz (the BBC's time pips are 1 KHz) but we often lose the higher frequencies as we get older.

British bats use frequencies from about 20 KHz to 115 KHz so some people – particularly the young – can hear the calls of some bats. Other calls made by bats – chattering in the roost site or social and mating calls – are often within audible range. Of the 980 species of bat worldwide, 16 are resident in the UK.

A. M. Hutson, Bat Conservation Trust, London.

❓ HAS one of those fire-fighting flying boats ever scooped up a scuba diver, or is this a tall tale?

THIS tale is taller than a Chicago skyline. It usually involves the discovery of a diver's body in full underwater rig many miles from the sea, with no signs of burning, in the middle of an area where firefighters have been tackling a blaze.

Only when police discover his car at the beach do they realise he has been accidentally scooped up by a water-carrying plane and dropped onto the inferno.

The tale has many versions, including a water skier, fisherman or dolphin as victim, with locations as far apart as Canada, Australia and the Mediterranean.

In fact, fire-fighting aircraft use only a 4in to 6in pipe in the water to fill a 1,400-gallon tank. Aircrew work with firefighters on the ground and generally have a person at the landing site to assess any potential danger for the plane.

Forest fires are a regular occurrence in this part of the world, with an average 8,000 each year. My own region alone spends an annual $1,340 million on fire protection each year and has deployed teams of up to 10,000 firefighters at any one time.

Karen Terrill, California Dept of Forestry and Fire Protection, Sacramento.

❓ HOW are airports given their identification codes?

CODES are used in all airline operational departments, including baggage and cargo consignments. Anybody or anything moving from one airport to another should be appropriately coded; but spare a thought for the harassed check-in clerk or baggage handler, as there's much room for confusion.

Many codes readily identify their city and airport: DUB, MAN, FRA, AMS, BRU, VIE, for example, but if you fly to Costa Rica, where SJO is the code for San Jose, make sure your bags aren't tagged for San Jose, California – SJC.

Some use letters from the city name which may be easily identified by the layman: CPH, MUC, PRG, STL, PHL, JNB etc but cities with more than one airport or airports with local names complicate matters. LHR and LGW are well known in Europe, as are Paris's CDG and ORY, but Oslo now has FBU, Stockholm has ARN, Rome has FCO, Chicago ORD and New Orleans MSY.

All Canada's airport codes begin with Y – YVR for Vancouver, YYC for Calgary, YYZ for Toronto and YMX and YUL for the two Montreal airports.
A.W. Smith, Windsor, Berks.

? FROM where do we get the word 'tuxedo'?

THE millionaire community of Tuxedo Park, 20 miles north-west of New York City, was noted for its formal parties, held at Tuxedo Park Country Club, at which men wore tailcoats.

In October 1886, however, one dandy, Grisold Lorillard (descendant of tobacco magnate Henri Lorillard – the first person described as a 'millionaire') was so fed up with the cumbersome tails that he ordered a tail-less dinner jacket, modelled on the smoking jackets popular in Britain at the time.

Eyebrows were raised but the fashion caught on and, though described in *Harpers* magazine in 1894 as a 'hybrid garment', it became known elsewhere in the U.S. as a 'Tuxedo coat'.

The name Tuxedo Park can be traced to the Delaware Indian *p'tuksit*, a wolf, a totem of one of the tribe's three groups. When Europeans settled the area, they adopted the Indian word, anglicising it to 'tuxedo'.

Glenn Miller's hit 'Tuxedo Junction' popularised the word in this country during World War II.

James Addis-Vaile, Durham.

? WHICH country first adopted the red beret for its paratroops? Who has followed suit?

THE history of the beret can be traced back to the 12th-century Basque country where stone carvings depict lords and shepherds wearing it. It is thought to have originated among Pyrenean shepherds though a quaint local legend claims it was invented by Noah. Having sheared the sheep on the Ark, he left the fleece on the floor where it was pounded by the hooves of the other animals until it became felt, which Noah turned into a hat.

By the early 18th century, use of the beret had spread across France and in this century some military units found it practical to wear in confined spaces, such as inside tanks.

It acquired a fashionable edge in World War II when Field Marshal Montgomery introduced as standard military gear the black beret beloved of tank crews.

Marilyn De Keyser, Kangol Hats, London.

BRITAIN'S first Airborne Forces were formed when Churchill, prompted by the success of German parachute and glider forces in the assault on the Low Countries, asked the War Office to raise a force of 5,000 parachute troops.

The commander of this force once it came into being in 1942, General 'Boy' Browning, is credited with instigating the distinctive maroon beret and blue arm flashes for its paratroopers. Browning's personal racing colours were maroon and blue or he may have recalled how, on leave in 1939, he attended the shooting in Cornwall of the film of his wife Daphne du Maurier's novel *Jamaica Inn*, the leading actor of which wore a distinctive red bandana.

The red beret created a distinction which inspired other countries' airborne forces and the British style was followed by the U.S., France and, eventually, Germany.

Belinda Brinton, Airborne Forces Museum, Aldershot.

❓ I HAVE enjoyed eating carp on holiday in Hungary. Why isn't it available to eat here or in France?

CARP are available to eat in this country and in France, but demand is very low. We sell about 30 a year for consumption, mainly to the ethnic minorities, particularly people from the Balkans and other Eastern Europeans states.

The British don't eat carp for cultural reasons but also because of our delicate taste buds. Carp are bottom dwellers, can contain significant amounts of detritus from the pond and need to be thoroughly cleaned before being eaten.

Nevertheless, the proper preparation of this fish will ensure an excellent meal.

Tony McKenna, Rockingham Fisheries, Corby, Northants.

❓ GIVEN that steel had yet to be invented, of what were the swords of knights-in-armour made?

IRON Age swords were made of iron and Roman historian Pliny remarked on how the iron swords of the Celts were prone to bend in battle.

By the Middle Ages, however, knights-in-armour fought with steel swords and wore steel armour. Steel, an alloy of iron and just under two per cent carbon, has been known since Roman times but, being difficult and expensive to make, had limited use until the advent of improved blast-furnace technology in the 14th century.

By the second half of the 15th century, most weapons and almost all of the better-quality armour worn by noblemen were being made of steel.

David Edge, Armoury Curator, The Wallace Collection, London.

IF you were in a Morris Minor dropping at terminal velocity from 30,000ft, would it be physically possible to get out of the vehicle to use your parachute?

THE biggest obstacles to parachuting from an earthbound car would be the orientation of the vehicle, the wind resistance to opening the doors and the differing air resistance of the vehicle and the exiting passenger.

The car would fall at whatever angle offered least air resistance to its fall, probably nose or boot first. An exiting human would have a different air resistance to the car and therefore fall faster or slower.

A slower fall rate would mean the car would fall below the parachutist, a faster fall rate would mean being below the car, a point worth noting when opening the parachute.

Assuming a constant terminal velocity of 100mph, the fall would last just over three-and-a-half minutes, so there would be enough time to get out.

Ian Robshaw, Castleford, West Yorks.

IS it Uluru or Ayers Rock?

ARCHAEOLOGICAL evidence suggests that the monolithic tor in Australia's Uluru-Kata Tjuta National Park has been a place of cultural significance for more than 22,000 years.

Composed of sandstone, generally regarded as the world's largest monolith, and traditionally called Uluru (great pebble) by the Aborigines, it changes colour according to the position of the sun.

The Anangu tribe, traditional owners of the site, believe ancestral spirits formed it during the creation period.

The first white person to reach and climb the rock was William Christie Gosse in 1873. He named it after Sir Henry Ayers, then Chief Secretary and later Premier of South Australia.

It remained Ayers Rock until 1985 when the area was handed back to the Aborigines, its sites resumed their traditional names and Ayers Rock officially became Uluru.

P. Carter, Sydney, Australia.

WE know it's not illegal not to vote at a General Election but if I try to persuade others not to vote, am I committing an offence?

PERSUADING another to do something illegal is an inchoate offence, known as incitement. The rationale behind such offences is that the police can punish those who encourage others to commit crime.

If a person incites someone to do an act which isn't criminal but the inciter believes it is, then no crime has been committed. Nor has a crime been committed if the inciter suggests a crime be committed by impossible means – such as killing someone by pinging an elastic band at them.

So, as a person can't be guilty of an incitement offence if the action is a legal one, such as not voting, it's not illegal to persuade others not to vote.
Phil Burnham, Thame, Oxon.

INCITEMENT exists along with another inchoate offence of conspiracy which is regulated by statute rather than common law. Under section 1(1)(b) of the Criminal Law Act 1977, someone can be found guilty of conspiracy despite 'the existence of facts which render the commission of the offence impossible'.

For example, if you conspire to extract cocaine from a harmless substance which contains no cocaine, you can still be guilty of conspiracy. But you would need to have honestly believed that what you were doing was illegal, since conspiracy itself is not an offence, only conspiracy to pursue a criminal course of conduct.

So, although it would not be illegal to incite someone else to commit a crime, if you conspired to stop people voting and honestly believed that by doing so you were doing something illegal, it is possible that although you would not be guilty of incitement, you could be guilty of conspiracy.
David Anderson, Manchester.

❓ THEY say you never remember those who came second. Who has been remembered for coming second?
EVE.
Jill Lyle, Street, Somerset.

IN a Miss Naples contest in the Forties, the runner-up was Sophia Loren. I'd be surprised if anyone remembers the winner.
John Dobson, Surbiton, Surrey.

❓ IS it possible to weigh accurately a human head without removing it from the body?

ATTACH a pulley to the ceiling and pass a rope through it, then fill a large container with water. Suspend your subject by the ankles from one end of the pulley and counterbalance his mass by weights on the other end of the rope. As you gradually remove the weights, so his body will lower and become immersed in the container of water, which will overflow.

Once his head is fully immersed, count up the mass of the weights removed from the counterbalance. This will equate to the mass of the water displaced which provides an upthrust equivalent to the mass of the individual's head.

NB: he may need to take a very deep breath before you start.

John Prescott, Callington, Cornwall.

❓ DID napalm inventor Dr Louis Fieser spend years developing a bat bomb?

IN 1943, the U.S. Army took two million Mexican free-tail bats from the Carlsbad caverns in New Mexico and gave them to research centres studying how to equip the creatures with delayed action explosives.

The plan was to attach a bomb weighing less than 1oz (30g) to each bat by a piece of string fastened to its chest.

The bats would be released over enemy cities where, it was hoped, they would fly into attics or under the eaves of buildings and wait until the delayed fuse ignited.

At first, the bats kept chewing through the string but, after two years experimentation, a trial run was staged. The first wave of bats was released prematurely and set off fires, blowing up a general's staff car and destroying a $2 million hangar.

The U.S. Navy suggested that the bats could be artificially cooled to trick them into going into hibernation so they wouldn't chew through the string. They could then be dropped from an aircraft flying at 35,000ft to wake up as they hit warm air further down and fly to their targets. But the bats stayed asleep and fell to their deaths.

The specially converted $50 million aircraft was then blown up by a few 'bat bombs' which blew back inside it and the project was abandoned.

Mike Davies, Nuneaton, Warwks.

WHY do surgeons wear green when performing an operation?

AS an amateur artist, I often use this shade of green for a similar effect. The colour is known to have the optical capability of neutralising the blinding patches that occur in the eye after looking into a bright light, such as the sun's rays.

Operations are performed under powerful lights and the green make the procedure safer by keeping the surgeon's vision clear.

Terry Vaughan, Rugby, Warwks.

WHERE did the term 'hippie' come from?

THE expression 'hippie' dates from 1930s America, when opium smoking was still a popular pastime.

The Chinese community purveyed the drug through opium dens. Participants visiting a den were supplied with a pipe of opium and shown to a plank or bed where they could lie on one side or hip to smoke the pipe. This gave rise to the expression 'being on the hip', later shortened to 'being hip', describing someone who was knowledgeable in such matters.

The drug-use allusion soon became associated with marijuana and the psychedelic drugs common in the Sixties. The term 'hippie' was an indirect carryover from hip and soon came to mean anyone of bohemian dress or persuasion who, possibly, indulged in drug use. It generally replaced its 1950s cousin 'beatnik' in common descriptive use.

Paul Briscoe, author: When The Chinaman Spoke, *Perth.*

WHAT became of Anita Bryant, the U.S. answer to Mary Whitehouse?

ANITA Bryant was born in Oklahoma in March 1940, began a musical career at an early age and was winning talent competitions and appearing on TV at nine.

She became known as Oklahoma's Red Feather Girl and made her professional debut in 1956 with the album *Sinful To Flirt*. In 1958, she was crowned Miss Oklahoma and came third in the Miss America pageant.

A year later, she released 'Till There Was You', her first chart-topping hit, following it with several albums in the Sixties. In the Seventies, she turned to gospel and religious music.

In 1977, the Miami-Dade County Commission passed an ordinance making it illegal to discriminate on the basis of sexual orientation. Bryant, a devout Baptist, organised the protest group, Save Our Children. A referendum was held and the county's citizens voted to overturn the ordinance.

This galvanised the gay community and Anita lost her job as spokesperson for Florida orange juice after activists organised a boycott.

Bryant's celebrity slowly faded. She continued campaigning through the Eighties and Nineties but the gay rights measure was eventually passed in 1998.

In her campaigning days, she could be seen daily, performing in the Anita Bryant Theatre in Branson, Missouri, but she has now disappeared from the public eye and her theatre has closed down.

Mark Ashton, Newcastle upon Tyne.

DID astronomer Tycho Brahe have a silver nose?

TYCHO Brahe was born on December 14, 1546, in Knudstrup, then in Denmark but now in Southern Sweden.

Fascinated by the stars since his youth, he discovered that existing astronomical tables were highly inaccurate and set about making his own meticulous observations of the heavens, a project that occupied him for most of his life.

He accumulated an impressive body of astronomical data which his assistant, Johannes Kepler, used later to deduce the laws of planetary motion. Brahe made all his observations with the naked eye – the telescope hadn't yet been invented.

He had had a turbulent life since the age of one, when he was kidnapped by his uncle. A headstrong and adventurous young man, in 1566 he got involved in a sword duel in pitch darkness with fellow student Manderup Parsbjerg over some astronomical argument.

Tycho's face was slashed and he lost the bridge of his nose but he had a false one made out of gold and silver and stuck it to his face with tape. His love of drinking and feasting contributed to his early death at the age of 55.

When Tycho's body was exhumed for medical research in 1901, copper stains were found around his nose. It's not known if the copper was used to help obtain a flesh colour, whether the original false nose was replaced in a time of financial hardship or if he used the gold/silver nose only for special occasions.

Denis McGuire, Llantwit Major, Vale of Glamorgan.

? WHAT'S the most unusual way in which someone has asked for their ashes to be disposed?

MY children were walking along the promenade when a gust of wind covered their ice creams with ash. Turning round, they came face to face with a red-faced gentleman who was scattering his mother's ashes over the sea.
Mrs M. Jones, Eastbourne, Sussex.

WHEN keen shooter and Sotheby's specialist James Booth passed away after having been in a coma for two years, there was no stipulation in his will as to how his remains were to be dealt with other than that he should be cremated.

His wife Joanna thought it fitting that he should be able to 'go out with a bang' so his ashes were mixed with a mound of lead shot by the Caledonian Cartridge Company and loaded into 275 12-bore shotgun cartridges, to be used by a group of his best friends and family at a game shoot in Aberdeen.

The ammunition was blessed by a Church of Scotland minister, before being rattled off on a 100-bird day.
R. Calcutt, Leamington Spa, Warwks.

I ONCE scattered the ashes of an old aviation chum from an open glider. To avoid blow-back into the cockpit, I put his remains in a long cardboard tube, sealed both ends then, at 2,000ft above the Solent, released one end and, whoosh, he was gone.

He had a keen sense of humour and would have chuckled at the disrespect-ful transfer of his ashes from the regulation urn to the tube using a paper fun-nel cobbled together for the purpose, with the tube firmly clamped in a vice in the airfield workshop.
John H. Stanley, Bognor Regis, Sussex.

MY father Charles Gould passed away in 1986. His office had overlooked an island on the river Welland in Lincolnshire and he had asked a firm of under-takers to scatter his ashes into the river by the island.

After the funeral, the undertaker collected the ashes, put on his waders and early one morning walked into the river and started disposing of the ashes.

Unfortunately, someone had seen him and assumed that he was throwing some chemical into the river that might pollute it, called the police, who arrested the poor undertaker.

The police thought the undertaker's story was invented to cover up some other activity and it was hours before he was released when one of my father's relatives confirmed that the story was true.

The undertaker vowed never again to get involved in fulfilling the wishes of his deceased clients.

Anthony Gould, Rickmansworth, Herts.

BONNEVILLE salt-flat racers are an unusual breed. In 2003, the ashes of the official starter Bob Higbee were packed in the parachute of racer Mike Cook's car.

At the end of a 250mph run, Mike released the 'chute to slow down his streamliner, scattering Higbee's ashes over the salt flats.

Former record-breaking legend Fred Larson was given a similar send-off the same year, having his ashes scattered over the hallowed course by the Nish team.

David Tremayne, Harrow, Middx..

❓ HAVE women ever fought a duel?

THE duel as we know it in Western Europe had its earliest form in 'trial by battle' or the judicial duel, established in law by Burgundian King Gundobad in AD 500.

The development of the chivalrous duel came about after the spread of knighthood. A strict code of conduct was enforced and by the early 16th century this had evolved into duels of honour.

The peak of these duels came in the 17th century when a gentleman who took offence at another would make an official challenge, agree a time and place and appoint a 'second' to witness fairness.

Contrary to popular belief, most duels ended as soon as blood was drawn from one of the parties, rather than carrying on to the death.

Several 'petticoat duellists' emerged, one of the most famous being Julie d'Aubigny, better known as opera singer La Maupin (1670–1707) though, as a notorious bisexual, she rarely wore a petticoat.

She had been taught by her father how to handle a sword and won several duels, while dressed as a man, including at least one against a man, Louis-Joseph d'Albert de Luynes.

Having run his shoulder through, she felt sufficiently sorry for him to tend his wounds and begin a lifelong affair with him.

Other 'petticoat duellists' included Madame de St Belmont, Lady de Nesle and the Countess de Polignac. The latter two met at Versailles in 1721 to contest a duel over the affections of the Duc de Richelieu. Their first pistol shots were erratic but in the second round the Countess wounded de Nesle.

In Britain, the most famous duel between women was in 1792 between Lady Almeria Braddock and Mrs Elphinstone, at London's favourite duellists' haunt, Hyde Park, after an argument about their respective ages.

Both ladies missed their shots but fought on with swords until blood was drawn from Mrs Elphinstone. Honour restored, they curtsied to each other and left with their seconds.

Stephen Gregory, Perth.

❓ AFTER all the warnings about looking at the Eclipse, did anyone actually suffer eye damage after 1999?

MOORFIELDS Eye Hospital noted permanent eye damage to six people. In the early Fifties, there was a partial eclipse of the sun and I heard that by covering one eye and staring into the sun, I would see the eclipse.

I did this for a minute or so, successfully, but within a day or two I realised I had suffered eye damage. If I look at a dart board, I can clearly see all of it except the bull's eye which is a black spot and invisible.

Over the years, I've acquired the knack of looking half an inch to the side of any small object and seeing it momentarily but clearly.

Now in my 60s, I have no need of specs for distance nor for reading in daylight but have to wear weak lenses for reading indoors.

I just wish the abundance of good advice given now had been available then.

R. E. Findlay, Faversham, Kent.

❓ SOME time ago there was a competition to find the worst opening sentence in a novel. Who was the winner?

SINCE 1982, the English Department at San Jose State University in California has sponsored the Bulwer-Lytton Fiction Contest, a whimsical literary competition that challenges entrants to compose the opening sentence to the worst of all possible novels.

Few entrants have reached the dizzy heights of the original composed by the inimitable Edward George Bulwer-Lytton in his 1830 novel *Paul Clifford*: 'It was a dark and stormy night; the rain fell in torrents – except at occasional intervals, when it was checked by a violent gust of wind which swept up the streets (for it is in London that our scene lies), rattling along the housetops, and fiercely agitating the scanty flame of the lamps that struggled against the darkness.'

A recent winner was Dave Zobel, a software developer from California, who wrote: 'She resolved to end the love affair with Ramon tonight, . . . summarily, like Martha Stewart ripping the sand vein out of a shrimp's tail . . . though the term "love affair" now struck her as a ridiculous euphemism. . . not unlike "sand vein", which is after all an intestine, not a vein... and that tarry substance inside certainly isn't sand ... and that brought her back to Ramon.'
Scott Rice, San Jose State University, California.

? WHAT'S the difference between the Qassam rockets being fired at Israel from the Gaza Strip and the Katyusha rockets currently used by Hizbollah in Lebanon?
THE Katyusha multiple-launch rocket system was created in the Soviet Union in World War II and named after a popular Russian song about a girl longing for her beloved who is away fighting.

The weapon, resembling a pipe organ, was known to the Germans as 'Stalin's organ'. A highly versatile weapon, it could be mounted on trucks, tanks or even tractors.

It was a relatively simple design and lacked accuracy though it was often massed in large numbers to create a 'shock and awe' effect on enemy forces.

'Katyusha' is now used to describe any of the small artillery rockets often used in guerilla warfare. Hezbollah has long shelled Israel from Lebanon using Katyusha rockets, hitting cities and farms as well as military targets in the sparsely populated northern border zone.

Qassam rockets are a far more rudimentary single-rocket system consisting of a simple steel rocket filled with explosives, developed by the Palestinian organisation Hamas. Three models have been used, all lacking a guidance system.

These missiles are named after the Izz ad-din al-Qassam Brigades, the military wing of Hamas, and have been used to attack various Israeli towns.

Despite the Qassam's meagre characteristics as a rocket, its first use shocked the Israeli military and public, who were used to the Palestinians lacking any method of long-range warfare.
Keith Hill, Maidenhead, Berks.

Q **A SOUND rarely heard these days is the tap-tap-tap of an old-fashioned typewriter. What other everyday sounds have been lost to modern day technology?**

WHEN did you last hear a young man whistling as he walked or cycled along? These days they all seem to be plugged in to personal stereos or mobile phones.

M. P. Smith, Bromham, Beds.

Q **FROM what is the white cross that is piped onto hot cross buns made?**

THE white cross is made from flour, water, cooking oil and a little baking powder, mixed to a thick batter consistency and then piped onto the buns before they are baked.

Charles Burton, bakery technologist, former Master Baker, Tonbridge, Kent.

THE recipe for the white cross on buns at my bakery was melted lard, warm water and soft white flour mixed to the consistency of a batter. This was then piped over the buns after they had been proved.

Dennis Wetherly (retired baker).

Q **WHY is the hole in the ozone layer above the least industrialised parts of the Earth?**

THE hole in the ozone layer usually occurs over Antarctica, a somewhat surprising place given the untouched beauty of the continent. Most of the chemicals that lead to the creation of the ozone hole are manufactured and released in the northern hemisphere. From here they diffuse throughout the Earth's atmosphere – North Pole to South Pole.

What's special about the Antarctic lies in the winter temperature of the ozone layer. Over Antarctica it gets cold enough for thin clouds to form at 14 to 20km. Chemical reactions take place on the clouds that convert chlorine (and bromine) from the ozone-depleting chemicals into an active form.

In the Antarctic spring, these chemicals, with the help of sunlight, convert ozone back to oxygen, forming the Antarctic ozone hole. The atmosphere elsewhere is normally not cold enough for the clouds to form and last.

If it is particularly cold in the Arctic ozone layer, clouds form quite extensively within it. The same chemical reactions that create the Antarctic ozone hole take place and ozone values over Greenland have been known to drop to 40 per cent lower than normal.

But ozone values over the Arctic are generally higher than those over the Antarctic: they haven't dropped far enough to call it an ozone hole though this is a significant ozone depletion on our doorstep.

To complicate matters, the greenhouse gases that are warming the surface of the Earth have the opposite effect in the ozone layer, so it is getting colder which means we could see more long-lasting ozone depletion in the future.

Jon Shanklin, meteorologist, British Antarctic Survey, Cambridge.

? MANY years ago, we had our wedding reception at the Pinder of Wakefield pub at King's Cross. What is a pinder?

THE pinder was a town official responsible for the control of stray animals. He would impound them in a 'pinfold' where they would stay until the owners paid a fine for their release.

The ballad of 'The Jolly Pinder Of Wakefield' ('George a' Green') records his victory over Robin Hood and his Merry Men, whom he fought single-handedly. He so impressed Robin that he was invited to join his select band.

The public house of that name in London's Gray's Inn Road was a marvellous establishment. Once through the bar area, one emerged into a theatre which in its day played host to many up-and-coming stars of music and entertainment. Bob Dylan appeared there in the 1960s and The Pogues made their debut gig here.

Many 'resting' actors would appear on the occasional Friday evening when it became the Aba Daba Music Hall. I used to turn up there frequently in the Seventies for a good old singsong.

It still plays host to many musicians, including Oasis, but is now called The Water Rats Theatre.

M. Dunning, Wilton, Yorkshire.

? WHY do crabs walk sideways?

CRABS' legs are attached to the side of their body, like our arms are to our shoulders. While we have shoulder, elbow and wrist joints which move relatively freely, a crab's joints can move only very slightly in the front–rear direction so they can walk forward and backwards but only slowly but move well at right angles to this.

The joints are actually more like the fingers on your hand, which move well up and down, but only slightly from side to side. Try moving your hand across a table with the palm facing down and see which direction it is easiest to move it in.

Crabs evolved in this way probably because it was more important to develop a very hard and flat shell (or carapace) to protect them and to allow them to crouch down on and under rocks, than to have back and forward motion of their legs. As everyone knows, together with their large claws, crabs are very well protected.

Richard Harrington, Marine Conservation Society, Ross-On-Wye, Herefordshire.

? HAS enough alcohol been consumed on the QE2 to float her?

FOR the QE2 to float, the amount of liquid available must be heavier than the ship and the density of the liquid (the weight of one cubic metre) must be higher than the density of the ship. When the ship floats it has to displace its own weight of the liquid.

The QE2's owners, Cunard Line, say 600,000 litres of alcoholic drinks are consumed on the ship each year. In the 42 years the ship has been at sea, this amounts to 25.2 million litres. As the drinks are normally not pure alcohol, we can assume they have a density of 90 per cent of that of water and weigh 22.68 million kg.

Fully loaded, the QE2 weighs 70,327 tonnes – 70,327,000kg – which means the QE2 would have to be in continuous service for about 130 years before the alcohol drunk on board would allow her to displace her own weight.

However, if the ship were unloaded of its cargo, passengers and engines then it weighs 11,590 tonnes or 11,590,000kg. At this weight it could actually float in the alcoholic drinks already consumed.

Bhagwant Singh, Xperiment! Museum of Science and Industry, Manchester.

ONE doesn't need to define the amount of fluid displaced when the ship is lowered into an alcoholic ocean. Archimedes, lowered into his brim-full bath, caused his own weight of water to be displaced and was then floating in what remained, not what overflowed.

A bath moulded closely to his own shape would allow him to float in a minimal amount of liquid, be it beer, gin or asses' milk (an experiment which would have been highly popular at my school, had it been performed by Cleopatra rather than by an ancient Greek).

In the extreme case, a mould made to the exact shape of the QE2 would allow her to float in a single pint of Guinness, or less. Given containers of the right shapes, the alcohol drunk aboard the QE2 would be more than enough to float every ship that has ever been built, while leaving enough for me to get very drunk indeed.

Try this little experiment: a plastic coffee cup with an inch of water in it will comfortably float another identical cup that is three-quarters full. Label the inner, heavier cup as the QE2, and you have a ship floating in less than its own weight of water.

J. Spilsbury, Stockport, Cheshire.

WAS America's famous Liberty bell made in Britain?

THE Liberty Bell, now in its own special building in Philadelphia, isn't the original bell cast by Whitechapel Foundry of East London, though it's made from the melted-down metal of that bell.

In 1751, to mark the 50th anniversary of William Penn's charter of liberties and privileges, the Pennsylvania Assembly of what was then still a British colony ordered a bell for its State House, now known as Independence Hall.

When the bell arrived, it was hung from a nearby tree and tested for tone, but it cracked. Attempts to repair the crack failed and the bell was melted down to make a new one. The new bell didn't have a very good sound so it was remelted with an extra 80lb of brass added. This made the present bell, which sounded good and was hung in the State House tower.

Sadly, during the day-long bell ringing to mark the death of U.S. Supreme Court Chief Justice John Marshall, who died while visiting the city in 1825, the bell cracked and all attempts to repair it failed. It was removed to the entrance hall of the building, now renamed Independence Hall.

It was given the name 'Liberty Bell' in the 1830s when the Abolitionists took it as their symbol in their campaign against slavery, citing the words on the bell (from Leviticus 25:10): 'Proclaim liberty throughout the land and unto all the inhabitants thereof...'

Andrew Kevorkian, London W1.

HOW would a total eclipse appear to an observer looking at the Earth from the centre of the Moon?

AN observer standing on the Moon's surface with the Earth directly overhead would be able to see the Moon's shadow on the Earth's surface. It would appear as a penumbra (the lighter shadow – where a partial eclipse is seen) surrounding a much smaller central umbra (the darker shadow – where the total eclipse is visible).

As the Moon orbited the Earth, the shadow would move from west to east across the earth.

The GOES-7 weather satellite actually photographed the Moon's shadow passing across the Earth during the total eclipse of 1991.

Dr Massey, Royal Observatory, Greenwich, London.

? WHY are horse-racing bookmakers' odds quoted at 100 to 30 rather than 10 to 3, and 6 to 4 rather than 3 to 2?

THERE are two traditional patterns of offering odds, one of which has been largely discontinued. The offer of 'Burlington Bertie', as John McCririck always calls 100/30, in the old days was matched by 100/15 and by 100/9, 100/8, 100/7 and 100/6.

In the past 30 years, the last four have been largely replaced by 11/1, 12/1, 14/1 and 16/1, leaving the punter slightly worse off in all cases.

On the racecourse, when a layer is offering 100/8, it's easy to place a bet of £4 or £8 and know exactly how much to expect if the bet wins, and many course bookmakers will still accept bets calculated by the old system. But for settlers in betting shops, dealing with doubles, trebles and accumulators, the fractions are complex and less profitable. Try working out an each-way treble at 100/8, 100/7 and 100/6 and you'll appreciate the simplicity of a similar bet at 12/1, 14/1 and 16/1.

The shorter a horse's odds, the more important it is to have slight differences between them. Evens, 21/20, 11/10, 6/5, 5/4, 11/8 and 6/4 are all very close together but the differences can be crucial to profit and loss.

Punters are familiar with the 'quarters' going regularly from evens to 5/4, 6/4, 7/4, 2/1, 9/4, 5/2, 11/4 and 3/1 – the next price after this ought to be 13/4 but maybe that's unlucky and the next step used is 100/30, then 7/2. There is no logical reason for 5/2 being used and not 3/2 – it's just custom and habit.

In betting slang, 11/10 is tips, 5/4 wrist, 6/4 ear'ole, 7/4 on the shoulder, 2/1 bottle, 9/4 top of the head and 3/1 carpet.

David Elias, Nottingham.

SHOULD I ADVERTISE FOR A WIFE?

DEAR *Answers*,—I have often cogitated with myself on the advisability of advertising for a wife. With the immense superfluity of the feminine sex in this country today, the average man may consider the question ridiculous but it is not so by any means.

Although in a good position from a financial point of view, and possessed of every qualification necessary in a husband, I have not, up to the present moment, succeeded in meeting with a lady who fully answers my expectations, perhaps because my opportunities for doing so are exceedingly limited.

Should I therefore send an advertisement to the matrimonial and other papers?

On The Brink, Norwich.

In reply to this question, I would repeat Mr Punch's celebrated advice: 'Don't.'

In much the same position as him, I decided to insert an advertisement and accordingly penned one in these words:

MATRIMONY. – Gentleman, 30, independent, well connected and of prepossessing appearance, would be glad to correspond with a suitable lady with a view to matrimony.

I won't dwell too long on the result: sufficient to say that although I received over 100 replies, not one seemed in the least degree satisfactory.

Matrimonial agents sent voluminous circulars offering, in return for a small commission, their valuable assistance, which I respectfully declined.

Domestic servants replied by the score and one informed me that she, like myself, was well connected, having for two years been head scullery-maid in the Duke of B— —'s establishment.

Another lady thought our religious views might clash, as she was not an Independent.

Facetious correspondents remarked on the becoming modesty which characterised my advertisement, and one lady magnanimously offered to consider my lonely case if I was prepared to pay her return travelling expenses from the North of England.

I have come to the conclusion, after wading through a heap of correspondence, that matrimony by advertisement is a mistake – at least, such is my experience though others may have fared better.

Experience, Salisbury.

I think it a great error to attempt to advertise for a wife. It could not possibly turn out to be a happy marriage in the proper sense of the word, as making it such a business sort of arrangement would not be conducive to perfect happiness.

Where would be love for one another and those nonsensical little episodes which go to make a love affair so divine?

I do not think that any really nice, modest girl would answer an advertisement of the sort. I grant you that the girl might be pretty and charming but probably your money will be the most-thought-of item in her negotiations with you. I say wait until Dr Cupid pricks you with the fiery dart; it will be sure to come if you wait long enough.

It is a pity there are so few chances of the upper middle classes meeting gentlemen in social ways. I am 20 and have never had a lover but I would never dream of obtaining one by the means of advertising.

Forsaken Twenty, Yarmouth.

Here am I, an orphan bachelor, aged 33, not bad-looking, tolerably agreeable, domestic, eminently well-suited for married life and possessing a very substantial income and yet wholly unable to find a wife.

No maiden approaching the 30s ever wished for matrimony as I do, yet I find it absolutely unattainable.

How shall I ever get a wife except by advertising? I am sure there are many girls in the world who would be eminently suitable but they are not here and how can I meet them or hear of them save by advertising?

Having settled that I should advertise, a far more difficult question is where should I advertise? In a matrimonial journal? Certainly not, I tried it once.

'Gentleman, 33, dark, good-tempered, fairly good-looking, £ ___ per annum, desires ... etc., etc...'

Result? A typewritten agreement to sign from a 'manager,' a request for a fee, a bundle of rules and regulations about ambassadors and so forth and, of course, the usual letter that there were just then several eligible ladies on the books.

That is nearly a year ago and I am still,

A Batchelor, Dublin.

This question brings to my mind an amusing incident that occurred to a friend of mine some years ago. He was a lonely man, his continued bachelorhood probably being attributed to his abrupt and sometimes overbearing manner. Not finding a lady congenial to him, he decided to advertise, and ultimately made an appointment with a lady who, by her photo and letter, seemed likely to be the possessor of a temperament as brusque as his own.

This lady was in fact the spinster aunt of one of the few of his friends (including me) who had formed a secret plan. We had determined, if possible, to cure him of his bad manners and the lady in question aided us in our intention.

A meeting and a token of recognition were duly arranged between the two and, by the lady's account, the following brief conversation took place in a secluded corner of one of the public parks:

'You're the woman?' 'Yes!'

'Think you'll do?' 'Sure!'

'Cook?' 'No!'

'Sew?' 'No!'

'Economical?' 'No!'

'What?' 'No!'

'Keep house?' 'No!'

'Then what on earth can you do?' 'Teach elderly boors manners. Good-morning.'

With this effective retort the lady departed and retailed the story to us, much to our delight. As was to be expected, our secret ultimately leaked out and the 'guying' H—— received evidently produced its intended beneficial effect for from that time H——'s manners improved and he is now quite a presentable member of society.

In On The Joke, Limerick.

? DOES the production of cashmere wool involve any cruelty to the goats from which it comes?

CASHMERE goats in Great Britain are farmed in a similar manner to sheep. They are kept outside in free-ranging grazing conditions and shelter is provided to allow them to escape from bad weather.

In the springtime, the goats naturally shed or moult their fine downy undercoat and the cashmere fibre is harvested by combing, just as one would do for long-haired dogs.

Combing removes the undercoat but leaves most of the coarse hairy outer coat on the goat.

Some producers choose to shear the goats, like sheep. In this case the goats are kept indoors for a few weeks to protect them from bad weather while their coat regrows.

After combing, or shearing, the fibre has to be washed and processed to remove the valueless coarse hair. The best goats yield about 300g of 'pure' cashmere which is then spun into a yarn for knitting or weaving.

There is certainly no cruelty involved; most producers keep small numbers of goats which are known individually to their owner.

John Barker, Scottish Cashmere Producers Assoc Ltd, Helensburgh, Dunbartonshire.

? WHY is America called 'Uncle Sam'?

THE original Uncle Sam was Samuel Wilson, nephew of army contractor Elbert Anderson, who owned a slaughterhouse in Troy, New York, and had a contract to supply the army with salt pork and beef.

Wilson and his uncle Ebenezer, Elbert's brother, were army inspectors who often inspected the meat Elbert packed in barrels with the initials 'E.A. – U.S.' (Elbert Anderson – United States).

When a soldier asked what the initials meant, a comrade joked that they stood for Elbert Anderson's 'Uncle Sam'. Some scholars dispute this story, though it was widely accepted in Wilson's lifetime.

The term's first use was in the *Troy Post* of September 7, 1813, which accepted the Samuel Wilson theory but said only that the words derived from the initials on Government wagons. The name 'Uncle Sam' was soon adopted as a symbol of the army and then as a national nickname to counter the UK's John Bull.

The first visual representation or caricature of Uncle Sam, attired in stars and stripes, appeared in political cartoons in 1832. The character came to be seen as a shrewd Yankee, possibly the Brother Jonathan character in Royall Tyler's 1787 play *The Contrast*.

'Uncle Sam' gained further currency in World War I when he was painted by James Montgomery Flagg on a recruiting poster as a stern figure with a short beard and high hat pointing a finger with the message 'I want YOU for the U.S. Army.'

In 1961, the U.S. Congress adopted the figure of Uncle Sam as a national symbol.

Kevin Heneghan, St Helens, Merseyside.

? WHERE and when in Britain was the first electricity pylon erected?

THE first 'grid tower', a pylon which looked very much like the ones seen everywhere today, was erected outside Edinburgh in July 1928.

Before 1928, there was no high voltage grid system connecting the numerous local electricity networks which had spread across the country.

In 1926, the Government passed the Electricity Supply Act, setting up the Central Electricity Board to establish national coordination of the electricity system.

The CEB was asked to concentrate electricity generation in selected stations and begin work on a national high-tension mains transmission system.

The country was divided into areas and, in 1927, the South of Scotland scheme was the first to get the go-ahead. What became known as National Grid – a huge leap forward for electricity supply in the UK – was largely completed in just seven years. As a result of the new network's ability to transport electricity around the country to where it was needed, the amount of generating plant lying idle fell from 80 per cent to just 15 per cent by 1935.

Neil Williams, Electricity Association, London.

? WHAT is the highest altitude at which trees will grow? Is the tree line much the same in different parts of the world?

THE tree line is determined by site conditions, maximum and minimum temperatures, times of the last frost in spring and the first frost in autumn, depth of soil, precipitation and, most significantly, exposure to wind.

Above the tree line, any tree is more likely to look like a shrub growing close to the ground.

In Britain, the high ground of the Pennines creates sheltered conditions on the east (leeward) side and trees can grow at a higher altitude than on the windward west slopes.

The tree line in Britain is around 1,400ft on the west of a hill and between 1,500 and 1,600 on the east.

In world terms, moving north from the Equator has a similar effect as increasing altitude.

Derek Patch, The Tree Advice Trust, Wrecclesham, Surrey.

THE Sagarmatha National Park in Nepal, which ranges in altitude from 2,845m (9,334ft) at Jorsalle to 8,848m (29,028ft), at the top of the world's highest mountain, Mt Everest (also known as Sagarmatha), comprises about 3 per cent forest.

This forest has blue pine above 3,000m (9,842ft) and birch-rhododendron above 3,600m (11,811ft), reaching to the timberline (the line where trees start to look more like shrubs than trees) at 3,800–4,000m (12,467–13,123ft). Parts of this forest, the highest in the world, have a tree line at more than eight times the altitude of the tree line in the British Isles.

James Bannerman, Edinburgh.

———

HOW did Maltesers get their name? Do they contain malt?

MALTESERS do indeed contain malt extract. They were invented in 1936 by Mars and were first sold in November of that year, selling 500 tonnes in the first 12 months.

They were originally marketed as a 'portable malted drink in a box' – hence the name Maltesers – as malted drinks were very popular at the time but were very expensive. Maltesers were very inexpensive by comparison and quickly caught on.

Today, Maltesers are the number-one bite-sized brand in the UK (and quirkily enough number-one confectionery brand in Malta!) with more than five billion eaten every year, which works out at 14 million every day or 9,500 eaten every minute.

Kay Nicholls, Mars Confectionery, Slough.

? A BRITISH man called Brian Head enjoyed visiting the town of
• Brian Head in Utah; has anyone else visited a namesake town?

I'VE come across many place names that sound more like people including Allan Bank in Strathclyde; Anna Valley in Hampshire; Bryan Stone in Dorset; Cherry Hinton in Cambridgeshire; Chester Blade in Somerset; Dick Le Burgh in Norfolk and Dudley Hill in West Yorkshire.

There's also Felix Stowe in Suffolk and Fletcher Green in Kent. Frank Fort is found in Norfolk and Fraser Burgh in Grampian, which also has Kitty Brewster.

Penny Hill is in Lincs; Kenny Thorpe in North Yorkshire; Jemima Ville in Ross-Shire; and Ray Leigh in Essex; Rose Ash is in Devon as is Rosemary Lane; Scot Landwell is in Tayside; Sid Brook in Somerset; Lily Hurst in Shropshire. Logan Beck is in Cumbria; Lucas Gate in Lincs; and Lyn Chat in the Highlands.

Those who prefer to be known by their titles are Countess Cross in Essex and Countess Wear in Devon.

Jayne Clayton, Sutton, Surrey.

THE list may also include Mavis Enderby in Lincs; Hanna Ford (no relation to the newsreader) in Devon; Harriet Field in Tayside; Harold Wood in London; and Hayley Green in the West Midlands.

Oswald Kirk and Patrick Brompton are in North Yorkshire; Hazel Grove is in Greater Manchester; Kingsley Park in Northants; Olive Green in Staffs; Norman Cross in Cambs; Wally Ford in Lothian; Virginia Water in Surrey; and Tom Low in Warwickshire.

Jason Ogden, Oldham.

YOU could add to the list: Edmond Thorpe in Leicestershire; Edward Stone in Staffs; Paul Ersbury in Lincs; Russell Green and Saffron Walden in Essex; Lyn Hales in Hereford, Margaret Marsh in Dorset; Lee Brockhurst in Shropshire; and Ross Keen and Roy Bridge in the Highlands.

Danni-Jean Holgate, Chigwell, Essex.

? WHY is it considered unlucky to put red and white flowers
• together in a bouquet?

I AM well into my 80s and was told as a child that this rule applied specifically to roses and dates back to the time of the Wars of the Roses when Yorkists and Lancastrians adopted as their emblems the white and red rose, respectively.

Eileen Luker, Coopersale, Essex.

❓ IF I travelled the distance covered by every phone call made on the planet in one day, how far would I be from Earth?

THE current estimate is that there are about 800 million telephones on the planet (33 million in the UK) which works out at roughly one for every seven-and-a-half people (or enough, put side to side, to stretch from London to Singapore).

Worldwide, if we extrapolate from British experience where the average number of calls made each day on each of these telephones is three, there are 2,400 million calls a day. Each call covers an average distance of ten miles so this works out at 24 billion miles of calls every day.

To get an idea of how far 24 billion miles actually is, it would get a person on Earth to Mars and back 350 times. It would easily get us to the Solar System's outer planet Pluto, with more than 20 billion miles to spare. But it would not get us to our nearest star, Proxima Centauri which, at 5,878 billion miles away, means that our calls would total only 0.4 per cent of the distance.

For one person to call every telephone presently on the planet would take you up to the year AD 3520 – and that's without sleeping or breaks.

Alexandra I. Black, Prees Heath, Shropshire.

❓ AN old Scottish expression runs: 'We are all Jock Tamson's bairns.' Who was Jock Tamson?

THE usual meaning of the saying as defined by the *Concise Scots Dictionary* is 'the human race, common humanity; a group of people united by a common sentiment, interest etc' but this gives no clue as to where the name Jock Tamson comes from.

Among three possible explanations we have come across are that he was a philanthropist who founded orphanages in the West of Scotland; that it is linked to a minister in Duddingston called John Thomson; or that it is the Scots version of the slang word 'John Thomas' (male genitals), so in a sense we are all his children.

Derek Hoy, Jock Tamson's Bairns Folk Band, Edinburgh.

THE Jock Tamson referred to in the expression was Rev John Thomson of Duddingston church, Edinburgh (1778–1840), a landscape artist of renown, a contemporary of Turner.

He was my great-great-grandfather and the story was handed down through the family that he was a widower with children and married again a lady who also had children. They then had another five children. When introducing someone, he would always say: 'These are mine, they are hers – and these are ours – but they are all Jock Tamson's bairns.'

David Philp, Surbiton, Surrey.

❓I HAVE recently moved into a house named Rake End. Might there be any meaning behind this name?

WHEN I lived in Wallasey, Merseyside, a 'rake' was another word for lane, so Rake End is Lane End. There's a Rake Lane in Wallasey which means residents of that road live in Lane Lane.

Andy Brizell, Sutton Coldfield, West Midlands.

MY guess would be that this house is – or once was – located at the end of a lane or track. 'Rake' is a word not uncommonly found in the Norse (Viking) settled areas of England, deriving from the Old Norse *rak* – a stripe.

As a footpath or driveway leaves a clearly visible mark across the land 'rak' came to have the meaning of 'path, track or drove'.

'Rake' doesn't appear in English until the late Middle English period but is possibly a genuine Viking usage: Norwegian dialect preserves a word *raek* of similar meaning.

Karl Wittwer, The English Companions, London.

IN the Derbyshire Peak District, where I grew up, the word 'rake' refers to the surface workings of a lead mine. A rake is an open working following a vein of mineral, usually narrow, ranging from as little as 10ft and normally no more than 50ft wide.

The length of these workings varies from less than 30 yards to more than a mile in some cases. Frequently, shafts were dropped to exploit reserves not accessible from the surface.

In the Peak District, a house called Rake End would be at the end of one of these workings and not necessarily at the end of a lane.

The mining community migrated from Cornwall (tin mines) through

Derbyshire/Yorkshire (lead mines), up to Cumbria (copper and iron) and eventually to Scotland (lead and silver).

Ralph P. Cooper, Kirkby-in-Furness, Cumbria.

? IS there any county in Britain that doesn't have a breed of sheep named after it?

THERE are 18 recognised sheep breeds which take their names from British counties: the Cambridge, Derbyshire Gritstone, Devon Closewool, Devon and Cornwall Longwool, Dorset Down, Dorset Horn, Hampshire Down, Hebridean, Leicester Longwool, Lincoln Longwool, Oxford Down, Shetland, Shropshire, Suffolk, Wiltshire Horn, Kent Halfbred, Shetland-Cheviot and Black Leicester Longwool breeds.

Taking replications into account, only 15 British counties can lay claim to their own breed of sheep.

Margaret Barrow, National Sheep Association, Malvern, Worcs.

? SIR John Betjeman's lovely Christmas poem includes the line 'The tortoise stove is lit again . . .' What is a tortoise stove?

MY great-grandfather Charles Portway, an ironmonger from Halstead, Essex, invented the Tortoise Stove in 1834. It consisted of a round sheet-metal cylinder, internally protected by firebricks, with a cast-iron feed door at the top and cast-iron frame and ashpit door at the bottom.

It was called the Tortoise Stove because its heat came from the very slow combustion it promoted. Made in nine different sizes, many thousands were used in churches, schools, industrial and commercial premises using coke as fuel to heat large areas. It's still in production today, virtually unchanged after 163 years.

Michael Portway, Taylor and Portway Ltd, Halstead, Essex.

TORTOISE stoves were a common sight in the middle of Army Nissen hut barracks where, on cold evenings, the lads would huddle for warmth. I remember one night when some bright spark put a live 3oz round in the stove before it was lit. With all the soldiers huddled round as usual, it ignited with an almighty bang which blew the cast-iron feed door up to the ceiling, returning to strike a clanging blow on the head of an unfortunate lad dozing on his bed.

David Taylor, Canterbury, Kent.

RECALLING his Gloucestershire schooldays just after World War I, Laurie Lee writes in *Cider With Rosie*: 'One made pacts and split them, made friends and betrayed them and fought for one's place near the stove.

'The stove was a symbol of caste, a tub of warmth to which we cleaved during the seven months of winter. Made of cast iron, it had a noisy mouth which rattled coke and breathed fumes. It was decorated by a tortoise labelled 'Slow But Sure' and in winter turned red hot.'

My grandfather, W. F. Mon, started work for the firm which made the stoves in August 1899 at the age of 13 and remained for 52 years until his retirement in March 1952, his last 12 years spent as general manager.

Michael Ruskin, Jersey.

? WHAT did Andy Kaufman (Latka in *Taxi*) do to merit Jim Carrey making a film and REM singing a song about him?

BORN in New York City on January 17, 1949, Andy Kaufman was the first son of Stanley and Janice Kaufman and grew up on Long Island. He's probably best remembered in this country as Latka Gravas in the Eighties comedy *Taxi* but in America he achieved cult status for his stand-up comedy routines, appearances on the David Letterman show and as one of the original (and Elvis's favourite) Elvis impersonators.

Kaufman preferred his shows to be referred to not as comedy but as 'performance art' and his audiences were as likely to be left shaking their heads in bewilderment as roaring with laughter. Lorne Michaels asked him to appear on the inaugural broadcast of *Saturday Night Live*.

In the course of his bizarre 'performance art' Andy proclaimed himself Intergender World Wrestling Champion. Between 1979 and 1983, he wrestled more than 400 women, famously provoking Southern Heavyweight Wrestling Champion Jerry Lawler into challenging him to a bout which ended in near disaster.

On April 5, 1982, at the Mid-South Coliseum in Memphis, Tennessee, Kaufman took on Lawler and within six minutes was floored by a vicious piledriver which sent him to hospital with seriously injured cervical vertebrae.

His legendary wrestling antics earned him a mention in REM's 'Man On The Moon': 'Andy Kaufman in the wrestling match, yeah, yeah, yeah' and 'Andy, did you hear about this one?' which juxtaposes modern mythology with traditional religious iconography.

Kaufman's Elvis impersonations were legendary. His voice wasn't great but the mannerisms were perfect. In one of his best-loved stage personas, 'Foreign man', Kaufman played a disorientated Eastern European who transforms himself into Elvis. This features in the song as 'Andy, are you goofing on Elvis?'

In May 1984, Kaufman succumbed to a rare form of lung cancer and died at the age of 35. Reports of his sudden passing were thought by many to be another cleverly crafted performance piece and several friends and associates remained unconvinced until they viewed his body. Kaufman is buried at Beth David Cemetery, in the Long Island town of Elmont.

His madcap career, cult status and tragic death made him a good subject for Hollywood film treatment.

Brett Stevens, New York.

❓ HOW many counties are there in the USA compared with the UK?

THE U.S. has 3,097 counties with an average size of 1,168 square miles, which means an average U.S. county is roughly the same size as Lancashire.

In the UK, England has 47 counties, Northern Ireland 6, Scotland 32 and Wales 22. The average size of a UK county is 808 square miles.

Stephen Thornton, Blandford Forum, Dorset.

❓ WHY was Queen Victoria's father, the Duke of Kent, buried at Windsor at night? Why did his wife not attend the funeral?

THE practice of holding royal funerals at night began in the mid-17th century and continued for 200 years. Many associated customs developed until by the mid-18th century, women seldom, if ever, attended and the sovereign never did, even the funeral of his predecessor. It would have been most unusual for the Duchess of Kent to have attended the funeral of her husband.

With the ascension of Queen Victoria, torchlight funerals ended and ceremonies took place earlier in the day. The Queen didn't attend her beloved Prince Consort's funeral (the future Edward VII acting as chief mourner) but she subsequently developed a great interest in funerals and by the 1880s regularly attended royal burials with some of her daughters and ladies of her court.

The Duke of Kent's funeral was a low-key affair, taking place just four days before that of his father, George III.

Leslie Grout, Windsor, Berks.

THE attendance of women at funerals is a relatively recent practice, still not accepted by some elderly people and conservative communities.

The Duke of Kent's brother, the Duke of York, Commander-in-Chief of the British Army, was also buried by night, in St George's Chapel, Windsor, on a freezing cold night in January 1827.

The cold and damp were responsible for several other deaths and illnesses among those who attended. Post-funeral fatalities included two bishops, five footmen and several soldiers. Other high-ranking attendees including the Duke of Wellington, the Foreign Secretary and the President of the Board of Trade were confined to their sick beds.

This outcome may have been one of the reasons why the practice of conducting funerals at night gradually ceased.

Timothy Brain, Cheltenham, Gloucs.

☍ ARE there any ancient volcanoes in the UK? When were they last active?

THERE has been volcanicity throughout the UK during most of its geological history. The Ordovician/Silurian period (400 to 500 million years ago) saw volcanoes in North Wales (Cader Idris) and the central Lake District (Borrowdale) with minor eruptions in the Southern Uplands and Midland valley of Scotland (Arthur's Seat). This activity was a result of the closure of the ancient Lapetus ocean, and subsequent collision of two landmasses.

The collision resulted in a chain of mountains from North America (the Appalachians) through north-west Europe (North Wales, the Lake District, Highlands of Scotland) into Scandinavia – the Caledonian Mountain chain.

In the Tertiary period (2 to 65 million years ago), volcanic activity arose from the opening of the North Atlantic ocean (Europe and North America had been part of the same continent). It produced the volcanic rocks of West Scotland and Northern Ireland (Giant's Causeway, Skye, Rhum, Ardnamurchan).

To see what the area might have looked like then, you need go no further than Iceland, situated over the point at which the North Atlantic is still opening.

Andrew Southworth, Preston, Lancs.

TWO extinct volcanoes, Berwick Law and Traprain Law, which rise dramatically from the flat land on the south bank of the Firth of Forth, have gained a reputation with UFO enthusiasts as supposed 'antennae' for extraterrestrial life.

Tom Davies, Kidderminster.

? WHO first said, 'Cometh the man, cometh the hour'?

THE nearest to this we have in *Oxford Dictionary of Quotations* is: 'The hour is come but not the man' in Sir Walter Scott's *The Heart of Midlothian* of 1818.

There's a fairly extensive if not very conclusive discussion in Nigel Rees's *Phrases and Sayings*. After listing various uses from the sports pages of recent newspapers, he mentions John 4:23: 'But the hour cometh, and now is' and various more or less distantly related quotations. Harriet Martineau called her 1840 biography of Toussaint L'Ouverture *The Hour and the Man*.

The nearest early version seems to be Scott again: Meg Merrilees in *Guy Mannering* (1815) says, 'Because the Hour's come, and the Man.' Scott's own footnote to *The Heart of Midlothian* suggests it may ultimately derive from an old Scottish folk-tale, now lost.

Susan Ratcliffe, Oxford University Press.

? MY credit card number has 16 digits, enough for every person in the world to have about one million credit card numbers each. Why so many digits?

THERE are 16 digits making up the number on all Mastercards and most Visa Cards (some have 13 digits). Diners Club and Carte Blanche have 14 digits, American Express cards have 15, Discover have 16 and JCB 15 or 16 digits. The digits are used to help the validation of the card.

In general, the first four digits show what type of card is being used.

Any card that begins 51, 52, 53, 54 or 55 is a Mastercard. Any card beginning with the number 4 is a Visa, 34 or 37 is an American Express Card, etc.

The remaining numbers determine who provided the card, what type of product it offers and what the terms and conditions are for the cardholder. The last four digits are the individual customer number.

Dr Ron Jones, Stanford-le-Hope, Essex.

? WHEN is the best time for a work-out for the human body: morning, noon or night?

EVERYONE'S 'body clock' operates on a 24-hour cycle, the 'circadian rhythm'. The clock is composed of specialised brain cells which work in harmony with the hormone melatonin, produced during darkness, promoting a fall in body temperature and a desire to sleep.

Exercise at any time of the day or night is better than remaining idle and personal circumstances determine the time best spared for exercise, but most people can take advantage of circadian rhythms to organise their fitness programmes.

In the morning, you may feel refreshed after a good night's sleep but your joints are still stiff and muscle temperature is low. Any work-out at this time should be light or moderate and be done only after a good warm-up. If you're in a coronary-risk group, avoid early morning exercise as cardiac events are most often triggered at this time.

Midday is fine, if you can manage it. Adrenaline levels tend to be naturally high and help to cope with high intensity work-outs.

The best time, however, is between 5pm and 7pm when the body temperature is highest and the body is prepared for sustained exercise.

Once melatonin levels increase, overcoming the urge to slump becomes more difficult. An intense work-out too late in the day – near midnight – may hinder rather then help subsequent sleep.

Prof Tom Reilly, Research Institute for Sport and Exercise Sciences, Henry Cotton Campus, Liverpool.

? CAN germs live on soap?

GERM is an emotive term. Most micro-organisms are benign or beneficial, very few are harmful and only a few of those cause problems for humans.

Soap is a harsh, alkaline environment, with few nutrients other than fatty acids. It has mildly antiseptic properties and very few organisms would grow on such an environment.

Micro-organisms, however, are astonishingly versatile and there may be some harmless ones which can grow slowly, even on soap.

If a person has a specific worry, such as the possible transfer of a skin infection between people, it would be sensible for the infected person to use a separate bar of soap until the infection has cleared up.

Dr Brian J. B. Wood, Dept of Bioscience and Biotechnology, Strathclyde University, Glasgow.

? WAS Hitler genitally normal, or was the song we used to sing not so scurrilous after all?

MOST early literature points to Hitler being genitally normal but Prof Fritz Redlich in his book *Hitler: Diagnosis Of A Destructive Prophet* is convinced that the results of a Russian autopsy, substantiated by other circumstantial evidence, show that, in line with popular Allied troopers' theory in World War II, he had in fact only one testicle.

This is unlikely to have contributed to his apparent megalomania as this condition, perhaps surprisingly, is said to lead to little embarrassment.

One testes appears to function perfectly adequately and there's unlikely to be any infertility or lack of masculinity.

Another genital problem for which there is better evidence is Hitler's suffering from hypospadias, in which the aperture of the urethra opens on the underside rather than at the end of the penis. But this too is rarely uncomfortable or embarrassing, though it may become inconvenient and can easily be treated by a urologist.

As to venereal disease, though in his speeches and writings Hitler appeared to have a disproportionate interest in syphilis and popular rumour suggests he may have been a victim, it is now thought more likely that he suffered from severe syphilophobia.

Dr G. S. Murray, Golspie, Sutherland.

❓ HOW many X-craft were built in World War II? Did they have any success?

X-CRAFT were ingeniously designed midget submarines commissioned by the Royal Navy, 16m long and holding a crew of four in very cramped conditions. They displaced 30 tonnes and could make six to eight knots (11–15kmh) submerged. They had a 2,000–3,000km range and could dive to 90m.

They carried two amatol side charges weighing two tonnes apiece which could be detached and planted under an enemy ship.

These craft were designed to attack enemy ships in harbour. They were towed to the target by larger submarines before being released to carry out an attack.

Mr I. Richardson, Durham.

THE Royal Navy built 31 X-craft in World War II, in four distinct types. X3 and 4 were prototypes, the first completed in August 1942. X5 to 10 took part in Operation Source on September 22, 1943, attacking three German warships in Norwegian fjords. Xs 5 to 7 were intended to attack the *Tirpitz*, Xs 9 and 10 the *Scharnhorst* and X8 the *Lutzow*.

In the event, X8 suffered defects and was abandoned en route and X9 was lost while under tow. Mechanical faults forced X10 to abort and X5 was probably sunk while approaching her target, though it's possible she completed her attack. The remaining two craft carried out successful attacks and were scuttled in the fjord. The *Tirpitz* was repaired after the attack but was never fully seaworthy again.

Xs 20 to 25 were completed in 1944. Xs 20 and 23 were used to mark the Juno and Sword D-Day invasion beaches while X24 attacked and destroyed a large floating dock in Bergen harbour. X22 was lost in collision with the Royal Navy submarine *Syrtis* on February 7, 1944.

Xs T1 to T6 were training vessels. XEs 1 to 9 and 11 and 12 were built to an improved design, with air conditioning, for service in the Far East.

By the time of their arrival, the Japanese surface fleet had virtually ceased to exist and there was little employment for them but on July 31, 1945, XE4 cut the submerged telegraphic cables from Saigon to Hong Kong and Singapore and on the same day XE3 attacked and crippled the already damaged Japanese cruiser *Takao* in Singapore harbour.

Geoff Hewitt, Preston, Lancs.

X24, the only surviving example of a wartime X-craft which saw active service, is on display at the Royal Navy Submarine Museum in Gosport, Hants. There's a series of displays recording the wartime exploits of the X-craft and Chariot flotillas.

George Malcolmson, Royal Navy Submarine Museum, Gosport.

❓IS there a real story behind the ghostly tale about a hitchhiker vanishing as a driver stops to pick her up and later discovering a hitchhiker had died on that spot years before?

THE closest thing to this story is found in Brian Innes's book *A Catalogue Of Ghost Sightings*. He says a family called Hendrix were going with friends in a car to a dance along a coast road in the U.S. in the Fifties when the driver, Joy Hendrix, saw a girl thumbing a lift and picked her up.

They say she looked natural and got in the car complaining of being warm, winding down her window. The girl went along to the dance and seemed totally normal but when the men asked her to dance they found her hands icy cold. She said her name was Rose White and even gave out her telephone number and address.

As the family went back home, giving the mysterious Rose a lift, she thanked them but insisted on being dropped off at exactly the same spot where they picked her up. The next day, the Hendrixs' friends went to the address their new friend had given and were amazed to be shown a picture of the girl – said to have died 15 years earlier.

James Ward, Sheffield.

AS a child living in Moorside, I recall a similar tale about a man who was flagged down on a quiet local road, Bulcote Lane, by a woman who had crashed her car just over the lip of the railway bridge. As he went to the boot of his car to get a tow rope, another car came speeding over the bridge straight at him.

He woke up in hospital to discover that the other car had hit him, crushing his legs between it and his car, and the doctors had had to amputate his legs.

The other driver couldn't understand why he had parked his car just over the bridge where it couldn't be seen from the approach. He and his passengers saw no other vehicle or stranded lady in the area.

The injured man was later told by a doctor at the hospital that his accident was almost identical to one that had happened ten years earlier at the same location, in which a young lady driver had lost both her legs. In a distraught state, she committed suicide on the same bridge just hours after being discharged from hospital.

This story scared the life out of me as a child – and I never walked down Bulcote Lane.

Peter Hanley, Leeds.

? **WHEN and by whom was the 999 emergency phone number invented?**

THE 999 emergency operator service was first introduced in London on July 1, 1937. Telephones had grown in number and the GPO, forerunner of BT, needed a way of giving priority to emergency calls.

A minimum of three numbers was needed to match city exchange codes and the number 999 was chosen not, as is often thought, because the 9-hole was closest on the dial to the finger stop but because it could be easily remembered and didn't clash with other established codes.

Dialling 000 got the operator and 222 was London's Abbey exchange. Using 111 was considered likely to give rise to more false dialling. A major consideration was technical. The emergency number needed to be free from public call boxes and 9 was next to 0, the no-charge code for calling the operator. It was easier to adjust the mechanical exchanges of those days for two adjacent free codes.

Neil Johannessen, BT Museum, Queen Victoria Street, London.

DOES anybody know the full words to a song my late father Bill Wingfield used to sing, which had the first line: 'There was Old Van Damm and young Van Damm and the whole Damm family from Rotterdam ...'?

THE Van Damm song was about a Dutch girl, Gretchen, who was deserted in London by a family from Holland. She was left sitting in a London terminus, singing:

There's old Van Damm and young Van Damm
And me Van Damm from Rotterdam.
Old Van Damm repairs the dams,
So dams the Damms in Rotterdam.
Where, oh where can the Van Damms be?
Where is the Van Damm family?
With Pa Van Damm and Ma Van Damm
And the whole damm family from Rotterdam.

British troops off to war in Egypt took up the song, which dates it to the time of the war in Sudan, about 1885.

Mrs Mary Hunt, East Grinstead, Sussex.

AS a British citizen, would I be free to go and live in one of Britain's dependent territories or colonies, such as Bermuda, St Helena or the Falklands?

BRITISH Citizens do not automatically have the right to live and work in one of Britain's Overseas Territories. The locally elected Governments of our territories have a substantial measure of responsibility for the conduct of their own internal affairs, including issues such as immigration and work permits.

British citizens are subject to immigration control in the same way as other visitors to those islands and would have to apply in advance for the necessary permissions from the appropriate Government.

Janet Duff, Foreign & Commonwealth Office, London.

AS Gibraltar joined the EEC (now EU) at the same time as the UK in 1973 under Article 227(4) of the Treaty of Rome, any EU national is free to settle and work in the Crown Colony of Gibraltar.

Michael Brufal de Melgarejo, Friends of Gibraltar Heritage Society, Fleet, Hants.

？WE have seven days a week for Biblical reasons. Do all other cultures have seven days in their weeks?

MOST ancient cultures based their calenders, hundreds of which exist from areas such as Mesopotamia, Greece, Rome, India and China, on the 28-day lunar cycle. Some, however, used other astral bodies to help determine the passage of time. The Mayan calender, for example, used Venus as well as the moon. Their year was divided into 18 20-day months, with a five-day period at the end. Even if weeks had existed, they were unlikely to have been split into seven-day phases.

France's preoccupation with all things metric in the late 18th and early 19th centuries led to the adoption on October 5, 1793, of a revolutionary calendar which ran retrospectively as from September 22, 1772. It consisted of 12 months of 30 days each with five intercalary days, called *sans culottides* and every fourth or Olympic year was to have six such days. Its weeks lasted ten days.

But it didn't catch on and on January 1, 1806, Napoleon ordered the restoration of the Gregorian calendar we know today.

Michelle Posner, Hassler Calendars, New York.

？MY brother lives at Northfield Close, South Cave, in East Yorkshire – an address with three points of the compass in it. Does anyone have all four points in their address?

IF I moved in with your brother, I could make it the full 360 degrees.

Jenni West, Horncastle, Lincs.

WHEN I began work for West Yorkshire Metropolitan County Council after local government reorganisation in April 1974, one of my jobs was listing outstanding road improvement schemes from the constituent local authorities. One such scheme was for 'the improvement of the East Side of North Street, South Kirby for West Yorkshire council'.

Frank L. Appleyard, Shepley, Huddersfield.

THE software programme GB Accelerator, incorporating the national register of the UK Electoral Rolls, delivers several such addresses when combining the name of the occupant with the address but the only address which appears to qualify in its own right is a house called North Shore, at South Strand, East Preston in West Sussex.

John Wynn, Peterborough, Cambs.

FRIENDS of mine had a weekend cottage called East Gubbs, at West Buckland, South Molton in North Devon.

Shirley Cheevers, Sneyd Park, Bristol.

? DID the Ancient Romans or Ancient Greeks leave any records of their athletic achievements?

THERE'S a wealth of information on athletics tournaments in ancient times but they didn't have clocks so they don't include times.

Most prestigious of these were the Olympic games held in Olympia, a rural sanctuary in the western Peloponnese, performed as a salute to the Greek gods, principally Zeus.

The earliest reliable date for these games is 776 BC, though there's good evidence that they began earlier. They differed from the modern equivalent in featuring music, oratory, poetry and theatre as well as athletic performances.

Olympic sports included running, wrestling, boxing, equestrian (chariot racing, riding etc), pankration (a martial art) and a pentathlon of discus, javelin, jump, running and wrestling. Aristotle was a particular fan of this last event, claiming its participants had 'a body capable of enduring all efforts, either of the racecourse or of bodily strength. This is why the athletes in the pentathlon are the most beautiful.' (*Rhetoric* 1361b).

The first recorded winner of an Olympic event was a cook called Coroibus of Elis who won the standion, a foot race of 600ft.

In Homer's *Odyssey*, the Phaeacian nobles entertained the hero Odysseus by competing in athletics. 'A course was marked out for them from the turning point and they all sped swiftly, raising the dust of the plain, but among them noble Clytoneus was far the best at running. He shot to the front and the others were left behind.' (*Odyssey* 8.121ff.)

The popularity of the Games fostered 'professionalism' among competitors and the Olympic ideals waned as royalty began to compete for personal gain, particularly in chariot events. Human beings were glorified rather than the gods and many winners erected statues to deify themselves.

The Games were officially ended in AD 394 by Roman emperor Theodosius, who felt they had pagan connotations.

Rory Webber, Dale, Haverfordwest.

MODERN sporting events are held to be too commercial but this is nothing new. In ancient Greece, coins were struck to commemorate chariot races and sculptors were commissioned of stylised images of athletes. Pliny complained that most of the images set up in the Sanctuary of Zeus were idealistic athletic poses.

Poets were hired to eulogise their employers, the most famous being Pindar (*c.*522 BC to *c.*440 BC) whose Epinikina (triumphal odes) ran to four books celebrating victories won in the Olympian, Pythian, Nemean and Isthmian games.

The ancient Greeks were also prone to other vices associated with modern sport. Comic playwright Aristophanes describes the troubles of a father whose son has over-expensive tastes in horses: 'Creditors are eating me alive ... and all because of this horse-plague!' (*Clouds* 1.240ff.)

John Lister, Feock, Cornwall.

ACCORDING to legend, in 490 BC a Greek soldier named Philippides ran the 36.2km (22.5 miles) from the site of the battle of Marathon to Athens, where he announced the Greek victory over the Persians – before dropping dead on the spot.

The modern marathon commemorates this feat and, appropriately, a Greek, Spiridon Loues, won the first modern Olympic marathon.

Caroline Godber, Birmingham.

———

SHOULD the name The Wirral be preceded by the definite article?

THERE'S no such place as The Wirral. The name of the area is Wirral. As eminent local historian J. E. Allison has pointed out, Wirral has been known by this name – without the definite article – since at least AD 895, when it is mentioned in *The Anglo-Saxon Chronicle* under the form Wirhael.

Wirral is, however, on The Wirral Peninsula, and this has led to the mistaken belief that the area is called The Wirral.

Weaver Sheridan, Birkenhead, Wirral.

? WHAT became of the Mennonite group whose members I helped ferry from Britain to Paraguay on the Blue Star Liner _Avila Star_ in 1941?

MY mother and eldest sister were part of the Brundenhof group of 158 men, women and childen who embarked from Liverpool on the _Avila Star_ in 1941, bound for Buenos Aires and on to Paraguay.

The Mennonites gave them temporary accommodation and help while they set up their settlements near Puerto Rosario, where they farmed the land, raised cattle, built and ran a hospital for the local inhabitants and ran their own schools.

In about 1960, the three settlements were uprooted and moved to England and the U.S. to join communities there. They are now in Sussex, Pennsylvania and New York State. A number of the people who travelled on the _Avila Star_ are still living in community life today.

Chris Beels, Windsor, Berks.

? IS the efficiency of a bicycle dependent upon wheel size? What is the optimum size?

A LARGER (27in, for instance) spoked bicycle wheel does add to overall efficiency and its strength/weight ratio is phenomenal. Tests at the Raleigh factory found that such a wheel could support well over 400 times its own weight without inelastic distortion at the rim.

The significant factor often overlooked in discussions of bicycle efficiency is that a cyclist's body weight is entirely carried by his machine, so almost 100 per cent of his expended energy goes into forward propulsion. Add to this the low rolling resistance of larger bicycle wheels and the very low frictional losses in bicycle technology (there are around 200 ball bearings in a high quality machine) and you have an energy conversion system of almost unparalleled efficiency.

Alec Grace, Guildford.

? IS there any truth to the old story about a Tokyo store depicting a crucified Father Christmas as its main festive feature?

OUR son has lived and worked in Tokyo since 1993 and on his first Christmas away from home telephoned and told us he had seen a cross in one of the department stores with Father Christmas attached to it. Our daughter, visiting her brother, went to The Oriental Bazaar where there was a Christmas Tree decorated with small crosses.

So the tales are true though we should remember that Japan isn't a Christian country and Christmas isn't one of their usual festivals.
Mrs J. Allan, Romford, Essex.

WHEN I worked in Japan in the late Eighties, my office was in Nihonbashi, close to the Japanese equivalent of Harrods. I don't recall it being a main feature of this store's Christmas decorations but it certainly displayed in its windows small versions (about 6–7in high) of poor old Santa being crucified.
Allan Jamieson, West Wickham, Kent.

THE mythical status of this story is demonstrated by the endless differences in its various versions. The date has been put at anything from 1945 to 1990 and the store and type of the display is regularly changed between versions. How could the Japanese have believed that a man nailed to a cross would be so cheerful?

The story is believed by some to be spread simply to deride the Japanese or as a joke, aimed at demonstrating how Jesus has been replaced by Santa at Christmas time.

Japan has been known, however, to adjust images and themes from Western holidays in all sorts of ways – a Halloween-style card, for example, showing Santa standing in a graveyard, while the Virgin Mary flies overhead on a broomstick.
Edward Martland, London.

IS it possible to use a super telescope to see the Stars & Stripes on the Moon?

THERE'S not much hope of this with any current telescope and even with advanced optics, atmospheric disturbance would probably make it impossibile.

The Hubble Space Telescope, orbiting above the atmosphere, can resolve detail of light and shade on the surface of Pluto, corresponding to an object which makes an angle on Earth of 0.1 deg of arc (1/36000 of a degree). The flag on the moon would appear 100 times smaller than that; a telescope capable of resolving it would need at least 100 times more light-gathering power than Hubble, probably 1,000 times if the flag is to be recognised as such.

Given the advances which produced Hubble, this is not outside the bounds of possibility and I'm sure such an instrument will be built one day but by that time people will probably be travelling to the Moon every day to see the flags for themselves.

Keith Matthews, Crystran Ltd, Poole, Dorset.

IF you watch the film of the first Lunar Landing Module blasting off on its return to Earth, you can clearly see the Stars and Stripes being blown out of the ground and flying off towards the horizon – a fact that the Americans didn't altogether like.

Mr C. Moult, Fleckney, Leics.

? WHAT is the origin of the dots over our letters 'i' and 'j'?

THE dot first appears in manuscripts of about the 11th century and was used to distinguish the letters and to help in reading words in which 'i' was close to letters like 'n' or 'm' – inimicus, for example.

The dot sometimes took the form of a dash and it also became the custom in medieval manuscripts to distinguish an initial or otherwise prominent 'i' by continuing it below the line. The distinct letters 'i' and 'j' arose from that differentiation.

E. A. Freeman, Thorpe, Surrey.

THIS superscript is a diacritical mark, introduced by medieval scribes to differentiate between letters that looked similar. The letter 'j' was originally a variant of 'i', emerging as a letter in its own right in the Middle Ages but still used as an 'i' in Shakespeare's original scripts and until the 18th century.

Suzanne Blumsom, Writers' Monthly, Turnpike Lane, London.

? I HAVE a Christmas Card from the Welsh Guards, depicting the altar cloth of the Welsh Guards Cloister in the Guards' Chapel. On the cloth are the arms of the five Royal Tribes of Wales. Who were, or are, they?

THE five Royal Tribes of Wales are the descendants of the most prominent Welsh rulers from the Dark Ages (9th to 11th centuries). Wales at the time was a patchwork of principalities in a state of perpetual flux. Through a combination of conquest and inheritance, different families would rise and fall from power. The most durable and powerful of these have been ascribed 'royal' status.

The tribes were the descendants of: Gruffudd ap (son of) Cynan who claimed most of Gwynedd and the Western region of Ceredigion before his death in 1237. Rhys ap Tewdwr who was Prince of Deheubarth (South-West Wales) until 1073. Iestyn ap Gwrgant who was Prince of Morgannwg (South-East Wales) between 1072 and 1093. Bleddyn ap Cynfyn, King of Powys between 1063 and 1075 and Elystan Glodrydd, Lord of Builth until his death in 1010.

These rulers lived before the time of heraldry, and their arms were created posthumously in the high Middle Ages (13th to 15th centuries) when prominent families wished to add a symbol of their ancestry to their arms, drawing on knowledge provided by scholars and bards of the time.

Clive Cheesman, Rouge Dragon Pursuivant, College of Arms, London.

OF what does 'anti-climb' paint consist and how does it work?

ANTI-CLIMB paints are a security measure, providing a slippery surface which is difficult to grip and may also be designed to stain the hands and clothing of anyone who tries to clamber on protected surfaces.

This paint works by incorporating materials which will never dry and is applied by brush in a coating around 1 or 2mm thick. Because it's so slippery and marks anyone who touches it, the paint should be applied well out of range of normal accidental contact – not lower than 2m from the ground and warning signs should also be posted.

It isn't necessary to paint large areas, just those places where a hand grip is needed, such as tops of walls, window ledges, edges of flat roofs and on drain pipes.

This paint is much less dangerous than barbed wire or broken glass so it's a better option for buildings such as schools or homes.

Chris Storey, Paint Research Assoc, Teddington.

IS CRIMINALITY HEREDITARY?

DEAR *Answers*.—In the awarding of punishments for crime, our laws recognise to a certain extent the principle that an individual should not be held entirely accountable for that particular development of character which he exhibits nor the actions that it influences him to perform.

For this reason, we employ in the administration of justice men of vast experience and judgment and give them great latitude in the severity of their sentences.

Were it an absolute fact that every man is the sole architect of his own character and that he is totally uninfluenced in its development by circumstances beyond his control, all we would require would be a hard and fast criminal code, in which every known crime would have assigned to it its exact and due punishment – a code that any intelligent policeman could administer.

It may be said, generally, that no man is a willing lawbreaker. He becomes so by force of circumstances, of environment or strong influences at work within himself which he has not the ability to overcome or to even control. If, then, each individual case were especially studied, while in duration, by experienced, humane persons, it may be that in many instances the criminal on release could be placed in a groove that would enable him to become and to continue a law-abiding subject.

Prisons are in a transitory state. Formerly they were invariably places of pitiless punishment; now the punishment is sometimes almost humane; by-and-bye they will doubtless become asylums of gentle, yet effective, reformatory influences where the results of bad rearing and example will find their correctives.

R. M. O., Bexley Heath, Kent.

My bitter experience is that crime is hereditary and, unfortunately, I have, from my earliest days, been reared in the very midst of it. As the result of an hereditary tendency to crime I have already suffered 13 years' imprisonment. My last term of five years' penal servitude expired

? WHO decides exactly where one ocean ends and another begins?

OCEANS and seas, bodies of salt water, cover about 71 per cent of the Earth's surface, enveloping 80 per cent of the southern and 61 per cent of the northern hemispheres.

Centuries ago, the navigable oceans were described as the 'seven seas' – the Atlantic, Pacific, Indian and Arctic oceans, the Mediterranean and Caribbean seas and the Gulf of Mexico. Present-day oceanographers consider all other oceans and seas as belonging to the Atlantic, Pacific or Indian oceans. The Arctic Ocean, Mediterranean and Caribbean seas and the Gulf of Mexico are considered marginal seas of the Atlantic.

The boundaries between these oceans have nothing to do with physical water masses, they depend on geographic criteria set by cartographers. The Atlantic separates from the Indian Ocean at the 20 deg E meridian. It divides from the Pacific Ocean, in the south, by a line extending from Cape Horn at the tip of South America to the South Shetland Islands off Antarctica's tip and in the north by the narrowest part of the Bering Strait.

The dividing line between the Pacific and Indian oceans extends along an arc through the Malay Peninsula, Sumatra, Java and Timor to Cape London-derry in Australia, to Tasmania, and then along the 147 deg E meridian to Antarctica.

Deborah Walker, Edinburgh.

WHEN I lived in New Zealand, I was told that if I went to the very tip of the North Island I could actually see the Tasman and Pacific 'meeting' and distinguish them by their different colours.

I didn't know whether to believe this or not until I did go and see it for myself – one is green and the other blue – and I have photographs to prove it.
Andrew Bradstock, South Croydon, Surrey.

? WHO was the John Carpenter after whom the street in the City of London was named?

JOHN Carpenter was Town Clerk of the City of London when Dick Whittington was Lord Mayor. He died in 1442 and, in his will, left money for the education of boys born in the City.

Proceeds from his estate enabled the Corporation of London to build the City of London School in Milk Street in 1837. When a new school was built on Victoria Embankment in 1882, the street next to it was named John Carpenter Street.

The school moved again in 1986 to its present site in Queen Victoria Street, between St Paul's Cathedral and the Thames.
William Hallett, head porter, City of London School 1982–1996, Whitstable, Kent.

THE link between money and the name John Carpenter is strong. The first person to win a million on *Who Wants To Be A Millionaire?* was a John Carpenter who won $1,000, 000 in the American version. He was an agent for the tax service.
James Byrnes, Palm Springs, California.

? WHO (or what) is a wonk?

IN Australia, since the Thirties, 'wonk' has been the Aborigines' derisive term for a white man. In the Forties, it was a white Australian's name for an effeminate male.

In late Seventies America, it was adopted at Harvard to deride any excessively hard-working student, with the suggestion that it was derived from the word 'know' spelt backwards.

Here in Britain, it was used in the Royal Navy from about 1917 to mean a useless seaman or inexperienced cadet. From around 1930, it came to mean predominantly a junior midshipman. This may be connected with 'wonky', meaning shaky or unsteady. The Australians use 'wonkite' to describe a 'mad' person.

The naval term seems to have originated on the China Station in the early 1900s when wonk, meaning 'yellow dog', was applied by sailors to the Chinese mongrel or pi dog, from the Ningpo pronunciation of the two characters for 'y' and 'd'. In some circles it was still being used in the Sixties for any scruffy mongrel.

The latest use is described by the *Oxford Dictionary of New Words* which lists 'policy wonk' as slang for one who takes an obsessive interest in minor details of policy. It notes 'wonk' as an early term for a 'nerd' or 'anorak', one who pursues an arcane interest with excessive dedication.

This has been in use since the early Seventies though 'policy wonk' wasn't recorded until the mid-Eighties American political scene.

Kevin Heneghan, St Helens, Merseyside.

WHEN I was a child in the early Fifties, Wonk was the eponymous hero of the children's book series The Adventures of Wonk. I had the whole set.

There were two stories in each book and I read them so often I knew them all off by heart.

Wonk was a cute, plump, cuddly and lovable koala who spoke excellent English. He lived with a little boy called Peter as a sort of teddybear-cum-pet and was very mischievous, always getting into scrapes. If I see a koala on TV or in a photograph, my reaction is always: 'Oh, it's a Wonk!'

Gillian Taylor, Cambridge.

THE Adventures of Wonk were stories by Muriel Levy (described on the book as 'of radio fame') with illustrations by Joan Kiddell-Monroe, first published in 1941. The three books in the series were *Going To Sea*, *Fireworks* and *Strawberries And Cream*.

Josephine Collins, Doncaster.

WHY was Bob Dylan banned from singing 'John Birch Society Blues' on *The Ed Sullivan Show* in 1963?

PEOPLE in the post-war U.S. were paranoid about 'reds under the bed' and this anti-Communist feeling helped ruin many careers as individuals were accused by far-right politicians like Senator Joseph McCarthy, mostly falsely, of pro-Russian sympathies. Even after McCarthy was disgraced, most Americans remained suspicious of anything that appeared Leftist.

It was with this background that Dylan penned his 'Talkin' John Birch Society Blues' in March 1962, a humorous skit on an extreme right-wing group led by George Lincoln Rockwell. This verse gives some idea of why the song was controversial:

Now we all agree with Hitler's views,
Although he killed six million Jews.
It doesn't matter to me that he was a fascist,
At least you can't say he was a communist.

This was strong stuff, especially for national TV but Ed Sullivan was happy to have Dylan perform this work when invited to appear on his show on May 12, 1963. Network bosses, however, were not so keen and Dylan failed to appear after being refused permission to sing this song.

'Talkin' John Birch Society Blues' was also due to appear on *Freewheelin'*, an album scheduled for release on May 27 that year. Rumour had it that the Ed Sullivan ban was responsible for its removal, along with 'Let Me Die In My Footsteps', 'Ramblin' Gamblin' Willie' and 'Rocks And Gravel'. In fact, the highly prolific Dylan simply wanted more recent material to be issued instead.
Tim Mickleburgh, Grimsby, Lincs.

THE John Birch Society parodied in typical early Dylan style in 'Talkin' John Birch Paranoid Blues' was formed in 1958 to promote strong patriotic and anti-communist views. The studio recording of the song is one of the most sought-after tracks in the Dylan catalogue, being included on early copies of his second album, *Freewheelin'*, but deleted and replaced on later issues.

Only around 300 of the original pressing were released with stereo versions now valued in excess of £10,000.
Nick Bridge, Benfleet, Essex.

WHEN you buy frozen, peeled prawns, who has peeled them?
COLD-water prawns are trawled mainly in the North Atlantic, off the coast of Greenland, Iceland, Norway and Canada and are landed at our state-of-the-art factories in each of those countries.

On intake, the raw material is assessed for its standard and has to pass a quality test before being allowed to enter the premises. From this point on, the prawns are automatically transported through a process which cooks, peels, freezes, grades and packs them.

Four machines peel the prawns. An initial set of rollers, rotating in opposite directions, squeeze the prawn body from its shell and any remaining bit of shell are loosened from the meat by a mechanical agitating machine.

Air density is then used to blow away lighter shell pieces, rapidly followed by a highly sophisticated electronic machine which rejects any remaining shell by a combination of optical and laser technology.

Finally, a team of highly skilled personnel visually inspect the prawns to ensure they're clean and free from any residual shell.

Joanne Stobbs, technical services manager, Royal Greenland Ltd, Cheadle Hulme, Cheshire.

⍰ IS it theoretically Midsummer Day somewhere on Earth every day?

MIDSUMMER Day – the Summer Solstice – is the day of the year when the midday sun appears highest in the sky. In the northern hemisphere, this falls on June 21, the day favoured by Druids to hold their ceremonies at Stonehenge and other sacred sites.

In the southern hemisphere, the midday sun reaches its highest point on December 21 and antipodean Druids accordingly celebrate their Midsummer Day when we're celebrating Yule at our Midwinter. Over the whole Earth, the light of the Sun is always in balance.

Between the tropics of Cancer and Capricorn, the midday sun appears to rise higher in the sky day by day until it is directly overhead, then keeps on going – tipping over into the other half of the sky. Its movement stops at the Solstice (June 21 or December 21) and then it moves back to where it started six months before.

Everywhere in the Tropics therefore gets two days a year when the Sun stands directly overhead at midday – once early on the way up to midsummer, and once late on the way down to midwinter. Every day, there is one latitude where the Sun is directly overhead, but it is not correct to call this a midsummer. The extreme example is for anywhere exactly on the Equator, such as Ecuador or Kenya. An observer there sees the sun directly overhead on March 21 and again on September 21, neither of which could strictly be called either midsummer or midwinter.

Any Druids living on the Equator have special problems of their own.

Chris Turner, Druids of Albion, Ardrossan.

IF by 'Midsummer Day' is meant the day with the longest hours of daylight, then yes. Between the Equator and the tropic of Cancer, the longest day occurs twice per annum between March 21 and September 22. North of the tropic of Cancer, the longest day occurs only once on June 21.

Between the Equator and the tropic of Capricorn, the longest day occurs twice between September 22 and March 21. South of the tropic of Capricorn the longest day occurs once on December 21.

The variation in day length at the Equator is less than an hour but increases towards the poles. At Latitude 51.7 deg North (London) it's more than nine hours and within the Arctic/Antarctic Circles day length ranges from 0 to 24 hours a day.

John Haime, Mold, Flintshire.

CAN anyone complete the rhyme about South Wales locations which begins: 'I had an Uncle Mike and he had a motorbike. He could ride around the Gower in a quarter of an hour'?

THIS is 'Cosher Bailey', which has many versions and the chorus: 'Did you ever see, did you ever saw, did you ever see such a funny thing before ...'

Verses known to me include:

Have you ever been to Wales where they sell the beer in pails?
If you want a drink on Sunday you will have to wait till Monday.
Cosher Bailey's Uncle Matthew had the job of cleaning statues.
One day while cleaning Venus he fell off and broke his ... elbow.
Cosher Bailey's Uncle Reg went to go behind the hedge.
Uncle Reg is feeling better but the hedge is looking wetter.
Cosher Bailey's got a chimney but he had to build it higher.
*Cos the cat's were ****ing down it and putting out the fire.*
Cosher Bailey's Cousin Lanto went to see a panto.
He wants to be a fairy but his legs are far too hairy.
Cosher Bailey's Uncle Rupert plays outside half for Newport.
They think so much about him that they often play without him.
Cosher Bailey's Cousin Gus drives a motor bus.
If you press the bell Gus will go like ... lightning.
Coshers's train came into Gower doing 90 miles an hour.
It caused a great sensation as it tore down half the station.

Anne Dagen, Stanwick, Northants.

'COSHER Bailey' was the much disliked Crawshay Bailey, ironmaster at Penydarren, Merthyr Tydfil. There are probably as many different versions of the song as watering-holes in which it has been sung but the first verse is generally:

Cosher Bailey had an engine
And she always wanted mending
And according to her power
She would go five mile an hour.

This refers to the locomotive *Richard Trevithick* designed for the Crawshays' Tram Road, for which it was far too heavy. The tune to which the song is normally sung originally belonged to a Welsh folk song, originating in Ceredigion, called 'Y Mochyn Du' ('The Black Pig').

J. C. Diment, Dudley, West Midlands.

'COSHER' Bailey was a satire on Crawshay Bailey, a harsh employer whose brutality led to discontent and riots. Instead of listening to his workers' grievances, Bailey built two fortified towers in Nantyglo for his own protection. The towers exist to this day.

In the 1830s, as wages fell and the price of bread increased, the Chartist movement grew throughout Britain, calling for radical electoral and social reform. In South Wales, Bailey was among the factory, mine and estate owners who opposed the Chartists.

He delivered a speech in which he said: 'I owe what I have to my own industry,' ignoring the sweated labour of men, women and children who slaved in unspeakable conditions.

The most savage response to the Chartists was in Wales. On November 3, 1838, Chartists marched on Newport, gathering next day outside the Westgate Hotel and stoning it. Soldiers posted inside the hotel opened fire, killing 22 protesters and injuring a further 50. Organisers of the demonstration were arrested and tried for high treason. They were sentenced to death but their sentences were commuted to transportation to Australia.

Powerless to fight against him by other means, Crawshay Bailey's workers resorted to ridicule and their song has tickled the Welsh sense of humour ever since, as Crawshay was corrupted to 'Cosher', many more verses were added and the grim genesis of the satire was forgotten.

Dr Mike Lawrence, Chichester, Sussex.

Q I'VE recently heard birdsong at night, typically at 2.40am. Why do birds sing so well before the usual dawn chorus?

BIRDS sing for two main reasons – to attract a mate and to establish and defend a breeding territory. Birdsong reaches its peak in spring but usually starts early in the year. The drive to sing is largely controlled by hormones and these are triggered by increases in daylight length. The days start to get longer at the end of December and it's usually in early January that birds start to sing again.

Early songsters include mistle thrushes, song thrushes, blackbirds and robins. These birds pioneer the dawn chorus which builds as more species start to sing.

Some birds are so keen to proclaim themselves and their territories that they will sing at night, especially on bright moonlit nights. Song thrushes and some warblers which arrive later in the year do this but the prize for insomniac songbird is the robin.

Robins are very aggressive towards rivals and spend much of their time singing at the edges of their territories, often a garden boundary or road.

These midnight melodies often lead to claims of nightingales being heard in January but in every case it will be a robin, perhaps two, singing sweetly but threateningly for all they're worth.

Chris Harbard, RSPB, Sandy, Beds.

Q WHAT is the origin of the 'rubber' in bridge playing?

A RUBBER is a unit of measurement, possibly borrowed from lawn bowls, the game Sir Francis Drake was playing when the Armada was sighted in 1588 and is reported to have said: 'We can finish the rubber and beat the Spaniards too.'

The term came to the game of bridge via whist. A 'rubber of whist' is referred to in Fielding's *Tom Jones*.

Ann Mayhew, English Bridge Union, Aylesbury, Bucks.

THE origin of the term 'rubber' is uncertain but it may have transferred from the game of bowls, where the collision of the two woods is called a rubber, as they are said to rub against each other.

Irene Cathcart, Manchester.

? DO any of George Formby's ukuleles still exist?

AT an auction held in Lytham St Anne's on June 21, 1961, soon after George Formby's death, 19 of his ukuleles and uke-banjos were catalogued for sale and I've been able to keep a record of each owner of 16 of them over the years.

The other three have disappeared and I'm interested in locating them. I'm still looking for two small wooden ukuleles made by Jose Fernandez, which were lot Nos 441 and 445, and a melody uke-banjo bought by someone named Turner, which was lot 453.

The 16 ukes are owned mainly by members of the George Formby Society and I'm pleased that my family owns George's very first uke-banjo played in his films, a Will Van Allen which he used in the film *Off The Dole* in 1935, which has been shown on Channel 5.

Stan Evans, George Formby Society, Penketh, Warrington.

? WHY is the phrase 'marker's dry' used when scores are level in crib?

THIS is simply a good opportunity for a break in the game to have a drink and it's traditional in cribbage for the players to pay for the scorer's (marker's) drink when they're 'level pegging' (registering the same score).

The phrase was also used in darts for a short time, when darts was scored on a crib board, but has been replaced by 'chalker's beer' or 'scorer's dry' when two players are level.

Patrick Chaplin, Maldon, Essex.

? AS an Ice Hockey fan, I've twice been hit by the puck. Is mine the most dangerous spectator sport?

THE most dangerous spectator sports are, without doubt, various forms of motor sport. In rallying, for example, a spectator is constantly peppered by flying stones, suffers from various sprains from jumping into roadside ditches to avoid oncoming cars and has been known to be mown down and killed along the route.

In the World Rally Championship some years ago in New Zealand, a spectator trying to capture video footage of the cars was hit by 'Flying Scot' Colin McRae at 60mph plus and was lucky to get away with only two broken legs.

In Formula 1 racing a few years ago, after a crash, a wheel bounced over the perimeter fence and killed three spectators. This sort of thing used to happen quite frequently in the U.S. until extra perimeter safety measures were taken.

All this is a bit more dangerous than being hit by an ice-hockey puck.

Vicky Edwards, Westhoughton, Lancs.

❓ IN the film *Apollo 13* how did the actors achieve the weightless effect without going into space?

THE 1995 double-Oscar-winning film *Apollo 13*, starring Tom Hanks, Bill Paxton and Kevin Bacon, told the true story of the ill-fated attempt to reach the Moon for the third landing. Director Ron Howard couldn't buy a space shuttle in which to film and chose the next best thing to achieve the effect of weightlessness, a NASA KC-135 training aircraft, the so-called 'Vomit Comet'.

The KC-135 is a hollow aircraft with masses of padding inside the fuselage, a very fast aircraft with the ability to fly at high altitudes, making it ideal for creating short-term weightlessness.

The aircraft is flown in a series of long parabolas, the pilot flying a trajectory that creates a gentle free-fall for the passengers in the fuselage. The effect is similar to the feeling you get in a lift for a moment when it drops too quickly.

During shooting, the cast and crew averaged around two flights a day. On each flight a series of parabolas was conducted, enabling an average 23 seconds of weightlessness which meant a 23-second take of a film shot as if the actors were in space.

The crew and cast did 13 days of this kind of filming, on one occasion performing 97 parabolas. Afterwards Howard said: 'Once you're comfortable with weightlessness, you never really want to walk again.'

John MacDonald, Perth.

❓ HOW did the card game Newmarket get its name?

NEWMARKET, a mild unskilled gambling game, suitable for family play, was named from the racetrack frequented by Royalty and has proved a most enduring game.

In America, where the name Newmarket lacks significance, the game was originally known as Stops or Boodle but by 1920 it had developed into Michigan, which also commemorates a racetrack.

Major Donald Welsh, English Playing Card Society, Bath.

⊘ DID suttee (widow-burning) arise from a misprint in the sacred Sanskrit text?

SUTTEE, the self-immolation of the widow on her husband's funeral pyre, was a custom among Indian Hindus until suppressed by the British in 1829, though sporadic instances persisted into the 20th century.

The name 'suttee' is derived from the Sanskrit *sati* – faithful wife. The act was supposed to be voluntary and was intended to prove the wife's devotion and to ensure the continued union of the couple in the afterlife.

In practice, suttee permitted the division of the husband's property without the complicating presence of a wife who, in any case, as a widow had little status.

Clare Mackay, Dundee.

THIS inhumane rite is taken from the description of the funeral ceremonies of the Aryans in the Rig-Veda but the only two lines that refer to suttee have been deliberately changed in what Max Muller described in 1881 as: 'Perhaps the most flagrant instance of what can be done by an unscrupulous priesthood.'

The original text ran: '*Arohantu Janayo Yonim agre*' ('Let the mothers advance to the altars first') but by the alteration of two letters, *agre* (altar) became *agneh* (the genitive of fire), so the line became 'Let the mothers go into the womb of fire.'

The fact that this change was made can be demonstrated by reference to the context and to the earliest commentators on the Rig-Veda. The original text had no reference to widows or suttee but was an injunction laid on all mothers present. As Dubois said in 1879: 'Few false readings have had consequences so fearful.'

Dr Tim Healey, Barnsley, South Yorks.

⊘ DO the Seven Sisters cliffs near Birling Gap in Sussex have individual names?

THE Seven Sisters are chalk cliffs rising to about 155m above sea level, just west of the famous Beachy Head. The cliffs are high in this area because of the more resistant nature of the chalk compared with the softer Lower Cretaceous rocks to the east and Tertiary rocks to the west and south.

Flamborough Head in East Yorkshire and the White Cliffs of Dover form headlands for the same reason.

The individual names of the Seven Sisters, from east to west, are Wentbrow Hill, Bailey's Brow, Flagstaff Point, Brass Point, Rough Brow, Short Brow and Haven Brow.

Greame Cobb, Saltcoats, Ayrshire.

WHO designed the 'Keep your country tidy' logo?

THE international Tidy Man logo first appeared on UK wastebins in 1972 but was already being used in the U.S. by the Keep America Beautiful Campaign, funded by the sponsorship of numerous corporations, individuals and groups.

One major sponsor was Budweiser beer brewers Anheuser-Busch. As part of its commitment to the environment, it asked its advertising teams to design a logo to remind consumers to dispose of bottles and cans in a proper manner. They came up with the 'pitch-in' logo we see today. Copyright was waived so other companies were persuaded to adopt it.

The logo was brought to Britain by then Keep Britain Tidy director, David Lewis. With one small change (we use a solid bin where the original was a wire one) it has remained the same ever since.

Popularity of this logo increased in this country in the early 1970s when the Government began to take environmental issues seriously. Environment Minister Peter Walker boosted Keep Britain Tidy's budget to mount a substantial promotional campaign making people more aware of the litter problem. This helped establish the Tidy Man logo.

Celebrities who helped the campaign by appearing on posters included Dixon of Dock Green, Morecambe and Wise, The Two Ronnies and David Cassidy. The campaign is held to have been a great success.

Prof Graham Ashworth, director general, Tidy Britain Group, The Pier, Wigan.

MIGHT hand-hot water poured on my car on frosty mornings run the risk of cracking the windscreen?

MODERN windscreens are formed by a lamination of two thin layers of glass separated by a plastic inter-layer, which acts as a thermal insulator. When hot water is poured on the outer layer of the screen, it will tend to expand at a greater rate than the insulated inner layer. If there are any chips or small cracks in the area, the tension created by this uneven expansion will make them grow.

The classic crack we tend to see runs across the bottom of the windscreen immediately over the hot air vents. Anyone who continually uses this method to clear their screen should obtain my telephone number before doing so.
Pete Stevenson, Abbey Windshields, Portswood, Southampton.

I'VE been using the warm-water method since my first car in 1953 without ill effect – even when living in Germany at -19°C. It's ten times quicker than scraping and warms the glass so it doesn't refreeze.
Derek Mayell, Bourne End, Bucks.

I NEVER buy anti-freeze windscreen sprays. I always pour warm water onto my windscreen to clear the ice, just before setting off. To date I have not had any problems. When I was living in Russia, my driver would pour vodka onto the screen, as it was cheaper than anti-freeze. At -35°C, water was no help.
John Peart, Dorchester, Dorset.

? WHICH squadron was responsible for the attack on Rommel's vehicle in Normandy in 1944?

ON July 17, 1944, two Spitfire fighter-bomber pilots of RAF No 602 (City of Glasgow) Squadron reported that they had attacked a staff car in the vicinity of the village of Fey St Montgomerie and that it had been seen to leave the road and overturn in a ditch.

One of the occupants turned out to have been Field Marshal Erwin Rommel. He was thrown out of the vehicle and sustained injuries including a fractured skull. He was perhaps unwise to risk travelling by daylight while the Allied Air Forces enjoyed total air superiority over the area and any moving vehicle was likely to be attacked.

Although he was seriously ill in a French hospital when the attempt on Hitler's life was made on July 20, he was implicated in the plot by another general and was given the choice, on Hitler's orders, of taking his own life or being arrested and tried. Rommel committed suicide on October 14, 1944.
Peter Barrington, Brundall, Norwich.

ANOTHER source claims a different squadron's involvement. Norman Frank's book *Typhoon Attack* says: 'Another significant event on July 17 was that Field Marshal Erwin Rommel ... received wounds that effectively put him out of the battle.

'He had been inspecting front line troops and on his return to his HQ his staff car was strafed by Allied fighters. Although one of his officers thought the aircraft were Spitfires, history records it was Typhoons of 193 Squadron, led by Wing Co Johnny Baldwin.'

Jerry Eaton, Christchurch, Dorset.

THE year 2000 was expressed in Roman numerals as MM. How long was it since the Roman method had fewer digits than the Arabic?

THE last year to have fewer Roman digits than the Arabic was 1900 (MCM).

The previous three-digit year was 1600 (MDC). The longest in the last 2,000 years was the 13-digit, 1888 (MDCCCLXXXVlll).

Paul Elborn, Newcastle, Staffs.

IT has been suggested that the previous year – 1999 – should have been expressed MIM rather than MCMXCIX as used by the BBC and others but this depends on incorrect use of the Roman numeral subtractive principle.

The seven key symbols are: I V X L C D and M. We can use the subtractive principle as long as the two symbols used are less than two apart. So we can say XC = 90 as X is only two symbols away from C, or IV = 4 as I is next to V.

We cannot say VC = 95 because V is three symbols from C. We certainly cannot use IM as 999 because I is six symbols away from M.

Capt J. W. Bakewell, Valley, Anglesey.

HAS anyone ever met, fallen in love and married in less than two weeks? Did it last?

MY cousin Reg Greig, on embarkation leave in 1944 before being posted to Palestine, met his future wife, Lena, at a dance.

They decided to marry and the banns were called in church on the Sunday with a view to them marrying the following day, despite the fact that Reg had to return to his unit by 2359 hours. He applied for a 48-hour leave extension but it wasn't granted so, on the Sunday morning, the Minister gave him a letter to give the Registrar, allowing them to be married in the Minister's Manse at 10pm on that Sunday.

Reg left the following morning by train at 6am and didn't see his wife again for two years. They were reunited in 1946 when they planned a big wedding but limousines weren't easy to come by at that time and Reg ended up commandeering a hearse to drive his bride to their wedding.

Happily, Reg and Lena celebrated their Golden Wedding on June 25, 1994. 'Love at first sight' was certainly true in their case.
Mrs Alice Morrison, Aberdeen.

THIRTY-three years ago, I met my wife Mavis at my going away party for South Africa and we were so in love that we married by special licence within the week so she could travel with me.

On our return six months later, we bought an old cottage and started a family, with daughter Christine and son Peter coming along. I worked as an electrician and my wife gave up her job as a window dresser to bring the children up. We never had much money and went without holidays as I was often out of work through accidents, illnesses and redundancy. Our children went to the local comprehensive school.

Our daughter is now a barrister and a member of the Bar Council and Peter is Dr Peter Bispham after getting 1st Class Honours in Physics with Astrophysics and a PhD in Particle Physics. Both are gifted musicians on piano and violin.

Length of time knowing each other is no replacement for strength of feeling.
C. Bispham, Prescot, Merseyside.

MY wife Jean and I met in Edinburgh on Sunday, June 12 and the next day I was away on sea duty in the Royal Navy for five days. On meeting again, I asked Jean if she would marry me, she accepted and we were married on June 25. The year was 1945 and we're still as in love as we were at 19 years of age.

In 2000, we celebrated our 1,000th visit to a nightclub in Huddersfield to disco dance the night away – which we do four nights a week.
Jack and Jean Atkinson, Huddersfield, West Yorks.

I MET my husband at my sister's wedding on December 18, 1955, when I was 19 years old. The next day he returned to his naval base at Portsmouth, leaving his gloves behind. I returned them and he wrote back saying: 'Thank you, and will you marry me?' I wrote back: 'Yes'.

The next time I saw him was on Feb 9, 1955, when I travelled from my home in Kent to his parents home in Hampshire and we were married three days later. Three weeks after that he was shipped out on a tour of duty for 18 months.

He left the Navy in 1957 and we went on to have five lovely kids who have given us 16 delightful grandchildren between them.

The actual time we spent together between meeting and marrying was just four days. We're still happily married. Yes, love at first sight can last.

Mrs M. Warwick, Andover, Hants.

? WHO was the first monarch to travel in a submarine?

BOTH George V and Prince Albert (later George VI) travelled aboard K Class submarines in World War I. The K Class, built between 1916 and 1923, were giant steam-powered vessels designed to go to sea with the Grand Fleet, supporting battleships.

They displaced 2,565 tons and their steam turbines enabled them to reach speeds of up to 25 knots on the surface. They had twin funnels which had to be retracted when they submerged and their electric motors took over.

They suffered many mishaps, the most serious of which was, when in a steep dive the whole boat acted as a giant hydroplane, driving them straight towards the sea bed. Crews hated them and would do almost anything to get posted to another ship.

K8 held the record for the fastest dive – 3 minutes 25 seconds – against a normal time of about six minutes. A conventional diesel/electric boat would dive in less than a minute.

In 1916, K3 was the first of the class to undergo trials and Prince Albert (later George VI) came aboard to see how they were progressing. The boat submerged in Stokes Bay when she suddenly put her bows down at a steep angle and dived out of control. She hit the sea bed and dug her bows into the mud with the propellers above the surface thrashing through the air. It took 20 minutes to get her to the surface.

In the summer of 1917 King George V inspected K1 while alongside at Scapa Flow. The vessel didn't submerge: it was too risky for the King to go under the waves in a K Boat. But he was photographed climbing up the ladder leaving the vessel and the two funnels were retracted 'to fool the Hun' as the K Class were secret at the time. The sight of two funnels on a submarine would have given the game away that the Royal Navy had 'fleet' submarines.

Ian Richardson, High Shincliffe, Durham.

MIKE Ashley's *History of British Kings and Queens* indicates that the first ever submarine was the 12-man wood and leather submersible devised by Dutch scientist Cornelis Jacobszoon Drebbel (1572–1634) in the early 17th century. This clumsy machine, which subsailed through the water by means of oars protruding through sealed ports and had oxygen supplied via two long tubes, was demonstrated to James I in 1620.

It travelled the Thames for two hours and even took the King for a short trip, making him the first monarch ever to travel underwater.

Michael Wood, Tewkesbury, Gloucs.

? COMING from a large family, we get tied in knots trying to work out cousin relationships: first, second, once removed, twice removed etc. Can anyone help?

ONE'S first cousin is the child of one's parent's sibling. One's second cousin is the child of one's parent's first cousin; a third cousin the child of one's parent's second cousin and so on.

The term 'removed' applies to generations. Thus, a parent's first cousin is one's own 'first cousin once removed' (and vice versa). A grandparent's first cousin is one's own 'first cousin twice removed' (and vice versa).

A parent's second cousin is one's own 'second cousin once removed' (and vice versa); and a grandparent's second cousin one's own 'second cousin twice removed' (and vice versa). Similarly, a great-grandparent's first cousin is one's 'first cousin three times removed' ... and so on.

Dr Maureen Norrie, Stockton-on-Tees, Cleveland.

THE easiest way to remember is that your first cousins are people with whom you share grandparents but not parents. Your second cousins are people with whom you share great-grandparents but not grandparents; your third cousins are people with whom you share great-great-grandparents but not great-grandparents, and so on.

So your first, second and third cousins are all of your generation, even if their age is completely different.

A remove is a generation difference. So your first cousins once removed, are the children of your first cousins, or (less frequently) the first cousins of your parents.

B. Ganly, Glasgow.

ON WHAT INCOME CAN A COUPLE COMFORTABLY MARRY?

DEAR *Answers*,—I think £140 per annum a sufficiently large income to marry on, supposing that both husband and wife do not possess expensive tastes.

My husband earns £2 10s per week, out of which we pay 10s 6d rent weekly, keep a comfortable home going, a well-spread table, and manage occasionally to treat ourselves to an evening's quiet amusement.

We find also that we can keep up a good appearance, enjoy a week at the seaside annually, and, on the whole, take life very comfortably.

But to bring about such a happy consummation a couple must live and scheme in harmony, and let love smooth the petty troubles that occasionally arise in the course of wedded life.

A Happy, Contented Wife, London S.E.

The theory that it is possible to marry comfortably on £70 a year is absurd: matrimony on such a slender basis would be the sure forerunner of the workhouse. Such marriages as these are the curse of the country and bring about in very many cases the terrible struggle against poverty which is so often found in small households.

My estimate is as follows:

	£	s.	d.
Bedroom, sitting-room, and kitchen	0	10	6
Coal and gas	0	1	6
Clothing	0	7	6
Food	0	15	0
Insurance, societies, &c.	0	1	6
Sundries	0	2	6
Balance	0	3	9
	£2	2	3

From this I conclude that £110 per year is about the smallest income a couple can comfortably marry on.

Carlton, London.

The £70 a year figure appears to me as one which shows, only too plainly, upon what income a young couple (young and foolish, I should say) can uncomfortably marry. What can be more preposterous, risky, and foolhardy than such an act, especially when based upon so small a yearly income?

Here we have a young man, in receipt of the magnificent salary of £60 per annum (which fact leads me to believe he has not been a clerk very long), talking of and advising others (situated presumably as he now is) to 'commit' matrimony; and that, too, without loss of time.

The old saying 'Marry in haste and repent at leisure' seems to have quite escaped his apparently sanguine memory.

He undoubtedly looks too much on the bright side of things and leaves no margin for the 'rainy day' which may come in the shape of sickness, accident, loss of situation or some other unforeseen and undreamt-of disaster which would render his proposed weekly allowance of £1. 7s. only about half of what he would require in such an unenviable extremity.

Should such a calamity overtake a couple so married, what can result but an unhappiness and misery which may last for years, and perhaps until death puts a merciful termination to it all?

Before that takes place, however, the pawn-broker and money-lender may have appeared on the scene to add their quantum to the miseries already bad enough, and when the last scene of all shall have become un fait accompli, when, in short, the husband, we will say for example, has been conveyed to his 'long home,' what can or will remain for the stricken wife or family in that dark future which must then inevitably face them?

I am not, nor have I any wish to be, a 'croaker,' but being older in years and having seen 'all sorts and conditions of men,' I would say to those situated as he appears to be 'Don't commit matrimony until you can afford to do so without prejudice to your wife and a possible family.'

Veritas, Bristol.

I am somewhat astonished at the very unpractical views contained in the advice from the clerk who imagines he can marry on an income of £70 a year.

? IS there any record of where Van Gogh stayed while he was in Putney and Twickenham?

VINCENT-WILLEM Van Gogh was born on March 30, 1853, in Groot Zundert in North Brabant, Netherlands, the eldest son of the local pastor, Theodorus Van Gogh and his wife, Anna Cornelia Carbentus.

A loner throughout his early years, at 16 he went to The Hague to work in a branch office of Goupil & Co, an art house founded by his uncle. After four years, in 1873, Vincent was moved to the firm's London branch where he fell in love with Ursula Loyer, his landlord's daughter. Her rejection of him led him to take solace in religion.

In October 1874, he was transferred to the Paris office but returned to London in December. The following summer, he was back in Paris where he fell out with his employers and was fired. Returning to London, he took up teaching jobs in schools in Ramsgate and then Isleworth.

At Christmas 1876, having delivered his first sermon in a local Methodist church, he visited his parents in Holland and didn't return to England, taking instead a job in a bookstore in Dordrecht before trying theological school. Abandoning that course, he drifted for much of the rest of a life which ended in suicidal tragedy.

His works executed in England, referred to as his 'juvenilia', include *Ville d'Avray: L'Etang au Batelier* (April 1875), *Sketch of Westminster Bridge and the*

Houses of Parliament (July 1875), *Houses at Isleworth* (July 1876), the *Square at Ramsgate* (April 1876), *The Churches at Petersham and Turnham Green* (November 1876), and *Vincent's Boarding House in Hackford Road, Brixton, London*. Most of these can be seen at the Van Gogh Museum in Amsterdam.
David Franks, Manchester.

VINCENT Van Gogh stayed at a house at 160 Twickenham Road, Isleworth, Middlesex, in 1876 – there's a plaque to commemorate this on the outside of the house. It's next to L. Garvin & Co, opposite the junction of Worton Road/Twickenham Road, near Isleworth Day Centre.
Jenna Hill, Isleworth, Middx.

❓ WHAT is the piece of music played before the weather forecast on Radio 4?

THIS brief piece of music is 'Sailing By', written by Ronald Binge and played on Radio 4 since 1973.
Amy Mulcair, BBC Radio 4, London.

DERBY-born Ronald Binge (1910–1979), was one of the nation's best-loved composers of British Light Music. Largely self-taught, he began his career as a composer, arranger and organist with an orchestra at a small local cinema.

His big break came in 1934/5 when he became arranger for the popular Mantovani orchestra and his first big compositional success was the orchestral piece 'Spitfire' in 1940. After war service in the RAF, he returned to Mantovani before going freelance.

Binge was given his own radio series *String Song* between 1955 and 1963. He was a highly versatile composer with a string of well-loved classical pieces, including the two popular light orchestral pieces 'Red Sombrero' and 'High Stepper'; 'Daybreak', which featured saxophones; the serenade 'Love In A Mist' for harp and strings; the 'Cornet Carillon' for four cornets and brass band, which remains one of the most popular items ever composed for brass band and the piece for which he is best known, the immensely popular 'Elizabethan Serenade' for oboe and strings.
Nancy Jones, Wilmslow, Cheshire.

ROBERT Binge's 'Sailing By' was originally composed in 1963 as a piece of 'library music' for the BBC, intended for use as background accompaniment to radio or TV programmes. It was first heard on a dialogueless BBC TV documentary about a balloon race from England to Holland.

Ten years later James 'Jim' Black, head of presentation at Radio 4, chose it to precede the shipping forecast and the BBC was immediately inundated with requests from listeners for the name of the piece and information on where they could buy it.

The version used by Radio 4 is performed by the Perry Gardener Orchestra. The item is also available, recorded by numerous other orchestras, on several light music CDs.

'Sailing By' was played every night for 20 years. In 1993 there was an outcry when Radio 4 controller Michael Green, as a cost-cutting exercise, decided to use it only at weekends. Under the headline 'Sailing By' drifts off into the night', the *Daily Mail* reported: 'For years its sweeping strings lulled listeners to sleep and braced sailors for gale warnings. But Radio 4's nightly lullaby has been torpedoed by BBC spending cuts.'

Two years later the BBC relented and restored 'Sailing By' to its nightly spot before the shipping forecast.

Mike Carey, biographer: Sailing By – The Ronald Binge Story, *Tranter's Publishers, Derby.*

? HOW did Leighton Buzzard in Bedfordshire get its peculiar name?

THIS is an example of a hybrid name, showing the influence of the Norman incomers after 1066. For centuries, this settlement was merely Leacton, meaning 'leek farm' or 'herb-garden' to its Saxon inhabitants.

The leek was a highly-prized vegetable, one of the few eaten in this country 1,000 years ago, and was also believed to have medicinal and quasi-magical properties.

The Domesday commissioners of 1086, working in a language not their own, heard the name as 'Leston'. By about 1200, it was 'Letton' and as such could be confused with other similar names of different derivation.

The Norman family of Bosard were then in possession of the manor and it is from them that the second element in the name derives as a means of distinguishing this from other Lettons and Leightons.

Karl Wittwer, The English Companions, London.

WHAT is the meaning of 'Wight' in Isle of Wight?

THERE are two theories behind the origin of the word 'Wight'. The first is that in 1900 BC the island was settled by a pastoral Bronze Age race, the Beaker People, who named the island Wiht, meaning 'raised' or 'what rises out of the sea'. Later, in AD 43, the Romans arrived and translated Wiht into the Latin equivalent *veho*, meaning 'lifted'. During their occupation, the island was known as Vectis but following their departure it reverted to Wight.

The second theory is that Iron Age Celts from the Continent gave Wight its name in about 400 BC. The name meant 'place of division' because the island lies between the two arms of the Solent.

Sophie Jeffrey, Isle of Wight tourism, Ryde.

ARE Church of England clergy still obliged to allow a King Charles spaniel into a church?

THIS old chestnut is still put forward by owners of King Charles spaniels who are under the impression that Charles II, a great lover of what were originally known as 'toy spaniels', made an edict that this type of dog should be allowed to wander freely into any public building without interference from any human busybodies.

Nothing is enshrined in official statutes, though there's some evidence that he did make such a statement verbally, and diarist Samuel Pepys records the King's habit of giving his dogs the free run of Whitehall, even on state occasions.

Today, neither the House of Commons nor the Lord Chamberlain's office is aware of such unlimited freedoms being granted in law. The concept has been put to the test at least twice in recent years when journalists have taken King Charles spaniels on trips around the capital to see if anyone dared bar this 'royal' dog from their premises.

On both occasions, the dog was refused entry to many well-known clubs, public buildings and even Buckingham Palace itself. The only way a King Charles spaniel could expect to be given the freedom to enter public buildings today would be if it were accompanied by someone registered as visually impaired.

Lucy Tatton, Maida Vale, London.

? WHEN did the indigenous lions, lynx, bear, bison and beaver of this country die out?

THERE is no convincing evidence that either lion or bison returned to Britain after the maximum point of the Devensian Glaciation in about 8000 BC.

Lynx and brown bear seem to have died out during Roman times, in about AD 300. The beaver disappeared some time during the 1200s and the wolf seems to have died out in the early 1300s in England but survived until the late 1600s in Scotland.

Extinctions such as those of the lion and bison were due to climate changes while the decline of wolves was hastened by deforestation (probably human led) as well as hunting.

Georgette Shearer, The Mammal Society, Battersea Park Road, London.

? LE Mans in France is twinned with Bolton. How are they alike?

BOLTON was forging links with Europe long before it was possible to buy a baguette in Bolton and is now twinned with two towns; Le Mans in France and Paderborn in Germany. The link with Le Mans was established in 1973 and the one with Paderborn two years later.

Apart from the towns being of similar size, likeness isn't a key issue as the idea is to twin with somewhere which is different from your own town, culturally and in other ways.

All three are large towns with easy access to attractive countryside. Since the Seventies, Bolton has been home from home for thousands of visitors from France and Germany with numerous educational and other twinning exchanges taking place, involving a wide range of people from school pupils to pensioners.

The three towns take it in turns to host joint twinning meetings to cement ties and establish further friendships and promote better understanding.

Alf Atkinson, Bolton Borough Council.

? WHAT was Portland Sago?

THIS was a kind of sago used to make puddings or blancmange, prepared from the tubers (roots) of *Arum maculatum* – a British native with the common names of cuckoo-pint, lords and ladies and starchwort, among others.

This arum has large tuberous roots, resembling those of the potato. Eaten raw they taste insipid at first but soon produce a burning and pricking sensation. The whole plant can cause these reactions, so should never be eaten; it can be fatal.

Portland sago – so called because it was regularly made on the Isle of Portland – is prepared by drying and baking the peeled tubers.

Geoff Hodge, Garden Forum, Old Fletton, Peterborough.

WHO invented double glazing?

DOUBLE glazing was first patented in New York on August 1, 1865, by Thomas D. Stetson in a specification forming part of Patent No 49,167.

Double glazing is made up of two or more sheets or layers of glass which are hermetically sealed. The gap between the sheets is filled with an insulating air layer or sometimes inert gases such as argon.

With this process, heat loss can be halved, cold down draughts reduced and rooms made warmer and more comfortable. The warmer internal window surfaces are less prone to condensation and heating costs are reduced with the environmental benefit of reduced pollution.

Amy Band, Glass And Glazing Federation, London.

ARE there really only 36 possible storylines/plots to a film? If so, what are they?

THIS applies to all forms of fiction, not just film. I was given Georges Polti's book *The 36 Dramatic Situations* to help me achieve my ambition of becoming a writer. The book demonstrates that there are only 36 basic situations though each has many variations, and many film or book stories combine several situations to create an original tale.

Polti names the basic situations: Supplication; Deliverance; Crime Pursued by Vengeance; Vengeance Taken for Kindred Upon Kindred; Pursuit; Disaster; Falling Prey to Cruelty or Misfortune; Revolt; Daring Enterprise; Abduction; The Enigma; Obtaining; Enmity of Kinsmen; Rivalry of Kinsmen; Murderous Adultery; Madness; Fatal Imprudence; Involuntary Crimes of Love; Slaying of a Kinsman Unrecognised; Self-Sacrificing for an Ideal; Self-Sacrifice for Kindred; All Sacrificed for a Passion; Necessity of Sacrificing Loved Ones; Rivalry of Superior and Inferior; Adultery; Crimes of Love; Discovery of the Dishonour of a Loved One; Obstacles to Love; An Enemy Loved; Ambition; Conflict with a God; Mistaken Jealousy; Erroneous Judgement; Remorse; Recovery of a Lost One and Loss of Loved Ones.

Many people have tried to find just one more dramatic situation that doesn't fall under one of these 36 headings, so far without success.
Morgan Gudgin, Lyneham, Wilts.

I WAS surprised to learn on a creative writing course that the number of basic storylines can in fact be reduced to eight: 1. Cinderella – after many obstacles, the dream comes true. 2. Achilles – the heroic individual destroyed by a fatal flaw. 3. Candide – the 'good guy' innocent abroad. 4. Circe – the chase of the innocent and the victim. 5. Faust – secret past actions catch up with the hero. 6. Orpheus – the tragedy of loss. 7. Tristan – the eternal triangle, the man cannot have the woman he loves. 8. Romeo and Juliet – boy meets girl or vice versa in less-than-encouraging circumstances.

These basic plots can be applied to many genres and can operate as comedy, tragedy, whodunit etc.

Most films conform to a certain formula, with a beginning, middle and end (the 'rule of three') incorporating obstacles that create tension within the plot, eg, she tries – fails – tries again – fails – tries again – succeeds. Watch out for this pattern and you will see it all the time in films and on TV.
Nick Fletcher, Malton, North Yorks.

? WHY is Ragtime music so called?

IN the late 19th century, when the piano became an everyday feature of many American homes, poor blacks couldn't afford music lessons but many learned to play by ear. They applied the syncopated rhythms of their drums and work songs, dances and spirituals, accentuating what would normally have been the weak rather than the strong beat.

This lively style was regarded by purists as tearing a tune to tatters and the style became known as 'ragged time' or 'ragtime', later incorporated into jazz.

In 1899, Scott Joplin's 'Maple Leaf Rag' attained great popularity and started a craze for the music, spreading in those days mainly through the sale of sheet music and piano rolls.
Marlene Macowan, Glasgow.

? WHY 'tit for tat'?

THIS expression dates from the 14th-century phrase 'tip for tap' – a tip being a light blow. It was probably influenced by the French *tant pour tant* –

so much for so much – and possibly by the Dutch *dit vor dat* – this for that. Both are similar to the Latin quid pro quo – a reciprocal exchange.

The French *tant pour tant* also gives us the word 'taunt', a stinging rejoinder.

From the late 19th century 'tit for tat' became Cockney rhyming slang for a hat, shortened in the Twenties to 'titfer'.

Kevin Heneghan, St Helens, Merseyside.

———————

WE hear of celebrities' famous last words, but has any average person come up with an equally amusing final line?

A PATIENT at the hospice where I work told me he was about to 'shut up shop' and promptly died.

Helen Claypole, primary nurse, Cynthia Spencer Hospice, Northampton.

MY daughter is a staff nurse in Aachen, Germany, where one of her colleagues, a student nurse, said she thought one of the seriously ill patients on the ward had died.

My daughter decided to check before reporting to the doctor on duty. As she neared, the lady awoke and said plaintively 'Have you got a book I can read? I'm bored.' At that she died.

Jean Smith, Ringmer, East Sussex.

SOME of the more famous last words are: 'Oh, I am bored with it all' (Winston Churchill); 'I'll see you in the morning' (Noel Coward); 'Eighteen straight whiskies, I think that's a record' (Dylan Thomas); 'So little done, so much to do' (Cecil Rhodes); and 'Either that wallpaper goes, or I do' (Oscar Wilde).

My favourite is attributed to U.S. General John Sedgewick who, during the Battle of Spotsylvania in 1864 during the American Civil War, looked over a parapet towards the enemy lines and said: 'Nonsense, they couldn't hit an elephant at this dist ...'

P. J. MacLaren, Lower Wick, Worcester.

———————

AT midnight on December 30, 1899, the steamship *Warrimoo* lay on the Equator at the point where it crosses the International Date Line, which meant December 31 never happened. How is this?

FOR this to occur, the *Warrimoo* had to be travelling west. Imagine two ships leaving the UK, one travelling east, the other west. Both ships leave the UK with their clocks set to GMT (or UTC i.e. GMT+/- 0).

The ship travelling east advances its clock as she crosses the various time zones until she arrives at the International Date Line, when the clock reads GMT+12 hours. The ship travelling west retards her clock, and when she arrives at the date line, her clock reads GMT -12 hours.

If both ships meet at the date line but don't cross it, the time of day would be the same on both but the date would be 24 hours apart, the ship going east being one day ahead of the other.

Aboard the *Warrimoo*, the date is December 30, 1899, and the time is midnight (0000 hours). On the ship which has travelled east, the date is December 31, 1899, time 0000 hours – 24 hours ahead of the *Warrimoo*.

When both ships cross the date line, they swap times. The *Warrimoo* advances her clock by 24 hours, missing out December 31 altogether. The other ship retards her clock by 24 hours and has a double December 31.

Container ships travelling from the UK to Australia and New Zealand circumnavigate the globe in an east-about direction, continually advancing their clocks. If the clocks weren't retarded 24 hours on crossing the date line, the ship would arrive back in the UK 24 hours ahead of the country.

A typical voyage like this takes almost three months so, in a normal year, the ship experiences 369 sunrises. On each voyage, the crew work an additional day for which an extra day's pay, called a Date Line Payment, is received.

William J. Stoker, 1st Officer (Navigating), P & O Nedlloyd Shipping Line, Southport.

IN my schooldays in the late 1930s we learned a rhyme to help us remember the Mediterranean countries, beginning 'Long-legged Italy kicked little Sicily...' Can anyone help me complete the rhyme?

I LEARNED this rhyme as a child in the Sixties, growing up in the Far East. It dates back to at least the late Twenties and relates not just to other countries but to some of the participants in World War I.

There are many versions through its use as a playground skipping rhyme. The one I knew went:

Austria was Hungary,
Ate a bit of Turkey
On a piece of China

Dipped in Greece.
Greece was slippery
Slipped into Italy,
Long-legged Italy,
Kicked little Sicily
Right into the middle of the Mediterranean Sea.

The worst part of learning the rhyme was trying to get our tongues around the word 'Mediterranean'.

Carol Haselwood, Glastonbury, Somerset.

❓ I AM a triplet and when my siblings and I were born in 1954 my parents received £3 from the Queen's Privy Purse. Who were the last triplets to receive such a gift and why did it stop?

VISITING Ireland in 1849, Queen Victoria initiated the Queen's Bounty for Triplets 'to enable parents to meet the sudden expenses thrown upon them' by the multiple birth.

Until 1938, the grant was conditional on the parents being 'in necessitous circumstances'. After that, it was regarded as royal appreciation rather than as a payment to help the parents meet the expense.

During the reigns of George VI and our present Queen before 1957, a Bounty of £4 was paid to 19 families for having quadruplets and the £3 Bounty to 1,451 families for triplets.

In 1957, after the introduction of the welfare state and because the financial value of the sum had declined, the Queen's Bounty for Triplets was replaced by a congratulatory message to the parents.

The Congratulatory Messages now in force are sent only on request. Both parents must be British citizens and all three children must be born alive and surviving. The request for a Message must be made within six months of their birth.

Spokesperson, Buckingham Palace, London.

❓ WHEN I was at primary school in the Seventies, I learnt a type of handwriting called 'Marian Richardson'. Who was or is Marian Richardson?

MARION Richardson was a reformer of writing styles who brought out the Dudley Writing Cards in 1928 and in 1935 the Teacher's Book – *Writing and*

Writing Patterns. Various schools put forward students to provide samples of the script as a test of its effectiveness.

The cards were aimed at youngsters from six upwards and the book gave exercises of pattern drawing to encourage writing flow, with age-related developments. The idea was to provide an uncluttered and harmonious copybook style while retaining the writer's individuality.

Years ago, in the course of my work, I came across a lady who had been one of the children involved in trying out the writing style in the early 1930s. She said those chosen had three months to practise before their samples were submitted for appraisal.

Hers must have been one of the best because it was used as a definitive version. This lady was 70 when I met her and she gave me a sample of her writing to compare with her named script in the book at the ages of 10 and 14. Her current script still bore a resemblance to her pre-Marion Richardson script.

Most people recognise that the personality of the writer influences the script. The copybook provides the facility for clear and comfortable writing performance, leaving time and energy for the personality to shine through. This is the purpose of teaching handwriting, rather than to produce conformity.

Elaine Quigley, British Institute of Graphologists, Hampton Hill, Middx.

❓ WHY do the Japanese drive on the left?

THE Japanese adopted the left-hand side of the road for driving after a proposal by the first British minister in Japan, Sir Rutherford Alcock.

The inaugural issue of the *Japan Herald*, the first English-speaking newspaper in Japan (1861), carried a letter from Sir John informing foreign residents that he had represented to the Japanese Government that a rule of the road should be introduced to create an orderly flow of traffic in the somewhat chaoitic streets of Tokyo (then Edo) and Yokohama, and that the Shogunal authorities had consequently issued an order that henceforth traffic should pass right side to right side – driving on the left.

Graham Healey, School of East Asian Studies, University of Sheffield.

❓ SIR Alex Ferguson is one of the Freeman of the Scottish city of Aberdeen. What are such Freeman allowed to do?

SIR Alex Ferguson, former Aberdeen Football Club manager, was awarded the Freedom of the City for his outstanding work in football management in England and Scotland and his ambassadorship for the game throughout Europe and the world.

In days gone by, those receiving the accolade were allowed to graze their cattle free of charge on land owned by the city, were allowed to own arms and carry their muskets through the streets – and had to be prepared to use them in defence of the city.

Today, the Freedom of the City of Aberdeen carries no physical trappings: it's a mark of the respect in which the city and its inhabitants hold the person concerned.

Other people who have been bestowed with this honour include Mikhail Gorbachev, the late Queen Mother and Sir Winston Churchill.

Ray Gibson, City of Aberdeen District Council.

? WHO invented the can opener?

MY collection of 800 different tin can openers vary in age from Victorian to the present day. Older ones are sometimes difficult to date.

I've been collecting for about ten years, but had never found a fellow collector until last year. There are now four of us that I know of, one of whom lives in Holland, and rumour has it that there are many more in America.

The invention of the can opener by Ezra J. Warner is well documented. It was American Patent No 19063, dated January 5, 1858, and was a formidable instrument, a cross between a bayonet and a sickle.

It has been suggested that the bayonet itself was first designed in Bayonne, France, not as a weapon but as a method of opening tins and bottles.

Englishman William Underwood established the first cannery in New Orleans, America in 1817, and it remains to be seen whether we can unearth a British or French patent for a tin can opener which pre-dates that of Warner.

Canned food reached Australia in 1815 and they must have had a regular way of opening the cans so Australians may also have contributed to the history of the tin can.

R. L. Hardy, Anstey, Leics.

IS ALL FAIR IN LOVE?

DEAR *Answers*,—This is a popular saying and, undoubtedly, many people who on other points are strictly truthful and just, allow themselves to be wheedled by this sentence into actions they would under other circumstances never dream of performing.

Is it fair for papa to roll a rejected suitor down three flights of stairs into the road? Should George tell papa that he has been to a lecture on The Welfare of the Masses when he has in reality been romeoing up at the other end of the town? Is it right that Angelina should tip the baker's boy to bring her dear Edwin's notes, and thus shamefully hoodwink dear mamma?

These and many other little tricks are performed daily under the shelter of that saying.

I am in love myself and if it is the general opinion that 'all is fair in love', I shall lead my wretched rival to a lonely pool and compel him to give her up or swim for it.

In Love, Sheerness.

Vacillating, weak-minded and unprincipled must he be who asks such a question. If there is any passion in which honour, principle and strict truth should play leading parts, it is in the divine one of love.

What a delightful pass things will come to if the 'all's fair in love and war' saying is allowed. Little mean and paltry tricks on the part of anxious lovers will not only be condoned but actually held up as examples of loverlike procedure, and soldiers will receive medals for acts which would now disgrace the veriest scoundrel living.

The little subterfuges resorted to by lovers under the present order of things can scarcely be considered strictly honourable. How many couples now think unlimited exaggerations necessary and clever in love-making? The great majority, I fear.

I, for one, do not wink at such ruses and I fear those who practise them will not be above such subterfuges in their married life.

An Uncle, Dundee.

This is not a question that can be answered with a mere 'yes' or 'no'. It depends on circumstances. In my case, I think all strategy is allowable.

I am living with a guardian who has an interest in my not marrying and who puts every obstacle in the way of meetings between my lover and myself.

I have recently developed a great interest in geology – a subject my guardian hates. I may add that my lover is to be found on four afternoons a week in a certain geological museum.

Love Will Find a Way, Cork.

If a parent objects to a couple of young people becoming engaged, this is no excuse for the theory that they may exercise their own judgement in the matter simply because they believe all to be fair in love.

Parents' opinions in such matters deserve serious consideration. They have gone through the world; they know its ups and downs and are better able to judge of the advisability of a matrimonial alliance than the young people themselves.

A Parent, Dundee.

? HOW many Tom and Jerry cartoons were made?

WILLIAM Hannah and Joseph Barbera directed 114 MGM cartoons featuring the famous pair between 1940 and 1958. The first, *Puss Gets the Boot*, isn't strictly a Tom and Jerry as the cat is called Jasper and the mouse is un-named.

Of the others, all but one of which feature Scott Bradley's marvellous scores, four have new story footage as a framing device for excerpts from previous adventures and three are retitled Cinemascope remakes of earlier films.

The impact of TV on box office takings forced Hollywood studios to look for ways of cutting costs and MGM closed its animation department in 1958 but it continued to circulate Tom and Jerry shorts and the films remained so popular that it decided to make some new ones.

Between 1960 and 1962, 13 new cartoons directed by Gene Deitch and made in Prague, appeared. But budget constraints, the absence of Scott Bradley's music, and the unfamiliarity of the new animators made these cartoons pale shadows of the earlier ones. A feature length compilation, *Tom and*

Jerry's Festival of Fun, released at this time contained no new footage.

In 1963, MGM re-established an animation department and 34 more films were produced under Chuck Jones's supervision, with a higher budget than the Prague films but with the characters even further away from their established personalities.

By 1975, Hannah and Barbera, now firmly established as TV animation makers, bought from MGM the right to produce new cartoons for American TV network ABC. Despite the involvement of Tom and Jerry's creators and two of the original animators, Ed Barge and Kenneth Muse, TV budgets and deadlines and strict ABC broadcast standards and practices made these 48 cartoons a new low point in the duo's career.

In 1993, a full length Tom and Jerry movie was released – making a grand total of 210 cartoons.

Don Treadmayle, Rainham, Kent.

? IN Australia, Britain is sometimes referred to as 'the Old Dart'. What does this mean?

THE *Oxford Australian Dictionary* says the origins of calling Britain the Old Dart are uncertain but in the *Sydney Slang Dictionary* of 1882, 'dart' meant a fancy, a plan, or an enticing thing.

In 1895, a book on Australian English includes: 'Fresh strawberries; that's my dart!' said by a bushman arriving in the city. It seems likely, therefore, that the Old Dart was an ideal to be aimed at or an affectionate memory.

Baker's *Australian Language* of 1945 gives a typical usage: 'He would be less sentimental over Home, the old country, the old dart, or the old land, as Britain was known.'

David Elias, Nottingham.

I UNDERSTOOD the phrase to refer to Dartmoor prison, used as a 'transit lounge' for British subjects selected by Her Majesty for a new life in Australia. British convicts arriving in Australia would have been from 'the Old Dart'.

Garry Moore, Ilford, Essex.

? HOW many people earning the national minimum wage would it take to balance out a Premiership footballer in order to produce the average weekly wage?

THERE'S a large discrepancy between some of the 'journeymen' who make up the squads at some of the smaller clubs – even in the Premiership – and the highest paid footballers at the top clubs, such as Chelsea's Michael Ballack, reputed to be one of the highest-paid on around £120,000 a week.

The minimum wage is £5.25 an hour which, for a 40-hour week, gives a weekly income of £210. Comparing this with Ballack, it would take 571 people on the minimum wage to match this figure. No wonder Chelsea FC need an ever-increasing number of minimum-wage spectators coming through the turnstyles every matchday to keep the revenue rolling in.

At the other end of the scale, there are said to be a few Premiership players who are on only about 12 times the national minimum wage.
Mike Edelman, London NW3.

？ WHY should one 'eat one's heart out'?

IF you want to live a long and happy life you should never 'eat your heart out', as it means to grieve or worry where the situation is hopeless.

The symbol of someone gnawing at their most vital organ is a stark image of being consumed with worry but the phrase is, these days, most used as a frivolous taunt to a person one has supposedly bettered. For example, some-one who scores a good goal for their Sunday league football team may say 'Eat your heart out, Beckham!' leaving Mr Beckham to eat his heart out with jealousy.

The root of the expression goes back to the ancient Greeks. Their version (quoted by Plutarch as a Parable of Pythagoras) translates as 'eat not the heart' with the similar meaning, don't consume yourself with worry.

By the 16th century, the phrase had entered common English use and in 1535 English scholar and diplomat Sir Thomas Elyot gave the warning: 'Eate no Harte, what does it els signifie, but accombre not thy mynde and thoughtes, ne do not fatigue thee with cares.'
Charles Pritchard, Much Wenlock, Shropshire.

？ WHY do we swing our arms when we walk?

AS we walk, the centre of gravity shifts forwards and oscillates between the left and right sides. When the left foot is on the ground, the body shifts to the left so the centre of gravity is over the supporting foot; it shifts over to the right when the right foot is the weight-bearing foot.

Each step is accompanied by an alternating upwards tilt of the left and right hips, to help lift the foot off the ground, and alternating left and right forward projection of the hips as each leg moves forward.

These movements are transmitted to the upper body, including the head, but the amount of movement transmitted to the head is minimised by swinging the arms in the opposite direction from the legs, acting as a counterbalance.

Prof G. M. Morriss-Kay, Department of Human Anatomy and Genetics, Oxford University.

? **IS there any information on the number of birds killed by domestic cats each year? Are cats a threat to some bird species?**

IN 1997, the Mammal Society and its youth group Mammalaction ran a Look What The Cat Brought In survey to investigate the effect of domestic cat predation on animals. It ran for five months, during which 964 cats across the country took 3,383 birds.

A few were chance kills – one budgerigar, one red grouse and one Great Spotted Woodpecker – but in all there were 13 species of which more than 30 individuals died – sparrow, blue tit, blackbird, starling, thrush, robin, pigeon, wren, greenfinch, chaffinch, great tit, dunnock and collared dove. These aren't necessarily the most common bird species but are the ones that turn up in gardens. The top ten birds that feed from garden bird tables are all among the 13.

It's unlikely that cats alone will cause any species to become endangered in Britain but those which are already under pressure through habitat loss, pesticide use etc (such as the thrush) could find predation by cats significant. What we do know is that keeping your cat indoors overnight decreases the amount of predation.

Georgette Shearer, The Mammal Society, Battersea Park Road, London.

IN the U.S., we estimate that the nation's 40 million free roaming pet cats are killing hundreds of millions of birds each year – and that doesn't include kills by stray or feral cats.

Cats are killing threatened and endangered species, such as the Western Snowy Plover, California Clapper Rail, Piping Plover and Least Tern.

We encourage cat owners to keep their cats indoors, spay or neuter them at an early age and never abandon them.

Linda Winter, Cats indoors!, Campaign for Safer Birds and Cats, American Bird Conservancy, Washington DC.

❓ WHEN compared with satellite photos how accurate are maps made from the ground?

MAPS can't really be compared in any meaningful way with images created from satellite data. Satellite data can record the positions of features on the ground very accurately which is why many modern maps are based on information taken from satellites, but traditional surveying methods can also be very accurate. The trigonometrical mapping technique which created the Ordnance Survey maps of the British Isles in the 19th century are testament to this.

Maps include a lot of information which can't be collected by satellites: a road map, for instance, which didn't tell you the name of a town or the numbers of the main roads, or a walking map which didn't tell you about rights of way, would be of little use, however accurately features were positioned. This information can be collected only on the ground.

All maps and images of the world are a representation of a round world projected onto a flat piece of paper, so however accurately information is collected there will be some distortion.

A further problem with satellite imaging is that it is susceptible to environmental conditions, cloud over in the Tropics for example can make satellite mapping of these areas very difficult. So satellite data is now an invaluable source but satellite imagery can't replace maps and is generally used for slightly different purposes.

Debbie Hall, British Library, London.

❓ ARE Fire Brigade, Police and Armed Forces road-going vehicles subject to the same road fund tax as civilian vehicles?

FIRE Engines and Police vehicles form part of the Emergency group of vehicles, exempt from the payment of Vehicle Excise Duty (VED). They do however, have to display a vehicle licence disc.

Armed Forces vehicles are classed as Crown vehicles and are not subject to VED.

The number of emergency vehicles licensed at DVLA are: 10,435 ambulances, 11,377 other NHS vehicles, 5,446 Fire Engines, 3,716 other Fire Service vehicles and 21,208 Police vehicles.

Dagmar Wooldridge, Driver and Vehicle Licensing Agency, Swansea.

⍰ ARE there any hairy fish?

FISH do not have hairs in the way mammals do but they're covered in various types of scale which, like hair, also contains keratin.

Sharks have very different types of scale from perch, for example, and some are modified to appear hairy. The pogge (pronounced 'pogue'), common in British estuaries and seas, has a hairy-looking underside, possibly to help it anchor to mud and sand.

Some incredible-looking fish such as anglerfish, stonefish and frogfish are covered in 'hairy' appendages to help with camouflage. And a large number of species (cod, sturgeon, bearded rockling) have barbels on their chins which can look like a little goatee or projections that look like eyebrows (tompot blenny). Some other marine creatures do have human-like hairs – crabs you'll see at fishmongers have hairy legs, as do worms like the ragworm.

Richard Harrington, Marine Conservation Society, Ross-On-Wye, Herefordshire.

TRAVELLING from Michigan towards Toronto and Niagara Falls, we passed over the border to Canada at Sault Ste Marie. At the immigration terminal on the Canadian side of the locks, there's a small museum showing how the locks were made and the importance of being able to navigate them.

In a glass case there was a trout-like fish they had recovered while excavating part of the lock system – it was covered in hair.

Mrs J. A. Tokley, Braintree, Essex.

⍰ IN the children's TV programme *Rainbow*, Bungle was a bear and George was a hippo but what was Zippy supposed to be?

RAINBOW, made by Thames TV, was first broadcast on Monday, October 16, 1972, after the Government relaxed its controls over TV broadcast times and allowed programmes on weekday afternoons.

The original line-up included presenter David Cook, Bungle the Bear, Mooney and Sunshine and, of course, Zippy. George the Hippo appeared at the start of the second season and Geoffrey Hayes at the start of the third.

Zippy was originally voiced by Peter Hawkins and later by Roy Skelton, both of whom had been the voices of the Daleks and the Cybermen on *Doctor Who*.

It's always been fairly unclear as to what manner of creature Zippy is meant to be but it's believed that early promotional material produced for *Rainbow*'s first series indicated that he was supposed to be a snake.

Richard Bignell, Rainham, Kent.

I RECALL a similar question being asked of Thames TV some years ago. The response was something to the effect that Zippy wasn't actually meant to be anything – he was simply Zippy.

Nick Deakin, Fareham, Hants.

IS it true that polar bears cover their black noses to assist their natural camouflage when stalking prey?

THIS common myth, based on Inuit (Eskimo) folklore, arose because polar bears, captive and in the wild, often cover their noses with their enormous paws. But this is a matter of comfort, not camouflage.

A polar bear's nose is the only part of its body not covered in a thick layer of fur – even the soles of their feet are hairy. When resting, a bear covers its nose to keep it warm and help warm up the air it's breathing.

Looked at under an electron microscope, polar bear hair is solid and totally transparent, acting like a fibre optic, conducting light down the hair to the animal's black skin. It appears white because of the light reflected through it. This makes polar bear hair a favourite fishing lure for the Inuit in the Arctic.

Though polar bears are adapted to survive the cold they are mammals and, given the choice, prefer temperatures of 50 to 60°F.

Alison Ames, Monkey World, Wareham, Dorset.

WHAT happened to all the animals kept in zoos during World War II?

MANY animals from other zoos, circuses, travelling menageries, etc, were evacuated to Chester Zoo for the duration of the war. An appeal was made to the public for unwanted horses and goats which could be slaughtered to provide meat, as well as for stale bread and other food suitable for animals.

The response was heartening and many local tradespeople were generous in sending supplies of surplus foodstuffs. Members of the public donated coupons from their ration books to provide food for the animals. Gifts such as strong wire, railings, etc, were also gratefully received. Collections were made by staff at local companies and two free entrance tickets were given for each shilling (5p) collected.

By 1940, several of the staff had been called up for military service and many more girl keepers were employed. The stock of animals continued to increase as more 'evacuees' arrived and by 1941 there were 14 lions in the collection. As the war progressed, more difficulties were experienced, especially in finding food suitable for livestock.

Exotic fruits were unavailable for the birds and they didn't relish English fruit. Charlie, the black-footed penguin, didn't take kindly to strips of horse-flesh instead of his favourite herrings: he was an early casualty of the hostilities.

Notices were issued to the public advising them of precautions to be taken in the event of an air raid and staff members were trained in the use of firearms in case of any animal escape – but most of the animals didn't seem to worry too much about the air raids.

The majority of the animals came through the war surprisingly well, more than 90 per cent of them surviving it.

Pat Cade, Chester Zoo.

❓ WHY does tinfoil cause that horrible sensation when you bite it?

THIS sensation is the result of an electrical charge caused by contact of the tinfoil (aluminium foil) on the amalgam (mercury-based) tooth fillings, saliva being the catalyst.

This effect can be demonstrated on an electrical multimeter with two clean dissimilar metal coins, say, a 2p and a 10p piece. Wet a piece of newspaper the size of the coins with saliva and compress it between the coins. Applying the probes of the multimeter to each coin will indicate the presence of a small voltage. Sandwiching several coins and bits of paper in this way will create a small battery.

In the industrial world, the presence of dissimilar metals in areas like gas storage compounds is strictly forbidden.

George Lewis, London.

THE reason for not having dissimilar metals in contact in industry or construction, particularly in corrosive environments, is the risk of accelerated corrosion of the less 'noble' metal.

There are well-tested design techniques to prevent this and an aluminium roofing system with a steel framework will give years of good service.

There is no sparking hazard and, if correctly designed and installed, no corrosion hazard either.

Richard Mahoney, Aluminium Federation Ltd, Birmingham.

ARE there any pilots in the world who hold a pilot's licence, but not a current driving licence?

I OBTAINED my gliding certificate when I was just 17 and my private pilot's licence shortly after my 18th birthday. It took me another year (and three attempts) to pass my driving test.

Kieron Wood, Dublin.

I PASSED my private pilot's licence before I had my own driving licence. I got my licence in September 1999 and didn't get my driving licence until February the next year.

Julian Bridgeman, Reading, Berks.

I FIRST learned to fly in 1982 and was issued with my private pilot's licence when I was 17 years and 2 months old. It wasn't until a further 12 months that I gained my driving licence. There must many pilots around the world who have a pilot's licence but no driving licence. After all, who wants to drive when you can fly?

Darren Jones, Styal, Cheshire.

ONE of my friends, Eugene Mitchell, was a Lancaster bomber pilot during the war, winning the DFC. In civilian life he has never held a driving licence or owned a car.

Iris Benson, Bebington, Merseyside.

AT RAF Cosford in 1947 I shared a desk with an RAF Sgt pilot called Foxcroft who had been taken on for long-term service following the war. He had done most of his flying in the heaviest single piston-engined fighter plane at that time, the Republic Thunderbolt P47 but had never learned to drive a car and had never held a driving licence.

Today, flying a plane is easier – and much safer – than driving.

Ted Duck, Southampton.

HAVING been awarded the RAF Flying Scholarship and RAF Sixth Form Scholarship in 1998, I obtained my private pilot's licence at London Southend Airport that September.

I was among a growing group of 16/17-year-olds who are obtaining pilot's licences before learning to drive – the main reason being that under new European control the minimum age for solo flying is now 16.

It meant that although I could fly out for a holiday in France but had to ask my passengers to drive me to the local aerodrome.

Carl R. Franks, Gerrards Cross, Bucks.

I LEARNT to fly in 1972, finishing the course at the end of the year and sending off the paperwork for approval. On January 4, 1973, I took and passed my driving test and a couple of days later I received my private pilot's licence through the post – date stamped Jan 4, 1973, so I became a pilot and a driver on the same day.

Malcolm Derrick, Melbourn, Cambs.

❓ WHO painted the picture of the green oriental lady which graced so many lounges in the 1960s and 1970s?

THIS was one of many paintings executed by Vladimir Tretchikoff. Born in what is now Kazakhstan in 1913, Tretchikoff was working for the Ministry of Information in Singapore at the outbreak of World War II. When the Japanese attacked on December 8, 1941, he stayed at his desk while his wife Natalie and daughter Mimi were evacuated.

When Singapore fell, Tretchikoff was evacuated in a refugee convoy which was intercepted by the Japanese. At the time, he was minding a baby for a woman who was searching for another child and so was ordered into a lifeboat before the Japanese opened fire.

He was adrift in an overcrowded lifeboat for many weeks before being captured by the Japanese, imprisoned and subjected to the usual Japanese illtreatment of prisoners.

After many adventures, Tretchikoff was reunited with his family in Cape Town where he took up painting. One day, a pigeon came and perched on top of his canvas while he worked and he took this as a good sign.

His subject matter touched a universal chord and he became one of the first painters to have his prints mass-produced to meet an ever-increasing home interiors market. He painted the green *Chinese Girl*; the *Dying Swan*, posed by Alicia Markova; *Lenka*, a beautiful Japanese girl; and the *Black and White* girl, divided into a black girl on the right and a white girl on the left.

Copies of Tretchikoff's paintings sold in their millions and he held exhibitions throughout the world. More than 200,000 people visited his first exhibition at Harrods. He died in South Africa in 2006.

J. A. Hulme, Wirral.

Q WHO now owns the Inner Hebridean island of Inch Kenneth, once part of the estate of Lord Redesdale, and the place his notorious daughter Unity Mitford saw out the last years of her life?

THE beautiful island of Inch Kenneth came to us by luck. My wife Yvonne and I spent so many wonderful holidays on the West coast of Scotland that we decided to buy a small holiday cottage there. The agents accidentally sent us a brochure for the island of Inch Kenneth. On viewing the island and property we immediately fell in love with it and bought it from Jessica Mitford in 1967.

The beauty of the island has been well chronicled by two of Britain's most gifted authors: Samuel Johnson went there with Boswell in 1775 and wrote about it in his *A Journey To The Western Isles Of Scotland* and Sir Walter Scott described his visit in 1810 in his letters.

Industrialist and poet Sir Harold Boulton (who wrote the words of 'The Skye Boat Song') bought the island in 1935 and enlarged the house. He moved to this quiet corner of Scotland to seclude his alcoholic wife from the public and help cure her of her affliction but the locals took pity on Lady Boulton and, with true Scottish hospitality, helped her maintain her lifestyle.

Sir Harold died after completing the house and his wife died shortly afterwards. The property was purchased by Lord Redesdale, noted for his talented though troublesome daughters, including Diana who married Sir Oswald Mosley, Jessica, authoress and Communist, Nancy the renowned novelist and the notorious Unity, who became a friend of Hitler.

Unity survived a suicide attempt at the outbreak of war with Germany in 1939 but died in Scotland in 1948 from the late effects of the injury.

After the death of Lady Redesdale, the island passed to Jessica Mitford who was then living in America. She tried to give the property to the Communist Party of Great Britain but they wouldn't accept it, leaving the door open to us.

I have handed over ownership to my son Prof Martin Barlow and daughter Dr Claire Barlow, though my wife and I still try to spend as much time there as we can.

Dr Andrew Barlow, London.

Q WAS the Thirties table soccer game Newfooty an earlier version of Subbuteo?

NEWFOOTY was invented by William Keeling, of Fazakerley, Liverpool, in 1927 and, as a teenager in the Forties, I recall the disappointment when the game invented in my home city was supplanted by the newcomer, Subbuteo.

Birdwatcher Peter Adolph took the Newfooty idea and modified it in 1947 to create Subbuteo, named after the Latin word for the hobby hawk. The table and figures were virtually identical, Adolph making subtle changes to avoid breaching copyright. Both games were essentially the same.

Federation of International Sports Table Football president Dave Baxter said that if it wasn't for Keeling, Adolph probably wouldn't have got anywhere. But Adolph patented the game and, because he was younger and had more money than Keeling, was able to market it successfully.

Subbuteo fans in Merseyside still play for the Keeling Cup in the Keeling League. After England's 1966 World Cup triumph, Waddington's bought the rights, selling them to American company Hasbro in 1994.

Norman Coltham, Great Bentley, Essex.

? WHAT is the story behind the Ugly House on the A5 between Betws-y-coed and Capel Curig in North Wales?

THE Ugly House (Ty Hyll), built around 1475, is the best surviving example of a Yn yn y Nos – a 'house of the night'. To take advantage of a loophole in local law, these houses had to be built literally overnight.

Such hurried constructions were erected complete with fireplace and chimney between sundown and sunrise and if the builder could have smoke coming out of the chimney within that time, the property was his. The land surrounding the house was his too for as far as he could throw an axe in all directions from each side of the house.

The Ugly House (there were uglier ones all over Wales) is said to have been constructed overnight by four brothers from Capel Garmon, a formidable task considering the size of some of the boulders in the walls.

In the 19th century, the dwelling was used as an overnight stop by drovers taking cattle from Anglesey to the lucrative markets of England.

They travelled an average 15 miles a day and, before Telford's Menai Suspension Bridge opened in 1826, the cattle had to swim the Menai Strait. So for drovers and cattle alike, the Ugly House was a pretty sight.

It's now the home of the environmental campaigning organisation, the Snowdonia National Park Society.

Colin Adams, author: The Mountain Walker's Guide To Wales, *Newport Pagnell, Bucks.*

? ARE the large air holes often found in supermarket bread due to the baker's shortcomings or are they simply inevitable?

HOLES in bread are due to either a straightforward technical problem which can easily be identified and solved or else appear and disappear for no apparent reason when it can be difficult to discover the exact cause.

The most commonly seen holes are elongated 'handbag' holes under the top crust, either smooth edged or with strands of dough stretching across them.

This is due to excessive oven spring upwards so that the dough bursts apart – usually along one of the points at which the moulded surfaces came together. Strands of dough stretching across the hole are normally a result a lack of dough strength. The dough piece sets on the outside in the oven but is not strong enough. The unset dough below the crust collapses and pulls away from the top crust.

Triangular holes or dense patches just above the bottom crust are caused by air trapped at the base of the pan. Shiny holes appearing at random in any part of any loaf can be blamed on excessive oil being used, particularly to oil the hopper, but it's difficult to prove this.

Holes appearing regularly at the same point towards the end of loaves can be due to poor adjustment of the moulder pressure boards, particularly if the pressure board is curved.

Geraldine Griffiths, Federation of Bakers, London.

HOLES in bread are caused by the yeast in the dough respiring and giving off carbon dioxide, this is what makes the bread rise.

When the yeast is added to the dough and left to sit at a warm temperature (about 35°C) it feeds rapidly on the sugar in the dough and respires, causing large 'holes' full of carbon dioxide to form in the dough.

The dough is kneaded to release much of the carbon dioxide and this may be repeated so the yeast respiration forms smaller bubbles, as its food lessens. The dough is then baked, during which the yeast is killed off by the high temperatures and the alcohol given off as the yeast respires and evaporates.

So any large holes in supermarket bread are due to the dough not being kneaded enough to release the carbon dioxide from the larger holes.

Gemma McCulloch, Coleraine, Co Londonderry.

❓ HAS any top-flight goalkeeper been penalised for holding a football for longer than six seconds?

LAWS surrounding the handling of the ball appear in Law 12 – Fouls And Misconduct – of the Official Football Rules. This states under Decision 3 of the International FA Board: 'The goalkeeper is considered to be guilty of time-wasting if he holds the ball in his hands or arms for more than 5–6 seconds.'

The penalty for this misdemeanour is an indirect free kick.

Paul Jones, Manchester.

REFEREE Jim McCluskey penalised and booked Dundee United's Sieb Dykstra for this in the 1998/9 season in a league match against Hibernian at Tannadice.

S. McIntosh, Dundee.

NEVILLE Southall, playing for Everton, was penalised during an away game against Nottingham Forest in the League Cup in the 1992/3 season. Southall was booked for time wasting for holding the ball for more than six seconds. Stuart Pearce took the free kick, it was deflected into the net and Forest won 1–0.

TV coverage at the time took up the issue and, using other games that day, showed goalkeepers being timed holding the ball for longer than six seconds without any foul being given, showing inconsistency among referees that costs important games and frustrates the fans.

Ray Kennington, West Derby, Liverpool.

❓ DID Rolf Harris ever swim for Australia in the Olympics?

SADLY, I never reached Commonwealth or Olympic standard at swimming. I loved the sport but didn't have the dedication to be world class.

A school friend of mine back in Australia would swim for two hours before school and two hours after to be in the Australian team which seemed a bit excessive to me. However, I did win the World Junior backstroke championship of Australia in 1946 – a thrill I will never forget – and I was Western Australian Junior Champion in most strokes.

I first learned the importance of being able to swim when, as a child, I fell in the river at the bottom of our garden so my parents soon taught me.

Since then, I've always stressed the importance and the fun that can be had swimming and I still try to swim a bit though I can manage only a few hundred yards these days.

Rolf Harris, London.

? DID the Search for Extraterrestrial Intelligence (SETI) once record a 'wow' signal indicating that a radio signal of extra-terrestrial origin had been received? What was the conclusion as to its origin?

THE 'wow!' signal was one of a series of signals from space thought to have originated from extra-terrestrial civilisation. In April 1965, the leading story on ITN *Evening News* was Intelligent Life Found In Space. A Tass communique had stated that 'scientists of Steinberg Astronomical Institute believe that we are not alone in the universe'. They had found that an object in space was sending out intense radio emissions which were varying regularly over a period of 100 days.

Today the source, CTA-102, is known to be a natural phenomenon from a very distant galaxy known as a Quazar, billions of light years away.

In 1967, Cambridge University scientists found a much more intense radio signal which turned on and off with great regularity. They thought at first that it could be coming from intelligent beings in space but wisely delayed an announcement until February 1968.

They had christened it LGM-1 (for Little Green Men) and it became clear that LGM-1 was a new type of star known as a Pulsar.

The 'wow!' signal picked up on August 15, 1977, at Ohio State University radio telescope was where researchers wrote 'wow!' on the data sheet. It was never heard again and there is no obvious star at that particular point in the sky.

Since nobody has proved otherwise, it must remain a possibility that this was an alien signal but this is highly unlikely; the signal probably originated here on earth.

Other more recent examples have been picked up by META (Mega-channel Extraterrestrial Association) at the radio telescope at Harvard Massachusetts. These occurred on October 10, 1986; August 14, 1989; August 16, 1989; and most significantly on November 15, 1989, where a signal was received that looks either man- or alien-made and is yet to be traced.

Finally, on May 9, 1990, the Parkes radio telescope picked up a signal which scientists believe is most like a signal an alien would make.

Keith Park, London.

Q MY Father thinks he once heard lyrics to the *Match of the Day* theme tune. Can anyone confirm this?

THE theme tune known as 'Match of The Day' was composed for the programme by Barry Stoller in 1964 for the launch of the first series, performed at the time by Barry Stoller and the Musicians.

No words were compiled at the time though it is known that, as with many popular tunes, it was used by the public as the base for rugby, religious and camp-fire tunes.

Mark Barden, BBC Sport, London.

IN the late Sixties, as a Sunday School Superintendent in Wembley (of all places), I came across and taught to kids the following lyrics (accompanying them on piano accordion). It was a great favourite with them:

Why don't you give your heart to Jesus
And ask Him to come in?
He saw your need from up in Heaven
And died to cleanse your sin.
Why don't you take Him as your captain
And let Him take your hand –
He will keep you and He'll guide you
Till you reach the Promised Land.
And when the final match is over,
(I know that we shall win)
Because He died to beat the devil
And save us from our sin.
And when the ref has blown his whistle
And the final match is up
I'll stand beside my Saviour
And receive the winners cup.

No doubt there are other lyrics on a less religious theme.

John Hirst, Ilford, Essex.

ARE ROWDY CYCLISTS BRINGING CYCLING INTO DISREPUTE?

DEAR *Answers*,—Notwithstanding the fact that cycling is one of the most healthful and delightful of sports, hundreds decline to give it a trial on account of the large element of rowdiness in it. This adverse opinion is gained for the sport by the thoughtlessness and ill-manners of a few riders.

Two or three Sundays ago, I put up at a well-known cycling hotel, not many miles this side of Guildford. The inn was two doors from the village church and the men who put up there were evidently orderly, gentlemanly fellows, with a due respect for other people's feelings.

Next door to the church, however, is a coffee-house and in there a most riotous meeting was going on. One cyclist was presiding at the piano, playing the latest comic songs, in the choruses of which many were joining.

All this was taking place next to a church in which Divine service was being solemnised.

Such conduct is rapidly bringing discredit on cycling and will, I am afraid, ultimately result in its being shunned by respectable people.

Quite recently the local authorities in a little town passed a by-law warning cyclists not to ride at a speed exceeding four miles an hour through their town, a regulation which, put in other words, means dismounting and walking one's machine through the place. I sincerely hope that those rowdy cyclists will see that the exercise of thoughtfulness on the road is to their own as well as to others' interests.

A Lover of Cycling, London, S.E.

DO more species of animals live on land or in the sea?

SCIENTISTS have a better understanding of how many stars there are in the galaxy than how many species there are on Earth. Estimates of global species have varied from 2 million to 100 million, with a best estimate of somewhere near 10 million. Only 1.4 million have been named.

At present, fewer species have been described in the ocean environment but the marine realm is more diverse. It hosts 31 of the world's 32 extant animal phyla, 14 of them almost exclusively marine.

Specific marine ecosystems are revealing remarkable diversity, the exotic coral reef systems being well documented for their beauty and range of species. But these are highly localised areas, while the great mass of the ocean, specifically the area below the photic zone and above the sea bed, where giant squid, deep-sea sharks and many other species lurk, have hardly been surveyed at all.

Marine diversity may have been underestimated: the discovery of hydrothermal vent systems has led some scientists to believe there are more than a million species left undescribed on the sea bed.

Only 16 of the world's extant animal phyla can be found on land but the highly varied nature of terrestrial ecosystems, from tropical rainforest to desert, has forced these phyla to evolve into a far greater range of micro environments. In one study of just 19 trees in Panama, for instance, 1,200 beetle species were discovered, 80 per cent of which were previously undescribed. At least 6 to 9 million, and possibly more than 30 million, species of arthropods are now thought to dwell in the Tropics with only a small fraction currently described.

Richard Harrington, Marine Conservation Society, Ross-On-Wye, Herefordshire.

WHY are the Irish police called the Garda?

THE Irish Free State was set up in early 1922, under the Anglo-Irish Treaty of December 1921, the culmination of many years of bloody conflict between Irish nationalists and various branches of the security services, engendering strong feelings on both sides.

One of those security services was the Royal Irish Constabulary, an armed police force which had borne the brunt of the battle against republicanism and had, in doing so, attracted much odium to the very name 'police'.

The newly independent Irish state opted to avoid the words 'police' and 'constable' for its new, unarmed law-enforcement agency and preferred the purely Irish and more pacific-sounding titles An Garda Siochana or Garda Siochana na hEireann (The Guardians of the Peace or Ireland's Guardians of the Peace.)

Laura Byrne, Liverpool.

? WHAT'S the difference between 'repetitive', 'repeated' and 'repetitious'?

THE word 'repeated' may be used to signify something which occurs at least twice whereas 'repetitive' or 'repetitious' are indicative of a more continuous or lengthier recurrence.

The difference between 'repetitive' and 'repetitious' is less marked but 'repetitive' is an adjective which precisely defines an action for what it is while 'repetitious' is less exact, more suggestive of the action being repetitive-like.

Both 'repetitive' and 'repetitious' share the connotation of unnecessary tedium in the recurrence of the event they are describing. 'Repeat' is generally free of this inference except, perhaps, in the context of TV programmes.

Mike Hollingsworth, Co Wicklow.

? DOES the word 'buxom' have anything to do with Buxton in Derbyshire?

THE word and the name are related. 'Buxom' comes from the Old English *bugan*, to bend or rock, plus 'some' and originally meant obedient or compliant.

The name of the town of Buxton also comes from *bugan*, combined with the Old English *stan*, a stone, suggesting that the place was named after a rocking stone, though no stone of this kind has ever been traced in the vicinity.

Adrian Room, author: Dictionary of Place Names in the British Isles, *Bloomsbury Publishing, London.*

? IN today's money how much was William Shakespeare worth when he died?

SHAKESPEARE'S 1616 will has survived but not an inventory of his goods so it's difficult to gauge his wealth at his death but we do know that between 1597 and 1605 he invested about £900 in property and land in and around Stratford-upon-Avon and, on his father's death in 1601, inherited the family home of Henley Street.

His properties and investments included New Place, the second largest house in Stratford, which cost about £120, a copyhold on a cottage in Chapel Lane, about 100 acres of land at a cost of £320 and a £420 stake in the Stratford tithes.

A labourer in Shakespeare's time was lucky to earn 4 shillings (20p) a week and a small town property could change hands for as little as £25 to £30.

In 1597, when his purchases began, Shakespeare was still only 33. His will includes a bequest of £300 to one of his daughters, £20 to his sister and around £13 in other minor legacies. It also mentions his collection of plate and a few other valuables.

Dr Robert Bearman, Shakespeare Birthplace Trust, Stratford-upon-Avon.

IF Shakespeare's three properties were sold on the current Stratford housing market, without their specifically Shakespearean connections, he would be a very wealthy man.

His birthplace on Henley Street would be worth about £500,000. New Place on the corner of Chapel Street and Chapel Lane, would be worth about £600,000 and the property on Chapel Street would be about £400,000. The current price for an acre of pasture land is about £2,500, so 100 acres would be worth £250,000.

On this basis, Will Shakespeare would have been worth a healthy £1,750,000, plus house contents, etc.

Graham Carter, Bigwood Chartered Surveyors, Stratford-upon-Avon.

❓ HAS anybody ever called 'Bingo!' after just 15 numbers?

THE odds of getting 15 consecutive numbers on one card from the start of a 90-number random bingo draw start from 6 to 1 for the first number and get progressively longer for each successive number drawn.

The last number drawn would be 76 to 1, reflecting the number of balls left in the container against the fact that only one number will do to complete the 15. The odds for each successive ball multiplied together come to a staggering 45,795,673,964,460,000 to 1.

You have 234 more chances of winning the National Lottery twice in succession.

T. Cox, Malvern.

MY father, Norman Albert Wilson, was the first to do so. On June 22, 1978, at the Guide Post Working Men's Club in Northumberland his call of 'House!' was met with derision from the other players, believing he was calling for a line.

He insisted it was a full house and the card was checked: he won £48. My dad passed away in 1990 but will always be the first name in the record books to have achieved this feat. On August 17, 1982, Ann Wintle, of Brynrethin,

Glamorgan, became the second person to win on the 15th number.

Kevin Wilson, Blyth, Northumberland.

? HOW did the first explorers to reach the South Pole know when they had arrived?

ROALD Amundsen had to prove he was at the South Pole and set about it very methodically. He and his colleague Helmer Hansson had been taking sextant readings throughout their journey and their first observations when they thought they might be at the Pole showed they were about four miles from the exact spot.

With their position fixed, Amundsen sent out members of his team to 'box' the Pole, to ensure they had covered the area in which it lay. This involved focusing on the artificial horizon at an awkward downward angle and getting the direct image of the sun and its reflection to touch exactly.

To his surprise, he found he was on the 123rd meridian East longitude instead of the 168th West which he had been following. But at that latitude, a degree of longitude is only 200 yards so they weren't far out.

They finally calculated they were 5.5 miles from the Pole, lying in an area which had already been 'boxed'. Followed the route they had planned, they proceeded dead straight until they reached it. Amundsen pitched camp and constructed two snow pedestals: one to hold the artificial horizon, the other on which to rest the sextant when not in use.

From the middle of the morning, hourly observations were taken for 24 hours. To make absolutely certain they had reached the Pole, Amundsen 'boxed' the last remaining minutes of arc by putting pendants a few miles in each direction, erecting poles and marking the shadow of the sun at hourly intervals. When they made a complete circle, he could be sure he was at the Pole, with the sun circling at the same elevation for a complete 24-hour period.

Captain Scott, on the other hand, made an error in his calculations, mistaking one of Amundsen's 'boxing' pendants for the Pole itself. Amundsen returned in triumph while Captain Scott and his compatriots marched to their deaths, and undying fame.

Charles Bruce, Chatham, Kent.

? IF you had one grain of corn on one square of a chessboard, two on the next and four on the next etc, what would be the weight of corn on the 64th square?

THE number of grains of corn on any square can be computed from the equation $2^{(n-1)}$. With n being 64, the total number of grains would be 9,223,372,036,854,775,808 − an awful lot of corn. This large number can be written as $9.223 * 10^{18}$.

There are about 23,000 grains of corn in a kilogram so the total weight of our corn is 4.0×10^{14} kg = 4.0×10^{11} metric tons = 400,000 million tons.

The total worldwide annual production of corn is around 400 million tons so our chessboard corn represents more than 1,000 years of corn production − more corn than has been grown worldwide since the dawn of creation. This amount of corn would cover the whole of the U.S. to a depth of 6in.

Mike Toft, Hoddesdon, Herts.

? LAURIE Lee's book *Cider With Rosie* tells of the great drought of 1921. How bad was it?

THE year 1921 still stands as the driest year on record for most of south-east and south England. Many people recall the drought of 1976 but that was very different. The heat was more intense but the drought broke at the end of August and was followed by one of the wettest autumns on record.

In 1921, the whole year was generally dry and warm and its impact on memory was all the more powerful because it followed a run of generally wet summers.

In 1921, ponds dried up, fields turned brown and water rationing was introduced in many areas but there was no comprehensive Government policy to combat the great aridity, no 'minister of drought'.

Rain gauges were empty for weeks on end and for the first time in our weather-conscious history, the driest places received as many headlines as the sunniest, wettest, hottest and coldest. Margate had 9.29in of rain. The Isle of Grain a mere 7.94in − comparable with Almeria, the driest place in Spain which averages only 7in of rain a year. In London, total rainfall for the year was 12 to 16in, about half normal.

It was one of the warmest years on record with summer yielding only slowly to an Indian summer. Before July 1983, the only record in Britain of a mean monthly temperature as high as 70°F was 70.1°F at Camden Square in July 1921. No month in 1976 matched that, despite a long run of days in the

90s. The sunshine, heat and dryness continued through October 1921: temperatures plummeted in November but it was still very dry. H. G. Wells's novel *Men Like Gods* refers to the parched appearance of the landscape.

Britain survived all this with little official intervention. Reservoir keepers, farmers and gardeners coped, with patience. No gurus or mystics were called upon, no teams of rain dancers or water diviners, though some old village wells were revisited in desperation.

We English in those days faced nature's hardships fairly and squarely, without resorting to self-deceiving rituals and those practices popular nowadays which make a mockery of reason and science. The drought was a manifestation of the profound cycles of nature and of our puny attempts to evade its effects.

The following year was much wetter and colder and people actually found themselves missing the great drought of 1921.

Alasdair Maclean, Stourbridge, West Midlands.

THE 1921 drought was one of the longest droughts of the 20th century, lasting almost the entire year. Ten of the 12 months were drier than average, and some were exceptionally so. February 1921 was the third driest February in the 20th century and June 1921 was the second driest June.

Some suffered more than most. Margate, in Kent, recorded only 236mm of rain for the whole year, the lowest rainfall amount recorded at any UK weather station in a calendar year.

Travel restrictions were imposed on the Thames because of the low water levels and fires became a problem as several square miles of tinder-dry countryside blazed. Temperatures were high as well. May, June and July were very warm months and were followed by an Indian summer, with October temperatures as high as 29°C (84°F).

Nathan Powell, Met Office, Bracknell, Berks.

? WHAT type of grease was used in the cartridges that allegedly provoked the Indian Mutiny?

THE grease issued by the British Army for the Enfield Rifle Musket was not, as popularly rumoured, made from cow or pig grease. C. H. Rhodes, whose definitive book on the subject *The British Soldier's Firearm 1850–1864* discusses the matter in depth, describes how in 1857 a committee including Colonel Hay, Colonel Gordon, Mr Abel, chief chemist to the British Army and

Mr Gunner, chief inspector of small arms, concluded that a grease combining one part tallow and five parts beeswax was the best mixture to ensure smooth cartridge flight out of the barrel.

By 1858, the Army had settled on an optimum lubricating mixture of four parts tallow and one part beeswax. The grease issued by the Army was probably not the real cause of the mutiny, it was caused by the political pressures of that time.

Mark Murray Flutter, Royal Armouries, Leeds.

THE Indian Mutiny was sparked by a rumour that the British had begun allocating the Army with a new type of rifle cartridge (which had to be bitten before opening) smeared with beef fat (violating Hindu law) and pork fat (violating Muslim law).

It wasn't true but this barely mattered as tensions were already running high. The mutiny lasted 13 months, from the rising at Meerut on May 10, 1857, to the fall of Gwalior on June 20, 1858.

The mutiny, regarded by many as India's first War of Independence, had important consequences on the structure of British India, leading to its extensive reorganisation.

India came increasingly under direct Crown rule as the British East India Company was dispossessed of its functions, a process which culminated in 1877 when Queen Victoria was crowned Empress.

Charles Pritchard, Much Wenlock, Shropshire.

❓DVLA adverts for personalised registration plates say it's illegal to mis-space letters and numbers but there are dozens of examples on the roads. How many people are prosecuted for doing this?

IN the 1970s, my father Michael James, a number plate manufacturer in Leeds for 20 years, had the number plate 00 77 00. The first two 00s were letters, followed by the number 7700.

For several years, the number was on an Aston Martin DB5, like the James Bond car, and he had three sets of plates, which he interchanged, spaced 00 77 00, 007 700 and in italics.

He kept a ruler and a copy of the number plate regulations in the glove compartment. He was stopped three times and on each occasion proved that the officer's car's number plate was actually illegally spaced. He was never prosecuted.

The regulations state that the space between the nearest parts of two letters or numbers should be 7/16ths of an inch. If you place an L next to a T, for example, it's difficult to state where the nearest parts are.

Complying with the regulations would make many plates illegible and certainly difficult to manufacture.

My father claimed that at least a third of all number plates in this country are illegal, not just personalised ones. He was called as an expert witness at a court case in London against a Mr Hudson who had the number HUD5ON on his Triumph Herald with the 5 made to look like an S.

The charges were for illegal spacing and the more serious charge of not having the correct registration number for the vehicle. Mr Hudson was fined £5 for each of the two charges relating to illegal spacing but my father was able to prove that no number plate has yet been issued in the UK with more than three letters, so the 5 was a five and not an S.

But the Triumph Herald was parked outside the court during the case and Mr Hudson was given another summons for the spacing offence.

Fiona C. James, Bingley, West Yorks.

? WHAT'S the difference between an icon and an idol?

AN icon is a painting of a holy figure, venerated and used as an aid to devotion in a Christian church. Metaphorically, it's a person or thing regarded as a symbol of something.

An idol is an image or representation of a god used as an object of worship. Metaphorically, it's a person or thing that is greatly admired.

These overlap in two ways. In past religious controversies, some people regarded icons (religious paintings) as little better than idols (images that are worshipped). In the 8th and 9th centuries, the Iconoclasts in the Byzantine church tried to suppress icons for this reason.

Meanwhile, it is obvious that someone who is, metaphorically, an idol (say, a film star whom people 'worship') could also be, metaphorically, an icon because he or she symbolizes some cultural value such as sex appeal.

Edmund Weiner, www.oed.com, Oxford English Dictionary.

I HAVE a carved pipe with the name 'Ally Sloper's Half Holiday' stamped on the bottom. Who was Ally Sloper and what is a 'Half Holiday'?

A HALF holiday is simply a half-day holiday, a free afternoon after a working morning.

Ally Sloper was a 19th-century comic character created by C. H. Ross under the pen-name Judy's Office Boy in 1873, and illustrated by Marie Duval.

Ally had a very large nose and a sloping forehead, and was something of a wide boy whose dishonest schemes usually went badly wrong.

In 1877, Ross published *Ally Sloper's Book of Beauty*, followed in 1884 by *Ally Sloper's Half Holiday*, which the pipe would have been advertising.

In World War I, the Army Service Corps was commonly referred to as Ally Sloper's Cavalry and in James Joyce's *Ulysses* (1922), a character is described as having an Ally Sloper nose.

David Elias, Nottingham.

WHY do the four corner pillars at Salisbury Cathedral bend outwards by nearly two feet?

BUILT over a period of 38 years, Salisbury Cathedral is one of the finest examples of Early English Gothic architecture. Completed in 1258, it lacked the present soaring spire but had a squat lantern rising a few feet above roof level at the central crossing.

Between 1285 and 1325, an unknown master mason added two further stages of a tower and the spire itself whose top rises an astounding 404ft above ground level. Visitors on tower tours today can still see the windlass which raised the stone to the base of the spire and the 13th-century wooden interior scaffold of the spire itself.

The spire added a further 6,400-ton load on the four main Purbeck marble pillars which, despite additional internal buttresses and external flying buttresses, can now be seen to bend outwards above the spire crossing by two feet. Were these massive pillars not of Purbeck marble, it's likely that the spire would have fallen by now. Further stone arches were added in the 15th century.

Today, the top of the spire is stable but leans 77.5cm (29in) from the perpendicular while its base has settled 8.9cm (3.5in) into the bed of gravel which underlies the Cathedral and provided the 13th-century builders with the foundation.

Alun Williams, Salisbury Cathedral.

DOES any natural food substance contain nandrolone?

NANDROLONE is an anabolic steroid, related to the male sex hormone testosterone. It promotes the build-up of muscle but has undesirable side effects including liver, heart and circulation damage. It is banned in competitive sport.

Some dietary supplements contain compounds similar to nandrolone but it may not be obvious from the label that such banned substances are present.

Nandrolone is produced naturally in animals such as the boar and horse, accumulating in the liver and other organs, but isn't found in meat from animals commonly eaten in this country.

According to a report presented to the UK Sports Council by the expert committee set up to look into this issue, eating good quality unprocessed muscle meat is unlikely to cause a positive urine test but competitors should avoid boar and horse offal.

Nandrolone is not present in any vegetables.

My advice to anyone thinking of taking a dietary supplement is to have it checked out by someone with the experience and knowledge to give accurate and safe advice.

Jane Griffin BSc (nutrition), sports dietitian, Ealing, London.

I sometimes see squirrels on my 24th floor balcony. Is it normal for them to climb buildings so high?

OF the two types of squirrel found in this country, the native red squirrel and the introduced grey, both of whose natural habitat is woodland, the red squirrel spends a larger part of its time high up in the tree canopy, coming to the ground only occasionally.

Grey squirrels take to the open more readily and are commonly found in urban parks and gardens. They are superb climbers and as long as there are perches or footholds for them to use, climbing to that height shouldn't be a problem for them, particularly if they think there's food on your balcony.

Georgette Shearer, The Mammal Society, Battersea Park Road, London.

WHEN and where in Britain were birth certificates first issued, and whose name was on the first?

CIVIL registration started throughout England and Wales on July 1, 1837. Registration was carried out by thousands of local registrars, reporting to more than 600 Superintendent registrars so it's impossible to say which of the certificates issued on that day was first.

At the end of September 1837, copies of all births registered in the first three months were made, sent to the General Register office, and given volume and page numbers.

David Mayall, Ashton-under-Lyne, Lancs.

❓ IS there still a pub in Britain that is cut off from the road at high tide?

THE Ship Inn is on Piel Island, about half a mile off Barrow-in-Furness. The island, containing a ruined castle, a row of five cottages and the pub, is half a mile across.

The three- to four-hour foot access to the island at low tide is a one-mile sand trek, avoiding treacherous mussel beds, but the main access is by ferry.

The island's only mainland-connected utility is water so it has to rely on generators for power. It has little to offer apart from beer and grass but is very popular with boat and yachtsmen who travel some distance for the privilege.

Traditionally, the landlord of The Ship Inn is also the King of Piel. The title comes from 1487 when Lambert Simnel declared himself king after invading from Ireland. Roddy Scarr was the last landlord and King of Piel, a character and a half. He retired in April 2006 and the new landlord, Steve Chattaway, has overseen extensive renovations to the pub by its new owner, Barrow Borough Council.

Tony Morgan, Barrow boatman, Barrow-in-Furness, Cumbria.

VERY close to where we live is The Pilchard Inn, on Burgh Island, Devon. At low tide one can walk to the island along a sandy causeway but when cut off by the tide, the island is reached by the unique 'sea tractor' which can operate in up to 7ft of water.

Barbara Jesty, Plymouth.

MY local, The Old Point House in the village of Angle in Pembrokeshire is conveniently cut off at every spring tide.

Situated at the mouth of Milford Haven, it has a long association with the RNLI which is still maintained today with the nearby lifeboat station.

Roger O'Callaghan, The Lodge, Angle, Pembrokeshire.

THE Ship Inn at Noss Mayo in South Devon is at the side of an estuary. Its car park is on the estuary itself and if the tide comes in while you're enjoying your lunch, your car is likely to be submerged very quickly.
Jez Wadd, Bolton, Lancs.

HOLY Island is probably the most famous place in Britain affected by tides. When the tide is up, it's possible to gain access to the island only by boat or aircraft.

The island has two delightful public houses, The Ship and The Crown and Anchor. Twice a day, the island is cut off and everyone on the island is stranded until the sea retreats.
Simon Paul Haddon, Newcastle.

IS Errol Flynn the only famous person to come from Tasmania?
THE Australian island state of Tasmania, known until 1855 as Van Diemen's Land, is 150 miles south of the mainland, across the Bass Strait. It has an area of 26,178 square miles – about three times the size of Wales – but a population of only around 460,000.

Its weather is not dissimilar to that of Britain. The population is of mostly British ancestry and there are no full-blooded Tasmanian Aborigines.

Apart from Errol Flynn, its stars include Australian cricketer David Boon, two former prime ministers of Australia, Joseph Lyons and Eric Reece, and Truganini, a lady famous simply for being the last Tasmanian Aborigine.

Tasmania also lays claim to Britain's own World War II hero, General Bernard 'Monty' Montgomery, 1st Viscount Montgomery of Alamein, who spent a couple of years there as a child when his father was an Anglican Minister there.
Katey Holgate, Melbourne.

RONNIE Moore MBE, twice world speedway champion (1954 and 1959) is from Hobart, Tasmania. Moore led the famous Wimbledon Dons, partnering Ivan Mauger to victory in the World Pairs.

He was awarded the MBE in the late Eighties and now lives in New Zealand where he runs training schools and has a stadium named after him.
Mike Ford, Ringland, Newport.

ANOTHER famous Tasmanian was Frederick Matthias Alexander (1869–

1955), founder of the world renowned Alexander Technique. When his promising career as a Shakespearean recitor was threatened by voice problems, he found a solution.

Known initially as 'the breathing man', he arrived in London in 1904 and taught many actors his method to help improve their stage performance.

Alexander believed human beings had lost the art of natural movement, resulting in poor posture, compromising functions such as respiration, circulation and digestion. His radical theory on this cause of many ailments and conditions attracted medical attention.

In 1936, 18 doctors sent the *British Medical Journal* a letter urging that his technique be included in the medical curriculum.

He gained support from eminent scientists such as Sir Charles Sherrington, Rudolph Magnus and George Coghill. In the U.S. his pupils included John Dewey and the Huxley brothers.

Despite this, because of his Tasmanian origins, his theory was dismissed by others as 'the ramblings of an Australian with an original but uncultivated mind'. In 1948, he won a famous libel case in South Africa against Dr Ernst Jokl who had labelled his work 'quackery'.

Research has since confirmed much of his theory but his work has yet to be formally recognised by modern medical practice.

Roy Palmer, Society of Teachers of the Alexander Technique, Keysoe, Beds.

WHY do Americans say: 'I don't have...' rather than: 'I haven't got...'?

WHEN I started school in the Forties, the first rule of grammar instilled into us was that there is no such word as 'got'; also, 'seldom don't and seldom won't, never can't and never shan't'.

Bridget Hole, Maidenhead.

WHEN I was at school, spelling and grammar were important subjects. We were taught: 'got and what are wanted not and done is gone forever'.

I never use the words 'got' or 'done' but could never understand why 'what' was not permissible. We didn't question our teachers in those days. I have since realised that what was meant was that it should not be used as a single query: 'What?'

Winifred Henry, Fleet, Hants.

MANY Americans in fact say: 'I don't got...' They appear to have picked on the verbs: to have, to do and to get; they then mix and use them at random. They've even invented a new verb: 'gotten'.

So now we hear sentences like: 'I don't got a car, I've gotten a headache, can I get the cheque, please?' Their national pastime is to split infinitives but some at least know when to use 'whom' and not 'who'.
Terry Green, Ryde, IoW.

MY English teacher told the class: 'Never let me catch you using the word "got"'. Apparently, it is absolutely superfluous under any circumstances. For example 'Have you got a new car?' should be 'Do you have a new car?'

I've remembered her words all my life. It seems the Americans have got it right for once, I mean, of course, it seems the Americans are right for once.
Jean Spindler, Swindon, Wilts.

NONE of our great authors shares the inhibitions of such teachers of grammar. The words occur in most of the Sherlock Holmes stories, in the Bible, in Shakespeare, in *Alice in Wonderland* and in the poems of William Blake and Rupert Brooke.

And the *Mikado*'s Lord High Executioner sings 'I've got a little list.' Perhaps his list should be expanded to include teachers who take it on themselves to condemn perfectly good English words.
Ken Warren, Dorridge, West Midlands.

? WHEN did the Americans start putting 'In God We Trust' on their currency?

IN God We Trust replaced Mind Your Business as the motto on all U.S. coins large enough to hold it following two Congressional Acts of 1865.

It appeared on the eagle ($10 gold coin), double eagle ($20), half eagle ($5), silver dollar, half dollar and quarter. It still appears on the last three.

The motto was parodied by settlers who, made bankrupt by droughts from 1887 to 1891, painted on their covered wagons 'In God We Trusted, In Kansas We Busted' before returning to the East.

After the War of Independence, America adopted a decimal coinage system and the first dollars minted were issued in Philadelphia in 1794, following the Coinage Act of 1792.

The gold dollar, a small coin, issued only between 1849 and 1889, contained

24.75g of pure gold while the silver dollar contained 371.25g of pure silver –
but revisions changed the silver and gold content over the years.

Kevin Heneghan, St Helens, Merseyside.

❓ DO the Wasps have a B(ee) team?

WASPS Rugby Union Football Club, formed in 1867 at the now defunct
Eton and Middlesex Tavern in North London, before the Rugby Football Union
had begun as an administrative body, took its name from the fashion in that
Victorian period for naming sporting clubs after insects, birds and animals.

Presiding over the club in its embryonic stage was its first president James
Pain Elected and he was still at the helm when the Rugby Football Union was
formed on January 26, 1871.

As an established club, Wasps were invited to join the Union as a Founder
Member and would have acquired this status were it not for a calamitous
mix-up. The team turned up at the wrong pub on the wrong day at the wrong
time and so forfeited the right to be called a Founder Member.

The club's first home was in Finchley Road, North London, though subsequent years saw grounds being rented in various parts of London.

In 1923 Wasps moved back to an earlier home at Sudbury, eventually buy-
ing the ground outright. The team currently graces Loftus Road on home
matchdays but the Sudbury ground is still used for training and is considered
by die-hard fans and players alike as the club's spiritual home.

And, yes, we Wasps do have a B team.

Lucy Finnegan, Wasps RUFC, London.

❓ WHEN the Tyne pedestrian and cycle tunnel between Jarrow and East Howdon was opened in 1951, its escalators were reportedly the longest in the world. Are they still?

THE longest escalators in the UK are now the three parallel flights at the
Angel underground station in London, each measuring 197ft (60m) from top
to bottom. Built by French engineers as part of a station facelift costing £70
million, they broke down three days after being put into operation on August
12, 1992, but are now running smoothly.

The longest escalator ride in the world is the four-section outdoor escalator
at Ocean Park, Hong Kong, which has an overall length of 745ft (227m)
through a total rise of 377ft (115m).

Next longest is the single 729-step escalator on the underground at what was formerly Lenin Square station, in Moscow, which rises through 195ft 9.5in (59.68m).

Back in 1951, the Tyne Tunnel escalators were easily the longest in the world, rising through 85ft (25.9m) in an overall length of just short of 193ft. They remained the UK record holders until completion of the Angel escalators.
Tim Mickleburgh, Grimsby, Lincs.

❓ WHAT became of the missionary ship, *John Williams*, launched by Princess Margaret and bought with old 'ship' ha'pennies, collected by Sunday School children?

WHEN the *John Williams VI* was named by HRH Princess Margaret at Tower Bridge in 1948, it was one of seven John Williams ships, the first of which dated from 1864.

It sailed to the South Seas and was based in Suva, Fiji, with an annual sailing programme between the Gilbert Islands, Cook Islands, Ellice Islands, Samoa and Papua New Guinea. In November 1962, we needed a smaller ship to cut our costs and be more effective. We changed our base to Tarawa in Kiribati and sold the ship to Burns Philp. We were told the *John Williams VI* later sank.
Nina Orchard, Council for World Mission, London.

BORN at Tottenham in 1796, John Williams was only 20 when he and his wife sailed to the South Seas to work for the London Missionary Society. He was clever with his hands and helped the islanders build strong new houses.

He set up a school, teaching children and adults to read the Bible and soon many of them wanted to help him take the Christian message to other places.

Williams installed local teachers on other islands where they persuaded people to abandon their idols and learn the Christian life and worship.

Frustrated by his reliance on passing ships to travel between the islands, Williams began the difficult task of building himself a three-masted ship. In four months she was sea-worthy and he named her *Messenger of Peace*.

After 18 years in the Pacific, Williams came back to Britain, where his story drew large audiences and he raised the money for a college for his island pastors and for another ship, the *Camden*, in which he sailed back to the Pacific with other missionaries.

Leaving the others behind, Williams took the *Camden* to the New Hebrides islands, peopled by dangerous cannibals, where no missionary had yet set foot. He was clubbed to death on the beach at Erramonga in 1839.

Joseph Smythe, Leytonstone, East London.

❓ OUTSIDE Earls Court Underground station there's a *Doctor Who*-style police telephone box. Are there any others left?

THE Earls Court police box is a replica, unveiled on April 18, 1996. Local residents requested a police officer permanently on duty outside the tube station. As the budget wouldn't allow this, Brompton Crime Prevention Unit decided a new police box was the next best option.

The wooden box, constructed by London Underground carpenters, had a cylindrical closed-circuit camera on its roof and a push-button intercom link to the nearest police station behind a panel in the front door.

Police boxes began life in the 1880s as Police Signal Posts. Over the years, they underwent several variations. The *Doctor Who*-style was designed by Scotsman Gilbert MacKenzie-Trench and first appeared on the streets in 1929.

By the Fifties, the police box was a common sight in Britain, with almost 700 in London alone. By 1969 however, police communications had progressed, with two-way radios taking over. In that year, the Home Secretary ordered the destruction of London's boxes and police boxes rapidly disappeared from the rest of the country.

Very few are left today. Four remain in Glasgow (all listed buildings), in Buchanan Street, Wilson Street, Great Western Road and Royal Exchange Square. There's also a police box still standing in the grounds of Peel Centre, the Metropolitan Police Training Establishment at Hendon, which can be seen from the Underground train travelling on the Northern Line between Hendon Central and Colindale.

Richard Bignell, Rainham, Kent.

I'M a PC in Huddersfield, West Yorkshire, and we still have a *Doctor Who*-style police telephone box in Northgate, Almondbury, Huddersfield. This box is still operational and is a listed building.

PC Stephen Allen, Kirkburton, Huddersfield.

ON receiving our new kit issue two weeks into our training at Hendon a few years ago, we received among our handcuffs, whistle, etc – a key!

Our 'old sweat' instructor laughed that this was to the only two remaining police boxes, one in the grounds of Hendon and the other outside Earls Court Tube Station.

All police officers in the Met theoretically still carry their key with them (and have to produce it when so ordered).

PC Chris Parker, London.

THERE'S a well-preserved police box in the grounds of the police station and magistrates court of our beautiful floral market town of Wetherby in West Yorkshire.

Gerry Davies, Wetherby, West Yorks.

CHEPSTOW Road, Newport, has one of the old Thirties police boxes which is not only listed but has a colourful *Doctor Who* scarf painted around it.

Haydn Davis, Newport, Gwent.

❓ THERE were plans for a 500ft tower block to be built in Birmingham. How high would it have to be for a person to be able to see the sea from the top of it?

THE average person, standing at sea level, with eyes 5ft from the ground, sees the horizon at 2.9 miles away. A simple method of calculating the distance of the horizon is to take the square root of the height in feet above sea level and increase by a third, to give the approximate distance in miles.

From a height of 20ft, the distance to the horizon is 5.9 miles; from 50ft, 9.3 miles; from 100ft 13.2 miles; from 500ft, 29.5 miles; from 1,000ft, 41.6 miles; from 5,000ft, 93.1 miles; and from 20,000ft, 186.2 miles.

The nearest open sea (as opposed to river or channel) from Birmingham is the Irish Sea off the coast of Wirral in Merseyside, just over 80 miles away.

So, if Birmingham were at sea level, the tower would need to be almost 5,000ft high for you to see the sea from the top of it. The city of Birmingham is an average 400ft above sea level so the tower would need to be almost 4,600ft high, more than three times the height of the world's current tallest skyscraper, the 1,483ft Petronas Towers in Kuala Lumpur, Malaysia.

John Riley, Cannock, Staffs.

DOES THE STUDY OF SHORTHAND INTERFERE WITH THE KNOWLEDGE OF SPELLING?

DEAR *Answers*,—As a shorthand writer of four years' standing, holding one of Mr Pitman's certificates, I think I am competent to answer in the affirmative.

When a person is beginning to learn this valuable and interesting art, they have only to think of the sound of the word, and write as it is spoken, not as it is written.

For instance: 'The outcry because a few isolated kaces of kolera have okurred in England seems very absurd to one who has spent the last twenty years of his life in India. and therefore it is not surprising that a falling off in a person's knowledge of spelling accrues from the study of shorthand.

But when the learner gets further into his studies and obtains the mastery over shorthand, his knowledge of spelling will, as I have proved, return to him. Students do not then need to think so simply because they will have learned what are called the 'grammalogues' which are used instead of forming the whole words.

Robert M. Elliott, West Hill, Hastings.

As a teacher of shorthand for many years – my certificate is dated December, 1875 – I should like to place before you the result of some experiments which I have been rash enough to try on my own children.

From their earliest infancy they have been taught the phonetic spelling, and were kept in ignorance of the common alphabet until they were able to read by means of the phonetic or natural alphabet. When they were sent to school, it was thought their education had been ruined for life and that they would never be ale to spell in the ordinary way.

The scene is rather changed now, as, although unable to read the ordinary books when first entering school, they soon took their place among the best spellers and readers of their class. After the first term or two they have usually brought home reports showing them to have obtained the highest number of marks in spelling, reading, and writing

? WHERE is the longest wire fence in the world?

THE world's longest wire fence is the 3,299-mile (5,309km) Dingo Fence, which separates Australia's main sheep farming areas in the east from the deep outback.

The fence is well over twice the length of the Great Wall of China and came about after the earlier Western Australian No 1 Rabbit Proof Fence was built in the early part of the last century. This fence had been an unsuccessful attempt to stop the westward advance of the rabbit, an animal that had caused environmental havoc in eastern states when it was introduced in the 19th century.

One noticeable bonus of the fence was that the dingo population could be controlled, reducing the high number of attacks on economically important sheep. Holding back the predatory dingo required a much longer fence and so the dingo fence was constructed.

The dingo fence today is called the Barrier Fence in Queensland, where it stretches for 1,553 miles (2,500km). It joins the Border Fence in New South Wales and travels another 363 miles (584km) before being connected to the 1,383-mile (2,225km) Dog Fence in South Australia.

The fence is at least 6ft high and goes down more than 1ft into the earth. It costs £1 million a year to maintain.

Tina Harper, Perth, Western Australia.

? ARE sumo wrestlers physically fit?

COMPETITIVE sumo wrestlers are fit for sumo wrestling, but what is physical fitness?

A sumo wrestling bout usually lasts just a few seconds, the aim being to push the opponent off the circle, which calls for great strength and the perfect timing of a powerful push. Each competitor has to resist drives made by his opponent: the larger your opponent, the more difficult it is to shift him off the competition area.

So these wrestlers tend to be muscularly strong and powerful but they would be struggling very soon after the start of an endurance event such as a marathon. They aren't prepared for enduring exercise and don't need to be aerobically trained.

To make himself more difficult to move off the competition platform, a sumo wrestler bulks himself up by overeating as well as by muscular training. The extra energy taken in as food is stored as fat and the extra fat stores are obvious in the layers or folds hanging off the massive thighs.

The effect of the wrestlers' extraordinary diet includes raised cholesterol, increased blood pressure and the risk of cardiovascular disease and liver damage. Life expectancy among sumo wrestlers tends to be shorter than in the normal population.

Sumo wrestling has cultural and religious significance in its spiritual home, Japan. When accepted into a 'stable', the wrestler is considered a privileged person. It's not a sport which is open to all and those who enter it must be highly motivated to adopt its lifestyle.

Prof Tom Reilly, Research Institute for Sport and Exercise Sciences, Henry Cotton Campus, Liverpool.

? WHAT is the earliest known portrait of Christ?

THE Bible makes no mention of Christ's looks and there are no portraits from His lifetime. The earliest surviving Christian images represent Christ through symbols and metaphors. Images of the Good Shepherd in the catacombs outside Rome survive from about AD 200 but although they stood for Christ they were never intended to show what He looked like.

The earliest descriptions of Christ's physical appearance date from the 3rd century and describe Him as 'beautiful with long curly hair and eternally young' and the earliest images of Christ, as Christ, show Him as beardless, like representations of the Roman god Apollo.

One of the very earliest 'portraits' of this type is the mosaic pavement from the first half of the 4th century AD, discovered in Hinton St Mary, Dorset, in 1963 and now in storage in the British Museum.

The bearded face of Christ with which we are familiar was established as the predominant version of Christ's features in the 6th century. One of the most famous early examples is an icon that survives in St Catherine's monastery in the Sinai desert. This period also saw the emergence of legends surrounding certain images believed to be miraculous true likenesses.

The most important of these was a cloth known as the Mandylion of Edessa, claimed to have been made by Christ Himself, his features being miraculously transferred onto the cloth when He wiped His face with it.

A copy of the Mandylion, claimed by some to be the original, is in the Barnabite monastery of St Bartholomew in Genoa, Italy, and another is in St Peter's, Rome.

From the 13th century onwards, the most reproduced of these images in the West has been The Veronica, a cloth with which, according to legend, St Veronica wiped Christ's face when He was carrying the cross and on which his features were miraculously imprinted.

The most famous 'miraculous' image is The Turin Shroud which, despite the fact that carbon-14 tests have dated it to the 14th century is believed by some to be the cloth in which Christ was buried and onto which an impression of his body was transferred.

Cathy Hinde, The National Gallery, London.

WHAT happened to the crown which used to be on the top of the English national football badge above the three lions?

THE England football team's heraldic emblem of three lions derives from the royal coat of arms and there has been a lot of delving into history recently to establish the origin of the three-lion motif.

It's believed that Henry I was the first English king to adopt a lion as his heraldic emblem, a probable reference to the 'Lion of England' title given him by Geoffrey of Monmouth. Two additional lions are thought to have been added as consequences of marriages by Henry I and Henry II into families which also had lions on their crests.

Richard I is the first king known to have borne into battle the coat of arms of three golden lions on a red field and the royal lions and crown still feature in the crests of many English towns and organisations, sporting and other.

In 1948, an FA committee considered how to make the design unique to football and when Billy Wright led out the England team to play Scotland at Wembley in April the following year, his shirt carried the three lions within a shield – but no little crown on top.

David Barber, The FA, Lancaster Gate, London.

❓ HOW expensive would petrol have to get before it's worth my while trading in my Lotus Elise for a horse-and-gig for my daily nine-mile commute to work?

IF you were to make a straight swap for a horse and gig you will lose money. Assuming you work 250 days in the year and your only journey is to work and back (18 miles), you will travel 4,500 miles.

The Lotus Elise's fuel tank has a capacity of eight gallons and achieves about 30mpg in urban conditions, so a tank of fuel will cost about £38 and take you 240 miles.

To travel 4,500 miles you will spend about £1,400 on fuel. Add to this a yearly service £300, insurance £350, road tax, plus £120 for other sundries such as AA membership, screen wash etc you get a yearly running cost of about £2,500.

To run a stabled horse, you will have livery costs of £1,560 to £2,080, hay, straw and shavings at £780 to £1,300, feed at £260 to £520, vets' fees at £35, insurance at £240 to £480, farrier at £360 to £405 and worming at £90 to £135; a total of £3,300 to £4,950.

Bear in mind, however, that a new Lotus Elise costs £23,000 to £27,000, where you could get a good horse and gig for a fifth of the price.

Pauline Temple, Southend, Essex.

❓ WHICH country has been at peace the longest?

SWITZERLAND which, although it has been invaded, hasn't been involved in a foreign war since 1515, a few years earlier than almost all New World and some Old World countries were even formed.

Before that time, the area that now makes up Switzerland was constantly at war. The original inhabitants, the Celtic Helvetii, were overrun by the Romans, the Germanic tribes of the Alemanni, Burgundians, Ostrogoths and Franks and then came under the Holy Roman Empire.

In 1291, the cantons of Uri, Schwyz and Unterwalden declared their independence from the Habsburg regime and were joined a few years later by Lucerne, Zurich and Bern. The Austrians, followed by the Burgundians, tried to halt this move towards freedom but by the early 16th century the Swiss had emerged as a unified confederation of cantons, a military force in its own right, strong enough to take on the French for control of parts of northern Italy.

In 1515, the Confederation was dealt a serious blow when its forces were beaten by the French at the Battle of Marignano but, while this checked any outward aggression by the Swiss cantons, other countries remained wary of incursions into Switzerland.

In 1798, when Napoleon controlled most of Europe, the French entered Switzerland and set up a Helvetic Republic but after Napoleon's final defeat, the Congress of Vienna restored the Swiss control of their country and guaranteed its future neutrality.

This neutrality of Switzerland has been tested on several occasions, most notably during World War I when the French and Italian-speaking Swiss were at political odds with their German-speaking compatriots but the country held together and in 1920 was the obvious choice for the home for the new League of Nations.

In World War II, Switzerland the country was better prepared and, despite being surrounded by German-controlled territory, maintained its neutrality.

Switzerland backs up its neutral status by conscription of all males from the age of 20 and maintains a militia force of more than half a million men under arms.

Peter Owen, Cambridge.

❓ WHICH is the most valuable tropical fish in the world?

● RED Arowanas are freshwater bony fish of the family Osteoglossidae, known as 'Bony tongues' or 'Dragon fish'. The Asian versions of these, found in the slow-moving waters of Indonesia and Malaysia, are the most prized tropical fishes and their value can range from hundreds of pounds to tens of thousands depending on rarity and type.

The Arowana used to be divided by its colour variations into Red Arowana, Gold Arowana, Green Arowana, etc, and still is by collectors, but since the form and the behaviour of all of these colour morphs are the same, they are now treated as a single species.

Arowanas have a bony, elongated body which is covered by large, heavy scales and a mosaic pattern of canals, hence Dragon fish. For the Chinese,

Japanese and related cultures, the dragon is a symbol of good luck and prosperity and makes them highly sought after. The name 'bony tongues' is derived from a toothed bone on the floor of the mouth, the 'tongue', equipped with teeth that bite against teeth on the roof of the mouth.

The most expensive fish, a 7in golden albino Arowana, was sold to an unnamed Japanese buyer for 20 million yen, about £100,000.

Kurt Wallen, Slough, Berks.

? WHY do we celebrate April Fool's Day?

THERE are many claims about the origins of April Fool's Day – also known as All Fool's Day – the most common being that it stems from the culmination of the week-long celebration which began on March 25, our original date for New Year.

Other suggestions are that it is related to the Holi Festival which takes place in India at the end of March or that it derives from the Roman festival of Cerealia.

Leslie Meeching, Newcastle.

IN April, the cuckoo, emblem of simpletons, comes. So in Scotland, a victim is an April gowk, a Scots dialect word for a stupid person or cuckoo.

Alan Thorburn, West Kilbride, Ayrshire.

A REFERENCE to a Festival of the Fool can be found in the Bible, in Proverbs 32. This refers to a 'yearly celebration before the summer begins' when 'the fools of the world look for time to waste'.

The fact that a reference is made to a 'yearly celebration' suggests that the April Fool's Day we now know has grown from this Biblical tradition.

Rolf Paoli, Bonnie Rumeve, Tyrone.

? MY family has a goldfish that is 22 years old. Is this a record?

THE *Guinness Book of Records* reports several cases of goldfish (*Carassius auratus*) in China living for at least 50 years. Closer to home, it also gives the story of Fred, a goldfish owned by A. R. Wilson, of Worthing, West Sussex, which died in 1980 at the grand old age of 41.

Heather Hutton, Carlisle.

GOLDFISH can live for a long while, growing only to a size suitable for their surroundings. A goldfish in a lake may be 20cm long while a similar aged one in a fish tank may be only 5cm.

Scientists believe some goldfish still alive in France once belonged to Marie Antoinette, wife of Louis XVI. That puts them at between 200 and 230 years old.

Ben Clifford, South Croydon, Surrey.

AN aquarium goldfish is totally reliant on the care its owners give it. As a member of the carp family, goldfish should live 30 years and often do. Some carp, such as koi, can outlive their owners.

Dr David Ford, Aquarian Advisory Services, Elland, West Yorks.

❓ IS it true that if you don't wash your hair for months, it starts cleaning itself?

THIS is like saying that if your face or body weren't washed for months they would self-clean. Environmental influences and dust, together with body secretions which attract dust, build up progressively. The longer you leave hair without washing it, the dirtier it becomes. Unwashed hair would be lank, dull, greasy and smelly.

Philip Kingsley, author: The Complete Hair Book, Philip Kingsley Trichological Clinic, London.

THE root area of hair which has been left alone is generally very healthy because of the hair's natural oils but the ends get very damaged and so hair loses its overall lustre.

The most overwhelming characteristic of unwashed hair is an unpleasant odour. Some people have perceived benefits from leaving hair unwashed but you should use a good cleanser and conditioner regularly.

Bruce Masefield, Vidal Sassoon, Manchester.

A FRIEND who spent four months in the Tanzanian bush for Operation Raleigh was very enthusiastic about the merits of not washing one's hair for a long time. He said his group made a pact to leave their hair unwashed for the entire period they were in cahoots with nature.

Their hair became greasy and tangled at first but soon, he insisted, the natural oils made their hair 'clean itself' and restored it to normal.

Ben Lane, Aylesbury, Bucks.

MY husband has left his hair unwashed for a couple of years. It doesn't smell, has stopped falling out and he doesn't have dandruff. He used to suffer from an itchy scalp which has now cleared up.

Mrs I. Justin, Exeter, Devon.

? WHO was the 'King of Lampedusa'?

WHILE gathering witness reports for the audio cassette *The Siege of Malta*, we were told about a Swordfish pilot named Flight Sergeant George Cohen who, running short of fuel, put down over the small Italian island of Lampedusa, halfway between Malta and Tunisia.

He landed safely and had drawn his pistol with the intention of setting fire to his plane when the Italian Garrison Commander arrived. Thinking this was a precursor to an invasion of the island (it had just been bombarded) the Commander informed Cohen that they would like to surrender to the 'liberating forces'.

Cohen made the Commander sign a piece of paper to that effect, ordered his tank to be filled with fuel and flew back to Malta with the surrender of the island. He was subsequently nicknamed the King of Lampedusa and the Jewish community in London's East End wrote and performed a musical play in his honour.

Philip Evans, editor, Images of War Audio Series, Paradise, Gloucs.

I AM now the 'King of Lampedusa' having inherited the title after my pilot, Sergeant Sydney Cohen, was lost flying home after the end of World War II.

I was wireless operator/gunner aboard the Swordfish he landed on the small Italian island on June 12, 1943, when we were surprised to be presented with the surrender of the garrison. The third crew member, navigator Peter Tait, survived the war but died some years ago.

Sgt-Pilot Cohen wasn't my regular pilot but we were called out from Malta that morning to help search for survivors from an aircraft which had ditched in the sea. We found nothing and set course for base but arrived over an unfamiliar island which was being bombed by American Lightnings.

We wanted to return to Malta but, with our instruments malfunctioning and limited fuel, we decided to land on Lampedusa and give ourselves up. As Sgt Cohen put the plane down on what was left of the runway, we saw white strips fluttering and I kept the machine gun trained on the very odd couple who approached us.

An elaborately dressed member of a crack Italian regiment, accompanied by a fellow who looked as if he had spent the night sleeping in a ditch, came up and jabbered away in Italian, which none of us spoke, until we understood that they thought we had landed to accept the garrison's surrender – all 3,000 of them! They had been bombed and shelled a lot and had had enough.

After some 'negotiations' with Sgt Cohen in their HQ, interrupted by more Allied raid warnings, they gave us a scrap of paper with a signature on it declaring their intention to give up. We flew to Tunisia and handed the Italian surrender chit to the Americans there.

Les Wright, Bournemouth, Dorset.

I WAS one of the RAF personnel hurriedly assembled to garrison the island after it surrendered. We sailed from Sousse, Tunisia, for the short trip across the Mediterranean on a tank-landing craft.

My abiding memory of Lampedusa was that it was overrun by fleas. Several of us had our hair completely cut off by an Italian barber to gain some relief.

J. Euston, ex-RAF wireless mechanic, Prestatyn, Clwyd.

I KNEW Sydney Cohen well through my duties as briefing officer at 17 Staging Post, Tripoli (Castel Benito). On August 26, 1946, I was due for demobilisation when Cohen came through on his way home and I requested permission to fly home with him. This was refused and I had to come home by boat.

In the event, Cohen's plane crashed in the Straits of Dover and nothing was found of the wreckage. His name is inscribed on the memorial at Runnymede.

Gabriel Dinerstein, Finchley, London.

THE play *The King of Lampedusa*, at the Grand Palais Jewish Theatre in London's Commercial Road, was highly successful in the late 1940s, enjoying the longest run of any Yiddish-language play in Britain and attracting many non-Yiddish speakers to see a top cast including Meyer Tzelnicker and his daughter Anna. There are still occasional revivals of it at Jewish venues.

Ray Peentner, Edgware, Middx.

I GAINED a unique insight into this from the enemy's point of view. While on guard duty in Tunisia, I picked out PoWs Gino Tatorini of La Spezia and Joe Donato of Genoa, for general duties.

Joe had been the main English speaker on Lampedusa. He said when

Swordfish pilot Syd Cohen ran short of fuel and landed on the island, he was met by a crowd of Italians and put up his hands to surrender.

But the Italians shouted 'No no! We surrender!' He said: 'No, we surrender!' They said: 'No, we surrender!' And thus it was.

T. Parkinson, London NW5.

❓ IS there any evidence, apart from the Bible, that the Romans used crucifixion as a form of execution?

THERE is a considerable amount. Following the defeat of the Spartacus revolt in 71 BC, an estimated 6,000 captives were crucified on the Via Appia between Capua and Rome.

Things didn't change under the Empire: the account by Josephus of the seven years it took the legions to crush the Jewish rebellion that started in AD 66 has numerous references to crucifixion. On one occasion, 800 were condemned to it, 2,000 on another, 'too many to count' on yet a third – while the threat of torture and crucifixion ('the most pitiful of deaths') of Jewish leader Eleazar within sight of the walls of a besieged city was enough to secure its surrender.

Crucifixion was the primary form of punishment for slaves, bandits, pirates and foreign dissidents. It was banned early in the 4th century AD by the emperor Constantine, a convert to Christianity. He replaced it with the furca – a wooden fork from which the victim hung by the neck until dead.

H. J. P. Arnold, Legio Secunda Augusta, Havant, Hants.

❓ ARE ants, wasps and other sugar-loving insects fooled by sugar substitutes such as Nutrasweet?

BARRY Bolton, world expert on ants, tells me that to the best of his knowledge, no one has ever experimented to see if sugar-feeding ants are fooled, though he believes they would probably be attracted to, and feed on, such substitutes.

The common black ant that comes into our kitchens will take any sugary food and should easily be fooled by Nutrasweet.

Gina Dobson, Natural History Museum, London SW7.

WHO needs detailed research to work this one out? I know sugar-loving insects aren't fooled by Nutrasweet.

While on holiday in Jersey with a friend who drank the 'real thing', I stuck to drinking the diet version. When we put our cans down beside our deckchairs, ants immediately gathered to sup the remnants from my friend's can and studiously ignored mine.

Miss P. J. Hayes, London E6.

⍰ IS there anybody who has to cross a time-zone boundary in their regular daily journey to work?

IT might be possible to get yourself an extended lunch hour, or a very short one, if you were employed on the Hoover Dam, which straddles the Arizona-Nevada border, and crossed it to pick up your sandwiches. There's a one-hour time difference spanning the 415 yards between both ends of the dam.

There would also seem to be possibilities of short shifts or generous overtime, depending on where one clocked on and off.

P. B. Jones, Hadleigh, Essex.

⍰ WHY is the BBC known as Auntie?

THE nickname 'Auntie' sprang from the idea that, rather like a favourite aunt, the BBC was always there to 'pour out hot cups of tea' and let you know everything was all right even though, compared with others, she was rather bland and gentle.

In the late 1970s, entertainer Arthur Askey claimed he first used the term 'Auntie' for the BBC during a Band Wagon programme in the Thirties; but the nickname gained currency from 1955, when commercial TV was introduced to our screens.

It started among BBC employees but was soon taken up by newspaper journalists, including the late *Daily Mail* TV critic Peter Black, who in 1959 became one of the first journalists to mention the 'auntie' image when he interviewed the new head of the BBC, Hugh Carleton Greene.

Jeff Raglan, Queen's Park, London.

⍰ WHY are flat-footed people not accepted by the Army?

FLAT-FOOTED people certainly weren't rejected by the Army in 1943. I have completely flat feet, but was accepted as A1 when I volunteered and successfully completed infantry officers' training, including a 35-mile march in full equipment. I then commanded an infantry platoon in Europe.

My success was down to the Army boot which was designed to fit a properly formed foot, with the result that my foot arches were virtually suspended from the ankle, creating artificial arches which enabled my feet to act efficiently. My ankles were very painful for the first week or so, but after that I could do anything any other soldier could. Now I have to wear arch supports.

Ex-Capt John Amsden, Seaforth Highlanders, London NW3.

I APPLIED to join the Tank Corps in 1931 but the Medical Officer told me I had flat feet and was unfit for military service.

Being in a reserved occupation, I was exempt from call-up at the start of World War II but I allowed the exemption to lapse in 1942 and was accepted into the Army as A1 fit. I did 20-mile marches and a bit of boxing in training, then landed on Gold Beach on D-Day. As far as the Army's concerned, when you're needed, you're fit.

S. G. Fryer, West Wellow, Hants.

❓ARE there any good alternatives to the sentence 'The quick brown fox jumps over the lazy dog' incorporating all letters of the alphabet?

IN our calligraphy class, we used 'a large brown fawn jumped quickly over white zinc boxes' and 'many big jackdaws quickly zipped over the fox pen'.

Mrs R.V. Battersby, Eastcote, Middx.

I OFFER: 'Pack my box with five dozen liquor jugs.'

K. F. Chappell, Bristol.

A FURTHER option is 'Jackdaws love my big sphinx of quartz.' The 'fox' has 35 letters, 'liquor jugs' has 32 and 'jackdaws' just 31.

The only one I've ever encountered which uses just the 26 letters of the alphabet, admittedly with proper names, is 'Z. D. Burk might vex J. Q. Plow's fancy.'

Colin Partis, Grimsby, Lincs.

ANOTHER 26-letter example is: 'J. D. Schwartz flung V. Q. Pike my box.'

There may be many other such pangrams (sentences incorporating every letter of the alphabet) by merit of the fact that the alphabet's 26 letters can be

combined in 403,290,000,000,000,000,000,000,000 different ways.
A. J. Alexander, York.

PEOPLE who endeavour to produce short sentences containing all the letters of the alphabet are known as pangrammists.

In 1984, Michael Jones of Chicago produced a 26-letter sentence to describe the situation in which a wryneck woodpecker from the grasslands of Africa climbs up the side of a male bovid grazing on sacred Moslem-owned land: 'Veldt jynx grimps waaf zho buck.'
Tim Mickleburgh, Grimsby, Lincs.

ANOTHER example of a holo-alphabetic sentence describes the annoyance of an eccentric in finding inscriptions on the side of a fjord in a rounded valley: 'Cwm fjord-bank glyphs vext quiz.'

All the alternatives to 'the quick brown fox...' show what a cleverly devised, concise, grammatical and utterly normal sentence it is.
James Anderson, Penarth, South Glamorgan.

I SUGGEST: 'Every zealous pangrammist becomes justifiably excited acknowledging such requests.'
Roy Harris, Harrow, Middx.

MY favourite is: 'Wet squid's inky haze veils sex of jumping crab.'
Mrs J. M. Page, Benfleet, Essex.

THE International Telegraph Alphabet provides the French version: 'Voyez le brick geant que j'examine pres du wharf' for Latin alphabet teleprinters. It was used regularly by French military radio systems.
R. D. Thompson, Kirkcudbright.

THE most common sentence French typists are given to practise is: '*Max a bu le whisky que tu as vu jadis chez le forgeron due pays.*' This roughly translates as: 'Max drank the whisky that you once saw at the local blacksmith's.'
Mrs C. Amarasinghe, Slough, Berks.

WHEN I die I would like to be buried in the Land of the Free. Is there such a place?

THERE are three references to the Land of the Free in the poem 'The Star Spangled Banner' written by Francis Scott Key on September 14, 1814.

He wrote it while a prisoner of the British, seeing his beloved American flag survive a bombardment of Fort McHenry. It was later adapted to an English air and became the U.S. national anthem in 1931.

Trevor Atkins, Keighley, West Yorks.

THE music of 'The Star Spangled Banner', which includes the words Land of the Free, was composed by Gloucester composer, organist and tenor singer, John Stafford Smith. It became the national anthem of the United States by a 1931 Senate Bill.

B. Bullock, Tuffley, Gloucs.

LIBERIA in West Africa is the Latin word meaning 'Land of the Freed'. Ashby de la Zouch, Leicestershire and Washington, West Sussex, were part of the Freeland estates. The pub in Washington is The Frankland Arms, with a sign bearing the motto: 'Franke Minde, Frankeland', *franke* meaning 'free'. It comes from the Latin *franca* originally applied to the North European tribes beyond the Elbe. This derivation would make Saxony, Brandenburg and Prussia the 'lands of the free'.

Frank McGlasson, St Leonards, East Sussex.

ANY Briton who wants to be buried in the Land of the Free need look no further than his own country. In 1942–43, I was in a Boy Scout show, raising funds for Wings For Victory Week, trying to buy a Spitfire for the RAF. Our grand finale concluded:

Britain our island home, Land of the Free,
Britain unconquered yet On land or sea.
God of the heaven above, answer our prayer.
God, make Britannia's sons, Lords of the air.

J. M. Farrow, Bolsover, Chesterfield.

❓ IN what language did Jesus speak?

THE language of Palestine at the time of Jesus was Aramaic, which belongs to the same group of languages as Hebrew and Arabic. A large part of the Biblical book of Daniel is written in Aramaic.

Spoken Aramaic today is divided into two dialects, Western, spoken in several villages in Lebanon and Syria, and Eastern, spoken in northern Iraq around the city of Mosul.

One of the reasons why Aramaic has survived is that various Eastern churches adopted liturgies written in the vernacular Aramaic of the time, called Syriac. The first kingdom to adopt Christianity as the state religion was Syriac-speaking Edessa (now Sanliurfa in south-eastern Turkey).

The New Testament was written in Greek, the lingua franca of the Near East in Jesus's time. Jesus's sayings were originally in Aramaic and were translated into Greek by the authors of the New Testament.

Simon Fishburn, East Grinstead, Sussex.

JESUS is believed to have spoken Aramaic in everyday life, and Hebrew, the language of the Old Testament, when preaching.

Jesus would also have spoken Greek, common among upper-class or better-educated Jews, and the language in which the Gospels were written some years after his death and resurrection.

Sidney Manches, London NW8.

IN addition to speaking in Aramaic, Jesus read classical Hebrew (Luke 4:16–19) and like everyone else he would have known the everyday Greek of the part of the world called Koine. Our expression 'coining a phrase' refers to this lingua franca.

Ivor L. Challis, Brighton, Sussex.

? WHAT is the origin of the place name New Invention?

THE name New Invention for the small residential area near Short Heath, Willenhall, between Wolverhampton and Walsall, arose when a local man, fed-up with smoke billowing from the fireplace into his house, hit on an idea to improve his chimney's up-draught.

He positioned an old bucket, with the bottom rusted out, on top of his chimney and found that it drew up the fumes far more efficiently: he had invented the chimney pot – hence the name New Invention.

Willenhall is known in the Black Country as 'Humpshire'. Pubs in the area used to have hollowed-out wooden seatbacks to accommodate customers who worked in the town's main industry, lockmaking. Their intricate skills meant they were always bent over at work benches and many had spine curvatures giving them humped backs.

Terry Andrew, Marsworth, Bucks.

DO WE FALL IN LOVE WITH OUR OPPOSITES?

DEAR *Answers*,—I have often heard this question asked and by 'opposites' I mean people of different temperament – of an opposite disposition to ourselves.

We frequently hear of couples marrying who are, according to the opinions of their friends, so unlike each other and yet, when married, these same couples seem to be the happiest.

I know now a married couple of entirely different tastes and inclinations, as opposite as one could well imagine, and those who know them cannot have two opinions about their happiness.

Querist, Blackpool.

We do, but we ought not to. Couples of opposite opinions and temperaments, except in the minority of cases, are rarely happy. It is unnatural that they should be so.

Literary men, poets, artists and musicians have been and still are only too often unhappy in wedlock. Why? The question scarcely needs answering. Their wives are uncongenial.

They may be the best of women, the most accomplished in some things, the most kindly, but still the awful fact remains that they are in many ways of opposite temperament.

A man should in his choice of a partner be most careful that that kind of work which constitutes his profession, or more particularly, perhaps, his hobby, should be of deep interest to his prospective wife, so that a mutual sympathy should exist between them in the subject.

Unless this is so, no union can be a perfectly happy one. Men and women need sympathy, and without congeniality it cannot exist.

Litterateur.

❓ WHY did Winston Churchill wear high-ranking forces uniforms in World War II?

CHURCHILL'S Army uniform was as Honorary Colonel of 5 (Cinque Ports) Battalion of the Royal Sussex Regiment. The unit's badge can be seen clearly on his hat in pictures of Yalta and the Rhine crossing. He visited the Battalion at El Alamein with Generals Montgomery and Alexander. His rank of Honorary Colonel was bestowed on him through his office as Lord Warden of the Cinque Ports and the Battalion helped line the route at his funeral.

The Battalion was founded in 1795 by William Pitt the Younger to counter the anticipated French invasion. Its successor is the Company of the Princess of Wales Royal Regiment in Hastings, Sussex.

P. G. Harrington (Major retd), Sittingbourne, Kent.

? WE were married in June 1957 and I still have the top tier of our wedding cake? Is this a record?

WE married in 1938 and I still have the whole top tier of our wedding cake, made by my mother. It last went on display for our Golden Wedding. I still have my wedding dress and veil, too.

A. L. Powell, Kirk,Yorks.

I WAS married in 1924 and still have a piece of my wedding cake. At the time, it fitted into a small box but looking at it today, I find it's about the size of a walnut and has become as hard as a fossil.

Mrs O. Durrant, Bournemouth, Dorset.

? HOW are ball bearings made?

BALLS for modern ball bearings are not made by dropping molten metal down a tall tower (that's lead shot). The process actually involves a short sharp punching action followed by many hours of grinding in machines. It is very reminiscent of mill stones grinding flour.

Billets are sheared off the end of a rod of high-grade steel and formed into rough ball shapes. These are then fed through specialised grinding machinery which recirculates thousands of budding balls around grooves in a side-by-side pair of revolving grinding wheels.

The constant, random rolling of each ball ensures that every part of the surface has its 'high points' slowly ground down.

The balls, which have to be very hard, are then heat treated in furnaces followed by even finer grinding – 'lapping' as it's known. This results in steel balls with a mirror finish and absolute precision in size and sphericity.

Charles Reed, NSK-RHP Bearings Ltd, Newark, Notts.

? HAS anyone ever tamed a crocodile?

AS children we had living next door to us a Mrs Roberts and Miss Davis who kept a menagerie of animals including an alligator and a crocodile. The alligator had starred in the film *Daisy The Alligator* and the crocodile was called George. We often called on the two ladies and talked to their animals.

They all came from the wild but none of them caused us any fear. Though not really 'trained', during the summer fete season, Daisy and George were shown as exhibits: George had a lit cigarette placed in his mouth and Daisy a huge pink bow around her neck.

Margaret Mitchell, Guildford, Surrey.

ABOUT 60 years ago I recall seeing on two occasions at my local theatre in Northampton a variety act involving a highly mesmerising lady with a large Afro hairstyle who went by the name of Kanga.

Her act consisted of swimming in a huge tank with several crocodiles, carrying out various manoeuvres and tricks. She also wrestled with them on the stage floor.

Alan A. Ashton, Middleton, Manchester.

IN 1805, eccentric naturalist Charles Waterton (1782–1865), of Walton Hill near Wakefield, captured a 10ft 6in cayman in the Essequibo River and rode on its back for 40 yards. Asked how he managed to keep his seat he answered: 'I hunted for some years with Lord Darlington's fox hounds.'

His aim was not to tame the creature but to dissect it.

Kevin Heneghan, St Helens, Merseyside.

? IN *Pride and Prejudice*, reference is made to a card game called Lottery Numbers. What was this?

JANE Austen used this game as a metaphor to highlight Lydia Bennett's scatterbrained nature. Described by Aunt Philips as 'a nice, comfortable, noisy game of lottery tickets', it's difficult to discover the actual rules but it was obviously less intellectually demanding than whist.

No doubt the indulgent Mrs Bennett would have advanced her youngest daughter a small sum of money to bid for lottery tickets in successive games. Lydia would have enjoyed the fun of bidding and counter-bidding and would have looked vivacious and desirable in the delightful anguish preceding the draw where, of course, only some of the tickets were worth prizes. It was an innocent form of gambling, rather like our present-day bingo sessions.

Lydia even sacrificed the attentions of Mr Wickham for the game.

Ironically, at the end of the novel, he is the prize she draws in the lottery of marriage, though as Jane Austen points out, one of low denomination.

Susan McCartan, The Jane Austen Society, Hants.

THE game referred to is called lotto, not a card game as such, but one in which players drew cards printed with a grid of numbers. It was then played in a similar way to bingo but using counters or little coloured wooden 'pawns' to cover the numbers called.

Over the years, the name of the game changed from lotto to house or housey-housey and then to bingo as it is played today.

Denis Hardie, Great Yarmouth, Norfolk.

❓ COLCHESTER has signs welcoming visitors to 'Britain's Oldest Recorded Town' but a recent BBC *Songs of Praise* programme claimed Ipswich was the oldest. Which is right?

COLCHESTER is indisputably Britain's oldest recorded town and the first settlement to be like a town as we would understand it today.

Pliny the Elder, writing in AD 77, refers to Colchester in his book *Natural History* and there was a major Iron Age settlement at Colchester long before this reference. In the oldest surviving written reference to any town in Britain, Pliny wrote that it was 200 miles from Camulodunum, the ancient name for Colchester, to Anglesey, demonstrating the importance of the town in the Roman world. Pliny is confident his readers will know of Camulodunum and its location.

Camulodunum, meaning fortress of Camulos (a Celtic war god), was already an important settlement by 25 BC and became the seat of the most powerful kings who ruled Late Iron Age Britain, the most famous of whom was Cunobelin.

Ipswich claims not to be Britain's oldest town but rather the oldest English town, the first town built by the Anglo-Saxons who arrived in the area after the Romans had abandoned Britain. The Anglo-Saxon name for Ipswich was Gyppeswyk.

There are many English towns and cities founded by the Romans (Colchester, London, York, Lincoln, Cirencester, St Albans, etc) which are far older than Ipswich, whose claim might better be that it was the first 'new town' of the Saxon era.

Peter Berridge, Colchester Museum.

WHAT is the story behind the memorial in Worthing inscribed 'In memory of warrior birds who gave their lives on active service, 1939–45'?

THIS memorial is a tribute to the thousands of racing pigeons on active service during World War II, provided by civilian members of the National Pigeon Service or specifically trained by the Armed Services.

Pigeons were initially provided to each bomber crew to be released if the plane was shot down with details of the crew's last position to enable a rescue to be carried out. Thousands more were sent out with Special Operations Executive agents behind enemy lines to send information back to Britain of troop movements and fortifications.

A further tactic was the dropping of pigeons by parachute in the occupied countries to enable the Resistance and ordinary civilians to provide information of use to the Allies. Each pigeon parachuted was accompanied by special message containers, paper and pencil and a supply of food with instructions on how to care for the bird, when to liberate it and what information may be of use.

Pigeons successfully returned to England with messages from as far away as Denmark and the South of France. Many returned to their lofts with serious wounds and were awarded by the PDSA the Dickin medal for animal gallantry. More pigeons have been awarded this medal than any other animal.

Stuart Fawcett, Darlington.

THE memorial was paid for by actress and writer Nancy Price who lived in the town. A total of 31 Dickin Medals – the 'animal Victoria Cross' – were awarded to pigeons for various feats, most of which saved the lives of servicemen.

The memorial was unveiled in 1951 by the Duke and Duchess of Hamilton but fell into disrepair until restored by local stonemason and pigeon fancier Stewart Earl. It can be seen in Worthing's Beach House Park.

Peter Bryant, Royal Pigeon Racing Assoc, Cheltenham.

Q MY Grandmother gave up mustard for Lent. What is the most unusual thing given up during these 40 days of Christian fasting?

AS a former VAT inspector, now working as a consultant in the private sector, I always apply my knowledge of VAT during Lent in giving up any food which is subject to 17.5 per cent VAT.

This simple but very healthy habit means that, among other things, I can't drink alcohol or fizzy drinks or eat take-away food, chocolate biscuits or confectionery. However, if my willpower wavers, there remains the good old Jaffa cake, which as every 'man on the Clapham omnibus' knows, is a cake not a biscuit.

Keri A. Pay, Worcester.

IN my homeland of Spain, in several regions it used to be common for men and women to give up eating oysters for Lent, since they are considered aphrodisiacs and associated with love-making.

In the increasingly secular society of today's Spain, however, few people are willing to make any such sacrifice.

Sebastiano di Espinoza, Leamington Spa, Warwks.

I HAD a secretary once, a very devout lady called Sarah, who actually gave up croutons in her soup for Lent.

S. Andrews, London E11.

Q WHY do you have to wait a few minutes after the spin cycle has finished on a washing machine before being able to open the door?

A WASHING machine door won't open for a few minutes because as soon as you switch the power on, electric current runs through the door switch causing a bi-metal strip to heat up and enable the door to lock firmly.

After the machine has finished its programme, the current is cut from carrying on through the switch, allowing the switch to cool down, which takes around two minutes.

Russell Smithers, Thorn engineer, Wallington, Surrey.

THE reason for the safety device on the door is primarily to stop it from being opened during a spin cycle. It could be dangerous to open the door before the drum had stopped moving. The few minutes' wait is to make absolutely sure that the machine has stopped before allowing access to the clothes. Only then is it safe to put your hands inside the drum.

Ben Myles, Denton, Manchester.

? PEOPLE say 'laughter is the best medicine', but where does this saying originate and is there any truth in it?

THE 17th chapter of the Biblical Book of Proverbs contains two references: 'A cheerful heart is good medicine but a crushed spirit drieth up the bones' (v22) and 'A merry heart doeth good [like] a medicine' (v20).

More recently, Matthew Green has written 'laugh and be well'; Mark Twain's *Tom Sawyer* includes the reference: 'The old man laughed loud and joyously, shook up the details of his anatomy, and ended by saying that such a laugh was money in a man's pocket, because it cut down the doctor's bills'; Jonathan Swift says: 'The best doctors in the world are Dr Diet, Dr Quiet and Dr Merryman'; Henry Ward Beecher says: 'Mirth is God's medicine' and Voltair: 'The art of medicine consists of amusing the patient while nature cures the disease.'

There are numerous anecdotal accounts of laughter causing healing. Norman Cousins published in the conservative *New England Journal of Medicine* and elaborated upon in his book *Anatomy Of An Illness As Perceived By The Patient* how he healed himself of a potentially life-threatening disease by intravenous vitamin C and regular laughing.

But there are few hard scientific studies and what little is being done is primitive and biased.

As a psychotherapist for 30 years, I've seen remarkable shifts in perspective as a result of specifically directed laughter. Laughter as catharsis can relieve depression, anxiety and physical pain. I help people laugh about what isn't funny: hency the title of my book: *Laughter Therapy: How to Laugh About Everything In Your Life That Isn't Funny*.

Annette Jones, New York, USA.

? IF I select random on the CD player, what are the odds of it playing the tracks on a 12-track CD in their proper order?

IF it's completely random, there would be 12 x 12 x 12 possible sequences: nearly nine trillion to one.

However, if each track is played only once, the odds are quickly found by multiplying 12 x 11 x 10 x 9 x 8 x 7 x 6 x 5 x 4 x 3 x 2: making only 479,001,600 possibilities. The odds are therefore 479,001,599 to 1 against.
David Elias, Nottingham.

IF the CD was one hour long, it would take about 55,000 years to listen to each combination.
Chris Share, Stoke-on-Trent.

? HAS anyone ever died on their 100th birthday?

MY mother Margaret Maris died during the afternoon of her 100th birthday on February 21, 1999. We were sad but grateful that she had achieved her ambition to reach her century.
Betty Hoad, Ashford, Kent.

ADA Margaret Moore, who never married, was born on January 13, 1893, in London and died in the early evening on January 12, 1993, at a nursing home in Minehead.

From the day she moved into the nursing home in her mid-90s, it had been her ambition to be the oldest resident.

She achieved this status some six weeks before her death when the previous oldest resident died.

The family treasures the message of congratulations from Her Majesty the Queen, which she did not live to see.
R. Faux, Andover, Hants.

? IS there a street in the UK that has different names on each side?

THE road that forms the border between Hove and Portslade in East Sussex has three different names. The Portslade (west) side is called Station Road south of the railway line that intersects it, and Carlton Terrace to the north. The Hove (east) side is called Boundary Road, both north and south of the railway line.

To confuse matters further, Portslade railway station is on the Hove side and therefore not in Station Road.
Judi Tilley, Hove, Sussex.

WHERE I live in Chirk, Wrexham, my side of the road is Coronation Drive while the opposite side is Princess Avenue. On the Princess Avenue side, where Walden Crescent meets it, both turn away from Coronation Drive opposite one another in a circular route until Princess Avenue meets Coronation Drive again, now on both sides of the road.

R. E. Carr, Chirk, Wrexham.

HERE in Larkhall, the road to my house from my son's school is called Charlcombe Lane on its eastern side and Frys Leaze on the west.

In Hooe, Plymouth, my parents' address is Westways, on the western side of the road while the eastern side is Church Hill Road.

Steve Nicholson, Larkhall, Bath.

WHEN I was a child, I lived at 24 Fernbank Drive in Bingley, West Yorkshire. This was the official postal address for the front of the house but the rear of the house was 24 Elizabeth Street.

Rod Allen, Nottingham.

? WHAT was first described as 'all singing, all dancing'?

THIS phrase which is now used to denote any product or service which claims to be the ultimate in its field, has its roots in the showbusiness world.

It can be traced back to Hollywood's first musical, MGM's 1929 hit film, *Broadway Melody*, which appeared at a time when 'talking pictures' were first bringing 'live' sound to the silver screen. Heavily promoted, the musical's posters boasted: 'The new wonder of the screen! All Talking, All Singing, All Dancing, dramatic sensation!'

Fiona Johnson, Inverness.

? WHO has given the longest speech in the House of Commons? What was the topic?

ON February 26, 1828, Henry Peter Brougham (1778–1868) spoke for six hours on Law Reform. On October 7, 1831, he went on to set the House of Lords record, speaking for another six hours, on the Reform Bill.

Under much stricter standing orders, on March 6, 1985, Conservative MP for Burton, Sir Ivan Lawrence (*b*.1936) spoke for four hours 23 minutes opposing the Water (Fluoridation) Bill.

The most impressive achievement of all was that of John Golding (*b.*1931) who, on the night of February 8/9, 1983, when he was Labour member for Newcastle-under-Lyme, spoke for a staggering 11 hours 15 minutes on small amendments to the Telecommunications Bill – but this was in committee.
Tim Mickleburgh, Grimsby, Lincs.

❓ HOW did the 12 horses in the horse-racing game Totopoly get their names?

HAVING had this game for well over 50 years, my horses and jockeys are now rather worn but are still played with, including a board which is taken to Boston at least once a year when I visit my daughter and her family.

We have often wondered about the horses' 1 Dark Warrior, 2 Flamenco, 3 Dorigen, 4 Marmaduke Jinks, 5 Leonidas II, 6 Overcoat, 7 Play On, 8 Priory Park, 9 Knight Error, 10 King of Clubs, 11 Jerome Fandor and 12 Elton and were surprised some years back to see that a horse called Marmaduke Jinks, from Mary Reveley's stable, was running at Newcastle. (It won, incidentally.)

There are two stables named on the board, Stevedon (no doubt named after Steve Donaghue) and Walroy named after? We can't guess.
Jack Merewood, Huddersfield, West Yorks.

THESE names are all taken from real horses, all past winners of the Lincolnshire Handicap.
Walter Ancel, Tewkesbury.

❓ APART from south-east England and north-east France, where else in the world are coastal chalk cliffs to be found?

A YEAR ago, my wife and I were in Germany and visited Rügen Island in the Baltic, off the coast of the former East Germany. We took a boat trip from Sassnitz round to the north-west side of the island, where there are beautiful white chalk cliffs, heavily wooded. These are rated one of the area's major tourist attractions.
George Sassoon, Warminster, Wilts.

? AIRLINE safety leaflets show an airliner floating on water and the passengers exiting into life rafts. Has it ever happened?

SOME time ago, a Ghana registered B707 cargo aircraft was landing to pick up a load of fish from Mwanza, a small port city in north-western Tanzania at the lower end of Lake Victoria.

After numerous aborted landing attempts in the darkness, the pilot approached from over the lake. With no visual reference, the control tower informed him he was too low but the plane continued to descend and, about three miles short of the runway, hit the water, tore off all four engines and landing gear, but didn't puncture its fuselage. With battery power and the taxi light on, the uninjured crew were picked up by a fishing boat.

The following day, the plane was still afloat, and was towed to shallow water near the airport, where it will probably be a beacon for many years.
Tom Colclough, Chapel Brampton, Northampton.

THE first successful ditching by a jet aircraft in open water was in the Caribbean sea on May 2, 1970. A Douglas DC9-33 leased by Overseas National Airways to ALM of the Dutch Antilles, ran out of fuel while trying to divert during a thunderstorm.

It ditched intact and the escape chutes deployed, enabling evacuation. One of the chutes, however, deployed inside the aircraft and the flight crew had to escape through the cockpit window.

The most publicised failed ditching took place in the Indian Ocean a few years ago. An Ethiopian Airlines Boeing 767 ran out of fuel after being hijacked and the incident was captured on camera by holidaymakers on the beach.

The only time a pilot would land on water would be after a total engine failure due to fuel starvation or contamination. Modern aircraft are designed to stay airborne on one engine and normally carry sufficient fuel to circle the intended landing airport for 45 minutes before diverting to a suitable airfield and still landing with sufficient fuel reserves.
Ian Clarke, Horton, Berkshire.

? EUROPEANS introduced many new diseases to native Americans. Did any diseases travel in the opposite direction?

SYPHILIS was the first, and most major, disease introduced into Europe from Central America as soon as the first conquistadors returned from the New World.

Following Columbus's return to Europe, the first outbreak was reported in Barcelona in March 1493. As the European population had no natural resistance, its effect was devastating.

Only as the population acquired resistance did the disease develop its characteristic and long drawn out primary, secondary and tertiary stages.

Anthony Cooney, Liverpool.

? IS the island of New Britain in Papua New Guinea, in any way like the Britain we live in?

THE crescent-shaped island of New Britain was named in 1700 by English navigator William Dampier (1652–1715). After control by the British, the Germans, who called it Neu Pommern, the Australians, the Japanese, the Australians again until 1975 and finally its own people, it is now part of the independent country of Papua New Guinea.

The island covers an area of 14,100 square miles about one-sixth the size of the island of Britain. The present population of 312,000 is about 182 times smaller than that here.

New Britain is a narrow, mountainous island, more than 300 miles from end to end. The interior is harsh, densely rain-forested country, split by steep gorges and fast flowing rivers. The east of the island is dominated by active volcanoes. The capital, Rabaul lies in the shadow of Matupit Volcano.

The west is sparsely populated and relatively undeveloped with the main road system concentrating around the Williamez Peninsula.

Economic activity centres on copra and cacao cultivation, logging and coal, copper, gold and iron mining.

The only similarity between Britain and New Britain is that both employ a large number of people in the tourism industry and both drive on the left.

Clive Spinney, Brighton, Sussex.

? IN the original *Star Trek* series, did Lieutenant Uhura have a first name?

LIEUT Uhura, played by actress Michelle Nichols, never had a first name on screen but in later *Star Trek* literature the name Nayota appears.

Supposedly born in the United States of Africa in AD 2239, her name was derived from the Swahili word *uhuru*, meaning freedom. She first appeared in the episode 'The Corbomite Manoeuvre' and was a regular minor character in virtually every subsequent episode. On appearance in the first six *Star Trek* films, she had risen in rank to Lieutenant Commander and accepted a teaching role at Starfleet academy.

Star Trek creator Gene Roddenberry took quite a chance with the character. She was the first black female to appear in a role of any importance on American TV and, with William Shatner, took part in the first on-screen multiracial kiss. This led to her being a figurehead for ethnic minorities and women's rights groups.

Chris Gornall, Penwortham, Preston.

THE Uhura/Captain Kirk kiss was the first multiracial kiss on American TV but had been preceded five years earlier in the British TV series, *Emergency Ward 10*.

The claim by *Star Trek* fans that this series was the first to give us a multicultural crew/cast is only partially true. When *Star Trek* was first shown in September 1966, *I Spy* (first shown in September 1965), featuring Bill Cosby and Robert Culp, was already the first American TV series to give a lead role to an African American actor.

J. Buss, author: A Collector's Guide to Television: The Sixties, *London.*

? CAN postage-paid envelopes for junk mail be legally recycled to another address?

POSTAGE-paid envelopes are treated in the same way as envelopes with stamps. The postage is paid before delivery and the item is delivered to whatever address is on the front.

This type of envelope is identifiable by the numbers 1 or 2 or the words First Class or Second Class alongside a picture of the Queen's head.

Most companies, however, use business reply envelopes which are identified by the number 1 or 2, denoting class of service, and the licence number of the company. With these envelopes, postage and a handling fee is deducted after delivery, so only those companies with the licence receive them.

Royal Mail will deliver business reply envelopes to other addresses only after a surcharge has been paid by the addressee and the item will be handled as a second class letter.

C. Wade, postman.

❓ IS there any way to estimate the altitude of aircraft from the ground?

DURING the 1939–45 War, the magazine *Aeroplane Spotter* gave away a 6in section of wood marked with the relevant sizes at various heights of the most common aircraft of the time.

This allowed the user to gauge the height of an aircraft by holding the stick at arm's length and lining up the aircraft with the appropriate section of stick.

As these aircraft flew lower and slower than present-day aircraft, they were easy to identify and this proved a reasonably accurate estimate of their altitude.

Mr R. Swift, Littlestone, Kent.

❓ DRIVING to Oxford in heavy rain, I discovered two sections of the M40 had no water spray from traffic wheels. What material achieves this? Why isn't it used on all roads?

THESE sections are covered not with the traditional wearing course in the UK, hot rolled asphalt (HRA), but porous asphalt (PA).

On roads surfaced with HRA, water drains slowly and is splashed into the air as spray when a vehicle passes. These roads are also noisy as sound waves caused by tyres rebound off its surface.

PA is designed with open pore spaces between the aggregate particles, allowing water to enter, leaving the surface almost dry. As well as reducing spray, PA is also quieter.

However, because it's porous, PA doesn't contribute as much to the structural strength of the road pavement so a thicker layer is required to support the traffic, making it more costly. New materials are being tested providing similar benefits at lower cost.

Steve Rimmington, Barnsley, South Yorks.

THE presence of air voids in the porous asphalt offer markedly reduced spray and improved visibility.

Headlight glare is reduced from reflection on wet surfaces and there may be a slight improvement in vehicle fuel consumption.

However, air voids are quickly filled with detritus and the lifetime of porous asphalt is only eight years compared with 20 years for conventional material.

In winter conditions, the presence of air voids, can reduce the temperature of road surfaces to 1–2°C below that of adjacent roads, causing the surface to freeze sooner and thaw later. Two to three times the amount of road salt is required to maintain ice-free conditions and the dangerous situation of mushrooming is more likely to occur. This is when rain is followed by freezing conditions. Water in the voids expands when it freezes, pushing up above the adjacent road surface. Salting is ineffective and the road can become highly dangerous.

Kevin Cathcart, Moston, Manchester.

WHY are 'mad scientists' in films so often played by people with German accents? What accent do they have when these films are dubbed into German?

IN most cases, Hollywood films in which the English language versions have a German-accented madman/scientist/terrorist/baddie, when dubbed for the German market, tend to give them a specific German minority accent.

One of the best examples of the German accented mad scientist was portrayed by Peter Sellers in *Dr Strangelove or How I Learned To Stop Worrying And Love The Bomb*, made in 1964. In the German version, Sellers was given a German Yiddish accent.

In more recent films, the tendency has been to dub the German accent with a Bavarian or Austrian accent. *Die Hard With A Vengeance*, for instance, which starred Jeremy Irons as an ex-baddie, ex-STASI member from East Germany, when dubbed into German, gave him a Viennese accent.

Klaus Schuette, journalist, Hamburg, Germany.

WHAT is the history of the network of tunnels below the site of the old Chatham Royal Naval Barracks, now occupied by the Medway campus of Greenwich University?

THERE are a surprising number of tunnels under the former naval base at Chatham and the adjoining barracks. The oldest ones were made by the forerunners of the Royal Engineers, the Sappers and Miners, who used the area in the 19th century to practise digging trenches and tunnels.

Unfortunately these were neither recorded nor filled in and to this day small sections of them occasionally collapse, causing holes in the ground.

Other tunnels are associated with wartime defensive works built in anticipation of aerial bombing. These include a telephone exchange and workshop areas. None of these tunnels is particularly well recorded or publicised. The

location of some of these tunnels was identified only by dowsing.
A. Reeds, Gillingham, Kent.

THE tunnels used in World War II as day-time air-raid shelters and at night for sleeping quarters for sailors not on duty were lined with corrugated iron, supported by curved girders.

Hammocks were taken from the mess decks after tea and slung from the girders. In the morning they were lashed and taken back to the messes.
J. A. Milner, Bromley, Kent.

I SLEPT my first night at Chatham Barracks in these tunnels. Hammocks slung on hooks were so tightly packed that anyone getting up in the night had to push the next hammock to make room to get out. That created a knock-on effect all down the tunnel.

The stench from the buckets, placed at intervals along the tunnel was unbelievable. I soon learnt to volunteer for the fire party which was allocated a room in the barracks.
Edward Aked, Bridgnorth, Shropshire.

? IF a phone call starts within one charge rate but doesn't finish until after the rate has changed, is it all charged at the initial rate or does the charge change with the time of day?
THERE are many telecommunications companies in the UK, some functioning as network operators, others as service providers. Under current regulations, each company is allowed to decide its own policy on how charges are worked out.

There are no rules, other than to ensure that any claims they make about their charges (or any other terms and conditions) are factual.

The most common approach (used by BT and most reputable operators) is to change the rate of charge during the call. But some service providers have been known to charge the higher rate for the duration of the call.

We advise clients to ask service providers for this sort of detail (preferably in writing) before signing up, but in some cases there is reluctance to provide it.

Where the rate does change during the call, it will normally do so just before or just after the 'official' time (always in the customer's favour), to avoid errors or misunderstandings.
Richard D. G. Cox, telecommunications engineer, Mandarin Technology, Penarth.

HAS ANYONE SEEN A GHOST?

Dear *Answers*,—Christmas is coming and with it is ushered in the ghost season, that time when the family circle, seated by the blazing fire, listens in open-mouthed wonder to weird stories of spirits, spectres, ghosts, and other denizens of the spirit world.

Such is the effect of these tales that the hearers turn in terror at the slightest sound and direct their affrighted gaze into the black shadows out of the ken of the firelight, expecting some apparition to appear and confront them. Yet these are but tales, without one atom of fact in them.

Personally, although no spook or spectre has appeared to me, I cannot, in the face of the evidence of the Psychical Research Society and others, doubt but that spirits do exist and that there are more things in heaven and earth than are dreamt of in our philosophy.

Spook, London.

I share a belief in supernatural apparitions. To my own knowledge, the child of a gentleman who is a medium died and, as the body lay on the bed, the father declared that he could see the form of the child standing in a certain corner of the room, although the spirit was totally invisible to the other occupants of the apartment.

The father seemed so positive of his remarkable statement that it was suggested that a friend of the family who was an amateur photographer should photograph the corner indicated.

The camera was erected, focused on the spot pointed out by the medium and a photo taken. The result was extraordinary. On the negative being developed, a distinct outline of the child's figure was produced, just as described by the father.

I cannot account for this phenomenon but I am prepared to personally vouch for its occurrence.

F. S., Southampton.

The late Lord Tennyson was an interested member of the Psychical Research Society and at the present time it numbers among its many members Mr Gladstone, Mr Ruskin, Mr Balfour and quite a number of prominent English and foreign scientific men.

I presume that the very fact of such men having allowed themselves to become members of the society is more or less proof positive, at least, of their belief in a spiritual form of some sort, whether we call it a ghost, spectre or spook.

H. Cuthbert, West Kensington.

I am reminded of a curious incident related by an old friend of mine, to whom it occurred.

While seated with his parents and sisters at breakfast one morning, their attention was called to a dog barking loudly in front of the house and, on looking at the animal, to their surprise they all recognised it as the favourite terrier of my friend's brother, supposed at the time to be in Burmah.

All instinctively rushed to the door, expecting to find the dog the advance guard of its master. On opening the door, however, the dog was seen rushing through the garden gate and at the same time a figure – which all recognised to be the brother – disappeared round the corner of a hedge into the road.

A second later the whole family were looking down the road, which is quite half a mile long and perfectly straight, with an open view, but nothing was visible.

The next mail from Burmah brought news of the supposed visitor's death, which occurred at the same time as the apparition appeared to us.

The dog in question was later on brought to England by a friend of the deceased and is at the present time alive.

I offer no theory about this; sceptics, perchance, will call it coincidence. Maybe, but I doubt it. It is uncanny, certainly.

Doubtful, Glasgow.

IS there a complete list of bingo calls from one to 90?

NO Gaming Board regulations define bingo but the game has evolved to a point where it is played in much the same way throughout Britain. These days, the selection of numbers is usually made by an electric random number generator and the caller simply announces each number as it's selected.

The Bingo Association advises members that 'bingo lingo' shouldn't be used in licensed clubs. Traditional calls are discouraged lest they confuse players. With prizes of up to £200,000 at stake, if a player missed a winning call through confusion over a number, one can imagine the uproar.

These calls are still used in fun games: Kelly's eye, No 1; On its own/Baby's done it/Doctor Who, No 2; I'm free/Debbie McGee, No 3; On the floor/The one next door, No 4; Man alive, No 5; Tom Mix/Chopsticks, No 6; I'm in heaven, No 7; Garden/Golden gate, No 8; Doctor's orders, No 9; Brown's (or whoever's) den, No 10; Legs eleven, No 11; One dozen/Monkey's cousin, No 12; Unlucky for some, No 13; Lines in a sonnet, No 14; Rugby team/Red balls in snooker, No 15; Never been kissed, Sweet 16; Often been kissed/Old Ireland, No 17; Now you can vote/Key of the door, No 18; 19 to the dozen, No 19; Getting plenty, No 20; Royal Salute, No 21; Dinkie do/All the twos/Two little ducks, No 22; Duck and a flea, No 23; Two dozen, No 24; Preston Guild/Cents in a quarter, No 25; Old halfcrown/Bed and breakfast, No 26; Little duck with a crutch, No 27; In a state, No 28; February leap, No 29; Burlington Bertie/Dirty/Flirty Gertie, No 30; Days in May, No 31; Water freezes, No 32; All the threes/Dirty knees/Feathers, No 33; Gallons in an oil barrel, No 35; Three Dozen, No 36; Shakespeare plays, No 37; Smith & Wesson, No 38; Those famous steps, No 39; Life begins at, No 40; That famous street in Manhattan, No 42; Droopy drawers, No 44; Halfway House/ Halfway there, No 45; Four dozen, No 48; PC/Nick Nick, No 49; Bull's eye/Bung Hole, No 50; I love my mum, No 51; Weeks in the year/Cards in a pack, No 52; Snakes alive, No 55; All the beans, No 57; 5 and 9, the Brighton line, No 59; Three score, No 60; Tickety Boo, No 62; The Beatles' number, No 64; Old age pension, No 65; Clickety click, No 66; The argumentative number, No 67; Your place or mine, No 69; Three score and ten, No 70; Crutch with a duck, No 72; Crutch with a flea, No 73; Bottle of wine, No 75; 7 and 6, Was she worth it?, No 76; Sunset Strip, No 77; 78 RPM, No 78; 79 Park Lane, No 79; Gandhi's breakfast, No 80; One fat lady and a little wee, No 81; Fat lady with a duck, No 82; Fat lady with a flea, No 83; 84 Charing Cross Road, No 84; Maxwell Smart, No 86; Fat lady with a crutch, No 87; Two fat ladies, No 88; Nearly there, 89; Top of the house/Shop, 90.

John Beard, The Bingo Assoc of Great Britain, Warrington.

☿ HAS anyone triggered a speed camera while riding a pedal cycle? Do they even respond to cyclists?

SPEED cameras are used to set designated speeds on the roads on which they are installed and, in theory, any vehicle breaking that speed limit could activate the camera and be caught.

We're not aware of anyone ever riding a pedal cycle being caught speeding by a camera.

Sgt Bob Davey, Camera Enforcement Unit, West Midlands Police.

? IS it a legal requirement that drivers who wear spectacles must carry a spare pair in their car in case they damage their normal ones?

THIS is not a legal requirement but it is an offence to knowingly drive with uncorrected defective eyesight.

The Highway Code states that you must be able to read a vehicle number plate from a distance of 20.5m (67ft) in good daylight.

If you need to wear glasses to do this then you must wear them all the time when driving. The police have powers to require a driver at any time to undertake an eyesight test in good daylight – so it's highly advisable to carry a spare pair of glasses.

Chris Lee, Driving Standards Agency, Nottingham.

? I HAVE a Caterpillar Club gold tie pin that belonged to my late husband. What was this club? Does it still exist?

THIS exclusive club was formed in 1922 by Leslie L. Irvin, with a membership limited to those of any nationality, race, creed or sex, whose lives have been saved in an emergency by an Irvin-designed or manufactured parachute.

He chose the name Caterpillar to denote the silk thread, produced by a caterpillar, from which parachutes were woven and the way in which the caterpillar lets itself down to earth by the silken thread. The club motto is: 'Life depends on a silken thread.'

Each member of the club is presented with an engraved gold caterpillar pin. By the outbreak of World War II in 1939, membership had risen to 4,000.

The UK roll now stands at a staggering 32,034, a large proportion being Armed Services personnel who were forced to bale out of stricken aircraft.

An individual file is maintained for most members and some make interesting reading, for example: 'Dear Sir, Will you please enrol me as a member of the Caterpillar Club. I baled out from a blazing kite over Holland on August

15 and made a wizard landing. God bless you, brother Leslie, on behalf of my wife and children, as yet unknown.'

'Dear Leslie, I'd like to thank you for the sweetest moment in all my life when my parachute opened and I realised I was not going to die. Your 'chutes are so good, I'm going to name my son (when I have one) Irvin.'

Famous members have included long-distance flyer Tom Campbell Black, who baled out over Egypt in 1935, Wing Commander Douglas Bader and Jimmy Doolittle, whose life was saved by Irvin parachutes three times.

Judy Adams, Irvin Aerospace, Letchworth, Herts.

? WHY, after the American War of Independence, were the Americans called 'Jonathans' by the British?

ONE theory is that when the Army Commander-in-Chief George Washington was short of ammunition, he called a council of officers, who could offer no solution.

He then said: 'We must consult Brother Jonathan' meaning Jonathan Trumbull, Governor of Connecticut, the only colonial governor to repudiate his oath of allegiance to the King and throw in his lot with the rebels.

Trumbull solved the problem, hence the phrase 'To consult Brother Jonathan'. He became the American equivalent of John Bull the typical Englishman, replaced by Uncle Sam in the early 19th century.

Kevin Heneghan, St Helens, Merseyside.

? HOW does a spider attach the first strand of its web across unconnected high objects?

SPIDERS produce silk from six spinnerets near the tip of the abdomen. Spider silk is very fine and light but very strong, with a tensile strength greater than steel.

Bridging the first gap is achieved in one of two ways: the spider may attach the silk to a piece of vegetation and then walk down the stem, paying out silk and pulling in the slack to form a bridge line. Or it may simply pay out silk from a high point and rely on air currents to drift the stand and attach it around vegetation several feet away.

Spiders can use their silk for ballooning, climbing to the top of a prominent structure and paying out silk to be caught by a rising air current which can lift the spider aloft. Spiders can be carried great distances in this way and are believed to have used it to become one of the first creatures to recolonise Krakatoa after its volcanic eruption 100 years ago.

Dr M. J. Roberts, author: Collins Field Guide To Spiders Of Britain And Northern Europe, Berwickshire.

❓ HOW can so many mobile phones operate without overlapping. Are there enough wavelengths?

IN theory there aren't enough wavelengths. However, an individual radio channel is allocated to each mobile phone only when making a call. As radio waves travel only short distances, the same channel can be repeated many times in non-adjacent cells, meaning that a finite number of channels do not mean a finite number of mobile phones which can operate on the network simultaneously.

In essence, someone in the centre of London could be talking on the same channel as someone 20 miles away without any interference between the two calls.

Carole Williams, BT Cellnet, Slough.

❓ WHAT is the greatest number of football players sent off a field for misconduct during a match?

ON June 1, 1993, referee William Weiler sent off 20 players in a league match between Sportivo Ameliano and General Caballero in Paraguay.

Trouble flared after two Sportivo players were sent off. A ten-minute fight ensued, culminating in Weiler dismissing a further 18 players, including the rest of the Sportivo team. The match was abandoned.

The most sendings off in Britain occurred at a Gancia Cup match at Waltham Abbey, Essex, on December 23, 1973, when the referee sent off the entire Juventus-Cross team and some club officials.

The most undisciplined game was a local cup match between Tongham Youth Club, Surrey, and Hawley, Hampshire, on November 3, 1969. The referee booked all 22 players, including one who went to hospital, and a linesman.

More unusually, Glencraig United had all 11 team members and two substitutes for their 2–2 draw against Goldenhill Boy's club on February 2, 1975, booked in the dressing room before a ball was kicked. The referee took exception to the chant that greeted him on his arrival.

At a specially arranged game between Glasgow and Sheffield in 1930, the referee realised that his shirt was the same colour as the Sheffield strip – and sent himself off.

Brian Madeley, Telford, Shropshire.

? **ARE there any surnames in the country that are held by just one family?**

I BELIEVE the name Didlick (aka Didlock) is unique. A distant cousin in Sydney has carried out a prodigious amount of work which I compiled into a huge tree with 500 names covering 14 generations to put on the Internet.

This tree links Didlicks living all over the world with one family living in a farm near Cleobury Mortimer, Shropshire, at the turn of 16th/17th centuries.

John Didlock, Spalding, Lincs.

WHEN my father's birth was registered in 1909, the registrar made a mistake with the spelling and it was never put right and has been used for the following generations. The family name is now Haslum but previous generations used the spelling Haslam. As far as we are aware there are no other families using this surname.

Mr F. Haslum, Donington le Heath, Leics.

THE name Audfroid is held only by my wife and I. To keep the name alive, my two daughters have decided to retain both our birthnames.

D. J. Audfroid, London.

OUR family surname is Babe. Only my father and brother remain, so my brother is the last remaining male heir.

Clare Babe, Two Mile Ash, Milton Keynes.

I BELIEVE Fatcher, my husband's family name, is unique. As both my husband's grandfather and father have now passed away, we believe there are now only three males with this name: my husband, his brother and our son.

A check made at Somerset House many years ago did not produce any further families with the name.

Margaret V. Fatcher, Bovingdon, Herts.

IN Thailand in 1916, King Vajiravudh said that all Thai families who had previously had only first names, should have surnames – all of them different.

The mechanics of ensuring this must have been complicated but in the three years that I lived in Thailand, I never found two families with the same name.

Thai phone directories list subscribers by their first name followed by the surname since almost all of the latter are different.

Mr N.T. Oliver, Wainfleet St Mary, Lincs.

? 'I DIED for beauty and was scarcely in my tomb, when someone who died for truth was laid in an adjoining room.' Where does this poem come from, and are there any further lines?

THIS is a poem by Emily Dickinson (1831–86), the recluse of Amherst, Massachusetts, nearly all of whose work was unpublished in her lifetime. It is No 449 in Johnson's standard edition, was written in 1862 and was among her first poems published posthumously in 1890.

The full text is:

'I died for Beauty – but was scarce
Adjusted in the Tomb
When One who died for Truth, was lain, in an adjoining Room –
He questioned softly 'Why I failed'?
'For Beauty', I replied –
'And I – for Truth – Themself are One –
We Brethren, are', He said –
And so, as Kinsmen, met at Night –
We talked between the Rooms –
Until the Moss had reached our lips –
And covered up – our names –

The punctuation of this poem is important, as are the capital letters – this was part of Dickinson's unique writing style.

Stephen Kellett, Eastbourne, Sussex.

? WHY do chefs wear checked trousers?

IT was the great master chef Auguste Escoffier who put cooks into check trousers while he managed some of the great hotels including the Grand Hotel in Monte Carlo and The Savoy and Carlton in London.

In his time, all the kitchen lackeys wore white or grey cloths and if any-thing went wrong and a complaint was made, the waitress didn't know who to complain to. Escoffier arranged for cooks to be wear check trousers to distin-guish them from the other workers.

Andrew Thorne, Walmer, Kent.

THE style of trousers now commonly worn by chefs was originally created for butchers in France. Chefs adopted the trousers but with a white coat.

Butchers in France can still be seen sporting both checked trousers and jacket to match, whereas chefs still wear the trousers.

Lucy Rundle, Academy of Culinary Arts, London.

IS there any particular criteria for the draping of a military flag on a coffin?

AT British military funerals the national flag of the deceased's nation is draped over the coffin before the funeral service and up to the moment before internment or cremation, when it is removed.

The flag is laid over the coffin with the hoist of the flag towards the head and the fly towards the feet of the coffin. It may be discreetly tacked or tied to keep it in place.

On the flag are then laid various accoutrements (medals, cap sword etc) belonging to the deceased. It is not correct to use ensigns or other flags for a military funeral.

J. H. Witherow, Squadron leader (rtd), Watford.

THERE are no regulations or laws governing which people, on death, may have a Union Flag draped over their coffin, but the protocol that has built up over the years that the flag be draped only over the coffins of those who have at some time been a member of the Armed Services, merchant fleet or the emergency services.

Gerry Vetriano, Black and Edgington flagmakers, Stratford, London.

IS it true that I can legally buy the birth certificate of any person in the UK?

THE indexes to all registered births in England and Wales since 1837 are available in the public search rooms of the Family Record Centre in Myddelton Street, London, and copies of these indexes are also available to the public at many libraries throughout UK.

Having identified an entry in the public indexes, it's possible to buy a certified copy of the certificate relating to that entry and this can be done in person at the Family Record Centre or by application by post, e-mail, telephone or fax to the General Register Office at Southport.

Alternatively, application can be made direct to the local Register Office for the district in which the birth was registered.

Certificates relating to people who are under 50 years of age or children who died before reaching the age of 16 years, are subject to additional security checks as to the identity of the purchaser.

All certified copy certificates contain a warning that a certificate is not evidence of identity.

Similar facilities exist for obtaining birth certificates of people born in Scotland or Northern Ireland.

John Wynn, People Finders, Peterborough, England.

ANYONE can legally buy the birth certificate of any other person whose birth is registered in the UK. But unless a person can supply every requested detail when applying for a certificate post 1950, they have to supply proof of who the applicants are in various forms.

Marriage and death certificates are also available, but the person applying need only supply their full name and address.

William Hall, Research UK, St Leonards on Sea, Sussex.

❓ WHY were the inhabitants of the region comprising Lanarkshire, Ayrshire and Renfrewshire sometimes referred to as the 'Strathclyde Welsh'?

AFTER the collapse of the Roman Empire, Romano-Britons came under threat from Saxon and other raiders coming from mainland Europe. They opposed them but could not prevent themselves being driven into the west of the country, into what is now Devon, Cornwall, Wales and the south-western corner of Scotland (then called Strathclyde).

So the inhabitants of Lanarkshire, Ayrshire and Renfrewshire are descendants of the Britons of Strathclyde who were ethnically and linguistically akin to the Britons of Wales.

One example is the Scottish patriot Sir William Wallace. When he was born in Elderslie, Renfrewshire, in about the year 1270, the medieval names Walays and Wallensis, from which the modern surname Wallace is derived, denoted a Welshman in the language of the English-speaking peoples in England and Scotland at the time.

In the same way, the surname Inglis denoted Scots of English descent and people surnamed Scott were Borderers from the Scottish side.

Matthew Adcock, Chelmsford, Essex.

❓ IF the Moon really was made of cheese, how many cows would it have taken to make it?

FIGURES supplied by the National Dairy Council give the average amount of milk produced by a dairy cow as about 6,000 litres a year.

It takes about 9,500 litres of milk to produce 1 tonne of cheddar cheese so one cow produces 0.63 tonnes of cheddar cheese a year.

The Moon has a mass of 73,480,000,000,000,000,000 tonnes (73.48 billion billion tonnes) so it would take 73.48 billion billion / 0.63 = 117,000,000,000,000,000,000 (117 billion billion) cows one year to produce a piece of cheddar of the same weight as the Moon.

The UK dairy herd in 1999 consisted of 2,439,000 cows so it would take 48,000,000,000,000 (48 thousand billion) years for it to produce the amount of cheddar cheese required to fabricate one Earth moon.

Iain Crawford, Bearsden, Glasgow.

TO answer this, we must take account of the relative densities of moon rock and cheese. The moon has a mass of 73.48 billion billion tonnes of moon rock: the equivalent mass of cheddar cheese would be at least ten times the size of the original.

Since traditionally the Moon would be made of Swiss cheese, one fiftieth the density of moon rock, only 1.47 billion billion tonnes of Swiss cheese would be needed.

Anthony Davis, London N9.

❓ IS there anyone born in this country who can truly claim to be of pure British stock?

ADRIAN Targett, the 44-year-old teacher from the Cheddar Gorge area whose 9,000-year direct ancestor was discovered in Cheddar Gorge and matched to him by DNA tests in 1997, would certainly be a good candidate.

His dead ancestor pre-dates the Celts by 7,000 years and the separation of Britain from the European landmass by 3,000. This continuity gives the lie to the fashionable suggestion that all Englishmen are Anglo-Saxon interlopers and everyone else the 'true British'.

Pat Poole, St Austell, Cornwall.

IT'S impossible to trace every one of your ancestors but all the 271 ancestors, paternal and maternal, I've traced in my family tree were born or baptised in England. So I can not only claim to be of pure British stock but also of pure English stock.

On some lines I've traced back to the 15th century, to my 13-times great grandparents. The number of ancestors in each generation doubles so to have found all of these would have meant studying more than 65,000 lives. So there's always a chance that some foreign blood may turn up somewhere.

Two-hundred-and-seventy-one ancestors may not sound much, especially after 30 years of hard work but as I like to find out all I can about each one it takes a lot of time and research. I don't have any noble ancestry, just yeoman, tradesmen and agricultural labourers.

June Biggs, Petts Wood, Kent.

WHICH is the closest football club to the open sea?

ARBROATH Football Club's ground at Gayfield is about 20ft (just two pavements and a single carriageway road) from the sea.

During rough weather, the sea waves have been known to actually hit the wall of the ground.

Rosemary Hoskins, Falkirk.

OVER the years many a ball has been lost at Gayfield Park when the tide is in. And it's probably the coldest ground in Britain when the North Sea winds get up.

Hamish Fairweather, Arbroath.

WHY do Hindus worship cows?

WORSHIP is too strong a word. Reverence for the cow is an important feature of Hinduism and, for believers, killing a cow is a serious crime.

In World War II, U.S. servicemen driving in Calcutta were told that if they faced a split-second decision between hitting a cow or a human, they should hit the human.

The concept of the sacred cow has been a part of India's culture from time immemorial. It stems from the many benefits rendered by the cow to ease the burden of the poor, with the animal's milk providing food and its dung serving as both fuel and manure.

The National Council of Applied Economic Research says cattle dung in India provides fuel equivalent to 35 million tonnes of coal or 68 million tonnes of wood.

To generate this amount of energy by modern industrial processes would cost three times as much as supporting the livestock. It's estimated that animal power accounts for 66 per cent of the energy used in India, against 14 per cent from conventional sources.

Charles Fernandez, London W I.

THE first value a Hindu child learns from his or her family is respect for the mother and this respect for motherhood is extended to other natural beings which provide sustenance for life.

The cow, the provider of milk, is considered holy and worshipped as a mother; similarly, the Earth and nature are treated with respect.

The cow was the first animal Hindus in India domesticated. In the Vedic age (more than 5,000 years ago), the cow was a great blessing to the rural community, providing milk and milk derivitives. Its dung was used for domestic fire fuel and mixed with mud as a plaster for walls and floors.

On the farm, the bull ploughed the fields and was also a means for travel and transport. It's hardly surprising that in the life of man the cow soon occupied the same position as a mother in the life of a child.

Hindu scriptures prohibit cow slaughter and in some states in India there is now a legal ban.

Dr Nawal K. Prinja, World Council of Hindus, Manchester.

IS London's Marble Arch actually made of marble?

MARBLE Arch, designed by John Nash (1752–1835) to commemorate Nelson and Wellington's victories in the war against France, is made of white Carrara marble and cost £80,000. Inspired by the triumphal Arch of Constantine in Rome, it was built in 1821 as a ceremonial entry to Buckingham Palace.

When Queen Victoria and Prince Albert enlarged the palace in 1851, it was moved to the north-east corner of Hyde Park, at the end of Oxford Street. In the move, Samuel Parker's metal gates within the Arch, at that time the largest gates in Europe, were damaged and had to have the semicircle at the top removed.

From 1851 to 1908, the Arch spanned the normal traffic route but road changes since have left it on an island surrounded by roads.

The top of the Arch was meant to display Francis Chantrey's bronze equestrian statue of George IV but this ended up in Trafalgar Square.
John Hutton, Twickenham, Middx.

? WHAT would happen if you opened a can of lager in space? Would it have a frothy head?

OPENING a pressurised lager container in a pressurised environment such as the Mir space station, would be no different from opening one normally under Earth conditions or in the pressurised cabin of an airliner in flight.

Taking the same lager can outside the space capsule into the vacuum of space would make the can explode like a fragmentation device.

The chief difference inside a space capsule would be that while some of the lager might froth out of the top under pressure, the rest of it wouldn't come out when you tipped the can upside down because there's no gravity in space.

To have a drink, you would have to put the glass over the top of the can and spin can and glass around by the base to force the beer out into the glass.
Dean Cooke, Allesley Park, Coventry.

? I'M allergic to yeast and tomatoes. When making bread, is there a substitute for yeast to make bread rise? And is there an alternative to tomatoes in dishes such as bolognese, chilli, etc?

TOMATOES are a member of the deadly nightshade family and are commonly the cause of an allergic response. The best replacement is red peppers, also members of the nightshade family but less likely to cause a reaction.

There are several yeast-free breads available. The most popular is no yeast sourdough bread. The recipe for this requires sourdough culture, which can be bought at most health food shops.

Other possible yeast-free alternatives include soda bread/soda farls, manna bread and some Indian breads such as chapattis but it's always advisable to check the ingredients.
Vicky Lee Millward, Southbourne Natural Health Centre, Bournemouth.

ARE SECOND MARRIAGES HAPPY?

DEAR *Answers*,—Although, of course, marriage for the second time takes place among all sorts and conditions of people, there are certain classes of society in which second marriages are the rule rather than the exception, and in these I believe the departure is usually a happy one.

A second marriage of course necessarily has its greatest effect upon the children of the first union, and I regret that although in many cases the parents are perfectly happy, the children rise up in unreasoning protest against the step-father or step-mother, as the case may be.

Given the absence of step-children, my own experience teaches me that second marriages are, as a general rule, most happy.

Twice Wedded, Dundee.

People who marry for the second time are usually more or less of a mature age and are thus, by reason of their greater experience, the more likely to allow for and understand each other's failings.

They are practical too and although the union may be what is known as a 'love match,' it in no way prevents them from looking at life in a staid, sensible manner.

These, I think, are the reasons why, as a general rule, second marriages are not only happy, but often happier than those first unions, in which want of experience and judgment are so fatal to happiness.

Answerite, Chester.

I am disgusted with those who consider marriage for the second time invariably a success. I am afraid those cases must be somewhat exceptional.

My own experience, and that of many of my friends to whom I have talked upon the subject, is that marriage for the second time is usually, as far as happiness is concerned, a dead failure.

The step-children are wronged and treated, more often than not, cruelly. Is it any wonder, then, if they have an abhorrence of step-parents?

Second marriages are, in nine cases out of ten, a matter of

❓ WHAT happened to the Council For Education In World Citizenship, to which I belonged at school in the Sixties?

WE have been preparing British young people for citizenship since 1939 and are still going strong in an increasingly interdependent world, serving more school and college students than ever. Through activities, events and publications we help them understand and confront global issues and challenges.

Originally part of the League of Nations Union, then the United Nations Association, we're now an independent charity with a membership including 1,500 schools.

Many prominent people say their contact with the Council For Education In World Citizenship (CEWC) while at school sparked their interest in public life. Michael Portillo, Virginia Bottomley, Glenys Kinnock, Jack Straw, David Steel, Lord Frank Judd, Melvyn Bragg and Jonathan Porritt have all been members.

Friends of the CEWC gather at Westminster in February each year. We welcome individual and groups as members, as well as schools and colleges.
Patricia Rodgers, Council for Education In World Citizenship, London EC1.

❓ WHEN did we stop using solid cannon balls and start using explosive shells in battle?

THE first recorded use of an exploding shell was by the Spanish at the siege of the Dutch fortress of Wachtendonk in 1588. These early shells were hollowed-out metal cases filled with gunpowder, lit by a fuse. The shell was propelled over a defensive wall using a high-angled cannon, such as a mortar or howitzer.

In the late 1700s, the case shot was developed for use with ordinary field artillery. These were light metal canisters packed with musket balls. The case burst after firing to pepper the enemy with projectiles.

In 1784 British artillery officer Lieutenant Henry Shrapnel invented a fused shell for the same purpose. It was first used at the battle of Maida in 1803. The shell could be fused accurately enough to be made to burst either directly in front of, or above, enemy infantry. Shrapnel's name came to describe all metal fragments propelled from an explosion.

The use of these shells is recognised in the American national anthem, 'The Star Spangled Banner', where the line 'the rockets bright flare/the shells bursting in air' refers to the war of 1812.

R. J. Cubitt, Byfield, Northants.

WHICH time zone has the most people in it?

OF the 192 independent nations of the world, 17 share the same time zone as the UK, with a combined population of 195,489 million.

The time zone with the most countries is GMT +1, which includes much of western Europe and large parts of Africa, having a combined population of 656,681 million.

The time zone with the most people is GMT +8 incorporating the most populous country in the world, China. Unlike the USA, Russia, Brazil and other large countries, it doesn't have separate time zones. It also includes Brunei, Malaysia, Mongolia, the Philippines, Singapore and Taiwan, and has a combined population of 1,375 million, almost a quarter of the world's people.

The second most populous time zone is GMT +5h30m, encompassing India alone, with a population of 1,001 million.

Kevin Cathcart, Moston, Manchester.

HAS an airline pilot ever mistakenly taken his passengers and plane to the wrong airport?

THE classic wrong way story was that of Douglas Corrigan. On July 17, 1938, he filed a flight plan for California, but 29 hours later landed in Ireland.

He had earlier applied for permission to cross the Atlantic but officials said his plane was not safe. He blamed a faulty compass for his error and became known for the rest of his life as 'Wrong Way Corrigan'.

John Atkinson, Douglas, Isle of Man.

BACK in the 1960s, when I lived near Northolt aerodrome in Middlesex, a Boeing 707 landed at RAF Northolt when it should have landed at Heathrow.

Landing instructions for pilots at the time advised them to get the gasometer near Harrow aligned with the runway and they couldn't go wrong. But this American pilot wasn't used to London and lined up the wrong gasometer with the wrong runway.

Having landed on the much shorter RAF runway, the Boeing had to have everything taken out, including the seats, to enable it to take off, and the nearby A40 Western Avenue was closed in case it didn't make it.

After this, the two gasometers were marked with large letters 'NO' and 'HR' to represent the the runways. Locals always laughed at the one in Harrow with NO emblazoned on it.

Clive M. Harvey, Brackley, Northants.

ONE hot evening at the small Army Air Corps helicopter strip in Cyprus, the only person around was the duty NCO when the peace was shattered by the roar of aircraft engines.

Going outside, the NCO discovered a Romanian Tarom Airlines twin-engined Antonov aircraft stopped with its nose right up against the fence at the end of the short airstrip.

The pilot had mistaken the small airfield for Larnaca Airport, 15 miles away across the bay. The runway was too short and the aircraft too heavy to take off, so the passengers completed their journey by bus.

The aircraft was eventually flown out by the company's chief pilot, after all the seats had been removed, the fuel had been drained leaving just enough to reach Larnaca, and the fence at the end of the runway had been removed.

Dave Braine, London.

THAT Romanian aircraft actually landed after dark, the pilot having mistaken the lights of Dhekelia garrison for those of Larnaca town. I was on guard duty there that night.

Jim Yeats, Brandesburton, East Yorks.

IN the film *Brief Encounter*, there are two scenes taken over a bridge in the countryside. Does it still exist?

FILMING started on *Brief Encounter* at Carnforth on February 5, 1945, and continued until February 18. There were about 70 people involved, and accommodation was a problem because of evacuees from London.

The cast and crew had to be spread out over six hotels, The Royal Station Hotel at Carnforth, The Royal Hotel at Bolton le Sands, one hotel at Morecambe and one at Lancaster. The main actors and senior production people stayed at The Low Wood Hotel or the Langdale Chaise Hotel near Windermere.

There are two scenes in the film where the lovers meet at a small bridge. The bridge has been difficult to locate but with the help of two local papers, the *Lancaster Citizen* and the *Westmorland Gazette*, the bridge near the Old Dungeon Ghyll Hotel, in the Langdale valley showed an exact match. Fifty-five years after the film was made the bridge looks exactly the same.

Peter E. Davies, Friends of Carnforth Station, Carnforth, Lancs.

WHAT causes the electric shock I often get when I open my car door, and is there any way of preventing this?

AIR is made up of atoms and electrons. By passing through air, people, cars, aeroplanes, trains etc, effectively rub against these electrons and gradually build up a static electrical charge.

The charge is not easily earthed or discharged from a car as it's insulated from the earth by four rubber tyres. When a passenger gets out and touches both the car and the ground, the passenger provides the earth for the charge, and a small static shock may be felt.

There is no danger of this charge ever building up to dangerous levels, at worst the person will feel a slight jolt, or perhaps hear a small crackle as the static discharges.

It has been suggested that the static build-up can contribute to travel sickness, but as it's the car body not the human body which becomes charged, this is highly unlikely.

David Stephenson, Newtown, Powys.

MOTORISTS often experience painful shocks because of the static generated as they slide out of their seat. The level of shock depends on their clothing and footwear, the seating material and the humidity. Synthetic materials can create 10,000 volts or more when rubbed together, so natural materials can alleviate the problem.

Gordon Rowlands, Statpad Ltd, Macclesfield, Cheshire.

IF you put your hand on a metal part of the door and keep it there when getting out of the car, the static electricity will still flow through you, but as the spark isn't jumping to your hand, it will be painless.
Debbie Rogers, Chelmsford.

DID anyone actually pay out, or get paid, the ridiculous sums of money being reported previously for babysitting, childminding, or other work done on Millennium Eve?

WE were forced to call out a plumber on the night in question. There was a burst pipe and we were expecting 30 guests for a party. After turning up within the hour, fixing the pipe and wishing us a Happy New Year, he sent us the dreaded bill. It came to the grand total of £25 – obviously not everyone was out to make a huge profit.
Alexia English, Monks Risborough, Bucks.

FOR Millennium Eve I advertised £45 each person for admission to the pub that I manage. This included 15 drinks, entertainment and a buffet. We sold all 250 tickets in the first 21 days.

On the night I had 14 staff working, and 250 of my closest pub friends and I danced all night. By the morning we had raised £800 towards the local village hall. I was paid £1,000 for the event, and gave £650 to charity.
Mike Loftus, Anderton Arms, Fulwood, Preston.

WHEN a horse is at full gallop is there a point at which all four of its hooves are off the ground at the same time?

A FULL gallop is not the only pace at which a horse has all four feet off the ground. Cantering also includes a brief 'moment of suspension' when the horse doesn't come into contact with the surface and even during a trot all four hooves can be suspended in the air.

However, it is in the gallop where this is most obvious. The gallop is called a 'four-time pace', meaning that there are four hoof beats, which can be heard as the horse puts each foot on the ground one after another, in this order: near hind, off hind, near fore, off fore.

Before the horse returns to its near hind to repeat the sequence, it is suspended in mid-air, its legs almost tucked right under the body. As the powerful hindquarters have to work hard pushing the horse forwards, it's best for the horse to lean forward. This is why jockeys almost stand up in the saddle – to allow the horse to move.

Shoshannah McCarthy, Stamford, Lincs.

? **WHY do we turn clocks back seven weeks before the Winter Solstice, yet wait till 13 weeks afterwards to move them forward again?**

THE dates have no specific connection with the Winter Solstice; they were chosen simply because they maximise daylight hours when using a 'daylight saving' scheme.

Although we've been using a version of daylight saving since 1916, our current scheme of using the last Sunday in March and the Saturday before the last Sunday in October as the beginning and end of Summer Time dates from 1981, when the UK accepted a European Council directive which bought us into line with other EU members.

Robert Warren, Royal Observatory, Greenwich, London.

? **'THE common cormorant or shag, lays eggs inside a paper bag' goes the rhyme. But is this true?**

THE cormorant (related to the shag, but a distinct species) breeds by the coast and at some inland wetlands. Its nest is made of seaweed by the coast and of sticks and reeds inland. As a bird which spends a lot of its time swimming and diving, a nest made of paper would soon become sodden, unable to hold three or four 60g eggs that the bird lays.

There are, however, reports of some very unusual nests including a mistle thrush which nested in a set of working traffic lights and a wren which nested in a bra on a washing line. Old kettles, jacket pockets, post boxes, even a human skull have been used as nest sites.

The materials for the nest can also be strange with such extremes as a carrion crow at Heathrow which built a typically tangled nest of metal wire and a thrush whose nest was made entirely of shredded plastic waste from a factory.

Chris Harbard, RSPB, Sandy, Beds.

THE nonsense poem is by Christopher Isherwood and goes:

The common cormorant (or shag)
Lays eggs inside a paper bag,

You follow the idea, no doubt?
It's to keep the lightning out.
But what these unobservant birds
Have never thought of, is that herds
Of wandering bears might come with buns
And steal the bags to hold the crumbs.

S. Andrews, London E11.

? ARE there any countries in the world which don't brew their own beer?

THE first known beers – probably porridgey brews like the traditional beers still made in African villages – were made by the Sumerians. Today's beers have their origins in the cooler nations where grains (barley) rather than grapes are cultivated – the Czech Republic, Germany, Belgium, Britain and Ireland.

The Czech cities of Pilsen and Budweis, in Bohemia, produced golden lagers; Germany (especially Bavaria) made dark lagers and wheat beers; Belgium made wheat beers, sour beers, strong bottle-conditioned ales in extraordinary diversity; Britain made cask-conditioned ales (hoppy in England, malty in Scotland) while Ireland made dry stouts. The traditions of those countries influenced a second stratum of adjoining nations and regions, notably The Netherlands and Denmark.

All of these traditions were transplanted by settlers in the colonial period. Most of the world's bland, mass-market, beer now is golden lager in a distant derivative of the Pilsner style.

Most countries have at least one brewery. Even Islamic nations have breweries for business visitors and tourists. The only countries without sanctioned breweries are Islamic states such as Iran, Iraq and Saudi Arabia or very small island nations like the sovereign island states of Micronesia in the Pacific Ocean.

The brewing of modern beer in the New World, intermediate economies and the Third World was largely a result of colonial influence but, in most cases, the original colonial aspect has long eroded and most beers from diverse countries are just bland standard lagers.

The few exceptions are the tastier lagers like Singha from Thailand and stouts in various African and Caribbean nations.

Among the new generation of micro-brews, the most exotic I've tasted from unlikely countries were a German-style smoked beer and Belgian-style fruit beers from a tiny brewery in El Bolson, in Patagonia, Argentina.

Michael Jackson, author: Pocket Guide to Beer, Mitchell Beazley Publishers, London.

❓ IS Cleopatra buried in Paris?

THE idea that Cleopatra is buried in Paris stems from the false rumour that Jean Francois Champollion (1790–1832), founder of French Egyptology and best known as the man who first used the Rosetta Stone to decipher Egyptian hieroglyphics in the early 1820s, discovered Cleopatra's sarcophagus in the French National Library cellars and had her buried in the library gardens at dead of night.

When Napoleon invaded Egypt in 1798, he had thousands of ancient artefacts shipped back to France and Champollion was appointed conservator of the Egyptian collections in 1826.

It's possible that a number of things were buried in Paris but not the body of Cleopatra. The location of Cleopatra's body hasn't yet been identified but is thought to be in an area of ancient Alexandria which is now submerged below the Mediterranean.

Prof John Ray, Oriental Studies Department, Cambridge University.

❓ HAS a tunnel to the Isle of Wight ever been considered?

THE idea of a Solent tunnel intrigued late Victorian entrepreneurs and engineers and an 1873 proposal involved a tunnel between Eaglehurst, near Calshot, and Cowes. Ten years later, a tunnel was suggested from Portsea to Ryde, followed by a Stokes Bay to Ryde Pierhead plan. None of these schemes got beyond planning stage.

In 1901, the South Western and Isle of Wight Junction Railway was formed to build a seven-mile line linking the Lymington branch of the London and South Western Railway to Freshwater, Yarmouth and Newport Railway through a single-track tunnel.

Further proposals appeared in 1912 when war looked likely and a link with the mainland was thought necessary in case of invasion. The next year, an electric tube line was suggested between Stokes Bay and Ryde.

In 1935, a postal referendum on the islands voted for a link but the idea was rejected when a levy was suggested for construction costs.

In 1961, a Solent Bridge between Gurnard and Calshot was on the agenda, at an initial cost of £7 million, but the idea was shelved. It returned in 1982, by which time the estimated cost had risen to £65 million and it was shelved again.

In 1990, an idea was put forward for a power-generating barrage across the Solent, which would also act as a road link, but it found little favour.

The idea of an Isle of Wight link splits our island community, one side regarding it as vital to the island's economic growth, the other suggesting a link would swamp the island with mainland traffic and destroy its character and charm.

A proposal by the Winchester-based consortium Linkland suggests a small-diameter tunnel between Gosport and Ryde, carrying a single line of traffic and bringing prosperity without affecting the island's character.
Chris Alldred, Isle of Wight Council.

WHAT has been the largest difference in size between two opposing armies in the 20th century in which the smaller force has won the battle?

TO its shame, Winston Churchill's government, under pressure from tin miners and rubber planters, sent the British 18th Division to reinforce the garrison on Singapore, regarded in February 1942 as an impregnable island.

Two capital ships, HMS *Prince Of Wales* and *Repulse*, hurriedly dispatched to the Pacific fleet, were sunk by the Japanese, with tremendous losses.

The Australians had already sent their 8th Division, and some 40,000 crack Indian troops also arrived to bolster the few hundred regular soldiers of the Singapore garrison.

But military leadership was faulty and morale was low. This total of 60,000 men, despite greatly outnumbering the enemy, surrendered to a very much smaller force of Japanese, who had landed on northern Malaya.

This campaign proved how little manpower mattered in modern warfare. Another 100,000 defending Singapore would have made no difference when we needed planes, ships, tanks and armoured cars.
Jack Caplan, Canterbury.

DURING the twin battles of Imphal and Kohima in Burma in May 1944, among the most desperate and bloody engagements of World War II, a force of 410 to 420 British Empire troops defeated 13,000 Japanese.

The Japanese were attempting to invade India but their advance halted at one side of the tennis court in the grounds of the Governor's residence in Kohima.

The defenders, who included cooks, clerks, military police and other administration staff fighting in the front line, stopped them there – and a tennis court is still maintained as part of the war memorial at Kohima to remind people of this.

W. Bagwell, Canterbury.

❓ WHY is some game hung for days before cooking yet a chicken treated in the same way would give us food poisoning?

IT'S common knowledge that game is improved by hanging but, for centuries, other meats and fish were also hung to develop flavour and improve tenderness. Beef, venison, fish, rabbit and even chicken and turkey can be hung.

They benefit from harmless bacteria in the meat breaking down muscle tissue. Some chickens and turkey are still hung, particularly at Christmas. So long as they are hung uneviscerated and cooked fully as soon after evisceration as possible, this is safe.

Prompt cooking destroys any salmonella that may have been released from the gut during evisceration. As people become increasingly demanding about the flavour and texture of their meat, we will see more hung meat on sale – and not just game.

Louisa Ayland, The Game Marketing Executive, London W2.

❓ ARE the horses in a race really trying to win or do they think they're out for a gallop with some friends?

NOBODY really knows. Anecdotal evidence from jockeys and trainers suggests many horses are aware they're in a race and want to get to the finishing line ahead of the rest but others say horses have very strong herding instincts and tend to want to stay together.

The herding characteristic is demonstrated when they fall or unseat their rider during a race, only to pick themselves up, chase after the pack and stay alongside them for the rest of the contest.

Horses are very bright animals and, like humans, have varied, complex personalities. Some display stubbornness, refusing to start a race or losing interest halfway round and pulling themselves up. Others seem to show a will to win the race and refuse to allow any other horse to run past them.

The most likely answer is that horses have no concept of being in a race as we would imagine it and instinctively run with the pack but their breeding over many generations has been honed to produce animals that not only run fast but also have a strong desire to run ahead of the pack.

Simon Clare, Coral Bookmakers, Barking, Essex.

? WHAT is the origin and meaning of the phrase 'crossing the bar'?

THIS saying springs from yet another piece of Britain's maritime history. The bar involved is the natural or man-made rise in the sea bed at the mouth of a river or entrance to a harbour. Any modern sailor entering a river or harbour will see the bar, as he crosses it, on his echo sounder.

In days gone by, when we were a great nation of sailors, a ship was considered to have begun or finished its journey when it 'crossed the bar' on its outward or inward voyage. Many sailors would talk of 'crossing the bar' when they were about to change their way of life, including getting married.

The saying was also used to mean death, the end of the human journey. In 1889, Poet Laureate Alfred Lord Tennyson took just 20 minutes while crossing the Solent by boat to pen his famous poem 'Crossing The Bar', which includes the lines: 'For tho' from out our bourne of Time and Place The flood may bear me far, I hope to see my Pilot face to face When I have crost the bar.'

Albe Lechley, Isle of Dogs, London.

? WHAT control has a barrister practising in the English courts over the cases he is liable to represent?

A BARRISTER (counsel) is expected to obey the 'cab rank rule' and take whatever case turns up next. Naturally, if it's a case on a subject in a specialist field in which he does not profess to practise he may – and indeed should – refuse it.

Certain counsel, known as Treasury Counsel, are retained by the Crown, for example, to prosecute at the Central Criminal Court ('Old Bailey') and are expected to do that.

It has been the practice for certain potential clients to pay a fee called a retainer to an individual to prevent him from acting against them. And, of course, he must avoid acting where he has a potential conflict of interest in so doing. So he has more restrictions than he has choice.

Christopher Nutt, (retired counsel), London.

WHAT DO THE FRENCH THINK OF US?

DEAR *Answers*,—The average Frenchman's ideas of our national characteristics are exceedingly humorous. The French people who reside out of Paris think the average Englishman is the John Bull of the children's picture-books, corpulent, stolid-looking, and attired in the regulation rig-out of a stumpy top hat, corduroys and tops.

Notwithstanding this idea, however, the Frenchman likes us very much and, in spite of his fixed notion that we are pig-headed and lack all refinement and sense of the artistic, is a firm believer in the power and ability of les Anglais.

We are not credited with the possession of any courtesy by the Frenchman whose knowledge of our ways is solely based on what he has read in very much overdrawn French novels and it would probably be the most difficult thing in the world to convince him that we do not live entirely on roast beef.

The secret of the Frenchman's liking for us probably lies in the fact that we possess one quality which is lacking in his own character – coolness and precision of nerve at a critical moment. Brave as the average Frenchman is, his coolness deserts him under such conditions and if a long steady shot is required to mark the turning-point to victory in a shooting match or in any other unnerving crisis, it is only the Englishman who will casually stroll up and, in the coolest possible manner, pick up his rifle and plank a bull.

One Who Likes The French, Hotel Metropole.

Although not in a position either to contradict or corroborate reported remarks anent the French view of les Anglais, this I do know, that the feeling between French and English naval officers and sailors is very cordial, and our Jack Tars are always ready to give Jacques a pleasant and friendly reception.

Some years ago, I was attached to a gunboat on the Panama station, where we spent our time in cruising about within a day or two's distance of Panama.

On one occasion when off the town, a French gunboat came in and during her stay we got on such friendly terms with her officers and crew that the former invited my brother officers and myself, with a certain number of the crew, on board to dinner, where we were received with that courtesy and open-heartedness so characteristic of the French nation.

No expense was spared in the endeavour to entertain us in the most sumptuous fashion. Not only the officers but the men were supplied with wine, and the dinner and entertainment provided afterwards were admirable.

On a French ship every seaman has his allowance of wine.

A short time after this little entertainment, we determined to entertain the French and, not to be beaten in hospitality, went so far as to invite every man aboard their ship to dinner. The vessel was gaily decked out with bunting, the fare prepared was of the best, and a rough-and-ready concert was arranged to follow.

At the appointed hour, the French crew came off to our gunboat and took their places at the long tables knocked up by our carpenters on board. We had so arranged it that every French sailor should sit between two of our own bluejackets and this arrangement was carried out.

The rough-and-ready concert was a tremendous success and the Frenchmen went back delighted with their treatment and their English confreres. On the next day they steamed away from Panama.

For years afterwards, no French ship ever visited the Panama station without showing the British sailors on the station all the hospitality they were capable of. Need I say it was reciprocated? It is, I think, a very nice and happy feeling their friendship between the two great navies, and, for my own part, I hope it may long continue so.

A British Sailor, Yarmouth.

WHERE do hiccoughs come from and how does one get rid of them?

HICCOUGHS are caused by a sudden, involuntary contraction of the diaphragm, coupled with a rapid closure of the vocal cords, which produces the sound.

People usually get hiccoughs through an irritation of the diaphragm or phrenic nerves, rarely through a medical condition, though hiccoughs can be caused by stomach disorders, pleurisy, hepatitis, pancreatitis, alcohol poisoning or a disorder in the oesophagus.

Numerous popular remedies include holding one's breath, drinking cold water or trying to sneeze. Drugs or surgery may be prescribed in severe cases.

The longest recorded attack of hiccoughing affected an American called Charles Osborne of Anthon, Iowa, who began hiccoughing in 1922 while trying to weigh a hog and continued every one-and-a-half seconds until February 1990. Despite his affliction, he had two wives and eight children. He died on May 1, 1991.

David Farmer, Carlisle, Cumbria.

YOU can cure hiccoughs by bending forward while standing and drinking water from the far side of a glass. This certainly does work.

David Jeffreys, Sutton Coldfield.

? WHY does peeling onions make you cry?

THE onion contains a compound called isothiocyanate and the enzyme allinase which react when they come into contact with each other, which happens when an onion is peeled or crushed.

The combination of the two produces a sulphur-based vapour which irritates the eyes. The horseradish and mustard plants contain similar products.

Dr Gordon Roberts, Food & Consumer Technology Dept, Manchester Metropolitan University.

? HOW did the American town called Truth Or Consequences come by its name?

THE tiny town of Truth Or Consequences, between Albuquerque and Las Cruses in New Mexico, has a population of about 6,221 and is popular with tourists and senior citizens because of its dry climate, proximity to lakes, mountains and historical areas, numerous restaurants and community recreational activities.

But it's best known for its unusual name. Formerly known as Hot Springs, it grew up around the hot mineral water springs in the area, expanding rapidly in the early 20th century when workers from the Bureau of Reclamation built Elephant Butte Dam on the nearby Rio Grande.

In 1950, one of the most popular radio shows in the U.S. was *Truth Or Con-*

sequences, hosted by Ralph Edwards. When the show had been running for almost ten years, to mark the anniversary Edwards announced that he was looking for an American town prepared to change its name to that of the show.

In return, he would host the anniversary show from that town and bring it to the world's attention. After careful consideration, Hot Springs volunteered and was chosen: 1,294 residents were in favour of changing the town name with only 295 against.

Every year since then, Truth Or Consequences – T Or C as it is more commonly known – has held an annual fiesta which Ralph Edwards, now in his 80s, has faithfully attended.

Cathy Johnson, Truth Or Consequences Civic Center, New Mexico.

❓ WHY is a hot dog so called?

IN 1904, Anton Feuchtwanger asked his brother-in-law to bake buns for sausages he was selling at the St Louis Exhibition. Before that he had been loaning gloves to customers to wear while they held the hot sausages.

In 1906, cartoonist Tad Dorgan caricatured the new snack by drawing a snapping sausage dog and, unsure how to spell dachshund, called it 'hot dog'. Today, our company supplies about 80 million hot dogs/frankfurters a year.

Iain Meldrum, Westler Foods, Malton, North Yorks.

LIKE many people growing up in the 1940s, 1950s and 1960s, I first came across hot dogs at fairgrounds, the seaside and the cinema. And the link between entertainment and this slightly dubious sausage product goes back more than 100 years to Coney Island, near New York City.

In the second half of the 19th century, three great amusement parks were built there and became America's national playground.

One of the attractions was electric bathing. Under primitive arc lamps, daring bathers swam in the cold waters of the Hudson and warmed up afterwards, eating a novel kind of fast food, basically sausage and chilli peppers, invented by Charles Feltman and available from his shore-line restaurant. He called them Coney Island Red Hots, others, less certain of their ingredients, called them hot dogs.

They were so well liked that 'hot dog' became a popular slang expression of approval.

Jonathan Hill, Bampton Museum, Devon.

? **DOES anyone have a remedy for getting rid of plagues of ants, when all powders, sprays etc have failed and the garden is over-run with them?**

ANTS are masterful in finding new ways out of their nests and other means to avoid sprayed areas. Even if you kill existing ants, there will be more eggs in the nest – they can lie dormant during the winter and hatch out from early April onwards.

Inspect for ant activity annually, from early April onwards. Choose a time of day when the sun has been out for two or three hours, when the ground is warm and the ants are active. Spraying infected areas early helps prevent the build up of fresh eggs in the nest.

Reinspect the infected areas every fortnight and spray as necessary. Remember to check under foliage across path edges and lawn edges. If you find the ants are getting smaller, you are winning, because these will be the newly hatched ones.

A week after spraying, fill a small plastic hand sprayer with paraffin and spray down cracks in any concrete paving being used by the ants. By the second year you should see a marked improvement and by the third year you should be just getting rid of the odd fresh infestation.

Kenneth Holford, Manchester.

TRY mixing vinegar and mint in a spray bottle. Put some around doors where they can get into the house etc.

My mother got this information from an American helpful hints book and passed it on to me. It's worth a try and it's non-toxic.

K. Giggal, Ipswich.

———

? **A STEEP hill in Harpurhey, Manchester, is called Factory Lane but is better known by locals as Factory Brew. What is, or was a 'Brew'?**

'BREW' probably derives from *bre* the old Welsh word for 'hill'. Old Welsh, or British, was the language of the whole of Britain for 1,000 years before the Angles and Saxons came from northern Europe in the 5th century.

Welsh survived in Cumbria and parts of Lancashire for several centuries after that. There are hundreds of Welsh place names throughout England and Scotland. Brewood (Staffs) meaning 'wood by the hill called bre' and Bredon (Hereford) 'Hill called Bre' probably have the same origins as 'Brew'. Modern

Welsh words for 'hill' are *bryn* and *rhiw*.

Lyn Jenkins, Cardigan, Wales.

A 'BREW' in Suffolk dialect is the edge of a field between the 'ridlum', headland, or turning point, and the ditch. It probably shoud be 'brow', the edge of a high place.

Old Suffolkers often changed their vowel sounds. Thus a 'shed' would invariably be a 'shod'.

E. Thorpe, Barking, Suffolk.

❓ WHAT is the exact role of a U.S. Marshal in relation to the numerous other law enforcement agencies in the USA?

THE United States Marshals Service is the nation's oldest Federal Law enforcement agency, a vital link between executive and judicial branches of government since 1789.

Federal agencies are centralised bodies which work across state boundaries. The service provides support and protection for the Federal courts, including security for 800 judicial facilities and 2,000 judges and magistrates, as well as trial participants, jurors and attorneys.

It's responsible for apprehending most Federal fugitives; operating the Witness Security programme; maintaining custody of and transporting Federal prisoners; executing court orders and arrest warrants; managing and selling seized property forfeited by drug traffickers and other criminals; responding to emergencies including civil disturbance, terrorist incidents and other crises situations through its Special Operations group, and restoring order in riots.

Bob Hammond, Islington, London.

❓ WHY is a packed lunch colloquially referred to in certain areas of the country as 'snap'?

THIS was originally a North Midlands dialect term for a mid-shift snack. 'Snap' originally meant a thief's share of the booty and is linked to 'snack', a snap or bite, especially by a dog. The image is of a snatched mouthful.

'Snap' seems to have been spread by railwaymen from the 1920s and was adopted by Lancashire miners. Snap was carried in a snap tin, which was flat at one end and rounded at the other to accommodate slices of bread.

Kevin Heneghan, St Helens, Merseyside.

? WHAT happened to the ships which attended the *Titanic* when it sank?

AFTER *Titanic* sunk, the 705 passengers and crew who survived in the lifeboats were rescued by the Cunard liner *Carpathia*, under the command of Captain Arthur Henry Rostron.

The 540ft *Carpathia* was constructed in 1902 and weighed 13,603 tons. She left New York on April 11, 1912, bound for the Mediterranean. On hearing *Titanic*'s distress call, she raced to the scene, arriving at 4am, and picked up survivors.

She headed back for New York, arriving on April 18. Two days later, after the captain had attended the American inquiry, she resumed her voyage.

After the disaster, commemorative medals were presented to each of the 320 crew members who took part in the rescue.

On July 17, 1918, *Carpathia* was torpedoed and sunk by a German submarine, with the loss of five crew members. On September 9, 1999, the wreck was reported to have been discovered 185 miles west of Land's End.

Jason King, St Albans, Herts.

THE large loss of life from the *Titanic* was thought (though never proved) to have resulted not just from the insufficient number of lifeboats but from the failure of the *Californian* to respond to distress signals sent from the *Titanic*.

During World War I, the *Californian* was torpedoed and sunk off the southern coast of Greece having sailed from Salonika.

D. M. Wood, Solihull, West Midlands.

? HOW many countries by the year 2000 had a different name from those they had in 1900?

THE political map of the world is constantly shifting. Ignoring the Pacific island groups, there are now 71 countries which didn't exist in 1900: Angola, Armenia, Azerbaijan, Bahrain, Belarus, Belize, Bosnia, Botswana, Brunei, Burundi, the Central African Republic, Chad, Congo, Croatia, Democratic Republic of the Congo, Djibouti, Estonia, Finland, Gabon, Georgia, Ghana, Guinea, Guinea-Bissau, Indonesia, Iran, Iraq, Israel, Ivory Coast, Jordan, Kazakhstan, Kenya, Kuwait, Kyrgystan, Laos, Latvia, Lebanon, Lesotho, Lithuania, Malawi, Malaysia, Mali, Moldova, Mongolia, Mozambique, Namibia, Niger, North Korea, Pakistan, Poland, Qatar, Rwanda, Singapore, Slovenia, Somalia, South Africa, South Korea, Swaziland, Syria, Tajikistan,

Tanzania, Thailand, Turkmenistan, Uganda, Ukraine, United Arab Emirates, Uzbekistan, Vietnam, Western Sahara, Yemen, Zambia and Zimbabwe.
John Campbell, Glasgow.

MANY countries adopted new names at the time of their gaining independence from colonial rule. Many have changed status more than once since 1900.

Ukraine, split between the Russian and Austrian empires in 1900, became united as a republic within the Soviet Union and is now an independent country.

There may also be minor changes to the official name of a country while it is referred to colloquially by the same name. Burma is the historic name for the area now officially called the Union of Myanmar. In 1900 it was part of the British Indian empire; the Union of Burma, an independent republic, was created in 1948; in 1973 it became the Socialist Republic of the Union of Burma and the current name was introduced in 1989. Throughout this time it has been colloquially referred to as Burma.
Debbie Hall, British Library, Map Library.

IS any heat produced by the friction of water flowing over a river bed. If not, why not?

ENGLISH scientist James Prescott Joule studied the relationship between mechanical energy and heat more than 100 years ago. He experimented on the amount of heat produced for a given amount of mechanical energy input. Today, a joule is used as a measure of energy.

Heat is produced by water flowing over an uneven river bed. When the water gets turbulent, it loses some of its movement or kinetic energy which is then changed into heat. But the continual flow of water means that there is no time for the heat to accumulate, so there is never more than a minuscule rise in temperature.

This friction also smoothes stones in the river bed into rounded pebbles: the force of the water rolls them along and the river bed acts as a large sheet of emery paper.

Water alone can smooth stones and rocks by knocking off bits as it flows over them. This is largely a mechanical action, like someone pulling and pushing something along.
Bhagwant Singh, Xperiment! Museum of Science and Industry, Manchester.

SHOULD CATS BE SUBJECT TO A 'PET TAX'?

DEAR *Answers*,—People talk very big about taxing cats but not a word as to the protection of the poor pussies. How frequently, for example, do people desert their old favourite mousers, upon moving from one neighbourhood to another, or leave them unattended and uncared for when taking their annual holiday?

I have myself fed daily for two months, out of doors, one of these castaways, and am only waiting now – my position here not allowing of my adopting her – for some friendly person to give her a permanent shelter, but have not come across the right party yet.

If properly fed and domesticated, cats would not become such a nuisance out of doors. Boys and even grown-up persons take a fiendish delight in disturbing a poor inoffensive pussy who has sought repose on some doorstep or other. Indeed, from what I have often seen, cats do not know where to get to for safety from the mischievousness of those whom they are ready to serve.

P. H. Echlin, Gray's Inn Road, W.C.

HAS a British football team managed not to draw a single match in an entire football season?

SINCE the Football League began in 1888, seven teams have gone a whole season without drawing a single game.

Aston Villa and Sunderland were the first, during the 1891/2 season, followed two seasons later by Small Heath in 1893/4.

In the 1894/5 season, Lincoln City and Walsall both achieved this feat, as did Stoke City in 1895/6 and finally Darwen in 1896/7. None of the teams went down in the year they had no draws but Sunderland, in 1891/2, is the only team to have won their League in a no-draw year.

This distinction was never achieved in the 20th century but in 1931/2 Barrow became the first and only team that century to go a whole season managing just one draw.

Ray Spiller, Assoc of Football Statisticians, Basildon, Essex.

❓ HOW high can helicopters fly?

THE maximum height a helicopter can reach, as with other aircraft, is referred to as its 'ceiling'. Helicopters are quoted with two ceilings: In Ground Effect (IGE) which means the downwash from the rotor is reflected off the ground and blown back against the rotor blades, generating extra lift – this ceiling figure is the maximum altitude at which the helicopter can sustain a hover directly above the ground – and Out of Ground Effect (OGE), used to determine the maximum altitude in normal service, normally where the helicopter is hovering more than 30ft above the ground.

Most service helicopters have a hovering ceiling of between 7,000ft and 12,000ft. The Boeing Chinook can hover at 14,750ft but the highest helicopter hovering ceiling belongs to the massive Russian Mil-Mi 26, the biggest, most powerful helicopter in the world. With two 11,400 SHP (shaft horse power) engines, it can be lifted to 15,092ft.

Ian Halliday, Chesterfield, Derbys.

THE highest altitude ever reached by a helicopter was 40,820ft when Jean Boulet flew an Aerospatiale SA3158 over Istres, France on June 21, 1972.

Tim Mickleburgh, Grimsby, Lincs.

❓ WHY are we told we must have a varied diet while some animals live on one type of food? Are they vitamin and protein deficient?

ANIMALS can be divided into three groups, meat eaters (carnivores), plant eaters (herbivores) and those that require both (omnivores).

External variabilities between these three groups can be illustrated by looking at the teeth. A carnivore such as a tiger has well-developed incisors for cutting, canines for tearing and premolars for shearing flesh but has little requirement for molar teeth with which to chew.

The teeth of a ruminant, such as a cow, are mainly molars on which to chew grass. An omnivore such as a human, has both, to cope with both food types.

Animal physiology has evolved so that a carnivore can meet all its nutritional requirements by eating meat, the herbivore can extract all its energy and nutrient requirements from plants while omnivores have developed the ability to extract nutrients from both meat and plants, perhaps through their once nomadic existence.

Jane Cleave, Cardiff.

BESIDES human milk, which supplies a baby with all the nutrients it needs for the first few months of life, no single food is nutritional enough to keep the human body healthy.

A varied, balanced diet consists of foods from five food groups: fruit and vegetables; bread, other cereals and potatoes; meat, fish and alternatives; milk and dairy foods; and foods containing fat and containing sugar.

Vitamin deficiency diseases can be a problem where people follow either a very monotonous diet or avoid certain foods. Vegans and vegetarians may be at risk of vitamin B12 deficiency since vitamin B12 is exclusively of animal origin.
Dr Wynnie Chan, nutrition scientist, British Nutrition Foundation, London.

? ARE the quick-draw gunfights we see in Westerns a myth or were there many such confrontations in which the slowest gun slinger was left dying?

THE traditional gunfights depicted in films have a strong basis in reality but the degree of lawlessness is often overstated – death from illness and old age was far more common.

Many films understate what the best pistoleros were capable of. The gunfighters, working from holsters, sleeves, sashes or even pockets were skilled and lethal adversaries, capable of killing someone in less than a second.

In one account, after being arrested, John Wesley Hardin demonstrated drawing his (unloaded) guns so quickly that the Texas Rangers were astounded, despite having been around top-class gunmen for years.

The hallmark of the truly fast men was the clapping trick. Someone faces a gunman with their hands about 9in apart and goes to clap. The gunman draws his gun and inserts the muzzle between the hands before the clap can be completed.

As many fights were at close range, some gunfighters didn't worry too much about fine accuracy but the saying 'speed's fine, accuracy's final' was still true, especially as no one wanted to waste expensive lead.

Some of the marksmanship in films is impossible in real life. In *Lethal Weapon*, Mel Gibson wouldn't have been able to shoot a smiley face. Bullets from a gun can only group: they land within a certain diameter on the target at a given distance and cannot be placed with such accuracy.
Malcolm S. Whatcott, Port Seton, East Lothian.

? WHAT is the correct use of the words 'Scot', 'Scots', 'Scotch' and 'Scottish'? I understand misuse can cause offence?

I AM a Scot and enjoy the company of other Scots, sometimes reading Scottish literature or listening to Scottish music while I'm relaxing with a glass of Scotch whisky.

As a Scottish woman, I'm proud of my Scottish heritage and Scottish roots and often discuss the meaning of life with a fellow Scot – but always over a glass of Scotch.

In other words, Scotch is a term used to describe many things of Scottish origin, such as whisky, broth, eggs, even dogs and mist – but never the people, who are 'a Scot', 'the Scots', or 'Scottish'.

Mary Buckley, Harrow, Middx.

? HOW much navigable canal does Britain have today compared with the height of the canal era?

BRITAIN'S canal network reached its height in 1850 with 4,500 miles of waterways. After that, the canals fell into decline and disuse as railways and roads took over. By the 1970s, there were only around 2,600 miles of operational canals.

Today, there are more than 3,000 miles of canals and waterways open and working. Thanks to the National Lottery, the EU and a partnership of public, private and voluntary bodies, canals are being restored at the same rate as they were built in the 1790s and British Waterways has reopened many miles of waterways including the Huddersfield Narrow, Rochdale, Forth & Clyde and Union Canals.

Ed Fox, The Waterways Trust, Watford.

BRITISH Waterways don't own all the canals and not all the navigable canals are joined up to each other. To complicate matters further, there is a difference between man-made canals and rivers that have been made navigable. These include the river Thames, the river Severn and the river Wey, without which there would be no network of joined canals.

If we are to include all navigable inland waterways throughout the British Isles, then the total mileage is 2,500 miles. I cycled it all over the course of 1996–97 to achieve a Guinness World Record.

David Cox, Shenstone, Staffs.

? HAS the explosive force of the Big Bang ever been calculated?

SINCE the idea that the Universe might have begun from the expansion of a small super-dense object similar to an atomic nucleus, the Big Bang has been described as a super-giant explosion. The expansion of the universe possesses many explosive characteristics but this is an analogy, not a description. In accord with a constant discovered by American astronomer Edwin Hubble, it merely illustrates something for which we know of no other equivalent.

A normal chemical or nuclear explosion occurs when energy is released from a mass of material, exceeding the forces that bind it. The energy appears in a number of forms – heat, light and the momentum of the material which is ejected from the centre of the explosion. The greater the energy, the more violent the explosion. 57g of fissile uranium releases the same energy as 1,000 tonnes of TNT.

Space, time and matter all came into existence at the instant expansion began – it was not a case of a body exploding and injecting an excess of energy into pre-existing surroundings.

The content of the Universe evolved from high energy photons (particles of light) going through a series of successive stages. Visible objects account for a small percentage of the total mass of the Universe. To merely consider the energy locked up in them, would be a great underestimation of the total energy within the Universe.

In a typical galaxy there is about 10^{11} times the mass of the Sun and there are at least 10^{11} galaxies known. As $E = mc^2$, the energy of the entire system – missing mass (dark matter) as well galaxies, stars, gas and dust – is prodigious.

Richard Taylor, Interplanetary Society, London.

THE energy in the Big Bang equals the total amount of energy in the Universe: energy in the form of radiation and mass added together.

So far, sums don't add up as there doesn't seem to be enough mass. This is one of the most fundamental questions in cosmology today, so no, it hasn't been done yet.

Keith Matthews, Crystran Ltd, Poole, Dorset.

? WHICH came first, the 1960s–1970s TV programme *Magpie*, or the rhyme about magpies which was its theme tune?

THE magpie, the black and white relative of the crow family, lives in noisy flocks, gathering in roosts when not tending its young. The name 'magpie' comes from pied, relating to the plumage, and the female name Margaret.

Magpies are found in North America and much of Europe and Asia. They build elaborate, domed nests with a thorny roof which can consist of as many as 1,500 sticks cemented together with a layer of mud.

Magpies are known for hoarding shiny objects and for stealing food from other birds. They pair for life and are rarely seen alone. There's a widespread European folk belief that your future can be predicted by counting the number of magpies you see at any one time. The rhyme, in many variants, goes back many years.

The most traditional, dating from the 16th century, goes: 'One's sorrow, two's mirth, Three's a wedding, four's a birth, Five's a christening, six a dearth, Seven's heaven, eight is hell, And nine's the devil his old sel.'

The most popular version today, stemming directly from use in the *Magpie* TV series is: 'One for sorrow, Two for joy, Three for a girl, Four for a boy, Five

for silver, Six for gold, Seven for a secret never to be told. Eight to wish, Nine to kiss, Ten is a bird you must not miss.'
Darren Hill, York.

THE TV programme *Magpie* began a 12-year run on ITV in July 1968, soon establishing in collective memory its signature tune – far more memorable than Murgatroyd, its magpie mascot.

Most child viewers at the time were loyal to either *Magpie* or *Blue Peter*.

Magpie's original presenters were Pete Brady (1968–72), Tony Bastable (1968–72) and Susan Stranks (1968–74). Later presenters were Douglas Rae (1972–77), Mick Robertson (1972–80), Jenny Hanley (1974–80) and Tommy Boyd (1977–80).
Adele Harrison, Chester.

? HOW far out at sea can the lights from Portland Bill Lighthouse in Dorset be seen?

UNDER standard atmospheric conditions, the light from Portland Bill Lighthouse can be seen 29 nautical miles out to sea. The accuracy of this distance depends on a variety of imponderables such as the height of the observer's eye above the horizon, the height and luminosity of the light, the arc of visibility measured in degrees from the ship, the effect on tidal height from the Moon and the degree of atmospheric visibility due to moisture content and pollutants of the air.

Fortunately, with modern radar and global positioning systems, most of these variations can be ignored.
A. F. Harris, Lower Bosoughan, Cornwall.

THE degree of moisture content and pollutants in the air may explain a phenomenon about Portland Bill Lighthouse.

We live at a point 100m high three to four miles west of Hope's Nose at the other end of Lyme Bay. This is around 35 nautical miles west of the lighthouse at its lamp height of 43m above mean high water.

On about 20 cool clear winter mornings of the year, with a telescope we can see the lighthouse tower clearly between one and three hours after sunrise and on five or six nights a year we can see the flashing light itself.

Rather more frequently, 30 or 40 times a year, in winter and summer, we can see long rows of what appear to be orange-coloured main road lights at night in the area of the Bill and further east on higher ground towards the Purbeck Hills.

Ron Abbotts, The Lincombes, Torquay, Devon.

? WHAT proportion of the UK population has odd-sized feet?

FEET in general are becoming longer and wider and the number of people with odd-sized feet is on the increase. This has arisen partly because of improvements in our diet resulting in a general increase in body size but also because of the popularity of less supportive shoes, such as trainers, among teenagers.

This type of shoe provides little lateral support and as children develop, their feet tend to spread. Only four or five years ago, the average shoe breadth was C–D. The average now is D–E and predictions show it will soon be E–F.

A problem arises in the marketplace where modern retailers mass produce shoes to cater for a majority range to optimise profit margins: we estimate that eight to ten per cent of consumers fall outside this range.

Until recently, the British Footwear Association used to send out about 25 copies a week of its *Footwear For Special Needs* booklet. We are now distributing more than 250 a week.

To counteract the problem, children should be fitted with a measured shoe: two British companies Clarks and Start-Rite pride themselves on this service.

Everyone has marginal differences in size between feet but conventional shoe sizes can cope with some variation. Of the 280,000,000 shoes sold last year, the number of people requiring different-sized shoes measured in the low hundreds.

Nicholas Parry-Billings, British Footwear Association, London.

I TAKE a 7 on the left foot and a 5 on the right and must buy two pairs of shoes to make one pair.

Some shoe shops look kindly upon me and offer discounts but my biggest problem is what to do with the odd shoes I am left with.

Sara Butler, Innsworth, Gloucester.

? WHY are aircraft hangars so called?

HANGAR is a French word, probably brought to this country by the *Daily Mail* in 1909, when Bleriot, who garaged his plane in a hangar, won Lord

Northcliffe's prize for flying the Channel.

A *hangar* is a kind of French barn; a *garage* is another. Plenty of French words for both motoring and flying (aviation, chassis, fuselage, grill, suspension etc) are used in English because they were first generally used at a time when French enterprise was at the forefront of mechanical innovation.
David Marland, Shipston-on-Stour, Warwks.

? WHICH two countries have the shortest land border?

THE total length of the world's international borders is 251,000km – the longest border being the 8,893km shared between the United States and Canada.

The shortest theoretical border is in southern Africa, about 30km west of Victoria Falls, at the meeting point of the national borders of Zimbabwe, Botswana, Namibia (Caprivi Strip) and Zambia. The point is located in the Zambesi River and is called Kazungula. This is the only place in the world where countries physically border each other but it is impossible for the border to be seen or passed through.

The shortest recognised international border is 1.2km, between Spain and Gibraltar. This is followed by the 3.2km border between Italy and the Vatican City, and the 4.4km border between France and Monaco.

Other short international borders are between Azerbaijan and Turkey (9km), Guadeloupe and Sint Maarten (10.2km), Egypt and the Gaza Strip (11km), and North Korea and Russia (19km).

The land border defined between France and England is, presumably, only as long as the Channel Tunnel is wide.
John Thorn, Cardiff.

? WHAT are the odds of meeting someone with an identical name and an identical birthdate to yourself?

I DISCOVERED another David H. Elias, born November 11, 1937, who lived in Merthyr Tydfil. We had no knowledge of each other until I phoned him, and we met for the first time on April 17.

We were very different in appearance, with different middle names, but we may be distantly related, as both our family histories include steel workers in South Wales.

Nowadays, roughly 1,000 boys and 1,000 girls are born each day in the UK. In each urban area there may be a dozen born on a particular date. If you meet someone who is within three years of your own age, the probability of you sharing a birthday is about a thousand to one. Odds against sharing a name are harder to calculate – much depends on the rarity of the surname, and the popularity of your first name.

The real problem is how you find each other. In our case, we'd lived 62 years before a computer brought us together.

David Elias, Nottingham.

IN our small town, unrelated and previously unknown (except at the local doctor's surgery where much confusion is inflicted on us all) there is another family where the husband's name is Michael Higgins, his wife is called Sheila, their two children are called James and Louise and to cap it all, their family car is a white Montego estate, just like ours.

Michael, Sheila, James and Louise Higgins, Ashby de la Zouch, Leics.

THE Internet abbreviation www. has many more syllables than the word for which it stands: World Wide Web. Is any other abbreviation similarly wordy?

ONLY one letter in the alphabet has more than one syllable so this unusual occurrence is limited to abbreviations containing a W.

Others longer in abbreviation form include WWF (World Wildlife Fund) and VW (Volkswagen), while WBC (World Boxing Council) and WB (Warner Brothers) are equal in syllables.

A more difficult alternative is to find an abbreviation not containing a W, that has the same amount of syllables as the definition. The best I can do is PAYE – Pay As You Earn. Alternatively, definitions with the most syllables per letter: Quango – quasi-autonomous non-governmental organisation.

Paul Spice, Cheshunt.

IN the TV series, *ER*, when well-meaning paramedics need their patients to be treated speedily, they call out 'GSW!' In fact, it would be quicker for them to say the full: 'Gun shot wound!'

T. MacDougall, Wallsend, Tyne & Wear.

SHOULD LADIES WEAR FEATHERS?

DEAR *Answers*,—I wish I could persuade ladies never to wear a bird on their hats, or even a bright wing to set off their rosy cheeks. If they realised how the cruelty of fashion which trims ladies' bonnets with song-birds is robbing the groves and woods of their music; if they thought of the fact that in many localities a price is set on the little feathered beauties; that they are trapped by the thousand and sometimes actually skinned alive, that their plumage may look the richer for ladies' adornment, they could not wear a bird at such a price.

I once had a lovely fan of swansdown, with a robin redbreast mounted in the centre. The robin, stuffed in a very lifelike manner, with his little mouth open, seemed just ready to sing. The fan having been a gift, I kept it as a parlour ornament with some pride.

One day, a tender-hearted baby girl, three years old, was looking at my fan, when suddenly her little lips quivered and her brown eyes filled with tears. I wondered a moment at the grieved look and was much troubled when the little one said: 'Poor birdie! The last song came from there' pointing to the open bill with her tiny finger.

When we think what a glad, buoyant life a bird's life is and remember the sweetness the birds bring to our homes, we cannot feel happy in reflecting that for a caprice of fashion the song-birds are murdered wholesale.

Don't let us forget that we as individuals can do something to make this barbarous style a thing of the past. Let us refuse to adorn ourselves with a dead bird.

The power of the unit is never more visibly shown than in a quiet persistence in doing right and making a wrong unpopular. If ladies will decide against it, this style of cruelty will soon cease to be profitable.

L. M. T., Bradford

One should make a few inquiries before quoting gruesome details. A short time ago a paragraph went the rounds of the papers to the effect that humming-birds were being roasted alive to maintain their brilliancy after death. I presume this is the species that is now reported as being skinned alive. I have made inquiries from a personal friend who has been engaged in many parts of the world bird-catching and he says in no case has he seen such vile practices resorted to.

Very many of the birds whose feathers are used for trimmings are pests to the farmers in the different countries from which they come and large quantities of wings and plumes are obtained from birds used for food – the goose, for instance, duck, ptarmigan, pheasant, partridge, snipe, woodcock, plover, pigeon, fowl and many others.

These are so bleached and dyed that their artificial colour excels that of Nature in many instances. Personally, I should like to see fewer feather trimmings worn, as the industry only supports home manufacture in a small way, most of these goods being manufactured on the Continent, from whence they come into this country duty free.

The fair sex have the remedy in their own hands. Let them wear feathers by all means but let them be those of the ostrich. They are now very fashionable, very becoming and cheap in comparison with what they were some years ago.

They are largely manufactured (or dressed) in this country and the labour, with the exception of dyeing, is exclusively female. The bird suffers no inconvenience or pain on being relieved of its lovely plumes and the farming of them helps to support the inhabitants of an English colony.

An Admirer of the Fair Sex, Manchester.

Some people have been led away by sentiment in discussing this subject. This morning, I took the trouble to look through the samples of a fairly large manufacturer of these feather trimming goods – the range consisted of some 250 designs, all different; and in no instance was a British song-bird used.

In every case, where a bird was mounted whole, it was a foreign one, and in cases where the plumage of any bird caught in this country had been used, the body had been utilised as food.

With very few exceptions, all birds adopted for millinery purposes come from China, Japan, Africa, India, America, etc. Some few years ago, British birds were tried but they were so roughly skinned as to be almost worthless to the manufacturer.

❓ AS an adopted child, how do I go about finding my birth parents? What percentage of these reunions are a success?

MAKE an appointment with a local social worker dealing with fostering and adoption issues. This enables you to discuss the situation and to apply for a copy of your birth certificate. You may also learn the name of the adoption agency.

On approaching the agency, you should receive full details from the adoption file. A search to find the family can then be conducted, using the public records for births, marriages and deaths.

Any person in this position should join the National Organisation for Counselling Adoptees and Parents (NORCAP) by sending an SAE to NORCAP, 112 Church Road, Wheatley, Oxfordshire OX33 1LU. Here you will find a contact register, help, support and advice.

Once the search is completed, an intermediary service is available to make contact on your behalf professionally and tactfully.

It's hard to quantify the percentage of success. Reunions vary enormously, but the vast majority of birth relatives are happy to have some type of contact.

Carolyne Carter, Chippenham, Wilts.

RECENTLY, I received an e-mail from a woman in America. She was adopted at birth in 1966 and had attempted for years to find her birth parents. She e-mailed me simply because we had the same surname and I lived near the area in which she was born.

Before offering to help, I made sure she realised that the search may prove fruitless and that she was prepared mentally to accept all the possible scenarios if her parents were traced.

After about six months of searching using the Internet, local knowledge and the help of various friends, I was fortunate enough to find her father in the North of England and her mother in Southern Ireland. She initially made contact with them by letter, then by telephone and finally flew over to meet them a few months later.

The reunion between mother and daughter was wonderful and the daughter moved from America to live near her mother. Her father, however, shows little interest but does now at least keep in touch.

During the time of the search, I was constantly worried about whether I was doing the right thing and how it would all end but the sheer pleasure of helping to arrange a happy reunion between mother and daughter is a fantastic feeling.

Stephen Frampton, Waterlooville, Hants.

WERE guinea pigs ever used as 'guinea pigs'?

AS a retired medical laboratory scientist I used many guinea pigs as a diagnostic 'tool' in the investigation of specimens of human tissue for evidence of tuberculous infection during the late 1940s and early 1950s.

This was at a time when cultural techniques were unable to grow the causitive organism micobacterium tuberculosis from tissue specimens and the samples were inoculated under the skin of the guinea pig, usually in the abdomenal area.

If the guinea pig didn't die from a tuberculous infection during the next six weeks then it would be humanely killed and examined for evidence of tuberculous lesions in areas such as liver and spleen.

The specimens examined were most often from vagina curretings removed from suspected cases of tuberculous edometriosis in women and from other situations where a tuberculous cyst or infection was suspected.

C. Watson, address supplied.

ARE sturgeon found in British waters?

STURGEON are found in British waters, though more rarely than in former years. The Fishermen's Museum at Looe, Cornwall, preserves a specimen taken in the nets of a local boat within living memory. In accordance with ancient tradition, the fish was offered to, but graciously declined by our present Queen.

Sturgeon were never very common: in the Middle Ages they were regarded, along with beached whales, as 'King's Fish', the property of the Crown or some highly favoured local nobleman. But there is some tangential evidence that they were more regular visitors to our rivers and estuaries than today, and may even have penetrated far inland.

Anglo-Saxon charters reveal that a 'Styrigian Pol' – possibly a 'Sturgeon Pool' – near Bessels Leigh in Oxfordshire in the 9th century.

Karl Wittwer, The English Companions, London.

? IS there a story behind Russian Dolls?

A TRADITIONAL Matryoshka is a decorated nesting doll, normally depicting a girl in a patterned sarafan and wearing a kerchief. She is called Matryoshka from the Russian name, Matryona.

The Matryoshka Doll, first made in the 1880s, was an idea borrowed from ancient Japan after a Russian merchant brought back a bone carving of a Japanese sage called Fukuruma. This contained several nesting images, symbolising the everlasting chain of life. It was taken up in Russia where the genuine Matryoshka dolls are created in three centres: Sergiev Posad near Moscow and Semenov and Gordetz in the Nizhny Region.

The creation of each doll is complex and is based on skills passed down from father to son. Traditionally, Russian silver birch or lime trees are used. Rings of bark must be left on the tree to prevent the trunk from cracking as it dries. The logs are piled off the ground to allow natural drying with enough humidity left in the wood to allow turning.

Painting techniques vary by region. In Sergiev Posad paint is applied directly to the fresh wood and a coat of varnish added. In Semenov and Gordetz, each doll is given three coats of potato glue as a base, hand painted with aniline paint before the final varnish.

Margaret Oram, Russimco Collection, Chilton Polden, Somerset.

? HOW many hours of drilling does it take a woodpecker to make a nest?

WOODPECKERS create permanent dwellings for rearing their young and for daily roosting. Excavation of the hole, undertaken by both sexes, takes from 10 to 28 days, depending on the species and method used. An excavated hole may be in use for many years.

The tapping and drumming signals of woodpeckers are unique, and are regularly heard in woods throughout the world during the breeding season.

In Britain there are three species of woodpecker; green, great spotted and

lesser spotted. They are absent from Ireland, but there is a possibility that the black woodpecker may soon become an occasional or even regular visitor.
Valerie Osborne, RSPB, Sandy, Beds.

⏥ DOES time really go faster as one ages?

MANY changes occur in the body as it ages but there is no single theory to explain why time seems to pass more quickly. It could be related to the death of brain cells which help in the perception of time, or it may be linked with the notion of a chemical clock and the speed of chemical reactions in the brain.

With age, there is a loss of short-term memory and increased gaps in concentration. More of each day is missed and the days appear to go by more quickly.

In the laboratory, we measure the perception of time by asking individuals how much time has passed between two events. We ask them to indicate when a specified period has elapsed. On such tests, older people are less consistent than younger ones in estimating correctly.

Activity also influences the feeling of how quickly time passes. Busy people run out of time each day; for bored people, time passes too slowly. Under stress, events can even seem to occur in slow motion when recalled.
Prof Tom Reilly, Research Institute for Sport and Exercise Sciences, Liverpool John Moores University.

TIME doesn't travel any faster or slower but our perception of time travelling faster as one gets older seems very real.

As we get older, a given period of time becomes a smaller percentage of the life we've lived so far. In the year it takes a one-year-old child to reach the age of two, the length of his/her life has doubled, while for a ten-year-old, that year had added just ten per cent. This relative time carries on decreasing as we get older.
Paul Saunders, Portsmouth.

⏥ WHY, when you take a cellophane wrapper off something, does it invariably stick to your fingers?

THIS is caused by static electricity. When two materials are rubbed together or separated, electrons move from one surface to the other, creating a positive static charge on one material and a negative charge on the other.

Both cellophane wrappers and the human body are good static generators, and when one is handled by the other, the resulting static charges of opposite polarities mean that one is attracted to the other.

Tony Hesford, Ropley, Hants.

? IS there any fossil evidence of giant plant life on Earth, to match the giant animals of the dinosaur period?

WE don't need to look back into the geological record for evidence of giant plant life. Conifers such as the Giant Redwoods of California and flowering plants such as the Mountain Ash of south-east Australia, can reach heights exceeding 100m.

Fossils provide evidence for giant plants throughout the geological past as well as giant ancestors of plants that are still growing today.

In the hot, damp swamps of the Carboniferous period 350–300 million years ago, giant club mosses dominated the vegetation, reaching heights of about 50m. Their living relatives today are usually only a few centimetres in height.

When dinosaurs were at their largest (about 26m tall) and conifers dominated the vegetation, herbivorous dinosaurs were able to reach up and eat the growing tips at the top of these trees, often killing the tree. Dinosaurs may have helped the smaller flowering plants take over the world by eating the competition.

Dr Imogen Poole, Linnean Society, University of Leeds.

? HOW many ants weigh the same as the human body?

THIS depends very much on the type of ant. A worker of the common black garden ant variety is 0.3cm long, 0.1cm wide and 0.1cm high. And an ant's body is mainly made of water and one cc of water weighs one gram so the black garden ant weighs in at about 333 ants per gram.

The average weight of a man is 75kg, so it would take 24,975,000 black ants to equal this. Assuming the average human female weighs 60kg, it would take 19,980,000 to make up a female.

The largest ant in northern Europe is the Giant Ant, with dimensions of 1.5cm by 0.5cm by 0.5cm. It would take 2.7 ants to make up a gram, so only 27,800 of these would be needed to make up an average male and 22,200 for an average female.

Ants can live in very large colonies; a single supercolony of *Formica yessensis* on the coast of Japan is reported to have had 1,080,000 queens and 306,000,000 workers in 45 interconnected nests. These ants have a volume of about 0.03cm cubed, so the biomass would be equivalent to about 12 men and about 15 women.

Katrina Mackay, Edinburgh.

? WHEN did the last workhouse close in Britain?

THE last workhouse shut in 1930. In 1928, Neville Chamberlain, then Minister of Health, passed a bill to repeal the Poor Law Amendment Act (1834 England, 1845 Scotland) which had made the poorhouses (known as workhouses in England) the only legal source of poor relief. This was enacted on March 31, 1930.

The buildings remain, many of them converted to hospitals. The central block of the Southern General Hospital in Glasgow, was originally the Govan Combination Poorhouse, known as Merryflats.

Rev Alastair Ramage, Heatherbank Museum Of Social Work, Caledonian University, Glasgow.

? HAVE the secret vaults beneath Rosslyn Chapel ever been opened?

ROSSLYN Chapel, the Church of St Matthew, between Rosslyn Castle and the village of Roslin, six miles south of Edinburgh, was founded in 1446 by Sir William St Clair, Grand Master of the Knights Templar. It is a mystical centre whose spectacular carvings many people feel hold great symbolism.

The principal authority on the history of the chapel and the St Clair family was Father Richard Augustine Hay, Canon of St Genevieve in Paris and Prior of St Piermont. He produced a three-volume study in 1700 in which he described entering the vaults and finding the bodies of armour-clad soldiers, probably St Clair ancestors.

Many believe the Chapel to be an exact replica of Herod's temple in Jerusalem, three floors of which were built below ground.

One mystery surrounding the Chapel concerns relics found by the Templars while occupying Herod's temple in Jerusalem. When the group was driven underground by the Spanish Inquisition, many believe Sir William secreted the relics at Rosslyn, possibly in its vaults.

The Rosslyn Chapel Trust was formed in 1996 to conserve this mystical building.

Stuart Beattie, The Rosslyn Chapel Trust, Roslin, nr. Edinburgh.

? IS begging legal or illegal in Britain?

BEGGING is illegal. The 1824 Vagrancy Act defines an offence of 'wandering abroad in any public place, street, highway, court or passage to beg or gather alms, or causing or procuring or encouraging any child or children so to do; shall be deemed an idle and disorderly person'.

The same Act authorises 'any person whatsoever to apprehend any person they see committing an offence under this Act'.

There are several offences related to begging but this is one which gives the general populace their opportunity to take some positive action themselves.

Peter Fairweather, Cambridge.

? HOW are horror films made without giving their child stars nightmares?

WHEN I was a busy child actress, it was very rare to be on a film set from beginning to end. You were not normally needed all the time, unless you were the star.

Most films in which I was involved were harmless adventure stories. There were odd days when we were employed to film more sinister scenes out of context. One I recall was called *Secrets Of A Door-to-Door Salesman* when I was on the set only to sing 'Don't Turn Around'.

My mum and I proudly attended the premiere at the Odeon in Leicester Square and it turned out to portray almost exclusively naked romps. My mum was horrified. I was fully dressed, fronting the band, but my appearance was filmed as a totally separate scene.

Throughout my childhood and early adult life, I kept on having the same nightmare: I was being threatened by a teacher in period clothes holding a whip. I often woke in a cold sweat.

One night my husband and I were watching a film called *Blood On Satan's Claw*. There I was in a classroom being threatened by an evil teacher in period clothes brandishing a whip. I never had the dream again.

Kelly Miller, Egham, Surrey.

❓ HAS anyone still got a *3-2-1* ceramic Dusty Bin?

MASSIVELY popular at its height, today the game show *3-2-1* is a reminder of how undiscerning we were as TV viewers in the late 1970s and 1980s.

The show made its host Ted Rogers a national icon. His 3-2-1 finger gesture was as well known as the thumbs-up sign and Dusty Bin, the show's booby prize and mascot, was more recognisable than most pop stars of the time.

Made by Yorkshire TV, the show began in 1978 and lasted until 1987. It was based on the Spanish game show *Uno, Dos, Tres* and involved three married couples, who, between short plays, sketches and songs, answered questions until just one couple remained.

The couple could then try to win the big prize, such as a car. If they were unlucky, however, they won Dusty Bin.

Carol Maconnachie, Dundee.

I DON'T have a ceramic Dusty Bin, but until a few years ago the real one lived in the post room at Yorkshire TV in Leeds. It has since mysteriously disappeared.

Shirley McIntyre, Marston, Lincs.

WE still have a *3-2-1* Dusty Bin in the family. I wasn't a contestant on the show but was given my Dusty Bin after making the props for the pilot versions, which were never transmitted.

Bryn Siddall, Bideford, North Devon.

❓ WHAT causes birthmarks?

BIRTHMARKS are either inherited or formed during foetal development.

Hereditary birthmarks are the result of genetic makeup. These lesions are usually multiple, run in families and can be associated with other developmental changes.

Non-hereditary birthmarks are more common. Their cause is unknown, but it is thought they are caused by a slight aberration during the foetal development cycle.

Dr Robin Russell-Jones, Ealing Hospital, London.

SHOULD LADY SHOP ASSISTANTS HAVE TO STAND?

DEAR *Answers*,—Taking as I do a great interest in the welfare of young women employed in shops, I wonder why it is that some arrangement is not arrived at whereby the young women employed in shops can sit down when not engaged in serving customers.

Recently, a lady who is well known among social reformers and who has been a Sister in a London hospital, told a thrilling tale of the number of girls whose health was ruined by shop labour.

Young women, from 19 to 25 years of age, are frequently knocked up completely after three or four months of the work, while others struggle on bravely for a year or two and are then obliged to give up business altogether.

The enforced standing is undoubtedly one of the prime causes of this disgraceful state of things, which is becoming more serious daily.

Looking at the question from an employer's point of view, I confess that I see no reason why the assistants should not be permitted to sit down.

A Lady Social Reformer, London W.

As an assistant in a large shop in Oxford Street, I have to be something like ten hours behind the counter and, during the whole of this time, am on my feet. I often feel so tired I can hardly stand – and all the other girls say exactly the same.

It would be of the greatest benefit to us were we allowed to sit down when not actually serving anyone. I think the reason we are not provided with seats is because our employers think customers would not like it.

One Who Stands, Oxford Street.

As a shop-walker in one of the largest establishments in London, where hundreds of young women are employed, I am certain of one thing that the common cause of humanity should urge the employers of feminine assistants to remedy the present state of things and provide seats for the young women.

As argument does not seem to influence them, legislation should compel them to provide the necessary accommodation.

I have frequently spoken to heads of firms on the subject, and their sole objection to the innovation seems to be that the young ladies would not look smart and business-like if sitting down. I am very strongly of opinion, however, that it is the initial expense that they consider before their employees' health.

I have, in the course of my shop life, seen dozens of young women completely broken down in health by enforced standing for many hours.

Shop-Walker, London W.

I fail to see how the employer reaps any advantage from the cruel and health-destroying system of forcing assistants to stand when not serving customers. If they were allowed a few minutes' rest every now and then, it would, in many ways, be advantageous to the employer.

The assistants would have more life and energy in them and be the better fitted for serving customers. The latter would receive more attention and be met with more cheerful faces and greater courtesy and it would undoubtedly be the means of placing both parties – employer and employed – on better terms with each other.

Shopkeepers should be respectfully asked to abolish this enforced standing. Some, I am sure, would act accordingly. The remedy for the others would be in the hands of the public, who would, I think, under the circumstances, grant their custom only to those employers who considered their employees' health by allowing them to sit down.

One Interested, West Bromwich.

As an old hand, I find seats behind the counter a nuisance in a busy establishment. Shorter hours in shops and additional time for lady-assistants to spend in the open air is the remedy I advocate for their bad health.

Long hours in shops are ruining the health of thousands of our young lady assistants. By pleading for seats behind the counter, social reformers will only create indulgences for assistants in high-class establishments, while those unfortunate third-class hands in 'pushing' shops, who are compelled to labour behind a counter with a limited walk of about two and a half feet wide, will yet toil on their weary way – a long day's tasks of 14 hours or more.

A Shop Assistants' Union has been formed but at present I am doubtful as to what its policy may be. If its officers will only pay a few visits to the East End of London and watch the pale faces of the tired shop-hands on a Saturday night as the hour of 12 approaches, their hearts will ache with pain to think that in the employers' mighty struggle to get rich, shop assistants are gradually being crushed against the wall, their health so undermined by long hours as to lead to premature death.

Sixty hours of labour in shops per week is the only practical remedy. Parliament has legislated for factory operatives; why not protect shop-hands?

O. QUIZ, Cardiff.

The National Union of Shop Assistants is a democratic society, its policy being made, altered or amended by its members. The Factory Act, as applied to millinery and mantle workrooms, almost every lady assistant can tell is evaded in a very large number of drapery establishments every year at the height of the season.

It has failed. The assistants, if they complain, are dismissed to make room for others. In ten years' experience, I have known only one young lady who refused to work after the prescribed hours and the employer told her that during 30 years he had never known such an action.

I do not think that public opinion or Parliamentary interference will do very much to reform life behind the counter. Only through the protection of an organisation can these cases be properly dealt with, and the employees gain their legitimate hours of labour.

As union is strength, our remedy is to bring the combined influence of all the assistants to bear upon the employers and thus gain the desired end. The union that is now formed will do well or ill for our class in proportion to the support or neglect we pay to it.

Alison Oxley, National Union of Shop Assistants, Newcastle-upon-Tyne.

Lady shop-assistants stand because ladies who frequent the shops will that they should stand.

There is not a shopkeeper in London – or out of it – who would dare to keep his assistants continually on their feet against the known wishes of his customers.

Burns speaks of 'man's inhumanity to man' but this is nothing compared with woman's inhumanity to woman. Women frequent shops and those who wait upon them stand all day. Men frequent offices and those who attend to them sit all day.

It's all very well to quote Hood about evil being wrought by want of thought as well as by want of heart but where want of thought inflicts upon others physical agony, broken health and premature death, want of thought is want of heart. An evil which you can remedy, and yet do not, that evil you cause.

Mr Gladstone speaks of the 'vast influence' of Answers to Correspondents and he is right. The readers of this paper alone could make a change in the shop-assistant's lot.

If each lady reader, the next and every time she entered a draper's shop asked for the proprietor and put it to him whether he could not allow his assistants to sit when not attending to customers, adding a hint that she had made up her mind in future not to deal at shops where a different rule was in force, the present barbarity would not hold another six months' lease of life and the cry from the counter would be heard no more.

But how many women will make the attempt and resolve to keep 'pegging away' in their neighbourhood for even a month? Scarcely one in a thousand out of all the ladies under whose notice the matter may come. Lady shop-assistants stand because it is lady shop-frequenters' will that they should. The responsibility is theirs alone.

C., London S.E.

Popular feeling in favour of shorter hours and greater comforts for over-worked shop assistants has proved in some degree successful at last. The triumph is substantial though not magnificent. It has taken the form of a statute dealing with the evil in a practical and sensible manner.

The new Act, known as the Shop Hours Act, 1892, the operation of which dates from the 1st of September (1892), is one of the most useful legislative legacies bequeathed to us by the late Parliament. The statute

? WHO coined the term 'bugbear' and on what topic did it surface?

THE term 'bugbear', now used for anything that causes obsessive fear or anxiety, was, in 16th-century English folklore, a hobgoblin in the form of a bear – said to eat naughty children.

Dating from about the 14th century, 'bug' probably comes from the Middle Welsh *bwg*, a ghost or spirit, and seems to be connected with such words as bogle, bugaboo, bogey and the Lancashire boggart.

Horses were believed to be hypersensitive to spirits, so a bolting horse would be said to have 'taken t' boggart'.

Miles Coverdale's Bible of 1535 was known as 'the Bug Bible' because

Psalm 91:1 was translated: 'Thou shalt not nede to be afrayed for eny bugges by night,' where 'bugges' meant terrors.

Kevin Heneghan, St Helens, Merseyside.

❓ HAS anybody ever been fined for cycling on the pavement?

SHORTLY before Christmas 1943, I was riding my bicycle on a footpath, because the cobbled street was uncomfortable to use.

On turning a corner, I bumped into a police constable. Although I explained my actions, I finished up in juvenile court, and was found guilty and fined 10 shillings (50p).

Lawrence E. Bellhouse, Horsforth, West Yorks.

AT 7am one morning in 1959, I was fined £5 for riding 50 yards along a pavement in the cul-de-sac where I lived. The policeman was hiding behind a large tree at the end of the street. Other residents were also similarly caught and fined.

Sam Turner, Barrow-in-Furness, Cumbria.

❓ REMBRANDT painted several canvases concerning Susannah and The Elders, a story said to be from the Book of Daniel in the Old Testament. I cannot find this in Daniel. Was it removed?

ROMAN Catholics and Orthodox Christians have retained the story of Susannah in Daniel Chapter 13 but it is relegated by Protestants to the Apocrypha, the series of Biblical books not considered canonical.

Susannah was a beautiful young woman, lusted after by a pair of elders. They attempt to blackmail her into sleeping with them and, when she refuses, accuse her of unchastity with a young man, each having the other as an unimpeachable witness.

All seems lost until Daniel cross-examines the witnesses separately, posing the simple question: 'Under which tree was this going on?' Having had no time to collude over their answer, they contradict each other, which frees Susannah but condemns the liars to the punishment they had intended for her.

The challenge to artists has been to portray these two aspects of human nature on the one canvas. The eyes of the pure see that which is pure; the eyes of the depraved see depravity. Susannah has been painted not only by Rembrandt but by several other artists, including Guercino, Reni, Carracci and Gentileschi.

Douglas Porter, Bridgham, Norfolk.

? QUEEN Anne is said to have been buried in a giant square coffin. Why was this?

QUEEN Anne, born on February 6, 1665, the second daughter of James II and Anne Hyde, was short, stout and short-sighted, which gave her a squint. She was generally regarded as dull but conscientious.

Anne's mother died when she was six and her father remarried the Roman Catholic Mary of Modena. In 1685, he succeeded to the throne as James II and tried to convert Anne to Catholicism but she resisted; she was very devoted to the Church of England.

In 1683, Anne married Prince George of Denmark, an asthmatic drunken bore. Despite his shortcomings, he and Anne enjoyed a happy marriage, marred only by her many miscarriages and the death of their children in infancy. She endured 17 pregnancies and it came as a severe blow to her and George when their only child to survive infancy, William, Duke of Gloucester, died in 1700 at the age of 11.

James II's abdication and the Glorious Revolution of 1688 put Anne's older sister Mary on the throne, alongside her husband, William of Orange. When Mary died, in 1694, followed by William in 1702, Anne succeeded them.

Anne had serious illnesses in 1711 and 1713 and her last years were troubled by the question of the succession. She died aged 48, on August 1, 1714, at Kensington Palace, suffering from suppressed gout, which led to Erysipelas, a skin disease marked by large lesions on the skin which caused immense swelling. This was why she had to be buried at Westminster Abbey in a large, almost square, coffin.

Christine Dewen, Clayhall, Essex.

? WHY is it so difficult to find blood oranges in the shops these days?

THE Blood orange (*Citrus sinensis*), thought to be the product of a spontaneous mutation, was discovered near Lentini in Sicily only in the 1920s. Experts believe its creation was triggered by a combination of terrain and climatic conditions unique to the area. This type of orange is called Tarocco.

Its main commercial rivals are the Sanguinello (native to Spain), and the Moro, which is grown in San Diego, California.

Sicily still produces 70 per cent of the total world crop. Blood oranges owe their distinctive appearance to the pigment anthocyanin not typically found in citrus but common in other red fruits and flowers.

The blood orange season is January to March. If you've missed them in the last few years it may be because they've been rebranded as Ruby Red Oranges.

Pauline Porter, Jedburgh, Borders.

? **IN the 1940s, I was stationed at RAF Weston Zoyland, Somerset. On the other side of the airfield was the village of Middlezoy. What does 'zoy' mean?**

THE names Middlezoy and Weston Zoyland are derived from the name of the river Sow, a pre-English name, which possibly arises from the Indo-European root *seu* meaning 'to flow'.

In a charter of AD 725, Middlezoy appears as Soweie – the *ieg* (island) in the river Sow. It didn't acquire the 'Middle' part of its name until the 12th or 13th century.

Weston Zoyland, in the 13th century, was Westsowi. Its name implies that it was a subordinate farm (tun) to the west of the main settlement.

Karl Wittwer, The English Companions, London.

? **IS anywhere in the UK still capable of making matches?**

OCTAVIUS Hunt Ltd is the last match manufacturer based in the UK. Founded in 1870 by Octavius Hunt, the company is a family run business based in Bristol.

The match industry in the UK has changed dramatically over the last few decades with most matches being produced in Eastern Europe and Asia. Octavius Hunt has managed to maintain its business in the UK by producing speciality matches such as the windproof/waterproof match used by UK forces.

This match can be used in all weather conditions and is impervious to wind or rain. All the matches produced at Octavius Hunt are dipped by hand and, given the complexity of the match, it takes three days to produce one match. Last year Octavius Hunt produced more than 30 million matches.

Kerry Healey, Octavius Hunt, Bristol.

WHERE is the church or chapel with a glass interior by René Lalique?

THIS is St Matthew's on Millbrook, Jersey, known by the locals as the Glass Church. Despite the name, the exterior of the church is very plain and compares poorly with the warm granite of many parish churches.

Hidden behind the poor exterior, though, is an architectural marvel. Glass front doors are a clue but the casual visitor could not fail to be amazed by the fabulous René Lalique-designed artwork inside.

Glass designer René Jules Lalique (1860–1945) was renowned for his stunning creations of perfume bottles, vases, jewellery, chandeliers, clocks and, in the latter part of his life, car bonnet ornaments.

He was also the neighbour, in the South of France, of Florence Boot, Lady Trent, widow of Jesse Boot, Baron Trent, founder of Boots the Chemists, whose principal residence was in Millbrook.

She wished to refurbish the church in her husband's memory and Lalique readily agreed to be architect for the project. Work began in 1932 and was completed by 1934 – and was a stunning success.

Opalescent panels bathe the faithful in a calming light, entirely fitting for a place of worship. There is a spectacular glass cross, a glass font, glass altar rail and Jersey emblem and, most spectacular of all, some perfectly angelic Art Deco angels.

Paul Crowther, St Helier, Jersey.

WHAT is the World Bank, who runs it and from where do its funds come?

THE idea of a World Bank was conceived late in World War II, at the United Nations Monetary and Financial Conference at Bretton Woods, New Hampshire, in July 1944. It came into formal existence in December 1945, following international ratification of the Bretton Woods agreements.

'World Bank' is an umbrella term encompassing five closely associated institutions: the International Bank for Reconstruction and Development, the International Development Association, the International Finance Corporation, the Multilateral Investment Guarantee Agency and the International Centre for Settlement of Investment Disputes. These, along with the International Monetary Fund, are sometimes called the Bretton Woods Institutions.

The Bank's original purpose was to help rebuild Europe after the war. Its first loan, for $250 million, was made to France for this purpose.

Today, the World Bank's activities focus on developing countries, in fields such as education, health, agriculture, rural development, environmental protection, infrastructure and governance. It offers low interest or no-interest loans for specific projects.

The Bank's work has been subject to the criticism that it is a U.S. or Western tool for imposing economic policies which support Western interests.

Its funds come from three main sources: subscriptions paid up by 184 member countries, bond flotations on the world's financial markets and net earnings on the Bank's assets.

Control of the Bank resides with its Board of Directors. Voting power on the board is based on a member's capital subscriptions: those members which make the greatest financial contributions have the greatest say in the Bank's decision-making.

The U.S. holds 20 per cent of the vote and is represented by a single executive director. The 47 sub-Saharan African countries have two executive directors but hold between them only seven per cent of the votes.

Les White, Weymouth, Dorset.

? WHAT is the biggest chocolate Easter Egg ever made?

THE world's largest ever chocolate egg was created by Belgian chocolatier Guylian to celebrate the completed renovation of Belgium's largest market square in Sint-Niklaas on Easter weekend 2005.

The egg measured 27ft 3in (8.32m) tall and weighed 4,299lb (1,959kg). Twenty-six Guylian master chocolate makers took eight days and used a total of 50,000 Guylian Praline chocolate bars, which feature the company's signature marbled seashell chocolates, to construct the egg. Metal scaffolding with wooden panels created a 'shell' to support the egg.

This beat the record set in 1996 by the The Rotary Club of Piet Retief, KwaZula-Natal, South Africa, whose egg was 25ft (7.65m) tall.

Liam Frank, Arklow.

? HAS anyone devised an alternative image for the word game Hangman? I'd like to play the game with my six-year-old daughter but don't like the idea of hanging the man if we fail to guess the word.

TONY Augarde, author of the *Oxford Guide to Word Games*, says 'the origins of Hangman are obscure, but it seems to have arisen in Victorian times'.

The game is mentioned in Alice Bertha Gomme's 1894 *Traditional Games* and in other early sources is referred to as Gallows or The Game Of Hanging.

My godmother used to play the game with me when I was little using a beetle instead of the hangman. We would first draw the round body, then the legs and then eyes and anything else we might want to add. I always used a beetle when I played and didn't know Hangman existed until I was introduced to it at school.

Sarah McFarlane, Edinburgh.

WHEN I was a teacher in the 1960s, I played a similar game called ten steps where, with each incorrect letter, the figure moved one step closer to a crocodile pit.

This was also a bit grisly but had the advantage that I could put the letter under each step so there wasn't anyone trying to use the same wrong letter more than once. You could vary the number of steps according to ability.

Margaret White, Harrogate, North Yorks.

———————

? WHO invented the wheelie bin?

THE first wheeled bins for garbage disposal – the forefather of today's wheelie bins – were introduced in 1937 by George Roby Dempster, Mayor of Knoxville, Tennessee, as part of his revolutionary Dempster-Dumpster system for the disposal of solid waste. They were large round steel bins which could be hauled onto trucks using a system of chains and pulleys.

In 1955, Dempster created the Dempster-Dumpmaster, the first commercially successful front loading garbage truck. This was the first garbage collection system under which smaller wheeled dustbins could be mechanically emptied into a garbage truck. His bins were technically called Mobile Garbage Bins but U.S. users soon started calling them Dumpsters – and still do.

The rectangular box on wheels, now made from injection moulded high density polythene, first appeared in the UK in the 1970s and quickly became known colloquially as the wheelie bin.

George King, Peterborough, Cambs.

? WHY is plastic surgery so called?

THE word 'plastic' originally meant pliable and easily moulded, derived from the Latin *plasticus* – of moulding, from the Greek *plastikos* from *plassein* – to form or mould.

As plastic surgery involves remodelling and moulding the features, this is how the term came about. For many years, the word 'plastic' has been also used to refer to a range of synthetic materials created by the polymerisation of simple molecules. They are called plastics because at some stage in their creation they are in a plastic (easily mouldable) state. For example thermoplastics achieve this state when they are heated.

So plastic surgery is so called not because of any connection with plastic material but because of the original meaning of the word.

Dr Colin M. Barron, Dunblane, Perthshire.

? WHICH figurehead was shown on coins when Oliver Cromwell ruled during the Commonwealth period?

THE standard design used on all coins during the Commonwealth period (1649–60) had the shield of St George in a wreath and the legend THE COMMONWEALTH OF ENGLAND on the obverse, with the date, value, legend GOD WITH US and shields of St George and of Ireland on the reverse.

Smaller denominations, two pence, penny and halfpenny omitted the date and legends. The conjoined shields on the reverse led to these coins being called 'Breeches money'.

The gold unite, double crown, crown, half-crown, shilling, sixpence, half groat, penny and halfpenny were struck in most years from 1649 to 1660.

From 1656 to 1658, some denominations were struck with a Cromwell portrait designed by Thomas Simon, one of the finest of England's medallists, but these coins never went into circulation.

The obverse shows Cromwell crowned with laurels, like a Roman Emperor, while the reverse has Cromwell's arms and those of the Commonwealth. In the legend, he's described as 'PRO', for his title as Lord Protector, rather than 'REX' (king). A good example can be seen in Oxford's Ashmolean Museum.

Len Graves, Oxford.

ARE TALL MEN MORE SUCCESSFUL THAN SHORT MEN?

DEAR *Answers*,—I say decidedly 'yes' – and there are scores of very good comparisons.

Take, for instance, the selected candidates for a situation and, presuming that each is possessed of the required abilities, in ten cases out of 12 the selection will fall to a tall rather than a short applicant.

Again, ask a young lady (if she is not already engaged to a short man) which of the two she prefers and you will invariably find that it is to the tall man she gives the preference.

My shorter brothers will naturally shrug their shoulders and say I am prejudiced but that is not so. I frankly admit that a person of short stature is quite as good as one of tall stature – but no better.

Six-feet-one, Southport.

Although it cannot be taken as an axiom that the fact of a man being tall enhances his chances of getting on, yet it is an indisputable fact that the greater number of our prominent men, while perhaps not being tall, are decidedly above the average height.

Among those whose names strike me at the moment are Gladstone, Harcourt, Chamberlain, Randolph Churchill, Tennyson, Rider Haggard, R. L. Stevenson, Henry Irving, Beerbohm-Tree and there are many others whose names for the moment have escaped my memory. Charles Dickens and Thackeray, too, were both tall men. It would probably, however, be revealed, if a close investigation were made, that the honours may be equally divided between the tall and short men.

There is no possible doubt that, in certain positions, tall men are desirable but as a rule this is only the case in situations where outward show is an important consideration.

A Medium-sized Man, Blackburn.

I am glad that a medium-sized man came to the conclusion that honours are equally divided between the short and tall men. He gave a list of great tall men; below will be found the names of some notable men who are short.

M. Zola, the French author; Audran, the composer of *La Mascotte*;
Lord Justice Kay is not a tall individual; Sir Arthur Sullivan is very short;
A.C.Swinburne, the poet, is also short and so is Rudyard Kipling.

Then there is H. M. Stanley, the explorer; Sir Edward Lawson of the
Daily Telegraph and last, though decidedly not least, Canon Knox-Little,
a wonderfully powerful preacher and a grand specimen of a great mind
in a small frame.

Short and Round, Wimbledon.

This greatly depends upon what the 'success' refers to. Assuredly in
either love or war or business, the commanding stature possesses an
advantage over the diminutive.

Salesmen have more influence, and their words have more weight
with their customers when they can to some extent look down upon
them. The same contention applies to professions.

The doctor must inspire the patient with a sense of his power,
inducing the faith which is said to be half the cure.

The eloquence of the clergyman or the politician is partly lost on any
audience who have the faculty of sight when the speaker is a short man.

What do we observe in our own day? Gladstone, Harcourt and
Chamberlain are not short men – neither was Beaconsfield.

Short policemen there are not any. Soldiers must reach a certain
standard. In the matrimonial world I do not think five-feet-seven is at all
above the ideal standard of the faire.

Five-feet-nine, Hampton Court.

My own experience teaches me that it is the short men who get on,
perhaps because there is not so much of them. In the offices of
cheeseparing employers they are invariably used because they take up
less room. The tall man, on the other hand, is a nuisance. He has a habit
of lounging and lolls on the first thing he gets near. He inconveniences
everyone in his vicinity. On a bus or in a cab, he is a misfit; pieces of
him hang out of all the available apertures.

It is a pleasure to travel with the short man, he takes up so little room
that, influenced by the additional comfort and room, one is inclined to

bless him.

If there is one thing I detest most it is the supercilious smile affected by the tall man when he gets inside some sort of uniform. As plainly as possible he says to the little ones: 'Look out, I shall tread on you' – the sort of thing commonly called 'commanding presence.'

The long man loses many of the little luxuries of life: he never gets slippers and smoking caps and jackets made for him. It takes an acre of stuff to fit him out with these so that unless the work is undertaken by a Mutual Admiration Society he is doomed to do without them.

I must, however, give the tall men their due; they made excellent firemen, they take people out of three-storey windows while the little man is running for the escape. In this they are an excellent institution, but as with the serial story, so with the tall man – we like him best in instalments. Personally, I like the tall man as a friend; he is good-natured and jolly, but in life he is generally unsuccessful – his reach is too long.

Five-feet-nothing.

I have often been struck with the fact that tall men of commanding appearance seem to have an aptitude for making headway, and when I call to mind those amongst my own acquaintances, I am compelled to admit that there is abundant evidence for the argument that tall men are more successful than short men.

In the office or the workshop how frequently we see a tall and stately person at the head of affairs in his special department.

I am not prepared to prove that they hold these positions on account of their 'six feet,' but still my observations prompt me to say that their abilities are not greater than those of their less fortunate co-workers, and, in a large number of cases, scarcely equal to them. Hence my contention that their positions are attributable to their tallness of stature and commanding appearance.

The difference is even apparent in Volunteer corps. Mark how obedient and well-controlled is a company of Volunteers under the supervision of an officer of tall and military bearing, whilst a similar company of men in charge of a short, thick-set lieutenant will most probably be found an untidy and careless set of fellows.

Five-feet-seven, Woolwich.

? HAS a cricket match in Britain ever been stopped because of snow?

ON May 31, June 2 and 3, 1975, Derbyshire hosted Lancashire in a three-day County Championship Match at Buxton. Lancashire won the toss and chose to bat – a good choice as the pitch was flat and the weather good, with temperatures over 100°F.

Derbyshire strike bowlers Mike Hendrick and Alan Ward were absent and their deputies Keith Stevenson and Mike Glen fared badly in the heat.

In just 115 overs, Lancashire made 477 before declaring with only five wickets down. Frank Hayes produced a solid 104 while Clive Lloyd hit a spectacular 167 including seven 6s.

June 1 was a rest day. And by 9am on Monday June 2 there was an inch of snow on the ground! Strong snow flurries followed throughout the day.

The pitch looked like midwinter and it was no surprise when play was abandoned for the day. On the Tuesday, the sun came out again and – remarkably – the umpires deemed the pitch fit to play on, though the Derbyshire players may not have agreed.

On the drying wicket, Lancashire's Peter Lee was almost unplayable and bowled 50 balls without conceding a run. Ashley Harvey-Walker, mindful of the bounce, gave his false teeth to the umpire before being caught by Lloyd off Lee's bowling.

Derbyshire made just 42 in their first innings with Lee taking 5 for 10 in 13.2 overs. Forced to follow on, they didn't fare much better in their second innings, making just 87 with Peter Lever taking 5 for 16 in 5.2 overs. Lancashire won by an innings and 348 runs.

R. G. Lee, Stonnall, Staffs.

? IS Ben Gurion Airport the same place as the Lydda Airport where I spent two weeks waiting to hitch a lift to Cairo in 1941?

LYDDA Airport, built in the 1930s, was served by airlines including Britain's Imperial Airways. In 1948, the year in which the state of Israel was created, British authorities withdrew from Lydda and Israeli military forces took over the airport's operation to resume air services, renaming it Lod Airport.

It handled about 40,000 passengers in Israel's first year of existence and over the subsequent decades acted as both a civil air transport gateway and a station for military operations.

After the death of Israel's first prime minister, David Ben-Gurion, in 1973, the Israeli Government agreed to commemorate him by renaming the airport again as Tel Aviv Ben-Gurion International, its present identifier. It now deals with about nine million passengers a year.

David Kaminski-Morrow, Air Transport Intelligence, London.

I WORKED at the former Lydda Airport in the early 1970s, by which time it had been renamed Lod by the Israelis. Lydda, used by the British, was the Roman name for the village of Lod (old Hebrew).

Lydda or Lod was the supposed birthplace of the mother of the patron saint of England, St George, in AD 270.

R. Banham, Ramsgate, Kent.

? IF the death penalty were ever reintroduced in the UK, what sort of remuneration might those who carry out the deed expect?

BRITISH executioners were paid per job. Albert Pierrepoint was Britain's most prolific executioner having dealt with 433 men and 17 women in his 24 years of service. He resigned in 1956 in a pay dispute. He attended Strangeways Prison on a bitterly cold day in January 1956 to hang Thomas Bancroft, only for Bancroft to be reprieved later in the afternoon.

Pierrepoint claimed the full fee of £15 but was offered just £1 in out of pocket expenses by the Under Sheriff of Lancashire. The hangman appealed to his employers, the Prison Commission, who refused to get involved. The Under Sheriff sent him a cheque for £4 in final settlement but this was regarded as a huge insult by Albert, as Britain's Chief Executioner, so he tendered his resignation.

As we are unlikely to see the reintroduction of the death penalty any time soon, £15 per execution is probably our best guess at what an executioner would be paid. If we multiply this up to today's prices using a standard measurement such as the retail prices index, this equates to about £270 per execution.

Stan Yeoman, York.

? IS it true that the prefix 'Fitz' indicates illegitimacy?

THE idea that the prefix 'Fitz' originated with the naming of illegitimate children, particularly of a monarch, is a common misconception. It in fact begun with the Anglo-Normans, possibly in the reign of Henry II, and meant simply 'son of' with no connotation of bastardy or royalty.

It arose from the Anglo-Norman corruption of the Latin *filius*, a son, hence *Robertus filius Jacobi*, Robert son of James, via the French *fils*, as in *Hugh fils de Walter*, Hugh FitzWalter.

By about 1300, *filius* and *fils* had become filz, fuiz, fiz and finally fitz.

Henry VIII, in 1519, was probably the first monarch to give the surname Fitzroy (son of the King) to his natural son Henry by Bessie Blount, a relative of Lord Mountjoy, in recognition of his royal paternity. Charles II also used Fitzroy for his natural children, while his brother, James II, called his Fitz-James. This later practice gave rise to the association of 'Fitz-' with illegitimacy.

The practice continued into the 19th century, the last to use it being George, Duke of Cambridge, Queen Victoria's cousin, who gave his natural children the surname FitzGeorge.

Clive Smith, Spalding, Lincs.

WHO performed the 'Piltdown Man'-style vocals on Mike Oldfield's _Tubular Bells_ LP? Is what he sings based on any known language?

THE 'caveman' vocals 11:55 minutes into 'Tubular Bells Part Two' are the result of a crazy idea Oldfield had after drinking rather a lot of whisky at the pub local to The Manor, the recording studio built by Richard Branson in an Oxfordshire stately home.

Oldfield had already recorded all the instruments on this section but thought it needed something more. The recording team ran the tape at a lower speed while Mike shouted and screamed drunkenly into the microphone and with this, the caveman was born.

The 'Piltdown Man' credited as an instrument on the album sleeve refers to the famous archaeological hoax in which parts of human and monkey skulls were put together and claimed as the 'missing link'.

Olivier Lebra, Tubular.net, Montreal, Canada.

MIKE Oldfield was obviously feeling the strain while making his complex album. If you listen carefully to Piltdown Man, you can hear the words 'sick of work – going home – sick of work – don't want no work – going home'.

A. Marston, Wellingborough, Northants.

❓ WHAT is the biggest freshwater fish ever caught on a rod and line?

ACCORDING to the International Game Fish Association, the largest fish caught using conventional tackle was a 9ft long, 468lb (212kg) white sturgeon.

It was caught by then 21-year-old Joey Pallotta III in the Sacramento River on July 9, 1983. His record may last forever as it's now illegal to keep fish over 6ft long.

Graham Murgatroyd, Otley, Yorks.

THE largest seawater fish ever caught on a line, as recognised by the International Game Fish Association, was the 2,664lb (1,208kg) Great White shark caught by Alf Dean off Ceduna, Australia, on April 1, 1959.

Several larger Great Whites caught by anglers have since been verified but were later disallowed from formal recognition by IGFA monitors for rule violations.

In Australia after World War II, catching Great Whites became a popular pastime. Fishermen set chum slicks from boats using fish oil, blood or offal and often waited at sea for days before a Great White picked up the trail and rose to the occasion.

Once a shark comes near the boat, guided in by the slick, it's in an excited state and hooking it is little more effort than leading lambs to slaughter. In 1997, the Great White and Grey Nurse sharks were placed on Australia's list of endangered species and fishing for them was banned.

Tom Davies, Sydney, Australia.

❓ WHO holds the record for the most divorces?

GLYNN 'Scotty' Wolfe, a former Baptist minister, holds the world record for the most divorces, having been divorced 28 times. His shortest marriage lasted 19 days, and his longest seven years. His youngest wife, Daisy, was just 14.

His last wife, Linda Essex, holds the record as the most divorced woman, having sundered 23 marriages. They married as a stunt for a TV documentary but remained married until his death in a nursing home in Redlands, California, on June 10, 1997.

He is known to have had a son, John Glenn Wolfe, from his marriage to Christine Camacho and there are reports that he had 19 children but on his death, the *New York Times* reported that no one visited him and no one collected the body.

John Glenn Wolfe said his father married so often because he was against living in sin and was picky and stubborn. 'He divorced one wife for eating sunflower seeds in bed', he said.

Finlay Nash, Arklow, Wicklow.

? 'HORSES sweat and men perspire, but ladies only glow' goes the old adage – but how do ostriches keep cool?

OSTRICHES, like all birds, do not have sweat glands so have adopted a number of strategies to keep cool. They drink at watering holes or feed on moisture-laden grasses in the cooler early morning, and rest during the day.

Thick plumage insulates their bodies from the heat and their body feathers and wings can raise to capture cooling breezes. In the afternoon, when temperatures are at their extreme, ostriches will pant, causing their respiration rates to increase from 4 to 40 breaths a minute.

Ostriches excrete uric acid, rather than urine, which requires no water loss, and they are the only known animals whose exhaled air is not fully saturated, making that air up to 40 degrees cooler than their body temperatures.

They are physiologically well adapted to very hot environments. They have been known to lose a quarter of their bodyweight in a single day without detrimental effect.

Dr Richard White, Glasgow.

? WHY are there so many statues of tortoises in Tuscany?

THE tortoise is a mark of a *contrade* (parish) in Sienna. Medieval Tuscan cities were split into separate administrative districts to supply troops to the military companies hired for defence against warring neighbours: in Sienna's case, this meant gaining independence from neighbouring Florence.

There were once 59 such districts in Sienna but over time their administrative and military functions have been lost and their number has dwindled to 17: Aquila (Eagle), Bruco (Caterpillar), Chiocciola (Snail), Civetta (Owl), Drago (Dragon), Giraffa (Giraffe), Istrice (Porcupine), Leocorno (Unicorn), Lupa (She-Wolf), Nicchio (Shell), Oca (Goose), Onda (Wave), Pantera (Panther), Selva (Forest), Tartuca (Tortoise), Torre (Tower) and Valdimontone (Ram).

Tartuca is at the southern end of the city and if you take a walk through that part of the city the tortoise is much in evidence.

Traditionally, its residents were sculptors. Tartuca's symbol is a turtle with alternating Savoy knots and daisies. Its colours are yellow and deep blue.

The Siennese are fiercely proud of their *contrade* and their role today has broadened so that every important event – baptism, death, marriage, church holiday, victory at the Palio, even wine or food festival – is celebrated within one's own *contrade*. Even marrying outside one's *contrade* is frowned upon.

Each year on August 18 the role of the *contrade* is celebrated in Il Palio Di Sienna (known locally as Palio della Contrade), a magnificent medieval pageant followed by a bareback horse race which involves three circuits of the Piazza del Campo, between riders dressed in the colours of their *contrade*. Tartuca last won in 2004.

Northern Italy is home to three species of tortoise: Hermann's Tortoise, the Marginated Tortoise and the Greek Tortoise. They are popular animals in Italy and that may also be reflected in the number of statues.
Justine Webb, Cheltenham, Gloucs.

WHAT happened to the original FA Cup that was stolen from a sports shop in Birmingham in 1895? Could it still be in existence?

THE trophy used today is the fourth in the competition's 134-year history. The first FA Cup, nicknamed the 'little tin idol', was collected 24 times, the last time going to Aston Villa, before it mysteriously vanished while on display in the window of football outfitters, William Shillcock of Birmingham, in September 1895.

A duplicate cup was hastily made which lasted until 1910, by which time the lack of copyright on the Cup's design and the numerous copies it had spawned, meant a new Cup, of unique design, was required. The old Cup was given to FA president Lord Kinnaird in recognition of his 20 years' service.

It recently came up for auction last year and was purchased for £420,000 by then Birmingham City Chairman David Gold. He presented it to the National Football Museum in Preston.

The FA Cup used from 1911 was made in Bradford to the now familiar design. It was the longest serving of the four Cups but after 80 years' wear and tear was replaced by the present Cup in 1992.

That old FA Cup is used today by the Football Association mainly for promotional purposes. The names of all the previous winners, back to Wanderers in 1872, are engraved on its base.

The original FA Cup never turned up after 1895, lending weight to the claims of Harry Burge who, at the age of 84 in 1958, confessed he had a hand in the theft and melted the cup down into half-crowns.

Mark Bushell, National Football Museum, Sir Tom Finney Way, Preston.

? WHY is Queen Elisabeth of the Belgians, grandmother of the present King, known as The Red Queen?

QUEEN Elisabeth Gabriele Valérie Marie von Wittelsbach (1876–1965) married Prince Albert, Duke of Brabant, heir to the throne of Belgium, in 1900. On her husband's accession to the Belgian throne in 1909, she became Queen.

She was beloved by her people and her regular visits to the front line in World War I were legendary. In 1934, Albert I died in a climbing accident at Marche-les-Dames, in the Ardennes region of Belgium near Namur but his wife's good works continued. During the German occupation of Belgium from 1940 to 1944, she used her German connections and influence to assist in the rescue of hundreds of Jewish children from deportation by the Nazis.

After the war, she was awarded the title Righteous Among the Nations by the Israeli Government.

During the 1950s, the Queen aggravated the Americans by visiting Communist Russia, China and Poland on humanitarian trips that led to her becoming known as The Red Queen.

Queen Elisabeth died on November 23, 1965, at the age of 89. She's interred in the Royal vault at the Church of Our Lady, Laeken Cemetery, Brussels.

Mrs H. Wright, Malvern, Worcs.

? AN inscription on an obelisk on Putney Common describes the award by Parliament in 1774 of £2,500 to David Hartley for inventing 'fire plates'. How did they work?

FIRE plates were iron plates fixed over the joists of the upper floors, below the normal floor boarding. In Hartley's own words: 'The efficiency of the fire plates depends partly upon their preventing the immediate access of the fire itself to the timbers of the house and partly on their preventing that exterior draught of air without which no house can be set on fire.'

He drew attention to other 'subordinate conveniences' such as cleanliness, the prevention of dust falling from floor to floor and the interruption of the free passage of vermin.

In 1776 Hartley gave a series of demonstrations of his invention in his 'fire house' near Tibbet's Corner, Putney Heath. In the first, witnessed by the Lord Mayor and Corporation of London, Hartley set fire to the lower floor, with no damage to the upper rooms. Suitably impressed, the Corporation stated that for new buildings in the City, 'the said Fire Plates shall be ordered as part of the plan'. Hartley was later given the Freedom of the City.

In a further demonstration, George III and Queen Charlotte are said to have taken breakfast on the upper floor of the house while a fierce fire raged below.

Keith Pemberton, London E5.

❓DID Winston Churchill's mother have a tattoo?

LADY Randolph Churchill was a noted society beauty who did indeed have a tattoo – a delicate snake entwined around her wrist. It was placed so that a diamond bracelet could be used to cover it.

Not to be outdone, her son Winston also had a tattoo – an anchor on his arm. His wartime ally Franklin D. Roosevelt proudly bore one also, an image of his family crest.

It was quite fashionable in the late 19th and early 20th centuries for aristocrats, including women, to be tattooed. At the time, tattooing was very expensive and people paid large sums for their designs. Later, as the costs were reduced, tattooing was adopted by the lower classes and the practice fell out of favour with the social elite.

Ian Henley, Peterborough, Cambs.

❓WHY is Lake Chad shrinking?

LAKE Chad sits across the boundaries of Cameroon, Chad, Niger and Nigeria, including some of the poorest countries in the world. Surrounded by marshes and encompassing many small islands and mudbanks, it's very shallow, only 7m at its deepest. It goes through regular seasonal fluctuations and its size is particularly sensitive to small changes in depth.

Its ancient basin, formed in the Cretaceous period, extends over 2.5 million km^2 and the lake used to be much larger extending to the Tibesti Mountains in north-west Chad at one point in the Pleistocene era. About 6,000 years ago, it is thought to have been 400,000km^2 in area.

Because of the variable size of the lake, people living around it are vulnerable to food instability and no significant infrastructure can be installed on its ever-fluctuating shores.

Its largest source, providing more than 90 per cent of its water, is the Chari River but severe drought and desertification through the 1970s led to decreased inflows into the lake and it shrank from a 25,000km^2 surface area in the 1960s (when it was the fourth largest lake in Africa) to a mere 2,500km^2 in recent years.

Intense drought has increased human pressure, including several ambitious irrigation projects, on the ever-dwindling lake. Once a highly diverse wildlife habitat, home to myriad migrating birds, fish, crocodiles, hippopotamus and land mammals, the entire ecosystem is now destabilised and the lake will dry up completely some time this century.

Gareth Miles, Nairobi, Kenya.

WHERE does the tradition of adding myrtle to the wedding bouquet come from?

THIS tradition is attributed to Aphrodite, Greek goddess of love, held to have arisen from the sea wearing a chaplet (wreath) of myrtle.

The attractive evergreen myrtle shrub (*Myrtus communis*) is regarded across a broad range of cultures as a deliverer of good luck and love. The ancient Britons held it as sacred symbol to their goddess of love and it's mentioned in the Bible, in Isaiah 55:13, as being associated with the continuity of life.

Jewish and Germanic brides took to including a sprig of myrtle in their wedding bouquet as a symbol that they were virgo intacta. Over the years, myrtle became symbolic of love, marriage, fertility (it roots very easily) and domestic bliss.

Myrtle became popular in the UK when Queen Victoria's daughter, the Princess Royal (also named Victoria but better known as 'Vicky'), married Frederick III of Germany in 1858. She adopted the myrtle-sprig custom of German brides, much to the delight of her mother.

Every bride thereafter, emulating royalty, had to have a sprig of myrtle in their bouquet until the custom died out due, it is thought, to restrictions imposed on society by World War I and its aftermath.

Royalty, with its own supply in the gardens of Osborne House, maintained the tradition that every royal bride since 'Vicky' has had a sprig of myrtle discreetly placed somewhere in her bouquet right up to the wedding of Prince Edward and Sophie Rees-Jones in June 1998. Sophie broke the tradition but the practice is slowly returning among non-royal brides.

Dunstan Davies, Nuneaton, Warwks.

❓ WHO was the last non-county or university player to play Test cricket for England?

THE last of just five people to play Test cricket for England without having played county or university cricket was Audley Montague Miller.

Born in Westbury-on-Trym, Gloucestershire, on October 19, 1869, Miller made his First Class (and Test) debut in the First Test of the 1895/6 series against South Africa at Port Elizabeth under the captaincy of Lord Hawke.

Batting as a tail-ender, he scored 4 not out and 20 not out but was not asked to play in either of the two remaining Tests. He appeared in both as an umpire.

An Old Etonian, he was usually a middle-order batsman and a right-arm medium-fast bowler for minor county Wiltshire for whom he played between 1894–1920, captaining them for 25 years as well as being Honorary Secretary.

After the South African tour, he went on to play four First Class matches for MCC, the last of which was in 1903. He died at Clifton, Bristol on June 26, 1959.

Andrew Burgess-Tupling, Pontefract, West Yorks.

❓ MY atlas shows a place in New Zealand called 'Taumatawhakatangihangakoauauotamateapokaiwhenuakitanatahu'. Does this name have a meaning?

THIS is actually a shortened form of the name. In full it is Taumatawhaka tangihangakoauauotamateaturipukakapikimaungahoronukupo-kaiwhenak-itanatahu, containing 84 letters, making it the world's longest place name.

Touring New Zealand in 2004, we spotted this name on the map and made a point of visiting it. It's near Porangahau in the Hawkes Bay area of North Island.

A sign board at the site says: 'Tamatea was a well known chief, warrior and explorer of his time, the ancestor of the Ngati Kahungunu people of the Porangahau who acquired many names to commemorate his prowess. While passing through the island district of Porangahau, Tamatea had to fight the Ngati people to get past. In the battle, known as "Matanui", his brother was killed and Tamatea was so grieved at his loss that he stayed for some time at that place. Each morning he would sit on a knoll there to play a lament on his Koauau. So the name indicates the hill on which Tamatea, chief of great physical stature and renown, played a lament on his flute to the memory of his brother.'

Fred Waite, Lichfield, Staffs.

⦾ IS there any connection between the two uses in English of the word 'coach'?

VERY few words originating in the Magyar language of Hungary have entered the English language but 'coach', 'goulash', 'paprika' and 'hussar' are among them.

'Coach' as a form of transport made its way into English from the village of Kocs, between the Hungarian capital, Budapest, and the town of Gyor, known for the very fine horse-drawn carriages it made.

In German, a carriage of this kind became known as a *kutsche* and in French a *coche*. English acquired the word 'coach' in the 16th century as the name for this style of carriage.

Use of 'coach' for a trainer, mentor, instructor or experienced helper was derived from the word used for the carriage. In the 19th century, students were 'coached' through a lesson, subject or exercise as though they were being 'transported' from unskilled to skilful.

Bob Marden, Hastings, Sussex.

⦾ IN 1940, the UK gave the U.S. land rights for 99 years to several military bases in exchange for 50 obsolete destroyers. Do the Americans still man these bases?

THE Destroyers for Bases Agreement between the U.S. and UK was signed in September 1940, more than a year before the U.S. entered World War II. At the time, Britain and the Commonwealth stood alone against the Germans, and Churchill was desperate for any possible assistance. The acquisition of 50 ageing destroyers was necessary to fight the Battle of the North Atlantic.

The ships were designated the 'town' class. Most went to the Royal Navy with some for the Royal Canadian Navy. In return, Britain and the Commonwealth offered bases or land for bases in Antigua, the Bahamas, Bermuda, British Guiana, Jamaica, Newfoundland, St Lucia and Trinidad.

Most bases built or run by the Americans were closed soon after the end of World War II though some, such as the Agentia Base in Newfoundland, and that in Bermuda, took on a significance in the Cold War. Even these eventually closed in the 1990s when the Soviet Union broke up.

Today, even though the leases still have another 35 years to run, most of the bases have been handed back to the host countries, many with severe pollution problems – although the U.S. Government has given large sums towards clear-up costs.

Antigua Air Station is still operational and is used to track spacecraft as they leave Cape Canaveral in Florida.

James Bright, Nottingham.

❓ WHEN were dog licences introduced and when and why did they cease to be required?

SECTION 38 of the 1988 Local Government Act abolished duty on dog licences and therefore the licence itself, a change which came into force on May 24, 1988. Since then, there has been no requirement on dog owners in England, Scotland and Wales to have a dog licence.

In Northern Ireland, however, where it is thought there is a greater problem with stray dogs and sheep worrying, a licence system still prevails under the 1983 Dogs (Northern Ireland) Order.

Before 1988, Britain's dog licence had been in force since 1796 when it was introduced as a means of increasing funds to help fight the French. When abolished in 1988, it cost 37½p a year.

Abolition of the dog licence was sharply criticised by many animal welfare groups which had to deal with the thousands of stray animals throughout the country, and was partly brought back with the introduction of the Dangerous Dogs Act of 1991, which required the registration of several types of dog thought to be a potential threat to society.

Today, most dogs are micro-chipped for identification purposes.

Janet Hutton, Pet Medics, Wardley, Manchester.

? ON *Eastenders*, I heard both Peggy and Dot call someone a 'flibbertigibbet' implying they were a 'strumpet'. Where do these words originate?

'FLIBBERTIGIBBET', normally applied to a person best known for their love of chit-chat, is derived from the sound of aimless chattering. Being so loosely based, it took from the 15th century, when it was first noted, to the 20th century before it had one spelling, having been fleper-gebet, flippergibit, fliberdigibit, etc.

The word represents one of the five fiends who possess 'poor Tom' in Shakespeare's *King Lear*.

The word 'strumpet' is applied today to a woman with an overt knowledge of sexual methods and language. It has its origins in the 14th century when it was of anyone involved in any illicit sexual relations. It came to be applied to prostitutes and this idea was further enhanced by the link between 'strumpet' and *strompen*, a Germanic word meaning 'to walk', as in 'streetwalker'.
Kirsi Laurio, Maida Vale, London.

? DID Winston Churchill ever own a bulldog?

CHURCHILL was an avid animal lover and is said to have seriously considered selling his bicycle to buy a bulldog puppy when he was a schoolboy at Harrow. Two letters in the Churchill Archive advise him against such action. His mother, Lady Randolph Churchill tells him: 'A dog is sometimes a nuisance' and his nanny Elizabeth 'Woom' Everest writes: 'You are not wise about money matters, my dear boy.'

But it was a different breed of dog which captured his affections later in life – Rufus, a red-brown poodle was Churchill's constant companion in World War II.

Sadly, Rufus was run over in 1947. Following this misfortune, a Sunday newspaper reported that Moira Abbott of Uxbridge had offered him one of her bulldogs as a replacement but she was told that 'if Mr Churchill has another dog, it will be a poodle again'. After this, Rufus II was given to Churchill by Walter Graebner, his *Life Magazine* editor for the war memoirs.

So Churchill never did own a bulldog but dogs weren't his only pets: he kept swans, chickens, ducks, cats, goats, fish, bees and pigs, of which he famously said: 'Odd things, animals. All dogs look up to you. All cats look down to you. Only a pig looks at you as an equal.'
Oliver Taylor, Edinburgh.

SHOULD THE NUMBER 13 BE CONSIDERED UNLUCKY?

DEAR *Answers*,—The materialistic mind is inclined to be sceptical on this and deem the holder in such beliefs simple-minded. However, a remarkable instance fulfilling the superstition that should 13 dine at one table, one member of the party will die within the year, occurred when I was a guest at the dinner in question.

I do not attempt any explanation; I have none to give.

On December 20 of last year, 13 young men sat at dinner in a luxurious flat in the West End of London. Of that Bohemian temperament that scorns etiquette and conventionality, they had failed to notice the fatal number at the table.

Suddenly the clink of glasses was hushed, the chatter subsided as quickly as it had begun and 12 of the young fellows were looking in astonishment at their host. He was pale and seemed unable to express something he wished to say.

'What is it, old chap?' said a merry-faced young fellow called Blake, 'Nightmare or ghosts?'

'Ssh!' said the young man. 'Do you see how many we are at table? Count!'

'Thirteen, by jove! But, my dear fellow, you look like a scarecrow on a March day. You don't mean to say that you believe in that trumped-up tradition. Drop superstition and forget all about it.'

But the young host still felt uncomfortable. Should anything occur to one of the party within the year prescribed, he felt he would be, in some measure, morally responsible. The others divined his thoughts and proceeded to turn the whole affair into a jest.

'Come, come, my dear fellow. It's nonsense worrying yourself in this way. There's not a man in the room who believes for one moment the truth of the popular superstition', said Blake. 'And, to prove it, come to my rooms to dinner on the 31st, and see the old year out and the new one in. What better proof of the fallaciousness of your superstitious ideas? If we all survive, as we unquestionably shall, till after the stroke of 12, good-bye to the truth of your old tradition.'

The host was relieved, and the dinner proceeded successfully.

The blaze of light pouring forth from Blake's windows on the 31st suggested revelry and such was, indeed, proceeding.

Again the young men sat round the festive table, 13 in number. The young man who had previously been the host was now thoroughly reassured and was soon engaged in the enjoyment provided with as much spirit as anyone. Time flew on with rapid strides and, as the midnight hour approached, the lights were turned out, with the exception of one, and all the guests gathered round the fire to await the striking of the clock in the adjacent church tower.

The great bell tolled the first stroke of the hour, and all instinctively leaned back in their chairs to count its measured strokes.

Twelve! The tension produced by the solemnity of the moment was over and as the lights were turned up again, all burst into a hearty laugh. Blake was asleep. 'The bells did it,' one said. 'No, no, 'tis love. Blake, we know, is shortly to be married. Those bells have brought him pleasant dreams,' and the speaker shook the sleeping young man by the arm. He did not move.

'Uncommonly pleasant dreams,' he added as he gave him a more vigorous push but still the young fellow did not stir. One and all shook him without success. Fear and anxiety were rapidly expressed on their faces, and whilst one was dispatched for the doctor, restoratives were applied, but without avail. The doctor came. His verdict, short and terrible, fell sharply on the young men's ears – 'He is dead.'

The sequel to my story is its strangest part. In the subsequent medical examination of the unfortunate young fellow, one of the doctors informed me in confidence that they were utterly unable to assign any reason for his death; the physical condition was perfect, and no signs of disease of any kind were apparent. Thus the whole affair will be for ever enshrouded in mystery.

No doubt it is needless for me to say that never again shall I sit 13 to dinner.

Arthur M., Cromwell Road, London W.

Three years ago, I was going out in a troopship to join my husband who was with his regiment in India. One night, at dinner, we discovered that we were 13 at table, and, while some made laughing comments on the fact, others who were superstitious seemed somewhat awestricken. I must confess that, personally, I was with the former number.

When the attention of everyone was drawn to this fact, a young subaltern who was going out with us jumped up and in a loud tone remarked: 'As we are 13 at table, we won't alter the present arrangement. I call upon you all to witness that I am the 13th. If anything is to happen to one of us within the year, it shall fall upon me.'

Whether it was only a strange coincidence or not, I cannot say, but within two months I heard of the death of the poor young fellow in a hill station.

I was curious to discover what disease he had died from. Some three months after his decease, I met the regimental doctor who had been with him till the end. I asked him what the sub had died of, and he replied that it was through some internal complaint, the nature of which they did not quite know. He had been quite well up to about four in the afternoon and three hours after his complaint that he felt 'seedy' he was dead.

Whether this is mere coincidence or not, I cannot of course pretend to say.

E. H., Sheffield.

I think the superstition concerning 13 at table quite a farce. I belong to a tennis-club, and I think all our club are of the same mind.

Last Whit-week but one, we had a trip to Windermere when there were 13 both to dinner and tea. All the 13 are still alive and well.

Since then we have had tea in our tent in the afternoons and 13 has been quite a common number. We have laughed about it several times and joked about renaming our club The Thirteen Club.

That fatalities have happened to people who have helped to make up this number at table I know is true, but still the same thing would have happened to them if they had not done so.

I think many people cling too needlessly to old superstitions. Why should 13 be more unlucky than 15. I think myself it is a lucky number; at any rate, as regards bakers it certainly is.

Atalanta, Manchester.

At this college here we are arranged in messes of 13 boys and for the last two years I have sat down with 12 more boys to breakfast, dinner and tea, up to the present with no fatal consequences to any of us.

Perhaps it would be impossible to give more conclusive proof of the fallacy of the old superstition.

L. R., Mersea Nautical College.

I have been greatly interested by the instances of how sitting down 13 to dinner has wrought bad luck. Allow me to mention a case in which good luck has been the result.

Two years ago I was at a certain dinner-party. Suddenly the lovely girl I had taken down exclaimed to the hostess: 'Oh, Aunty Mary, just count! We are 13!'

Some laughed and said the superstition was all nonsense, others looked ill at ease, while one old gentleman turned livid.

'It's all your fault,' laughed her aunt, 'for beginning your visit to me today, instead of tomorrow as you intended.'

'Then I take all risk upon myself,' said my pretty companion. The guests all looked relieved at this – and I hastened to assure her that I would willingly share the danger with her. We got on so well together that I resolved to put off my departure for my holidays the next day.

Three weeks later we were engaged and in another three months married. Had she not made the thirteenth on that memorable night I should never have met her, and could not therefore have signed myself.

A Happy Husband, Blackrock, Ireland.

? WHICH country has the most domesticated dogs per head of population?

THERE are thought to be around 5.8 million dogs in the UK, shared among a population of 60 million. Dogs are the third most popular pet after goldfish, with a population of more than 15 million, and cats with more than 7.5 million.

The country with the most dogs is the U.S. which, according to Russell Ash's *Top 10 of Everything* book, has 61 million pet dogs, followed by Brazil with

30m; China (23m); Japan (9.6m); Russia (9.6m); South Africa (9.1m); France (8.5m); Italy (7.6m); Poland (7.5m); and Thailand (6.9m).

The country with most dogs per person is South Africa which, with a population of 44.3 million people and 9.1 million dogs has one dog for every 4.8 people.

Caroline Johnstone, Newcastle upon Tyne.

❓ MANY years ago, the *Daily Mail* worked out how much it would cost to replace the imperial road signs in the UK with metric ones. Is there a current estimated cost for changing our road signs to metric?

THERE'S more to changing Britain's road signs to metric than just the physical replacement of existing signs displaying information in imperial units.

MPs and civil servants would have to spend considerable time and money drafting a swath of new legislation to cover all eventualities for the change-over. This will have to include criminal penalties to ensure motorists and other road users comply with the new laws. The location, dimensions, letter fonts and style of the new metric signs will have to be specified by Act of Parliament.

It's estimated that more than a million road and footpath signs would have to be replaced to complete the metrication process. Many hundreds, possibly thousands, of contracts would have to be placed for the manufacture of replacement signs to the new specifications. Most of the new signs would have to be relocated, requiring a myriad of road contractors to erect them at their correct locations with the old imperial signs taken down and disposed of.

No metrication process could be completed without a vast amount of money spent on advertising, informing the public about the change-over – with even more money needed for public safety campaigns.

Lord Howe's UK Metric Association suggested a ridiculously low figure of around £80,000,000 to complete the change-over to all metric road signs but the Department for Transport has suggested a figure of about £700,000,000. Bearing in mind the laughably low official estimates for the construction of the Scottish Parliament Building, the Millennium Dome and Wembley Stadium, I would suggest that a realistic estimate of the financial cost of replacing all imperial road signs in the UK would be in the region of £1.5 billion to £2 billion.

Derek Norman, Active Resistance to Metrication, Huntingdon.

? ARE Farsley Celtic the only club in football to have the tag FCFC?

FELTHAM Cowboys Football Club also use the FCFC abbreviation. Formed in 2004 as a five-a-side team, they were so successful they have now grown to become a strong squad of 18 and are currently in the Chiswick and District League.

According to their very well-made website, this fledgling club have a 15-year plan to become champions of Europe.

Jackie Smith, Chiswick, London.

AT Hyundai's huge Ulsan shipyard in South Korea, many expatriates working in shipbuilding, oil or gas projects live in the Foreigners Compound and are members of the on-site social club.

Foreigners Compound Football Club has been active for 25 years and has seen many players come and go over the years, all enjoying weekly games against the football-mad Koreans.

Patrick Leahy, Singapore.

BEIJING-based Forbidden City FC were champions of the IFFC (Chinese and English) League Division Two in the 2005/6 season.

John Hutton, Twickenham, Middx.

? THE 1981 Sylvester Stallone, Michael Caine and Pelé film *Escape To Victory* is supposed to have been based on the exploits of a group of Dynamo Kiev players. What was the real story?

THIS 1981 film, directed by John Huston, also featured Max von Sydow, plus a host of famous footballers including Bobby Moore, Ossie Ardilles, Kazimierz Deyna, John Wark, Russell Osman and Mike Summerbee.

The script was a Hollywood take on the real story of several former Dynamo Kiev players who, during the German occupation of the Ukraine in the summer of 1942, began playing football together as a team called FC Start.

The players mostly worked in a bakery in the city and quickly gained a reputation for beating all-comers, including German and Hungarian military sides. The German occupiers realised the team were quietly galvanising resistance among their fans and decided that a game between a top German Luftwaffe team, Flakelf, and the bakery boys should be arranged. A German victory would show who were the real masters.

On Sunday, August 9, 1942, thousands of fans arrived at Kiev's Zenit Stadium to watch a game which, though outwardly sporting was, underneath, a 'game to the death'. The FC Start players knew they would be better off losing to the Germans, bolstered by the best players the Luftwaffe could muster. On the day, however, the Ukrainians won 5–3, the final humiliation for the Germans coming when an FC Start player took the ball past the goalkeeper and, instead of placing it in the net, turned and kicked it back to the centre circle.

The Germans let the players have a couple more successful games before turning up at the bakery one morning and arresting every one of them for interrogation. One of the players, Nikolai Korotkikh, was killed in the process and the others were sent to the nearby Siretz Labour Camp where Nikolai Trusevich, Ivan Kuzmenko and Aleksey Klimenko were shot the following spring.

Callum Hansey, Colne Engaine, Essex.

? WHERE is the most well-trodden square foot of land on the planet?

THERE are many candidates for this title, the more frivolous being the area in front of the bathroom mirror at 10 Downing Street or the complaints office at Ryanair.

Thinking logically about this, the most well-trodden places are those which are constantly under foot, such as the sentry boxes outside Buckingham Palace or the Vatican. But these tend to have the same feet on top of them, unlike places such as the inner circle around the Kaaba, the small building in the middle of Mecca's Sacred Mosque, which is visited by two to three million people during the annual hajj.

Other locations, such as the base of the Eiffel Tower or Times Square in New York are always packed with people. One particularly busy point on the planet is the Las Vegas Strip which, in its 24/7 mode, has some pinch points such as the entrances to the MGM Grand or Bellagio hotels and casinos which are always filled with people.

But the square foot of land that has the most people standing on it every day of the year must be the pedestrian crossing outside Shinjuku railway station, where more than a million people a day are known to pass.

Barry Jenkins, Swansea.

?WHERE does the word 'Stetson', as in Stetson hat, originate?

THE Stetson or 'ten-gallon' hat, synonymous with John Wayne, J. R. Ewing and Brokeback Mountain, took its name from 19th-century New Jersey hat maker John Batterson Stetson, whose factory at Philadelphia began production in the late 1860s. The surname Stetson is thought to be a diminutive of Stephenson or Stewartson.

The 'ten-gallon' nickname originated with the fact that the hat was popular among the arriving peoples of the newly acquired lands in the western U.S. – Texas, New Mexico, California, Colorado, etc – better known as the Wild West. Nothing to do with its capacity, the hat got its name from the braided hats, normally sombreros, worn by many of the Spanish-speaking population in those areas.

The Spanish for braid is *galon* and John Stetson's hats were big enough to carry ten braids.

Invention of the 'cowboy' hat in general isn't always credited to the Americans. There's a suggestion that it had its roots in the less sunny climes of Stockport, Bermondsey and Frampton Cotterell, Gloucestershire.

Christys hat company had various works in these locations making, among its early products, a hat very much like a 'cowboy hat' which was used across the British Empire.

Keith Wilson, Didsbury, Manchester.

?IN 1946, my wife was a civil servant, posted to Cairo, and recalls being served camel steaks for dinner at her hotel. Is it possible to buy camel steak in Britain now?

CAMEL steaks are familiar to many who served in North Africa in World War II but I know of only one place that sells camel steak in Britain now – Osgrows, here in Bristol.

They specialise in all manner of exotic meats such as ostrich, kangaroo, crocodile, locust, snail, wild boar, bison, rattlesnake, buffalo, zebra, springbok, kudu, eland, impala, wildebeest and frogs' legs. Most of the meats are for novelty value and quite expensive compared with less exotic home-grown meats like chicken and pork.

According to the company's website, camel has a sweet, mutton-like taste and is imported, vacuum packed and frozen, from Africa. It costs about £7 for two 170g steaks.

Liz Cole, Bristol.

? HAS any soldier fighting in trench warfare had an enemy bullet enter his rifle from the far end?

NEAR Armentières, now in France, on Friday, August 13, 1915, Private W. J. Smith of the 6th Battalion, the Queen's Own Royal West Kent Regiment, was aiming his short Lee Enfield .303 at a German sniper in a trench 50 yards away when the German, using a gun of slightly smaller calibre, fired first and his bullet went straight along the barrel of Smith's rifle and smashed the bolt.

Smith was uninjured but missed death by a whisker that day. The slightest twitch by the enemy sniper would have sent the bullet on a fatal course. The gun, known as the 'miracle rifle', can be seen in a museum at Maidstone, Kent.

Christopher Benton, North Middlesex Hospital, London.

EXTRACT from the Catalogue of the School of Infantry Small Arms Museum, March 1967: 'Exhibit 234: British Short Magazine Lee Enfield rifle No 1, Mk 1, 1914. Weight 9lb, Calibre 0.303in, sighted to 2,800 yards.

'This rifle was damaged in an exceptionally unlikely way during the 1914–18 war when a German bullet entered the muzzle at the exact instant the rifle was fired. This resulted in both bullets stopping in the barrel, the breech being blown out, the bolt broken and the firer spending a week in hospital suffering from shock and cuts. X-ray photos have verified the positions of the two bullets.'

I have seen this rifle, the nosecap of which is undamaged while the muzzle shows a very slight distortion. Alongside the weapon is an X-ray photo which clearly shows the British and German bullets nose to nose in the barrel.

E. Casley, Cheltenham, Gloucs.

? WILLIAM Shakespeare was born on April 23, 1564, and died on April 23, 1616. Have any other famous people died on their birthdays?

SHAKESPEARE is the most famous person to have died on his birthday. Other less well-known contenders include physician and writer Sir Thomas Browne, born on October 19, 1605, and died the same day in 1682; Flemish painter Frans Francken, born on May 6, 1581, and died in 1642; Russian composer Alexander Glazunov, born on March 21, 1865, and died in 1936; clergyman and puritan Thomas Hooker, born on July 7, 1586, and died in 1647; and sculptor James Thom, born on April 17, 1802, and died in 1850.

Joan Elford, Chigwell, Essex.

WE don't know for a fact that Shakespeare was born on April 23 though we know he was christened on April 26 and people have assumed his birthday from that. I believe that had he died on his birthday, it would have been recorded by his contemporaries.

Ralph Leavis, Lincoln College, Oxford.

THE Renaissance painter Raphael was born in Urbino, Italy, on April 6, 1483, and died in Rome on April 6, 1520. Both these days were Good Fridays.

D. G. Lydall, London SE15.

FOOTBALLER and soccer manager Joe Mercer died on August 9, 1990, his 76th birthday. He played with Everton, Arsenal and Aldershot during the war years and managed Sheffield United, Aston Villa and, most famously, the great Manchester City side of the late Sixties which won promotion to Division One, the League Championship, FA Cup, League Cup and European Cup Winners' Cup within five years.

He was caretaker manager of England after Sir Alf Ramsey and, later, general manager of Coventry City.

David Bennett, Worsley, Manchester.

A GRAVESTONE in the churchyard of St Mary's, Whitby, reads: 'Here lie the bodies of Frances Hunt Rodds and of his wife, Mary, who were born on the same day of the week, month and year, September 19, 1600, married on the day of their birth and, after having had 12 children born to them, died, aged 80, on the same day of the year on which they were born, September 19, 1680, the one not above five hours before the other.'

J. Smith, Biddulph, Staffs.

？ WHY is there a street in York city centre called Whip-Ma-Whop-Ma Way?

THE full name of the street is Whip-ma-Whop-ma-Gate, a name which dates from at least 1546, when it was recorded as Whipnam-Whapnam.

Gate is from the Old Norse *gata* – a street or road, common in York, related to our modern English word 'gait', meaning 'walk'.

Whip-ma seems to be a corruption of Whip-man – the city official responsible for flogging offenders. A whipping post or pillory once stood at the top of the street.

Wap or Whap has the meaning of yelping or crying out. A small, yapping dog is sometimes called a whappet and this has led some to associate the name with the local custom of whipping dogs on St Luke's Day but it could equally well relate to the pitiful cries of the condemned as the York Whip-man carried out his duties at the pillory.

Karl Wittwer, The English Companions, London.

THE tradition of dog whipping on St Luke's Day is said to have arisen after a stray dog was seen to eat a consecrated Host, accidentally dropped by a priest, while celebrating St Luke's Day.

'Ye sayed dog was chased & slaide', said the chronicle, but this didn't fully atone and for years afterwards 'ye boyes hadde charge to whippe stray dogs on October ye eighteenth' – St Luke's Day.

Malcolm Cutter, Haxby, York.

? HOW are aircraft vapour trails in the sky produced and why do only some planes make them?

A CONDENSATION (vapour) trail is caused by hot exhaust meeting cold air – but it's not quite that simple. Exhaust from a jet at altitude forms ice crystals, hence the vapour trail. Depending on the amount of moisture in the atmosphere, the trail may be 'persistent' or 'non-persistent' at certain altitudes. This is of great significance to the military, as planes can be seen from a greater distance.

Altitude also has a bearing on the formation of vapour trails. They seem most prevalent between 28,000ft and 33,000ft, but can form at higher or lower altitudes. The trails seen during the Battle of Britain were probably pressure trails, or vortices, from the wingtips of manoeuvring planes, not true vapour trails.

Chas W. Hanvy, Dukinfield, Cheshire.

VAPOUR trails, otherwise known as contrails, occur with aircraft flying at high altitude through sub-zero temperatures, discharging water vapour from the engine exhaust, which freezes in the form of visible ice crystals.

Contrails are also formed by the reduction of pressure below the dew point of the air passing over the aircraft surfaces. These are not to be confused with trails known as wingtip vortices, which can occur at low level with air temperatures above zero, and are the result of high-pressure air below the wing spilling over at the tip into the low-pressure air above, resulting in a visible spiral trail following the wingtip.

This phenomenon can often be observed at air displays during low-level high-speed flypast manoeuvres, or from the windows of a landing jumbo.

A. F. Harris, Bosoughan, Cornwall.

LIVING in East Anglia during the last war I saw a lot of these con(densation) trails, a most spectacular sight when B17s and B24s were assembling for a raid, climbing higher and higher, with con trails forming when at a certain height.

In the course of research at the Public Record Offices at Kew, I came across many comments about these trails, which were particularly important to lone, unarmed Spitfires which carried out reconnaissance trips over Germany. If a trail formed it gave away the position of the aircraft and the flight was cancelled or the height or mission altered.

J. R. White, Spitfire P8141 research project, Rugby, Warwks.

Index

Acknowledgements

General Editor: Andy Simpson

Editorial Assistance: Margaret Jonas

Executive Editor: Trevor Davies

Managing Editor: Clare Churly

Executive Art Editor: Joanna MacGregor

Page make-up: Dorchester Typesetting Group Ltd

Production Manager: Ian Paton